Revisioning Philosophy

SUNY Series in Philosophy
George R. Lucas, Jr., editor

Revisioning Philosophy

edited by
James Ogilvy

STATE UNIVERSITY OF NEW YORK PRESS

Published by
State University of New York Press, Albany

For information, address State University of New York Press,
State University Plaza, Albany, N.Y., 12246

Production by Marilyn P. Semerad
Marketing by Theresa A. Swierzowski

Library of Congress Cataloging-in-Publication Data

Revisioning philosophy / edited by James Ogilvy.
     p. cm. — (SUNY series in philosophy)
    Papers from a series of conferences organized by the Esalen
Institute Program on Revisioning Philosophy.
    ISBN 0-7914-0989-9. — ISBN 0-7914-0990-2 (pbk.)
    1. Philosophy—Congresses. 2. Democracy—Congresses.
3. Individualism—Congresses. 4. Spiritual life—Congresses.
I. Ogilvy, James A.   II. Series.
B20.R48   1991
101-dc20
                                                  91-30803
                                                     CIP

10 9 8 7 6 5 4 3 2 1

for
Jean and Sidney
and Laurance

CONTENTS

Acknowledgements

The Revisioning Philosophy Program owes its origins to the will and imagination of Michael Murphy, co-founder of Esalen Institute. The name, Revisioning Philosophy, came from Jean Lanier. The program owes most of its sustenance to Laurance Rockefeller, whose founding grant was then matched by generous donations from Steven Rockefeller, Mark Dayton, William Sechrest, Friedemann Schwartzkopf, Sidney Lanier, and the Reality Foundation.

Several of the papers in this volume were previously published. Grateful acknowledgement to: *Cross Currents* for permission to republish essays by Steven Rockefeller and Roger Walsh, whose essays were first prepared for presentation at Revisioning Philosophy conferences; *Journal of the American Academy of Religion,* for Huston Smith's essay; *Public Affairs Quarterly* for Bruce Wilshire's essay. All other essays are appearing for the first time.

Many people have contributed to the Revisioning Philosophy Program since its inception in 1986, when Jean Lanier, Michael Murphy, Huston Smith and I first discussed the possibilities. Particular thanks go to Donald Rothberg for his role in organizing several conferences. For help in preparing and proofreading this volume, thanks to Cathleen Sheehan, Karen Greenwood, and Tina Walden. Thanks, finally, to Douglas Baxter of Pace Gallery, and to Jim Dine for permission to reproduce his art on the cover.

Introduction

The Need for Revisioning Philosophy

James Ogilvy

There's a good deal of talk these days about the death of philosophy. Though it may be hard to imagine humanity without at least a small minority intoxicated with the love of wisdom, I find it very easy to contemplate a world devoid of wise men and women. For wouldn't a truly wise person shine like a beacon for all the rest to see? And wouldn't the presence of such people put the rest of us so to shame that we would do everything possible to eliminate such people and erase their memory from the face of the earth? However much some of us may say we are in love with wisdom (*philo*=love, *sophia*=wisdom), we can nonetheless do without any wise guys in our own immediate neighborhoods.

Envy and shame are not the only retardants to the rooting and spreading of wisdom in our native soil. There is also the problem of whether the real thing is even possible. What is this thing called wisdom, after all? Maybe it is a mythical attribute, like the unicorn's horn: something we read about once, something certain men of old were supposed to have had, but didn't *really*. One hears of "the wisdom of Solomon," but he probably made his share of mistakes. Ask his mother.

What is this wisdom thing? Maybe it's overrated. But maybe not. Maybe now, just when grand theory looks terribly pretentious, and hoary chestnuts like Justice and Virtue sound slightly embarrassing in hip company, the love of wisdom is due for a revival, or better, a burst of fresh energy—a new exuberance to replace the stale old fossils of academic argumentation.

1. Historical Background

Philosophy-as-we-know-it has become fossilized. Plato's Heaven of ideal Forms, those "eternal ideas" that were to be the unchanging sources and standards of perfection in all things, have suffered the ravages of time and change. The invention of historical time and the discovery of evolution were unknown in Plato's day. Kant's "architectonic"—his architectural blueprint for a perfectly orderly flowchart for reason—has been replaced by a postmodern architectonic which, like postmodern architecture, makes reference to the balance and harmony of classical order only with a sense of irony. Hegel's System has fallen under the criticism of Kierkegaard and his heirs in the existentialist tradition. And as if that weren't enough, a line of Marxists begat by Karl and running through Lenin, Stalin, Mao and Deng Zhao Ping have shown us in ghastly and unmistakable detail just how horrible a systematically regimented, centrally planned life can be.

A whole generation of European intellectuals has finally woken up. After living through the decades between the 1930's and the 1960's, when to be an intellectual was to be a Marxist (and therefore to know just enough Hegel in order to be able to refute him), these same intellectuals and their students have come to the realization that the whole Hegelo-Marxist dialectical juggernaut was a vast clattering structure of abstractions bearing little relation to reality. It might be made to clunk along a little longer but, even less productive than Eli Whitney's original cotton gin, whose quaint antiquity Marxism bore like a museum piece, this dynamically structured mechanism, inspiring pride over all its moving parts, would never issue forth with anything more substantial than a seedless bole of cotton.

So deconstruction set in. The deconstruction crew—Heidegger, Derrida, deMan, Deleuze, all those big and little *De*'s and *de*'s— destroyed the edifice constructed over centuries of European philosophy. They argued, quite convincingly in my opinion, that the world wasn't put together in such a way that *any* elegant system of thought— static or dynamic, Platonic or Hegelian, ancient or modern—could represent the true nature of things. They demonstrated in different ways that "the true nature of things" was not a phrase that denoted some small and elegant set of principles from which all of the fine-grained detail of earthly experience would follow. No first principles are sufficient to define, articulate and guarantee every feature of the universe, from those regularities representable as laws right down to the contingencies we sometimes dismiss as mere details, but whose accretions finally determine the shape and texture of everything and everyone.

No first principles will determine the precise shape of such last things: the irregularities so evident in the shape of a shoreline, for example. No first principles can determine the shapes of such last things unless you consider so-called *chaos theory* such a set of first principles. But I find the wonder of chaos theory to lie, first, in the fact that its formulae determine certain curves in a most indeterministic manner, and, second, in the way that at each level of magnification, the same structures are revealed, all the way up and all the way down, in an endless circle of "self-sameness" such that the very distinction between *first* principles and *last* things ceases to have the significance it once had in a more hierarchical environment. Chaos theory thus implicitly deconstructs its own claim to be a meta-theory, for the principles of architecture that it shows us are principles that deny the determinism of meta-principles—first by denying determinism, and second by destroying the neat hierarchy that would distinguish the highest from the lowest, the first from the last, the meta- from the sub-.

To the extent that chaos theory is paradigmatic of new developments in twentieth century thought, philosophy *is* in trouble. For philosophy used to be the meta-narrative *par excellence*. It was the science of first principles, the queen of the sciences, next to theology as king, and thus related by marriage to the Godhead at the very top of the old Greco-Christian ontological hierarchy.

Philosophy has always vied for a place at the head of the line of disciplines, whether as top-dog on a hierarchy, or as *first* in the order of presupposition. Both metaphysics and epistemology make claims about *priority*. After Descartes and Kant, after the subjective turn away from a metaphysical order of being toward an epistemological order of knowing, philosophy's claim to priority shifted from aspirations toward access to the *highest* to an attention to what comes *first* in the order of knowing. Philosophers shifted their attention from the transcendent to the transcendental, from that which lies beyond objectivity to that which lies this side of subjectivity. What, in the structure of rational consciousness, is necessarily the case in order that knowledge and experience should be possible? This is the question posed by the transcendental-subjective turn that dominated philosophy from Descartes to Kant.

Then, with Hegel, Marx and Nietzsche, the task of philosophy took another turn. Philosophy fell into time. Kant's categories of understanding shared with Plato's Ideas an immunity to time. Kantian categories, too, were put forward as eternally necessary structures. Hegel doubted their permanence. He became preoccupied with the *history* of forms of consciousness. Marx recast the Hegelian dialectic in terms of the historical succession of different means of material production. Nietzsche inquired into the *genealogy* of morals. The focus of philosophy had shifted not only from transcendent objects to immanent subjects, but, during the nineteenth century, from a subjectivity that was ahistorical to a subjectivity that was intensely historical. Things change, and so does the structure of subjectivity.

To continue this high-speed historical setting of the stage for the current crisis of philosophy, let us follow Richard Rorty in speaking of the *linguistic turn* as the twentieth century's successor to the *historical turn* in the nineteenth century, and the *subjective turn* taken by Descartes and Kant in the seventeenth and eighteenth centuries. The linguistic turn has not *solved* all the problems that plagued philosophers of a more metaphysical or epistemological bent. Instead it has *dissolved* or relocated many of the old puzzles. In its Anglo-American version, with Wittgenstein and his followers, many of the old puzzles are dismissed as "language gone on holiday"—merely semantic confusions that could be cleared up once we get more careful about what we say and how we say it. In its continental version, with Heidegger and his followers, language, not subjectivity, is recognized as "the house of Being," but there is much less attention to keeping a tidy house. Poetry is permitted. Still, there is an equally vehement will to destroy the tradition of Western metaphysics. God is dead, and we will not let him live on as a stowaway in words and concepts that carry the baggage of eternity.

Where the Anglo-American tradition tends to trivialize the great questions that preoccupied philosophers of old by subjecting them to increasingly technical analyses of the language in which they are cast, the continental tradition has steered itself clear of the trivial only to end up in the box canyon of nihilism. Thus philosophy in the twentieth century, following the subjective, the historical, and the linguistic turns, has ended up in a double dead-end. Take your choice: technical trivialization or poetic nihilism. Neither is terribly appealing to the poor person in the street who, if interested in philosophy at all, is more likely to turn to Plato than to Donald Davidson or Derrida.

I don't want to dismiss the achievements of twentieth century philosophers. The forked path of twentieth century philosophy had to be played out, in English and in European. It was a dirty job and some people had to do it. But now it's done, and the rest of us are left with a need...and nothing to fulfill or satisfy that need.

2. The Need

What is the need? Quite simple, really. We want to make some sense of our lives. We want to be able to believe that what we do each day is neither trivial nor nothing worth doing. We want to have a sense of direction, and a way of distinguishing good from evil. We would like to have something to tell our children. We would like to think we are building a better tomorrow, and not just squandering the last of the wine before leaving a devastated earth in our industrial wake...And somehow, in our naivete, we thought that philosophy might help us with such questions. We don't like to hear that philosophers have proven that such questions are meaningless or unanswerable. We are not likely to cease asking such questions. And if philosophers refuse to help us in answering these questions, then too many people are likely to take them elsewhere: to the astrologers, or to the psychoanalysts, or to the mystics, or to the investment bankers. There are people out there with answers...for a price.

Academic philosophers have, for the most part, abdicated the field. It is not just a question of living after the linguistic turn. There is also the politics and sociology of knowledge in the contemporary academy to consider. Tenure was once a means toward the end of protecting non-conformity; now it has become an end in itself, to which the means are conformity—conformity to the confines of disciplinary specialization. But philosophers of old sought a synoptic vision. Even a technician as rigorous as Wilfred Sellars insists that philosophy is a matter of "seeing how things, in the largest sense of the term, fit together, in the largest sense of the term." This task of making sense of things, in a very large sense of the term, very few academic philosophers attempt. Academic deans are responsible for awarding promotions, but they are not usually students of philosophy. Because they need clear proof of incremental progress in an assistant professor's chosen field, there are far more rewards for finite steps than for valiant attempts to grapple with the infinite and ineffable. Better to build a career by figuring out how adverbs work than by seeking something as elusive as wisdom. Philosophy as the love of wisdom is as ridiculous in the academy as romantic love in a bordello. Which is not to condemn either academies or bordellos, but just to put philosophy in its proper place. But where, if not the academy, is philosophy's proper place?

3. The Setting

What about Esalen Institute? Founded in the early 1960's by Michael Murphy and the late Richard Price, Esalen occupies an Edenic site overlooking the Pacific Ocean in Big Sur, California. Esalen is a place of learning, but there are no professors and no students, no curriculum, no grades and no graduation ceremony. Instead there are workshops and conferences lasting sometimes a weekend, sometimes a week, some open to the public, some by invitation only. Some of the invitational conferences go on for years, gathering the same group of people together again and again to probe one question or another in an idyllic setting where it is hard to get a hold of a copy of *The New York Times* that is less than a couple of days old.

The contents of this volume are the result of a series of conferences held over a three year period, mostly at Esalen. With the aid of a generous three-year grant from Laurance Rockefeller, the Esalen Institute Program on Revisioning Philosophy was initiated in 1986. Michael Murphy, who majored in philosophy as an undergraduate at Harvard, but then fled from the technicians in the graduate program at Stanford, decided to initiate a series of conferences that would gather together a group of philosophers to entertain the great questions. He asked me to serve as director of the program, and, together with Huston Smith, we sought out a gradually increasing circle of searchers who were not embarrassed to wade in where more cautious inquirers might fear to tread. The discussions gained momentum, and in August, 1989, we gathered close to a hundred philosophers from around the world for a five-day meeting at St. John's College, Cambridge, under the conference title, "Philosophy and the Human Future." This volume contains a number of papers that were presented in a similar form at Cambridge, though several have been written, modified and reworked in light of what was heard during that memorable week.

Even a cursory look at the table of contents will reveal the fact that not all of the contributors are registered members of departments of philosophy. This is not the place to single out individuals or name names. Readers are encouraged to refer to the "Notes on Contributors" section at the end of the volume. This *is* the place to pause on the questions that brought this remarkable group of professionals and non-professionals together in dialogue, and to orient the reader toward what he or she will encounter in the pages that follow.

4. A Framework

At our first conference early in 1986 we found ourselves reaching for Aristotle's four causes as a framework for understanding the ways that contemporary philosophy has become constricted. In the *Metaphysics* Aristotle distinguished material causes from formal causes, and efficient causes from final causes. Let us take each in turn.

Material Cause

With a few notable exceptions such as the pre-Socratics, Marx, and John Dewey's rarely acknowledged fascination with the work of F. Mathias Alexander, philosophers have had very little interest in or patience with the material or bodily dimension of existence. Ever since Plato set philosophy on an upward course that shunned the body, philosophers have been much more preoccupied with Being rather than becoming, with mind rather than matter, with ideas rather than feelings, with form rather than content, with the necessary rather than the merely contingent. Physical existence, whether in the form of the human body, or the lowly means of physical production and reproduction, or the merely contingent contents of formal structures, has exercised far less attraction to philosophers than lofty concepts like Truth, Justice and Eternal Law. But the lowly contents of time and existence is where we live each day. And the body, as is nowhere more clearly the case than at Esalen, is more than a mere chassis to be steered by autonomous mind. Emotions and passions are not just ideas that have gone wrong by getting mired in the body. But philosophers, with only a few exceptions, have done little to sort out the roles of body, matter and passion in the affairs of mind. This shortcoming of philosophy we were committed to set right. Esalen is a place noted for its attention to bodies. Sulphur hot springs that were sacred to the Esalen Indians, and a tradition of massage, have attracted the world's leading practitioners of somatics to Esalen. What better place to integrate an attention to the body into the love of wisdom? What better place to revision philosophy in a way that would add the flesh and blood so palpably missing at meetings of the American Philosophical Association?

Nor were we constrained by literalism in the pursuit of flesh and blood. Among the material causes of contemporary life are the lowly mechanics and plumbing of life we call business and commerce. On the fringes of the academy one can find philosophers engaged in philosophy of law, philosophy of medicine, philosophy of religion, philosophy of art, philosophy of just about every dimension of life except for business. True, one can find the occasional "business ethics" course being ridiculed as based on an oxymoron. But aside from trying to operate as a conscience to greedy investors, very few philosophers have anything to do with the business world. Few ask questions about the ontology of information, even as we shift from an industrial to an information-based economy. Few inquire into the relationship between business and politics, even as corporations take over from governments in the driver's seat of history. Without becoming a Marxist or a materialist, a philosopher could do worse than inquire into the material causes of contemporary life to get a sense, in the largest sense of the term, of its direction, in the largest sense of that term. So this volume begins with a section entitled "Philosophy Incarnate." This section includes essays on the earth, the environment, the emotions, and the body.

Formal Cause

If the earth, the emotions and the body can be taken to represent a realm of material causes too profane to hold the interest of respectable philosophers, then mystical experience has been taken as too close to the sacred for philosophers to discuss. As Sellars succinctly put it, "You can't eff the ineffable." But surely there *is* more to say about the unsayable: how it fits into the rest of our loquacious lives; what role it does or does not play in the rest of existence; whether there is or is not some shadow of eternity that escapes the ravages of time; whether, in short, there is any content to a perennial philosophy? Such questions, which threaten to draw one onto the turf of theology, are generally relegated to the fringe of philosophy of religion. But if anything remains of *formal* cause, then a preoccupation with this northern point on the Aristotelian compass of causes calls for a bracketing of the questions of divinity. Whether God is dead or not, *something* may still retain the necessity of eternal forms. *Something* may transcend the historical relativism of different ages, the cultural relativism of different traditions, the linguistic relativism of different nations. But what? And how would we know it if we saw it? In what language would we describe it? Might our only access be through some mystic experience? In this overture I can do no more than sound a few notes that anticipate a leitmotif that will return in several of the essays that follow, a leitmotif I prefer to think of under a rubric as philosophical and a-theological as possible: *formal cause.* Taken together, Aristotle's formal cause and material cause represent the poles of a vertical dimension variously referred to as the 'ontological hierarchy,' or as the map of the 'hylomorphic tradition' (*hyle*=matter, *morphe*=form). For the moment let us not prejudge whether this map represents a territory. Let us admit that there is a danger of reifying words into Concepts, ideas into Ideas, talk of a material, physical aspect of things into Prime Matter. But let us also admit that in its eagerness to avoid these premature reifications, recent philosophy has outlawed inquiry into certain *experiences* that nevertheless remain an important part of human life. Somewhere between the neo-Platonist's insistence on eternal Ideas and the mystic's experience of the sacred, there is still a job for philosophy that is not theology. Somewhere between the businessman's talk of strategy and the masseuse's silent manipulations, there is room for a philosophical discourse that risks sounding too profane for the scholarly journals. Whether or not the hylomorphic dimension represents any real territory, its vertical reach from the sacred to the profane can serve at least as a way of referring to the sorry fact that philosophy in this century has been truncated to the safety of a middle realm where the risks of sacred form and profane matter are studiously avoided. This volume ends with a section devoted to the place of spirituality in experience, and to the question of the content of a perennial philosophy.

Efficient and Final Causes: Past and Future

If formal cause is the north pole and material cause the south pole on Aristotle's compass, then let efficient cause lie to the west and final cause to the east. Then the temporal dimension, from past to future, will point in the conventional direction, from left to right, and will serve as a horizon orthagonal to the vertical arrow towards eternity. Remember: it's just a map. But again it will serve as an orderly way of referring to what is too often ruled out of court in the middle realm of contemporary philosophy: the whence and whither of past and future.

The past is dismissed with several distinct but related arguments. Let us count the ways. First there is the fear of the *genetic fallacy*: just because you know something's origins—its efficient cause—it does not follow that you know it's true nature or value, which may be a function of its formal, material or final cause. Second, there is in some quarters a disdain for a kind of philosophizing that smacks of mere history of ideas—a survey of what was said by The Greats, but without sufficient analysis of the truth value of their utterances. Third, in roughly the same quarters there lurks a related belief that *real* philosophy began with Bertrand Russell, and that everything before him, with the possible exception of Frege, represents a hopeless muddle of metaphysics, theology, and the sloppy use of language. Fourth, in very different circles, where poetry is preferred to logic, there is nevertheless a will to deconstruct or destroy the tradition of western metaphysics. Fifth, there is simple forgetfulness, a kind of cultural amnesia bred of bad education, leaving treasures of contemplation lost in libraries only rarely visited. Sixth, in still other circles, there is an explicit rejection of so-called 'historicism,' which can mean too many different things to discuss in detail in this purposely cursory context. Suffice it to say that, consciously or unconsciously, philosophers often pride themselves precisely for the *ahistorical* nature of our discipline, as if philosophy, almost uniquely among other disciplines, were not meant to make progress through time, but only to offer alternative routes toward the eternal, necessary nature of things...in the largest possible sense. Perish the thought that we should become preoccupied with yesterday's headlines. But no less a philosopher than Hegel is said to have regarded the daily newspaper as his bible. The ebb and flow of daily events cannot be irrelevant to the nature of things; the contingent cannot be completely unrelated to the necessary. Nor is the more distant past without interest to those of us trying to make sure of the present. Whether or not philosophy makes progress in a cumulative way like some other disciplines, surely we still have a lot to learn both from the remembrance of the past and from the writings of past philosophers. Our whence gives a momentum to our whither. Despite the usual arguments and amnesia that remove history from the purview of contemporary philosophy, we need to overcome the truncation of tradition.

To listen to Allan Bloom (*The Closing of the American Mind*) or his teacher, Leo Strauss, *only* the reclaiming of tradition will save us. While agreeing with the lament for the loss of the past, I find their writings lacking in a recognition of the eastern point on the Aristotelian compass of causes: the future. To read Bloom and Strauss, it sounds as if the Western tradition has gone straight downhill since Plato, and that nothing will save us short of a Platonist philosopher-king who could, by rational argument rather than the use of force, restore the eternal order of things. But top-down restorations of order have a funny way of turning totalitarian. Philosophers have to watch their step when they claim to discern the pattern that everyone else must follow. Yet who else speaks for humanity when it comes to charting a path into he future?

Here we come to the thorny question that gave rise to the title of our conference at Cambridge, Philosophy and the Human Future. Once one begins to entertain the possibility that the human condition is not determined by some Platonic Form, once one has taken the historical turn and acknowledged that, at least since Hegel, we have fallen into time, then *final* causes—*teloi*, goals—become intensely interesting as constitutive of the meaning of the present. But what *are* these final causes, and how are they to be determined? Does any sophisticated thinker in modern and postmodern times seriously believe in anything like *destiny*? Can anyone since Spinoza seriously engage in the kind of teleological reasoning that explains anything by saying,"It is as it is because it was *meant* to be so," or "So it must be because it is for the best"? Shades of Voltaire's Candide!

No, today we do not believe in destiny. But we do believe in evolution, not only in the evolution of species, but also in the evolution of consciousness. And once one grants that human history's arrow may be headed *somewhere* , then it behooves one to do more than monitor the momentum of the past. It behooves one to ask, in short, "Where are we going and do we want to go there?"

A moment's attention to some of our global crises will be sufficient to raise a whole host of questions about the current momentum of history. Do we *really* want industrial development to lay waste the environment? Are we content to witness the extinction of countless species? Are we satisfied with a growing separation between the rich and the poor? Can we afford our current rates of population expansion for our own species? This litany of vexing questions is all too familiar, and one cannot quickly gainsay a Richard Rorty when he objects that, as far as he can see, philosophers are no better equipped that anyone else to deal with these issues. To the extent that contemporary philosophers *have* ignored the nitty-gritty content of the material and efficient causes of our current condition, we *are* ill-equipped to engage in useful discourse with technicians who know much more than we do about how the world around us actually works. But that doesn't mean we should give up on setting right what is out of joint. It only means that we should overcome our preference for formal causes to the exclusion of material and efficient causes, do some homework, and equip ourselves to engage the technicians without making fools of ourselves.

Someone ought to be asking these questions about where we are going as a species. If not philosophers, then who? Politicians? Heaven help us! Futurists? Having spent the last ten years working very closely with some of the foremost futurists, first at Stanford Research Institute and more recently with a wider network spread around the globe, I can report with confidence that the whole field of future studies is almost entirely preoccupied with descriptive scenarios, not normative scenarios—how the world is *likely* to be, not how it *ought* to be. When it comes to saying how the world *ought to be* , futurists—myself included when I don that hat— retreat to the specialization of the expert technician and mutter words to the effect of, "That's not our business, how the world *ought* to be. We leave that to the philosophers."

So, alas, we are back to where we started, at our own doorstep, and the buck stops here. Ill-equipped or not, philosophers have a job to do, and it has something to do with helping the rest of humanity frame the issues on which humanity as a whole—not only philosophers—must decide. This is an intensely democratic project. It is not philosophy's job to *tell* everyone else where they should be going and how to get there. That, I believe, is the dangerous delusion under which Platonists like Leo Strauss and Alan Bloom labor. Nor is it sufficient to lapse into relativism, let a thousand flowers bloom, and retreat into the university while self-seeking anarchy reigns in the marketplace. To a truly alarming degree, our collective future is now being determined by twenty-six-year-old investment bankers who could care less about what *ought* to be.

Philosophy can neither yield to the babel of countless individual preferences, nor announce some collective destiny by descending, like Moses, with tablets that were taken in dictation from some formal and eternal blueprint in the sky. Time is real. History happens. It is our responsibility as philosophers to see that history doesn't just happen to us, but that we human beings have a hand in shaping a future that is better than the past, not worse.

This business of *shaping the future* is what human freedom is all about. It's not easy. It can be left neither to overt tyrants, nor to the subtler tyranny of technical expertise. If either the tyrants or the technicians take over, the freedom of the many is sacrificed to the shaping ability of a few.

Shaping the future has been the preoccupation of Marxists and existentialists more than most other schools of philosophy. Marxism lies discredited by its historical consequences. Existentialism, as a philosophy, remains too caught up with the freedom and future of isolated individuals. What is needed, if you will, is a *social existentialism*—a philosophy that takes freedom more seriously that Marxism does, but also takes the needs of society more seriously that existentialism does. So far, the philosophy that seems closest to filling this bill is the philosophy—if such it may be called—of democracy. So this volume contains a debate over the demands made upon us by true democracy, and a discussion of the conflicting demands of the individual and the collective. What with the remarkable events of late 1989 and 1990 in Eastern Europe, it would seem that our discussions leading up tp Cambridge in August, 1989, could not have been more timely.

Though the contributors to this volume may be in agreement on the need to revision philosophy—to push out the envelope of contemporary philosophy from its academic constriction toward the sacred and profane, toward the past and the future—this spirit of agreement does not extend to a tidy description of what is to be found in those wider reaches. Important differences divide the approaches taken by the participants in these discussions. Raised voices and furrowed brows were frequent in our discussions. Deeply held beliefs were contested. The principles on which lives are based were put up for debate and rendered vulnerable to critique.

Among the issues that divide the contributors to this volume are the following. Some see the history of human consciousness as a path toward eternal truths that can be glimpsed through spiritual practice. Others are devoutly secular, and see the evolution of consciousness as more like biological evolution, branching off into many directions, not converging toward some pre-destined *telos*. Some see cultural diversity as a veneer over a deeper unity, others see cultural differences as more fundamental and less amenable to translation. Some see philosophy as a handmaid to onto-theology; others see philosophy as the best we can do after the irredeemable death of god. Some see the profession of teaching in colleges and universities as the proper calling for philosophers; others have left academia altogether. But the contributors to this volume are all very much alike in pursuing the love of wisdom with a combination of seriousness and playfulness, boldness and integrity. For their willingness to debate basic issues, and for their courage in deviating from the professional straight and narrow, I want to salute the contributors to this volume.

I.

Philosophy Incarnate

Epistemology and the Extinction of Species

Tyrone Cashman

A. The Great Dying

In February 1986, biologist Peter Raven gave the keynote address at the Annual Conference of the AAAS:

> How fast is extinction proceeding?
> In western Equador, for example, a region that was almost compeletely forested as recently as 1950 is now almost completely deforested. As extensive deforestation of this kind spreads in many other regions, we can expect the rate of extinction to average more than 100 species a day, with the rate increasing from perhaps a few species a day now (1986) to several hundred by the early years of the next century. The great majority of these species will not have been collected, and therefore will never be represented in any scientific collection, preserved, or known in any way. No comparable rate of extinction has occurred since the end of the Cretaceous Period, 65 million years ago; and the background level of extinction

[number of extinctions that naturally occur in an average century] is perhaps a thousandth of that we are experiencing now.[1]

These estimates were updated by E.O. Wilson in September 1989:

I have conservatively estimated that on a worldwide basis the ultimate loss attributable to rain-forest clearing alone (at a present 1 percent rate) is from .2 to .3 percent of all species in the forests per year. Taking a very conservative figure of two million species confined to the forests, the global loss that results from deforestation could be as much as from 4,000 to 6,000 species a year. That in turn is on the order of 10,000 times greater than the naturally occurring background extinction rate that existed prior to the appearance of human beings.[2]

It will be clear to future generations of humans that the present mass extinction, The Great Dying of the species around the world is the *defining crisis* of our epoch, as the defining crisis of the 1930s and 40s was the aggressive expansion of Hitler's exterminationist regime.

The chief historical task of any generation can only be determined, with certainty, from the perspective of its future generations. It was the historical task of our fathers to stop Hitler. Those of us now in our middle years, especially non-Aryans, would not have forgiven our fathers and mothers for allowing a long-term Nazi takeover of the Western world.

In our epoch, the human species is engaged in many reckless acts on a global scale. But only one of them is intrinsically unredeemable:

1. The exhaustion of the of world's fossil fuel supply by just three generations is partly redeemable—if it helps develop technologies of information and miniaturization which in the long run can give birth to high-quality solar economies for all peoples.

2. The reckless explosion of the human population is possibly partly redeemable—if, in the future, our numbers return to levels that match the earth's carrying capacity and if that carrying capacity has not been mostly destroyed.

3. The fact that our generation is leaving behind great reservoirs of radioactive waste which will still be deadly 100,000 years from now is possibly redeemable—if it succeeds in encouraging future generations

---

[1]Peter Raven, "We are Killing Our World," Keynote Address, American Association for the Advancement of Science, Chicago, February 1986.

[2]E. O. Wilson, "Threats to Biodiversity," *Scientific American*, September, 1989, p.112.

of people to undertake a form of mindful, watchful, respectful guardianship, for 100,000 years, of the places where the radiating substances are put to rest.

4. But the extinguishing of a million lineages of beings as ancient as we are is not redeemable.

The murder of a mortal is forgiveable. The murder of an immortal is not. No one knows the lifespan of a species. Although its lifespan cannot be considered infinite, it must be considered indefinite. Death is not intrinsic to the lineage of a species.[3] Unless their native ecological systems are destroyed, the vast majority of lineages will simply go on and on, most likely for millions of years.

It is clearly *our* generation's historical task to prevent The Great Dying. No subsequent generation will have the opportunity to do it, if we fail.

B. Anthropocentrism

I propose that the mass extinction of species not only constitutes the primary philosophical issue of our historical time, but brings us back to the primordial philosophical question of the human species: *What is our true place in nature?*

What part have philosophers had in bringing nature to this brink? What part can we play now to prevent The Great Dying? These mass extinctions are being caused by us. There is clear evidence that they are a direct result of philosophical error, an error which is to us humans what the medievals called a "besetting sin." A besetting sin is a type of moral fault toward which our internal predispositions and our personal habits so bend us that it takes enormous moral strength for us to keep ourselves from committing it. Our besetting philosophic error is *anthropocentrism.*

Examining anthropocentrism closely, we can perceive three kinds:

1. *Anthropocentrism proper:* Etymologically, "humans-in-the-center." Other species exist and live out their lives, but we are the only significant species. We are central in the sense that the *meaning* of everything derives from us. The universe, the earth, has systemic spiritual and philosophic meaning and that meaning is *humanity.* Individuals of each of the other species have their own restricted purposes related to their own ecological niches, but our purposes are

---

[3]My definition of a species lineage, here, is an inter-breeding population of animals or plants in which one generation follows another and produces a generation after itself.

the purpose of the *Whole*. Philosophically, the meaning of the other animals is us.

2. *Anthropic totalitarianism:* Other species, for all intents and purposes, do not exist. They have no status, no say, no rights, no value at all except for their usefulness to us. Any value that may accrue to them derives from us. The human is to the animal somewhat as an omnipotent god would be to his creatures. On the surface of the earth, no entity has rights or value except humans. Descartes, Berkeley, Fichte, and Maturana all end up in this camp because of their initial idealist epistemological stances.

3. *Anthropic chauvinism:* We are the smartest of the species on earth, all others are less innovative than we are. Our ways are more successful, more exciting, more lively, more interesting, more admirable. Other species are independent from us. They got here by innumerable generations of successful evolutionary coping, just as we did. They populate the regions of the earth with their families, their instinctual customs, their simple cultures, somewhat as we do—but they are nowhere near as wonderful as we.

Although some form of anthropic chauvinism is probably inevitable in the human species, philosophies of anthropocentrism and anthropic totalitarianism are without ground.

C. Three "Copernican" Revolutions

1. *Copernican Cosmology.* In the West, it is science alone that has been able to loosen the grip of our besetting philosophical error. Copernicus's heliocentric theory of the sun and planets removed the earth from central position and showed us that the world we inhabit is just one planet among others, orbiting around a common star. Without the scientific approach taken by Copernicus, Galileo and Kepler no Western religion or philosophy would have unseated us from our central position in the geography of the universe.

2. *Anti-"Copernican" Epistemology.* Some 250 years afterwards, Immanuel Kant compared his own epistemological revolution to that of Copernicus. But, in fact, Kant reversed the revolution of Copernicus. True to philosophy's besetting anthropocentric bias, Kant made the *human mind* the center and cause of order in the universe. Of course, for Kant, the earth still orbited the sun, but the earth and sun were themselves formed by the *a priori* forms of intuition and the *a priori* categories of the human mind. This anthropocentrism was even deeper than pre-Copernican anthropocentrism, since with Kant, the human

knower is considered, in large part, creator of the known universe. In the Ptolemaic cosmology, the Creator role was left to God.

3. *Darwin's "Copernican" Biology.* Within a century after Kant, scientists again showed us that philosophers had over-estimated the centrality of human beings in the scheme of reality. Darwin and Wallace, joined very quickly by hundreds of biologists, realized that we were not created special and separate from all other creatures, but that we are in fact an evolved form of primate. We are a species of animal which has evolved to our present form in the same manner that other animal species have evolved to their present forms. Where Copernicus had shown us that we live on one eccentric planet among several, Darwin showed that we are one natural species among millions.

да

Since that time there has been an odd dualism between the philosophic and scientific traditions. For the last 200 years European philosophical epistemology has derived largely from Kant's pre-Darwinian positions: German idealism, the two reactions to German idealism—Marxism and existentialism—then structuralism and various linguistic philosophies, down to deconstructionism in our time.

Not until 1941 was the classic Kantian way of distinguishing the *a priori* from the *a posteriori* in human knowledge brought into clear conjunction with the discoveries of evolutionary biology. In a paper published that year, Konrad Lorenz, student of animal cognition in natural habitats, observed that quasi-Kantian innate forms of intuition and categories exist *a priori* for the individual human being, ontogenetically. But he pointed out that *phylogenetically* these *a priori* forms and categories are *a posteriori*. They were formed during millions of years of interaction with the natural environment.

By acknowledging the validity of the central Kantian insights, and then showing how they fit within the larger frame of 500 million years of the evolution of nervous systems in organisms, Lorenz removed many of the assumptions that had provided support for philosophical idealism. For, the skeptical question that jogs us into idealism has to do with what warrant we might have that our sensations and ideas match a world outside. Kant was an idealist when he claimed that, since the forms we perceive are imposed by our minds, the noumenal world-in-itself is unknowable. For Kant, there is no reason to think that our perceptions of the world are in any way *like* the world-in-itself. Previously, Descartes had claimed that the nature of God as Truthful was the warrant, for a Truthful God would not present us with perceptions of a world if there were not, in fact, a world there that matched our perceptions.

In "evolutionary epistemology," the warrant for the empirical accuracy of our innate frames and categories is the fact that our ancestors survived for hundreds of millions of years in a dangerous world. Our innate cognitive structures have been formed, through merciless deselection, as coordinate systems for quite accurate maps of a world in which food was to be obtained, mates found and won, progeny raised. Organisms whose innate categories failed to frame, within a certain range of accuracy, the concrete environment with its myriad dangers did not survive.

Lorenz points out that our brains are adapted to the mesocosmic natural world, as the fin of a fish embryo in its egg is already adapted to water and the hoof of a colt *in utero* is adapted to grassy plains. Thus, in our epoch, it no longer makes the same sense to take the idealistic turn as it did for philosophers who lived after Kant but before Darwin.

Predictably, the philosophers ignored Lorenz. His threat to the human anthropocentric bias was too great. Intellectuals throughout Western society had made an uneasy peace with evolution, believing, inconsistently, that our bodies evolved in the simian lineage but that our minds have the universal scope and clarity of Descartes's angel-in-a-machine.

Gradually, however, a change is occurring with the development of what is now called cognitive science, which combines experimental epistemology, information theory, cybernetics, cognitive psychology, artifical intelligence theory, neurophysiology and other germane disciplines. Among academic philosophers in the English-speaking world there is now a "naturalistic" movement and in Germany and Austria a new philosophic discipline, inspired by Lorenz, called "evolutionary epistemology."

But anthropocentrism is going to die hard. A panoply of pop theories, religious movements from Christian and Islamic fundamentalism to Asian mysticism, patchworks of philosophic dogma based on scientific and pseudo-scientific metaphors have cropped up on all sides. Perhaps the only thread they have in common is that all of them help keep us humans, or a human-like consciousness, still at the the center of everything.

Oddly enough, one of the ways people in our scientific society have chosen to fend off de-anthropocentrism is to retreat to philosophic idealism. Let us, then, examine in some detail the recrudescence of idealisms in our time.

D. Idealism

Types of idealism:

a. *Subjective:* The universe does not exist, only human perceptions of a universe exist.

b. *Objective* or *Absolute:* The universe is not a material event, but is the grand mental event of a Mind or Consciousness which is of a higher order than the human.

ﺨ

The tradition of thought called "idealism" is exemplified, in its subjective form, by George Berkeley in the Anglo-Saxon world and Johann Gottlieb Fichte in Germany.

In 1710, Berkeley published a critique of John Locke's theory where that theory says we have "ideas" in our "minds" that "represent" external objects. Berkeley claimed there was insufficient evidence for the existence of external material substances. He chose to believe that only perceptions exist. "To be is to be perceived," he said. That which is not being perceived does not exist. Berkeley, a pious Anglican, supported his world of human perceptions, ontologically, with the perceptions of his All-Seeing God.

Near the end of the same century, in Germany, J.G. Fichte greatly admired Kant's thought, but perceived a weakness in Kant's theory of the "thing-in-itself." Once Kant had claimed that the *form* in human perception and cognition is mind-derived, he had to admit that the "thing-in-itself" is unknowable. It seemed to Fichte ignoble for a man to submit to an unknowable, autonomous world. So he denied its existence.

ﺨ

It might seem surprising that the 18th Century idealism of Berkeley and Fichte should find a welcome in America today, surrounded as we are by evidence of the extraordinary fertility of the empirical method based on realist assumptions.

But since the early 1960s there has been a series of cultural and historical factors that have led to a resurgence of idealism in our time:

The early '60s were marked by spiritual aridity in the established religions, and by both social irrelevance and aridity in the prevailing analytic philosophy in the universities. After the assassinations of President and Senator Kennedy and Martin Luther King, Jr. most young people lost faith in the traditional political avenues of effectiveness. The subsequent absurdity of the Vietnam War became obvious. At the same time there was an availability for recreational use of psychedelic substances. There was an influx of spiritual teachers from Asia. Popularized explanations of the ambiguities of quantum physics began to sell. As the '70s moved into the '80s, individuals felt increasing helplessness in the face of looming nuclear and environmental disasters.

A yearning came over a great number of people for an interior life with power: a belief that what I, as an individual, think and want will directly constitute reality. From this mood developed a new privatism, political and social quietism, subjectivism, occultism, spiritualism and ultimately idealism. Among fundamentalist Christians this mood manifested itself in millennialism and apocalyptic visions.

The '80s were a period of detaching from reality (sometimes conveniently redefining "reality" subjectively) and a dissolving of the individual's natural connection with the concrete world of responsibility, action and result.

A range of new idealisms has arisen from this matrix. I will discuss here only the three most credible ones.

By coincidence, these three idealisms are considered by a growing minority to be elements of a "new paradigm" for the sciences *and* for society. This "new paradigm" is thought to be more "ecological" than the previous paradigm. We will see if that is true.

The names I have given to the three idealisms are: Quantum Idealism, Neuro-idealism, and Buddho-idealism.

Quantum Idealism

Since the 1920s nuclear physicists have been encountering microcosmic phenomena so strange that most investigators have been forced to reassess the very nature of reality at those levels of tininess. The majority of elementary particle physicists now espouse the Copenhagen Interpretation, formulated by Niels Bohr, that there is, in fact, no deep reality that their mathematical formulations describe. Bohr was quite firm about this, insisting *"There is no quantum world. There is only an abstract quantum description."*[4] Werner Heisenberg interpreted quantum reality slightly differently. He, too, claimed there

---

[4]Quoted in Nick Herbert, *Quantum Reality*, Garden City, NY: Anchor/ Doubleday, 1985, p. 17.

is no deep reality before measurement, but there is a semi-real quantum world which becomes fully real during the act of measurement. "The probability wave...means a tendency for something. It's a quantitative version of the old concept of *potentia* in Aristotle's philosophy. It introduces something standing in the middle between the idea of an event and the actual event, a strange kind of physical reality just in the middle between possibility and reality."[5]

Unfortunately, I have space here to discuss only the majority opinions. The standard Copenhagen interpretation says two things about sub-atomic reality:

A. In the absence of observations there is no reality.
B. The observations themselves create reality.

Now it should be clear why I call this "quantum idealism." It is obvious that the Copenhagen Interpretation of the microcosmic world is a subjective idealism on the general order of Berkeley's or Fichte's. Heisenberg's has a slightly more Kantian flavor.

Of course, an elementary particle physicist has no need for an interpretation of the *ontological* status of elementary particles. Ontology is a branch of philosophy, not of physics. If the scientist does choose an interpretation it is *as a philosopher* that he or she does it.

Physics at the mesocosmic level does not suggest a subjectivist approach. It is only the odd behavior of the *sub-atomic* particles that leads to idealist interpretations. Yet, more and more books are being published suggesting that the epistemology appropriate to sub-atomic phenomena is also appropriate to the complex entities at the mammal scale.

The ill-informed use of sub-atomic metaphors for mesocosmic psychological, political, artistic and ecological realities is becoming common, proposed mostly by those who have never seriously studied quantum level physics.

Evolutionary Epistemology and Quantum Idealism

There are many assumptions that lead writers to claim the mesocosmic legitimacy of quantum idealism, but the deepest one is the (unspoken) Cartesian assumption about the human mind. That assumption is that the human cognitive system, i.e., sensory and conceptual apparatus, is *uniformly* adapted to all objects and events in the natural, material world. If this were true, the ambiguities we encounter at the level of the infinitesimally small should, indeed, lead

[5]Herbert, p. 27

us to doubt the validity of our cognitions at all levels—including the mesocosmic.

But when the Cartesian assumption is replaced by the understanding from biology that our sensory and nervous system is the result of long evolution, then the expectations change radically. It becomes clear that the innate cognitive abilities of the human brain and peripheral nervous system are highly adapted to mammal-scale events. But this evolutionary guarantee does not extend to the level of the infinitesimally small parts of atoms. There was no selective pressure to develop cognitive equipment adapted to those realities. Thus, if it turned out that we were able to comprehend the infinitesimal structure of the universe with ease, that would be something of a conundrum for evolutionary theory. What a cognitive evolutionist expects is that the sureness of our cognition will weaken, and things will begin fading in and out for us, as we penetrate further into the realm of the extremely tiny. And this is just what happens.

When the event we are examining is the kind we evolved to perceive well, our cognitive structures *enhance* the ability of the external world to get through to us. For example, there are inhibitory neurons at the retina that enhance our perceptions of the *outlines* of objects in our environment. But when the situation does not provide what our cognitive system requires, what we end up perceiving and comprehending is partly our own cognitive structures themselves. This is somewhat analogous to looking out the window from a lighted room as night comes on. The darker it gets outside, the more you see yourself reflected in the window.

Neuro-Idealism

Of all the three new idealisms, the most surprising is that of Chilean neuro-anatomist, Humberto Maturana.[6] Although his early work, while at MIT, was in experimental epistemology with scientific realists, J.Lettvin and W.McCullogh,[7] in his later work he made two

---

[6]Maturana has co-authored several pieces with his former student Francisco Varela. However, Dr. Varela has made it clear, e.g., in his presentation at the Conference on Philosophy and the Human Future, Cambridge University 1989, that he restricts himself to the scientific aspects of cognitive science where Maturana is dedicated to the philosophical (especially ontological) ramifications of his neurological stance. Since my concern here is confined to the ontological ramifications of the theory of the closed nervous system as Maturana expresses them, no reference is made, or intended, to Varela.

[7]J.Y. Lettvin, H.R. Maturana, W.S. McCulloch and W.H. Pitts, "What the Frog's Eye Tells the Frog's Brain," [1959], *Proceedings of the IRE* 47, No. 11, pp. 140-159.

decisions which landed him firmly in subjective idealism. First, consequent upon certain experiments in color perception, he decided "to close off the nervous system."[8] Secondly, he decided to explore the epistemological and ontological ramifications of that theoretic choice. As with Berkeley and Fichte, his subjective idealism does not result from being coerced by the evidence, but is a deliberate intellectual choice.

To quote some of his clearest ontological texts:

> Nature, the world, society, science, religion, the physical space, atoms, molecules, trees...indeed all things, are cognitive entities, explanations of the praxis or happening of living of the observer, and as such, as this very explanation, they only exist as a bubble of human actions floating on nothing.[9]

When asked what his relationship was to Kant's theory he wrote, in Fichtean style:

> I claim that the *Ding-an-sich* [thing-in-itself] cannot be asserted or accepted as having any kind of existence because existence is bound to the distinctions of the observer, and to accept the existence of what cannot be distinguished has no sense.[10]

How he understands his theory's connection with quantum idealism is revealed in this statement:

> As we recognize that we cannot experientially distinguish between what we socially call perception and illusion, we accept that existence is specified by an operation of distinction: *nothing pre-exists its distinction.* In this sense, houses, persons, atoms or elementary particles, are not different.[11]

With this claim he is essentially stating that nothing could have existed at all before human observers-in-language came into the world,

---

[8]Humberto R. Maturana and Francisco J. Varela, *Autopoiesis and Cognition: The Realization of the Living.* Boston Studies in the Philosophy of Science. Vol. 42. Boston: D. Reidel, p. xv.

[9]Humberto Maturana, "Ontology of Observing: Biological Foundations of Self Consciousness and the Physical Domain of Existence," in *Conference Workbook for "Texts in Cybernetic Theory,"* American Society for Cybernetics, Felton, California, October 18-23, 1988, 51.

[10]Humberto Maturana, "Some Reflections," *Continuing the Conversation* (5), Summer 1986, p.3. Gregory Williams, Route 1, Box 302,Gravel Switch, KY 40328.

[11]"Ontology of Observing," pp. 44-45. The italics are his.

a claim which implies the ontological impossibility of the existence of the world, or of biological evolution, previous to *homo sapiens.* Subjective idealism leaves one with strange bedfellows. Here the non-theistic, "closed system" biologist falls in with the fundamentalist theologians.

After "closing off the nervous system," Maturana explicitly took up the philosophical issues. Unfortunately, his attempt to develop an "ontology of observing" has led him into a series of errors that a trained philosopher would have seen coming.

It has been acknowledged by many thinkers that Berkeley's theory, which reduces the natural world to human perceptions, is not strictly refutable as long as one accepts Berkeley's faith in the All-Perceiving God who makes "common" perceptions between individuals possible. Nor, for that matter, can Leibniz's theory of organisms as "windowless monads" be refuted as long as his Divinely instituted "pre-established harmony" is accepted to account for communication between them.

But Humberto Maturana's ontological reduction of the natural universe to individual acts of "distinction" made by "languaging observers" whose nervous systems are "operationally closed" is a philosophically untenable position. With these starting principles he necessarily falls into *solipsism.* The problem of solipsism is one he does not seem to grasp firmly, for he claims that his theory of language and his theory of the outside observer protect him from it. Yet it can be rigorously shown by his own principles that language, as he defines it, can never arise.

Maturana claims that recurrent reciprocal perturbations between two organisms whose nervous systems are *closed* to information from the outside and are *structurally determined* from within, will eventuate in coordinations of actions between the organisms. In human organisms, these reciprocal perturbations are supposed to lead, at higher levels of recursion, to "languaging," which he defines as "consensual coordinations of consensual coordinations of actions."

However, he has overlooked the fact that, for a closed nervous system the order of whose operations is determined entirely from within, all perturbations will be received as *random* perturbations. There can be no pattern, or order, or rhythm of perturbations received *as ordered* by the structurally determined closed nervous system. Maturana admits as much with his claim that between organisms there is no "transmitted information."[12] What scientists mean by the phrase

---

[12]Humberto Maturana, and Francisco Varela, *The Tree of Knowledge.* Boston: Shambhala, 1987, p. 196.

"transmitted information" is patterned or ordered or rhythmic perturbations received *as ordered.*

Thus, in Maturana's theory, there can be no coordination between two organisms because there can be no *order* common to the two nervous systems. There is no way an organism, as Maturana describes it, could "coordinate" its actions with another, much less achieve "consensual coordinations of consensual coordinations of actions," which are supposed to constitute human language.

Maturana's subsequent attempt to bring the environment, and therefore the *inter-actions* of two organisms, into existence by grounding them in the observations of a third-party observer (remember, existence is entirely the result of observation) leads off into infinite regress. A fourth-party observer will be needed to bring the third party's environment into existence so that the third party (with his closed nervous system) can be really "observing" the first two parties inter-acting. Then, of course, the fourth party will need a fifth party, and so it goes.

Although most of his terminology comes from the biological sciences, and he claims to be doing a "biology of cognition," Maturana's Berkeleyan theory is in direct contradiction to evolutionary naturalist epistemology. The understanding, in evolutionary epistemology, of the nervous system as a highly evolved network of response capacities and sensitivities adapted over millions of years by successful interaction with already existing ecosystems is not available to him. He denies the autonomous existence of an environment in relation to which more perfectly adapted nervous systems could have evolved through natural selection.

Buddho-Idealism

Buddho-idealism, as found in American culture today, takes more than one form. The most widespread is the assumption that "you create your own reality" and that the world is really a state of your mind. Let me hasten to say that this is not what the Buddha himself taught 2500 years ago. As far as we can tell, what the Buddha taught was a *way* to experience liberation from suffering, suffering largely caused by reifications of our own conceptual and emotional constructions, especially by the reification which we call the "self." Gautama was extremely careful not to make any ontological claims as to the reality or unreality of the natural world.

Here I refer to three kinds of Buddho-idealism. One is simply a famous scholarly misinterpretation by Western philosophers of one particular school of Buddhism, the Yogachara School. Some Western philosophers read it as claiming that "only mind" exists, since "the independent existence of the universe, separate from its subjective perception, cannot be found."[13]

A second type of Buddho-idealism is what happens to nearly any Westerner who reads the Buddhist texts with an ordinary ego-driven mind. The Sutras, written from the point of view of ego-free mind, cannot be penetrated or grasped by the ego-oriented intellect. Thus, it is quite easy, almost inevitable, to interpret translations of the Sutras as idealism. One will be tempted to compare selected texts from Sutras with statements of, for example, the quantum idealists or German philosophers. As far as the words go, there is indeed a similarity of words. Not much more than that can be said. Certainly no epistemological or ontological conclusions can legitimately be drawn.

A third form of Buddho-idealism is found in some Westerners who have seriously dedicated themselves to the meditative practice. There is a famous saying by the old Zen Master Seigen that before he practiced Zen for 30 years mountains were mountains and rivers were rivers, but that later mountains were no longer mountains and rivers were no longer rivers. Then, finally, he returned to ordinary life and was at peace, and mountains were again mountains, and rivers were again rivers.

Those who practice Buddhist meditation for a length of time can easily become Buddho-idealists by getting stuck at Seigen's second stage where mountains are no longer mountains. If the meditator is simply passing through the stages without judgment about the ultimate reality of things, there is no idealism, even at the second stage. But to come to the second stage, and to believe that this is enlightenment, that this is in fact the ultimate nature of the world, this constitutes Buddho-idealism. This is already an advanced meditative stage, of course, since the fictional nature of the ego is seen as well as the fictional nature of mountains and rivers.

---

[13] Roger J. Corless, *The Vision of Buddhism.* NY: Paragon House, 1989, p.25

This is what is meant by *chitta-matra*, 'just thinking,' or *vijnapti-matra*, 'just recognition.'... the objective universe exists but its *independent* existence, separate from its subjective perception, *cannot be found*.

This system was misunderstood in its turn. In China and Japan the mists of Taoism bewitched the Yogacharins more and more to claim the illusory nature of the shifting world and to recognize mental events as alone real; in the West, Yogachara was straightforwardly identified with philosophical Idealism, and it was presumed that Yogachara overturned the nihilism of Madhyamika by teaching the supremacy of Universal Mind. 'Just mind' was misinterpreted as 'Mind Only.'

In all likelihood, most of those in our culture who claim a Buddhist spiritual direction, who have read and meditated some, still remain attached to self, residing somewhere in Master Seigen's first stage. If they take the texts seriously, but remain attached to the reified "self," they easily come up with cant phrases like "you create your own reality." This amounts to traditional Western subjective idealism. On the other hand, those caught in Seigen's second stage, who make ontological judgments about it, are holding a doctrine of objective idealism.

Evolutionary Epistemology and Buddho-Idealism

The correction of Buddho-idealism occurs through an understanding of Zen Master Seigen's third stage: when mountains are again mountains and rivers are again rivers. Vietnamese Zen Master Thich Nhat Hanh brings us right up to the edge of evolutionary epistemology with his comment on this old saying:

> Meditators realize that all phenomena interpenetrate and inter-are with all other phenomena, so in their everyday lives they look at a chair or an orange differently from most people. When they look at mountains and rivers, they see that "rivers are no longer rivers and mountains are no longer mountains." Mountains "have entered" rivers, and rivers "have entered" mountains (interpenetration). Mountains become rivers, and rivers become mountains (inter-being). However, *when they want to go for a swim, they have to go into the river* and not climb the mountain. When they return to everyday life, "mountains are again mountains, rivers are again rivers."[14]

Nhat Hanh's explanation of Seigen's words is most telling. Within an epistemology of evolutionary mediate realism there is a simple principle that is necessarily true. *We can never perceive the world directly, but our actions always affect the world directly.* The actions of our bodies *directly* move, disturb, change, refashion parts of the world. Yet, our perceptions and cognitions are only internally-generated *maps* of the world which are organized by the central nervous system from the ways that sound waves, light waves, and tactile pressures impinge upon the parts of our bodies.

When we experience in meditation, as Thich Nhat Hanh describes, that mountains "have entered" rivers and rivers "have entered"

---

[14]Thich Nhat Hanh, *The Sun My Heart.* Berkeley: Parallax Press, 1988, pp. 87-88. Italics mine.

mountains, we are becoming aware of the derivative nature of our perceptions. We notice that the mountain which we "see" is not substantial, it is not solid and three-dimensional and made of granite, but is a slightly shimmering, alive sort of thing. What I "see," what I directly experience in the act of seeing, is not a real mountain, but an image, a construction, a visual interpretation prepared by my highly evolved and sophisticated nervous system from the array of differences found in the upside-down images on my two retinas.

Evolution has provided us with a strong proclivity to reify these visual images, to treat them as "things" and not to take them for what they are, images of things. There are clear evolutionary survival advantages, in both swiftness of response and confidence in action, if we regularly mistake the images of things for the things themselves. There would have been little advantage for our animal ancestors, in whose skulls most of our brain architecture was designed to know that they were seeing only an image of a predator and not directly seeing a predator itself.

Yet, it is possible for us as humans to override the natural reification of our sensory images and to experience that the "stuff" of the world-*as-perceived* is not stone, wood and water, but an array of images not intrinsically separated from each other, a kind of shimmering curtain which can almost be felt to be made up of vast volleys of neural signals. To effectively de-activate our ancient imperative to reify, it is necessary to slow ourselves down a great deal and become quiet for a very long time. Only then can we notice the sensory images *as images* in detail.

Buddhist meditation is particularly well suited to this work. Those who have practiced it long enough have usually come to the experiential realization that what they see is not a substantial thing, what they hear is not substantial, even what they feel is of the nature of image and not of the nature of solid, three-dimensional objects in the world.

Yet, there has always been a catch, a catch that is normally not focused on in the Buddhist literature, but which Seigen so clearly pointed out. Realizing the insubstantial nature of the world-as-perceived is not the last step. The last step is seeing that mountains are again mountains and rivers are again rivers. Because, if you want to go swimming, you have to go to the river and not the mountain.

The great principle of evolutionary naturalist realism is that action is in *direct* contact with the independently existing natural world, even though cognition is only in indirect relationship with it. When it comes to *action*, mountains will necessarily always be mountains, and rivers will always be rivers. Thus, even for the most traditional Buddhists (although they do not write much about it), when it comes to action in the world like going swimming or planting crops or building a meditation hall, the real material world is there under their hands. They do not imagine they can walk through walls.

Thus, it seems to me that the Buddhist tradition accepts naturalistic realism, by default. There are three reasons I think this: (a) The Buddha refused to speculate on questions about the real existence of the natural world. (b) Since Seigen's saying is so widely quoted throughout the Zen tradition, at least that tradition makes a point of a third-stage return to realism. (c) Traditional Buddhist writers offer no *idealistic* explanations for why we can only swim in rivers and not in mountains.

The *"independent world is not found"* within cognitive awareness because cognition cannot get outside our retinas, our tympanic membranes and the nerve endings in our skin. But when we go swimming, an action of our whole organism, we are directly outside. Nothing in the Buddha's basic teaching is incompatible with naturalistic realism.

E. Conclusion

Wildlife biologists inform us that the vast majority of the species being driven extinct, especially in the tropical forests, *have never been observed*. We did not even know they existed. They have been foraging, feeding themselves, mating, giving birth, raising young for untold millenia—utterly without our knowledge. But now, because of our actions in the world, they are being driven extinct.

This tragic fact is the ultimate test of subjective idealism. A subjective idealist cannot admit that a species *could* exist if we did not know about it. Since these species did in fact exist without our knowledge, as their corpses show, they are a refutation of the entire subjective idealist enterprise.

As for the call-to-action to prevent The Great Dying—will a generation of "new paradigm" idealists rally to their historical task, when they are not even convinced that unobserved species exist? Subjective idealism saps our strength for action when the call is to prevent harm to "the other." Whether it is oppressed humans or dying wildlife, *we must know they exist in their own right if we are to want to help them stay alive.*

ঝ

Let us be very clear about it. Subjective idealism is probably the most virulent form of anthropocentrism known. It not only leaves out non-human creatures, but it is a seedbed for racism and other forms of oppression among humans.

Its failure, as a philosophy, to acknowledge the intrinsic rights, and existence, of others has led to the cruelest political systems in our history. If there is any doubt of this, I refer the reader to the book by American philosopher, George Santayana, *The German Mind: A Philosophical Diagnosis*, written in 1915. Solely by an examination of the deep subjectivist current in the writings of philosophers of the German idealist tradition, Santayana was able to predict the rise of the Fascist state twenty years before it happened.[15] The Nazis took especial interest in the thought of J. G. Fichte. The idealist philosopher Giovanni Gentile was a major theoretician of Italian Fascism. The Germans know this. In a recent interview in *Time* magazine, German Chancellor Helmut Kohl stated, "The term idealism was born here—it was the contribution of German philosophers, and it was abused terribly in this century."[16]

Philosophical idealism is not a toy to play with, as if it were simply something "new and different" and therefore "better." It is not new. It is not different. And we know where it leads.

As we attempt to envision a philosophical direction for the next epoch of our venture in this complex natural biosphere, let us call what is old and discredited by its true name—and think far more courageously, deeply and *inclusively* than we have ever done before.

[15]George Santayana, *The German Mind: A Philosophical Diagnosis*. New York: Thomas Y. Crowell, 1968. Originally published in 1915 under the title, *Egotism in German Philosophy*.

[16]*Time*, June 25, 1990, p. 38.

Beyond Reason: The Importance of Emotion in Philosophy

Robert C. Solomon

Where did philosophy go wrong? When did it cease to be "the love of wisdom" and aspire to be a science? How did Socratic enthusiasm and the urge to edify and give meaning to the untidy questions of life give way to a compulsion for clarity and argumentation for its own sake? Why is it that the best-read intellectuals in America now say that they no longer read or relate to philosophy even if—they quickly add—they still enjoy and seem to understand a little Plato, Kant or Nietzsche? When did philosophy give up its claim to be the key to the humanities, the heart of *Humanitas*, to become the heartless discipline it is today?

Enmity toward emotion is as old as philosophy itself, but to be down on emotions is to be against the stuff of life itself. Philosophy makes a fatal error when it begins to take more pride in its "detachment" than in its passion. Richard Rorty has recently suggested that the "death of philosophy" began with its turn to epistemology and its claim to be the Arbiter of All Knowledge, but I would argue that the exclusive emphasis on knowledge and polite "conversation" is itself part of the problem. What is wrong with epistemology is not what it claims but what it leaves out. Philosophy is still very much alive and lively, but it gives us an extremely limited vision of what used to be called "wisdom." Reading much of contemporary philosophy, it would seem that to be a full human being is to use syntactically sophisticated language, process information and acquire knowledge—but not to feel anything. To be a philosopher is to evaluate arguments but avoid (at least, "qua Philosopher") caring too much about any concrete conclusion. What has evolved is this bizarre public image of a discipline full of clever sophists who can refute every argument—and then be left with nothing. In one recent textbook in ethics, for example, the author efficiently dispatches every familiar argument concerning our knowledge of the Good and leaves the students, without apology, stuck with a candid, dispassionate nihilism.

The problem is not, as some embittered critics have claimed, the heavy emphasis on logical sophistication and "technique." The problem, as with technique in general, is that the technique comes to dictate the content, and obliterate the untidy and all-too-human questions that the technique evolved to clarify. The result: what philosophers have gained in skill and cleverness, they have lost in sensitivity. Or worse, compassion and conviction have become embarrassments, stretches of a philosopher's soiled underwear showing between the neat and clean lines of argument. Robert Nozick praises a recent book on a particularly emotional issue (Tom Regan on Animal Rights) for its "dispassionate treatment" of the subject. To be passionate about the subject (as Regan actually is) would be to give up one's claim to be a philosopher, perhaps even becoming what Nozick calls "a crank." And yet, there are hundreds of professional philosophers who pride themselves on their compassion and counseling rather than their logic. Why should they be so defensive?

One might suggest that this is nothing new. From the beginning, philosophy has taken pride in its 'detachment'. Socrates warned us against "getting carried away by our passions" and philosophy ever since has been the business of reason and the enemy of unthinking emotion. But the story is more complex than this—and more encouraging. Socrates may have warned us against the emotions but he was also, and he remains, a model of impassioned philosophy and commitment. We have drawn the history of philosophy one way rather than another, concentrating on Socrates the dialectician instead of Socrates the eccentric character and the brilliant, devoted teacher. So too, Heraclitus wrote dark sayings about Being and the Logos, but he also wrote concrete and useful observations about the passions of life. Aristotle flatly contested Plato's rejection of emotion, and the Stoics, while criticizing emotion, managed to develop enormous respect and a full-scale theory about them. There is a very different reading of modern philosophy from what my friends call "the tradition"—that imaginary line that begins (out of nowhere) with Galileo and the New

Science and splits to three rationalists and three empiricists then capped by Kant's first *Critique* with a quick skip over the epistemological abyss of German idealism and romanticism to John Stuart Mill. But Descartes and Spinoza wrote extensively on the passions, and Hume devoted the whole of Book II of his Treatise to them. Even Kant wrote extensively about *"Gefuhl"*, and the essential nature of the passions is a primary topic from Hegel and Schopenhauer to Nietzsche and Freud. The historical content of philosophy is what we philosophers decide it to be. Why don't we include Rousseau in the standard "history of modern philosophy" course—because he had no epistemology?

A half a century ago, the logical positivists insisted with considerable justification that society had lost its senses, that rationality had been buried by nonsense. The significant social task of philosophy then was to save reason with science as its guide, to separate knowledge from meaninglessness and save the world. We tend today to view the positivists as troublemakers and glib reductionists but, in their social context, they were up to something much more noble than defending a dubious theory of meaning. Philosophy always has a context, and its task—far from being determined by some eternal lines from Plato, depends on which way the world has to be moved at any given time.

The problem facing philosophy today is not a lack of rationality but an excess of it—government "think tanks" devoid of human feeling, academic exercises oblivious to motivation and eagerness, crimes not of passion but of indifference and pointless brutality. Philosophy echoes society, and the dominant philosophy of our society is a resounding nihilism, a void badly filled with abstract principles and disputes where feelings should be. Our world is the macrocosm of David Rabe's play, *Hurlyburly*, which David Denby reviewed a few years ago:

> ...the play is about callous people who fill the gaping space where their emotions should be with an elaborate kind of psycho-babble. They all know that in certain situations they ought to feel something: their language represents the enfeebled...superego at work—the homage that words pay to the *idea* of feeling, a discourse about emotion in place of having any.
>
> (*Atlantic Monthly*, Jan. '85, p. 50)

What Denby doesn't quite say, however, is that the discourse too is largely a misunderstanding of emotions. It is as if feelings have become illegitimate in the business of life, intrusions and distractions that interfere with one's skill at cool negotiation or sense of judicial fairness. Emotions are misunderstood and the result, in business, in government, in academic meetings, on the streets and in daily life, is a striking absence of compassion and concern.

Philosophy as "the love of wisdom" can do two things, both exemplified admirably by Socrates. It can set the discourse straight, and it can serve as an example. Even if the emotions are to be dismissed or demeaned, they ought to be understood, but to understand them is to see good reason why they should not be dismissed or demeaned. It is reasoned emotion, not reasoned discourse, that is missing from our lives—edification, encouragement, enthusiasm, compassion and caring. The current business of philosophy, accordingly, is not to adduce more arguments but to understand and encourage feelings. We need Elie Wiesel, not more Tarski and Quine. There have been many times in our history when the task of philosophy has been to impose reason and order, but the last thing that we need to do now is to insist upon more "dispassion."

This suggestion will be met, predictably, by a lampoon of emotion—a vision of mad philosophers screaming at each other in the hallways. The presumption, of course, is that the introduction of emotions in an argument means the breakdown of civility—shouting at least, if not bloodshed and the destruction of university furniture. But this is precisely that gross misunderstanding of the emotions that gives support to their supposed illegitimacy in the first place. David Hume, and before him Aristotle, pointed out that there are "calm" as well as "violent" emotions, and the former (at least) are the basis of most of our moral virtues and best traits of character. Civility does not disappear when emotions enter the arena, nor do arguments suddenly become unsound or inferences unfounded. Emotions motivate, they do not undermine philosophy. Understanding our emotions is not extraneous to wisdom but its very essence.

What I want to argue here is that philosophy has too long demeaned or ignored the passions. Emotions are essential to philosophy, both as subject matter and as a part of our philosophical style. We have had enough chopping logic down the old Chisholm trail. Good philosophy ought to move us as well as rebut other people's arguments. It is more important to understand our own passions than to criticize other people's claims to knowledge. Tedious, dispassionate thoroughness, punctuated by an occasional wisecrack, has too long been our ideal. In this essay I want to make a plea for sensitivity rather than cleverness as a philosophical virtue.

The Importance of Emotion in Philosophy

Philosophers have often contrasted "reason and the passions," typically championing the former against the latter and defending philosophy itself as the love of reason. By implication, at least, philosophy tends to display a contempt for the passions. "Appeal to the emotions" gets listed in almost every introductory logic text and ethics book as an "informal" fallacy, something to avoid, not at all costs, perhaps, but at least in term papers. Philosophy gets defined as the formulation and criticism of argument, the exclusive domain of reason. "Heated" argument, though not uncommon, is considered inappropriate. Dispassionate analysis is encouraged; passionate advocacy is not. Philosophy might still be dutifully described as the "love" of wisdom but this love is hardly the lusty enthusiasm with which Socrates, if not Plato, approached the subject. The ideal, then as now, is a kind of calm, a contemplative detachment if not full-fledged stoic apatheia.

Even when we find one of the great philosophers defending the passions against the excessive claims of reason, the result is less than edifying and the implication smacks of skepticism. David Hume, most notably, insisted that, "reason is and ought to be the slave of the passions," dismissing out of hand a long tradition of ethics conceived as the business of reason. But in doing so, he at least implied and certainly set the stage for others to argue that morals were beyond the grasp of reason and in some essential sense unarguable. In juxtaposing reason and the passions, Hume in fact fit in with a long line of philosophers who also set them off against one another and separated emotion from rationality. Descartes and his compatriot Malebranche, for example, analyzed emotions in terms of physiological "animal spirits," distinctively inferior parts of the psyche if indeed parts of the psyche at all. Leibniz thought of emotions as "confused perceptions" and Kant rather famously dismissed what he called "pathological love" (i.e. love as an emotion) from the love more properly commanded by the Scriptures and practical reason. Kant may also have said that "nothing great is ever accomplished without enthusiasm" (a comment usually attributed to Hegel), but it is clear that enthusiasm as such deserves very little place in his grand "critique" of the higher human faculties.

This suspicion concerning all things emotional continues in the current philosophical literature. Let me mention two illustrative examples—one a recent address by one of our most distinguished and intellectually open-minded moral philosophers, the other an essay by a well-known philosopher of mind.

In his presidential address to the American Philosophical Association (Pacific Division) Joel Feinberg asks, ("Sentiment and Sentimentality in Practical Ethics" (March 26, 1982)) "What relevance, if any, do appeals to sentiment have for issues in practical ethics?" He begins with the usual answer: "The abrupt way with the question is to respond 'none; sentiment is one thing and argument is another, and nothing fogs the mind as thoroughly as emotion'." (p. 19) Feinberg rejects this "abrupt" answer, but his conclusion is far less than an enthusiastic endorsement; he acknowledges that feelings may be 'relevant' or at least not irrelevant to ethics, and he concludes that he "finds no unmanageable conflict between effective humanitarianism and the maintenance, under flexible control, of the essential human sentiments." He adds, as if this is not already sufficiently cautious, "I hope that conclusion is not too optimistic" (*ibid.* p. 42)

Feinberg's careful analysis of the place of sentiment in ethics deserves a similarly extended and careful reply, but the only point I want to make for now is to call attention to the extreme caution and defensiveness he feels compelled to adopt in presenting his "optimistic" thesis—that sentiment may not be wholly irrelevant to ethical considerations. One notes the extreme effort just to clear a bit of room for emotion, as if a woman's feelings about her body and her baby and her "morals" and reputation and her feelings for the father were but personal anecdotes and distractions in the abortion debate while the philosophers' abstract arguments about the status and rights of the fetus were the only legitimate concern. Whatever the pros and cons of deontology, our ethics remains quite Kantian, the emphasis wholly on principles and the arguments supporting them, the inclinations as such contributing nothing—whatever their other virtues—to moral worth.

The second article worth mentioning here is "An Assessment of Emotion" by Jerome Shaffer in *The American Philosophical Quarterly* (Vol. 20, no. 2, April 1983). In that assessment, Shaffer begins with a most unflattering example of "undergoing an emotion."

> I am driving around a curve and see a log across the road. I take it that bodily harm is likely and I don't want that. I turn pale, my heart beats faster, I feel my stomach tighten. I slam on the brakes... (in Myers ed., p. 202-3)

Not surprisingly, Shaffer uses this and similar examples of emotion to conclude that emotions are not very pleasant or valuable experiences and, accordingly, are "neither necessary nor in general desirable for the main concerns of life" (220).

Now a moment's reflection should establish that this case of unwelcome surprise is not anything like a paradigm of emotion. Indeed one might object that surprise is not an emotion, despite its physiological similarity to certain emotions. And in any case not all emotions should be characterized, much less defined, by this "turning pale, heart beats faster, stomach tightens," etc.. Consider the very different analysis that would accompany taking as our lead example, say, experiencing a powerful sense that justice has not been done, or the possibly decades-long experience of being passionately in love. (Shaffer's analysis of love as an emotion in the same essay reduces love to "butterflies in the stomach" and other such "waves, currents, surges or suffusions," concluding that love too is an emotion of little value. This is hardly the passion that moved Tristan and Isolde.) Furthermore, we can readily agree that coming across a log in the road is an undesirable experience without concluding that the fear itself is an undesirable experience. Indeed, in safer surroundings, millions of people have been known to stand in line in order to pay up to six dollars each to have the wits pleasantly scared out of them not only by misplaced logs but by killer sharks, mad men, monsters and chainsaw murderers.

Shaffer's "assessment" of emotion is, in fact, an emotional hatchet-job. But the only conclusion I want to draw from his techniques and conclusion here is the shockingly glib way in which it is carried out. Imagine a philosopher publishing in the same or a similarly professional journal an assessment of logic (would that even make sense?), in which the paradigm case was an undergraduate using sophistry and self-deception (say, with a version of the prisoner's dilemma) to evade an obvious responsibility, concluding that logic, accordingly, played no very important or desirable role in our lives. But the prejudice against emotion in philosophy is so strong that an unfair or frivolous attack does not even provoke a defense, and a defense of emotion, no matter how dispassionate and responsible, tends to invoke the charge of soft-headed sentimentality.

I do not think that I would be overstating the case if I were to say that modern American philosophy in general has shown a profound distrust as well as disinterest in the role of emotions in philosophy. Philosophers should try to be reasonable, not impassioned or—much worse—sentimental. Philosophers should look at both sides of a dispute, evaluating arguments and not get "caught up" in one position or another. Indeed one begins to suspect that the criterion for respectability for current philosophical problems is the inappropriateness of any emotional reaction—the intellectual purity of the trans-world reference problem versus the emotional morass of most "applied philosophy" issues. Philosophical theses must be argued, calmly and, if possible, formally, thus neutralizing the seductive effects of rhetoric and avoiding appeal to the emotions. Not surprisingly, a philosopher such as Kierkegaard, who celebrates passion over reason and knowledge, is misunderstood or dismissed as a philosopher.

Insofar as emotions provide us with a topic in philosophy, it has been understood that their place is tangential, their analysis a side issue. Not surprisingly, then, the most noteworthy theories of emotion—in Descartes and Hume, for example—are parasitic on, and sandwiched between, more general metaphysical and epistemological doctrines. First let's get straight about the virtues of human rationality—the virtues that make us human; then, perhaps, we can be entertained by a little piece on the nature and importance of the emotions. But our approach to the emotions, of course, must then be like our approach to any problem in epistemology or metaethics—formal, objective, argumentative, dispassionate, in other words, wholly unlike the subject matter itself and in opposition to it. Epistemology has as one of its aims the expansion of our knowledge; studies of emotion often aim at defusing our passions—or dismissing them, once again, as no more than mere "feelings" and clearly inferior to our rational virtues. Indeed one can easily argue that the overwhelming emphasis on epistemology over emotion in modern philosophy betrays an uncritical and probably false assumption about the nature of both philosophy and human nature.

In this essay, I want to defend the importance of emotions in philosophy. This is part of but not yet, I should say, the less modest enterprise of trying to defend the importance of the passions in life. In particular, I should like to return to some old topics in ethics, and some new issues in the philosophy of mind, in order to argue that much of what is taken for granted or ignored about emotions may in fact be essential to philosophy. It should be pointed out that serious study of emotions is far more prevalent and respectable today than it has ever been in Anglo-American "analytic" philosophy, at least since the days of James and Dewey. Nevertheless, I think that there is good reason for continued protest on behalf of the emotions in philosophy, and that is what I should like to do here—in appropriately professional and reasonable terms, of course.

1. The Relevance of Emotions to Ethics

Outside of the philosophy lecture hall, a handy way of recognizing a *moral* dispute would be this: both parties *feel* very strongly about their positions. One might object—but this leaves out any question of distinctively moral content." It does. But it is a fact (merely empirical?) that (1) disputes concerning what philosophers identify as peculiarly moral issues do inspire the strongest emotions and (2) we usually do not hesitate to judge a dispute to be moral, whatever its content, when emotions run high enough. (An argument over Babe Ruth's total number of strike-outs [1330] becomes a moral dispute when both parties tend to think their character, and the obviously faulty character of their opponent, is on the line.) In most ethical disputes, strong and in some sense fundamental feelings are involved or at issue. Whether these feelings concern or are expressed in some universal principle is a strictly secondary, merely Kohlbergian matter.

The idea that ethics essentially involves feelings is not new, of course. Indeed, if it were not for Kant, one wonders whether the suggestion that ethics is anything else could even be made intelligible. But, of course, Kant is very much with us, and philosophers who do not consider themselves deontologists or Kantians of any kind nevertheless obey Kant's primary instruction: ethics is a matter of reason (albeit practical) and not inclination. Doing ethics is a matter of formulating arguments, not appealing to the sentiments. Emotions, if they do anything, tend to 'cloud' the issue, interfere with rationality and muddle the issues.

Consider, for example, the current abortion debate. No one would deny that the subject itself generates a great deal of unmanagable emotion, and philosophers are not alone in urging that these emotions be 'controlled' to allow more rational—that is, non-emotional—debate on the issue. But more rational debate may not be possible, and, it is important to note, the emotionality of the debate does not mean—and has not meant—that there are fewer arguments or more unsound or invalid arguments on the debating table. Emotionally feverish proponents are nevertheless still capable of formulating and recognizing valid arguments; indeed, their ability to do so is typically improved, not hampered, by their emotion. This is a point often denied (without evidence), that emotional advocates tend to be "less logical" than cool, calm and rational discussants. But though it is true that they tend to be less inclined to "view the problem objectively" and amiably accept their opponents' conclusions and they are much more motivated to attack their opponents' inferences and premises at any perceivable weak spot, emotional advocates do not excuse themselves and are not excused from the rules of logic by virtue of their passion. The problem is not lack of logic but rather that it is not a logical problem. What is at stake in the abortion problem(s) are deep emotional issues. To urge more rational debate, however essential for policy makers, may be to urge ignoring the issues at stake altogether, which is, of course, what much of the philosophy debate has been doing. ("Do fetuses have rights?" and "Does a woman 'own' her own body?")

Consider Feinberg's discussion of the abortion issue, vis-a-vis the question of sentiment in ethics. (I will use the terms "sentiment" and "emotion" interchangeably; Feinberg does not.) He admits that the most effective "argument" against abortion consists of photographs of "tender little faces and chubby paws of 'sleeping' ten-week old fetuses.." This sentimental argument has now, we know, been supplanted by the not at all sentimental tactic of filming a fetus—with a variety of camera speeds and angles for effect—at the moment of an abortion, so that we can see the poor creature "being torn limb from limb" as one anti-abortionist explained it. Feinberg objects to such tactics, but I do not see that his objections support his general suspicion of "sentiment" and appeals to emotion. His main argument is that appeals to sentiment of any kind require further justification by reasons. To show this, he gives considerable attention to various flawed, contrived, cheap, "romantic", self-deceptive and merely "sentimental" sentiments. He also raises the familiar anti-emotion counter-examples of the "rabble rouser" and the "manipulated patriot." But all of this is no more than an argument to the effect that appeals to emotion *as such* do not have deontological trump status. Emotions (like arguments and other reasons) must be warranted and relevant to the issue, but this is not in the least to cast suspicion on their proper role in ethics.

There is a legitimate objection that some emotions and some appeals to emotion, like some arguments, are unsound or simply irrelevant to the case. The mere fact that a description, picture or film elicits a spontaneous reaction does not guarantee that such a reaction is justified, and in the case of our reaction to the destruction of a ten-week-old fetus, it may not be. That does not mean, however, that all such appeals are irrelevant; it only signifies that the relevance of such a reaction must itself be justified or, at least, justifiable. For example, our empathetic reaction presupposes that the fetus is sentient and can feel pain, that it does in fact "resist" the taking of its life, that it would in all likelihood have a reasonably happy future which is now being destroyed. But even if our reaction is justified, the emotion may be irrelevant or inadequate, or it may just miss the point. I have been deeply moved by the sight of baby rats playing and suckling, but I would not take this sentiment as particularly significant when considering the extermination of pests in my country home. I am certain that I could be thoroughly repulsed by a slow-motion close-up of an anopheles mosquito being crushed very slowly under a fingernail, but I would not take my repulsion as a reason for reconsidering my attitudes toward mosquitoes. One of my students recently wrote a response to a newspaper column against abortion in which he pointed out that a detailed description of a routine life-saving operation would no doubt inspire disgust and repulsion, but this should not be considered a reason for rejecting modern medicine. The problem here is not the appeal to emotion. These are appeals to irrelevant emotions or, at least, to emotions which are inadequate to support the conclusion.

Is our feeling of sentiment toward a fetus irrelevant to the ethical issues of abortion? I would certainly think not, and Feinberg himself spends many pages reconsidering the implications of denying such relevance. He mentions the ancient argument that the gratification of the moral sentiments is, in itself, a good thing and he himself has often argued that the feelings of others (especially feelings of outrage, disgust and repulsion) are a key consideration in ethics. He invokes the sense of a "sacred object" (a flag or religious artifact) whose value is defined largely in terms of the emotions it inspires—and fetal life itself might be so conceived. He also discusses the argument that human-like beings (including recently dead human bodies as well as fetuses) are significant *symbols* of humanity, and he sympathetically considers the argument that sentiment itself is essential to our humanity and that, therefore, anything that violates our sentiments is *prima facie* wrong, pending subsequent moral evaluation. Feinberg rightly insists that all of these arguments are too strong as they stand; sentiment itself cannot make a complete case and one must have some sense of the "quality and nature of the sentiments" before proceeding with such arguments. But this does not presume or indicate any antagonism between emotions and reasons, and it does not weaken the case for emotions in ethics.

Feinberg rightly points out that any criterion for proper sentiment will need support by reasons as well. (So too the idea that sentiment acts as a *test* of moral wrong needs reasons to back it up in each case.) But it does not follow that these reasons and the sentiments are at all distinct, or that the sentiments do not themselves provide the reasons in question. I would argue that emotions are themselves reasons, both in the sense that the appeal to emotions provides an essential source of support for most moral judgments and in the more interesting sense that emotions have a logic too and must be evaluated and justified like any other evidence or argument. A person's repulsion to the murder of fetuses does not in itself make abortion morally wrong, but neither will it do to say that the reasons for condemning abortion (or for that matter for condoning it) can be stated, understood or justified independently of such sentiments. Our attitudes toward abortion are based on the contingent facts that fetuses resemble and turn into infant human beings. Our emotional reactions to infants provide reasons—whether or not they are conclusive reasons—for our attitudes toward fetuses. Such arguments may yet be misdirected or out of proportion, like William James's (Czarist) Russian lady who sobs at a play while her coachman freezes to death outside. But to deny such reasons or their relevance is not to make the abortion debate "more rational." It is rather to ignore its substance altogether.

Feinberg's worry can be mollified, I would suggest, by rejecting the unwarranted separation of emotions (sentiments) and judgment. Feinberg defines a "sentiment" (as opposed to "an attitude, thought or judgment prompted by feeling") as "an *affective state* without the explicit attitude or judgment." (p. 21) Sentiments may have "some cognitive mediation" but they, unlike judgments, have a "certain *passivity* to them; for the most part they happen to us, or get pulled out of us by external stimuli." Feinberg distinguishes sentiments from emotions but adds here that sentiments, like emotions, are "in some degree agitating or disturbing." but once this separation is accepted and the emotions are reduced to Rylean "agitations", the relation between reasons and emotions becomes problematic. And if ethics is conceived as the study and search for (valid) moral arguments, then it would be hard to see how emotions (sentiments) could be relevant to ethics.

Over 2500 years ago, Aristotle insisted—without making a big deal out of it—that emotions as well as judgments and actions were essential to ethics, to virtue and to eudaimonia. There is a redundancy here in that emotions already include both judgments and actions and neither judgments nor actions exclude emotions. Indeed, Aristotle provided (in his *Rhetoric*) a detailed analysis of anger in which judgment and action play a crucial role. Anger, he argued, was the perception of an offense (real or merely perceived), a kind of recognition coupled with a desire for action (namely, revenge). Moreover, the perception and the desire were not effects of emotion but its constituents.[1] Emotions are

---

[1] Against Feinberg's juxtaposition of sentiment and argument, Aristotle saw that an emotion is already something of a practical syllogism. (Cf. Donald Davidson's somewhat curious recasting of Hume's analysis of pride in the second book of the Treatise; Davidson, "Hume's Cognitive Theory of Pride," *Journal of Philosophy*, Vol. LXXIII, no. 19, Nov. 4, 1976, pp. 744-57.) The physiological disturbances that accompany anger—though

not mere feelings; they constitute a kind of knowledge. And though Aristotle's writings are hardly paradigms of passionate polemicising his views at least support the kind of enthusiastic advocacy engaged in, for example, by Socrates. Indeed, one does not have to be a Plato scholar to point out that one sure way to misread the Socratic dialogues is to read them as sequences of syllogisms and their evaluation. Socrates has not retained his two-and-a-half millenia old status as our leading philosophical hero by virtue of his bad arguments.

Ethics and Principles: Emotions and Character

Emotions, not principles, determine our ethics. It is at least difficult to imagine an ethical dispute that is free of emotion, not as a breakdown in argument but rather as its motive and as its essential ingredient. A dispute in which the positions are randomly distributed—for example, by lottery preceding a meeting of the debating club—does not strike us as an example of moral disagreement. "Thinking the unthinkable," in Hermann Kahn's phrase, is hateful not because the options are unintelligible or unimaginable but because they are presented as mere matters of fact, devoid of emotion, cold calculations concerning subjects which should never be cold or merely calculating. A purely rational approach to ethics ("pure practical reason") is at least as irrational as an emotional outburst, though the latter may have more "moral worth" than the former.

The idea that principles and not emotions define ethics has only recently been challenged by Bernard Williams, Alasdair MacIntyre, Charles Taylor and others. But the options in moral philosophy are still essentially two: neo-Kantian deontology and utilitarianism. It might be worth pointing out that these options are more alike than different. Both take ethics to be a matter of rational principles, and both take great pains to make those principles "objective" and impersonal (which in turn serve as the criteria for rationality and morality). If the principles themselves cannot be proved (as Mill feared), nevertheless all instances covered by them can be demonstrated—by appeal to the principles. Thus the demonstration itself becomes the substance of ethics. The emotions that define and motivate one's ethical position— that make it *one's own* ethical position—drop out of the picture. They become a distraction—or worse, a distortion or interruption of the moral argument. Kant still towers over us all with his authoritative dis-

they are mentioned—play no role in Aristotle's analysis. Thus he would dismiss out of hand Shaffer's reduction of an emotion to its physiological manifestations.

missal of "inclinations" from the substance of morals, against which Humean appeals to compassion and sympathy seem merely senti- mental. By the standard of this Kantian sobriety Nietzschean enthu- siasm strikes us as adolescent. Existential anxiety gets treated as pathol- ogy, not philosophy. Passionate moralizing is eliminated from philos- ophy. Moral philosophy is the defense and elaboration of the highest rational principles, not the emotional use of them.

In the tedium that counts as "rigor" in contemporary ethics it may be necessary to point out once again that the implicit moral hero of most current philosophical theories is at best an idealized bureaucrat who is, out of the office, a moral prig. The very idea that the good per- son is one who acts according to the right principles—be they categor- ical imperatives or the principle of utility—has always struck me as colossally out of tune with the manner in which ordinary people (and most philosophers) think about and judge themselves and their actions. As a matter of fact it makes my blood run cold. I don't have anything particularly radical in mind—although Nietzsche is lurking in one wing and Alasdair MacIntyre is impatiently waiting in the other. I have in mind, once again, no less respectable a moral philosopher than Aristotle, for whom *character*—in part composed of emotional states and dispositions—forms the heart of ethics, not in contrast to but as part and parcel of rationality. But this is not to say, as it is so often argued these days, that "virtue ethics" can be reduced to an ethics of principles (by establishing a one-one correspondence between duties and virtues). (e.g. G.J. Warnock, *The Object of Morality*, Methuen, 1971 pp. 71-86; William Frankena, *Ethics* (2nd Ed.), 1973, p. 68) The moral virtues in general have far more to do with "matters of the heart" than they do with ratiocinations in the head, and though a few moral emotions may be argued to already contain full-fledged moral principles (moral indignation, for instance) most of them do not (shame, pride, love and contempt, for example). If virtue ethics means anything it must mean that the clue to character is something other than (though not necessarily opposed to) acting on the basis of (or even in conformity with) moral principles. And it is not just the well-known examples of saints and heroes that illustrate this point (see, e.g. Feinberg, "Supererogation and Rules", *Ethics*, p. 71 (1961)). We see it too in the most everyday virtues of ordinary sympathy, love and loathing (of loathsome things, of course).

Character ethics is an important attempt to reintroduce into ethics a sense of morals that is not itself loathsome. Nietzsche's outrage about "morality" is at least in part an attack on conceptions of "the good per- son" which celebrate all and only the virtues of an assistant registrar or county clerk. Public policy is one thing; being a good person is another.

And what makes a good person is not just a question of right action on principle; it is also a matter of emotion, matters of caring and commitment, questions about love and hate and anger. What Carol Gilligan has now famously but mistakenly attacked as a one-sided male paradigm in ethics seems to me to be rather a falsification of the nature of ethics for any sex. There is nothing particularly female or feminine about the ethical importance of caring and nothing moral or male about a position that is devoid of sympathy, no matter how noble, categorical or utilitarian its principles. An unfeeling man cannot be a good man, no matter how universalizable his principles and no matter how consistent his actions. And in social philosophy, the concept of justice, which philosophers nowadays tend to translate immediately into some set of principles (principles of fairness, of equality, of natural rights) might better be understood as Hume and Aristotle understood justice, not first of all as a set of principles but as a personal virtue, a *sense* of what's fair. Justice is first of all a sentiment and in some people a passion. How principles of justice might be derived from or related to such a sense is not a question that I want to raise here, nor do I want to suggest what sorts of concepts and principles—as in moral indignation— might already be built into that sense. But what might a theory of justice look like, if we began not from a theory of rights or some impersonal "original position" (being no one and nowhere in particular) but rather that basic sense of compassion or empathy which seems to serve only as an unanalysed primitive in many philosophical theories? What if sensitivity rather than rationality were the issue—if, that is, these can be separated at all?

2. Emotions in the Philosophy of Mind

In a now-famous article, Elizabeth Anscombe polemicised that ethics, an already feeble subject at any rate, ought to be shelved and replaced by the philosophy of mind. (G.E.M. Anscombe, "Modern Moral Philosophy," *Philosophy*, 1958, pp. 1-19) The major questions of ethics, she argued, cannot be answered or even approached until we have solutions to certain problems in philosophical psychology. I do not propose shelving ethics, nor do I have solutions to the problems that concern Miss Anscombe. But I do find attractive her invitation to approach questions in ethics through the philosophy of mind. Questions of both virtue ethics and metaethics, I want to suggest, demand attention to the nature of emotion, and emotion, in turn, seems to me to be the most neglected topic in the philosophy of mind.

The importance of the study of emotion is nowhere more evident. For one thing, it is curious at least that the philosophy of mind has spent so much time on questions of sensation and belief and so little time investigating a set of phenomena that seems to encompass both. Even if you don't think that we've beaten the mind-body problem to death and even if you don't agree that functionalism is no more than a scientifically sophisticated version of eliminative materialism, there are limits to what can be said about the "mind" as a sensory receiver coupled with a computing machine and the philosophy of mind embraces much more than just the mind-body problem. The emotions have now become a legitimate topic in their own right, but what I should like to do here is to insert some of those considerations concerning emotion into the middle of three critical dichotomies too glibly accepted in the analysis of mind. Indeed, I sometimes wonder what the field of philosophy of mind would look like if emotions were taken as the paradigm examples instead of beliefs and (usually visual) sensations.

a. The Voluntary and the Involuntary

Philosophers who write about mental acts, states and processes quite naturally tend to distinguish between those that are voluntary— notably acts of will, acts of imagination—and those that are involuntary, for example, most sensations, pains and, according to at least some theorists, impulses, desires and attitudes. It is not at all clear, however, how emotions should be fitted into this dichotomy or, in other words, what we should say concerning the important practical question whether and how we can "control" our emotions and to what extent we are responsible for them. Should a person be blamed for his or her "bad temper"? Can a person choose to fall into or out of love? Clearly a decision to stop being envious or angry is not like a decision to perform what has been called a "basic action"—raising one's arm or winking, but neither is the envy or the anger like a pain or sensation for which one can be held responsible only in some instrumental sense (e.g. for carelessly stepping on the poisonous anemone or for not taking the prescribed dose of pain-killer).

Part of the problem is the crudeness of the dichotomy. On the one side, the paradigm is deliberate intentional action, exemplified in the realm of the mental by the so-called act of will, by a decision or a conscious choice. Questions here rarely concern the voluntariness of the minimal mental act itself (e.g. deciding to wiggle one's finger) but rather the 'spread' of responsibility (pulling the trigger, firing the bullet, killing the bystander, etc.). At the extremes, some theorists have argued that one is directly responsible only for the act of will itself, only indirectly for its consequences (Pritchard); a few others have insisted that one is responsible for *all* consequences of one's act of will (Sartre). But the seeming absurdity of both extremes brings us back to the realization that there is much that is our responsibility that is not simply willed, and much that is our "doing" that may yet not be our responsibility (e.g. unforeseen and unforeseeable consequences).

The "act of will," however, is by no means the incontrovertible pole of the voluntary. David Hume argued at some length that the supposedly "necessary" connection between such a mental act and the movement of my body is by no means so obvious. Nietzsche lampooned both will and free will, mainly attacking Kant (and defending Schopenhauer) pointing out how little in fact of our 'doing' there may be even in a deliberate act of will. I think that, first of all, they were both making a good phenomenological point: grammar aside—as Nietzsche would put it—it is not at all clear that we experience anything like the 'doing' that an act of will is supposed to represent. This is awkwardly obvious in that favorite classroom example, "I will now wiggle my finger...there, I've done it." The effort of will is most in evidence when we don't succeed, for example, for most of us, in the frustrating and foolish-feeling attempt to wiggle our ears. (Exactly what does one *do* when one performs the mental act called "trying to wiggle one's ears?") Too often, the test of willfulness is preceding deliberation, but as any reader of Dostoevsky or Alvin Goldman knows, deliberation is neither a necessary nor a sufficient condition for voluntary action. Most of our acts, indeed, are not preceded by any thought whatever, nor even accompanied by the conscious recognition of what we are doing. The conclusion of such questions, I take it, is that voluntary action is something more of a mystery than we usually get in the standard account of full-blown intentional actions.

Such questions about the nature of voluntary action illuminate the nature of emotion and control of emotions. It is quite true that we typically experience our emotions as "spontaneous," as states or episodes that happen to us, sometimes against our will or our "better judgment." Prior articulation and deliberation are not necessary for an act to be voluntary and intentional and the lack of articulation and deliberation do not make an act involuntary or unintentional. A great many of our actions, physical and mental, are clearly voluntary and intentional without articulation and deliberation, presumably if they fit into a "plan" that makes sense in the context of our other actions. A tired office worker signals the left hand turn into her driveway at 5:30 in the afternoon, her mind on nothing but the martini she is about to mix for herself (Vodka, very dry)—as soon as she calls her brother-in-law about

Saturday evening. Her signal is unthinking, unnoticed, undeliberated, inarticulate; indeed if challenged afterward ("did you signal?") she may well not remember (although we can be sure that she will be sure that she did). But do emotions—sometimes the most important acts of our lives—not fit into such plans and contexts? It often seems not, but then: could it be that we are conceiving of our plans and context on too small a scale? A sudden burst of anger or romantic passion may indeed disrupt the routines of an afternoon, but do they not often betray a covert plan of action and a context of far more significance than the everyday rituals thus disrupted?

Philosophers discussing emotions sometimes seem to talk as if the alternative to an intentional and deliberate act of will is total passivity—like having a migraine headache or a seizure. Part of the problem lies in the fact that one aspect of some emotions is an intense and distinctive physiological experience, and this—like a headache or seizure—surely does seem to be beyond our control. But the emotion is not the physiology and the voluntariness of emotion does not depend on denying our physical passivity. Paul Ricoeur, in his phenomenological study *The Voluntary and the Involuntary,* continually pushes the emotions to the side of the involuntary on such a basis, and R.S. Peters, in a well-known essay on emotions and the "category of passivity" and elsewhere in his writings on education insists that the emotions are not to be construed on the model of activity. William Lyons is one of the more recent writers to develop a full-scale analysis of emotion on the passive perception- physiology- feeling model classically developed by William James at the end of the last century. But our whole tradition, since the medieval doctrine of "humours" and Descartes's and Malebranche's "animal spirits," similarly takes emotions to be physiological and therefore involuntary episodes, not acts of any kind. But the physiology involved in emotion is much more complicated than, say, a reflex action or a straightforward desire (hunger or thirst), and it should be clear that the physiological aspect of emotions is no obstacle to their voluntariness. (All actions are physiological too.) That our emotions *seem* passive to us is at most one of the least interesting observations to be taken into account in a careful and detailed study of the extent to which we "do" our emotions. But first it would seem that the whole glib paradigm of the voluntary and the involuntary must be rejected, along with "acts of will" and the category of "passivity." And it is by no means settled what is voluntary and what is not: If a few yogis can willfully control the functions of the autonomic nervous system, then that should say something about all of us. And if some of us have a hard time controlling our anger or coping with love, why should our incontinence serve as a model for emotion in general?

Part of the resistance to thinking of the emotions as more willful than not stems from the fact that, most of the time, we can change our emotions only instrumentally, that is, "by doing something else"—as opposed to "simply changing them." But quite apart from the problematic sense of "basic actions" invoked here, the notion that an emotion is voluntary only if it can be 'simply done' just won't do. It is clear that there are very few acts that can be simply done, and controlling anger surely need not be so instrumental as taking a tranquilizer or a cold shower or, even, counting to ten. What does one do when one counts to ten? It is not just a matter of waiting a few seconds for the anger to abate (like letting nausea pass). It is rather time in which we *do* something else, namely think. We go beyond anger (or get angrier) by gathering new evidence, by gaining perspective, by revising our conception of the circumstances. It is clear that we do control our emotions; Spinoza and Seneca suggested that we do so with thoughts—emotions themselves being thoughts. William James insisted that one can control emotions by acting *as if*— act angry to get angry, act calmly to get calm. Perhaps we can't just decide, "I am now angry," or "I will not get angry," but to suggest that anything we might do in order to get (or not get) angry is just "instrumental" is like arguing that John Hinckley wasn't guilty of the shooting the President because all he did was to (will to) move his finger.

Sometimes trying to get (or not get) angry is like trying to wiggle your ears but, nevertheless, the question of control of emotion seems to me to be wide open. We may not have "direct control"—whatever that means, and the connection between an act of will and an emotion may be obscure (as obscure, in fact, as the notion of an "act of will")— but one can refuse to get angry and one can let oneself get angry (it really is like giving oneself permission to do something) and one can decide that one *should* be angry and then go ahead and get angry. We need to examine this middle ground between the voluntary and the involuntary, those critical emotional acts which are neither deliberate nor intentional but nevertheless express our most fundamental concerns and desires. To insist that we are not responsible for our emotions while maintaining uncritically that we are the authors of our most random and petty thoughts seems to me to be the height of *mauvaise foi.* As Nietzsche famously pointed out, "A thought comes when it will, not when I will." But Nietzsche would have been the first to say that his thoughts as well as his emotions were, nevertheless, very much his own.

b. The Two Aspects of Mind

In recent philosophy of mind, the realm of the mental is divided up into two unequal categories: sensations on the one hand, and intentional states on the other. (See for example Fodor's review of a book on recent work in the subject, *Scientific American*, Jan. 1981.) It is not difficult to see how tradition-bound this distinction is (consider Hume's distinction between impressions and ideas, Kant's division of the faculties of sense and understanding) and, so long as we have classic epistemology in mind, the division may seem to have some plausibility. But it is with the emotions that the distinction becomes questionable, at least. No one would deny that emotions have a "felt" quality, whether or not (like myself) one wants to deny that any of the usual accounts of emotions as "feelings" will do. But it is one of the most obvious features of emotion—providing the first paragraph of many a journal analysis—that emotions are intentional phenomena—that one is always angry *about* something. There may be a class of "objectless" emotions (moods) but it is a poor argument indeed (however common) that generalizes these exceptions to the conclusion that emotions need not be intentional. "Objectless" emotions are emotions with generalized objects (joy and depression) or those whose objects are displaced or confused (anxiety or dread).

Emotions are not like sensations. Thus Hume takes considerable pains to distinguish the "indirect" and "secondary" impressions from those that are evident in perception and he weaves a complex tale of impressions and ideas in order to account for the intentionality of the passions. Kant treats *"Gefuhl"* in the third *Critique* quite differently than he deals with *"Empfindung"* in the first. The standard discussions of the "quality" or "content" of conscious experience will not do for emotion, for while an isolated sensation can plausibly be treated as a discrete event, an emotion is an irreducibly *structured* phenomenon. Descriptions of emotional experience tend to be primarily descriptions of the situation ("he looked like a monster to me") or one's behavioral tendencies ("I could have killed him") or metaphorical ("I felt as if I were going to explode"). There may be some commentary on physiology ("I felt as if my knees were going to give out under me") but such descriptions turn thin quite quickly. The content of the emotion is in the experience, and the experience is an experience *of* a certain situation of a certain kind. Romantic love would surely be a poor emotion if, as we are so often told, it did indeed consist of the blind arousal *cum nausea* that affects teenagers, all but devoid of an object. Anger would hardly be an emotion at all if it consisted solely of the felt tendency to "explode." The phenomenon of rage provides an illuminating contrast. One can easily imagine (or remember) the physiological experience of that concatenation of reactions, but rage (which can be neurologically induced) is not yet anger, and insofar as rage is anger it also has an object—a reason. Again, one must be wary of absolutes: there is no emotion without physiology and, usually, some physiologically based sensation; but there is no emotion without an object, however peculiar, no matter how dramatic the bodily reaction.

The standard examples of intentionality are belief and other "representational" mental acts. What is so convenient about this choice of paradigms—in addition to fitting into an age-old philosophical tradition and highlighting those aspects of consciousness in which philosophers most pride themselves—is the fact that beliefs really do seem to be mental states without "quality," that is, without a "feeling" component. Quine and other writers on the subject have had an easy time lampooning those straw authors who would suggest that belief is any kind of an experience or mental act; it is rather a dispositional state, a theoretical construct, whose whole existence resides in the utterances to which it gives rise, the affirmations and denials it permits. The object of a belief is a bloodless proposition, and though we might occasionally say that a proposition is exciting, it is clear that it is we who are so enthused and not the proposition itself. Belief is happily devoid of not only sensation but emotion too, and thus it appeals to the oldest prejudices of philosophers. But the truth is rather that intentionality without emotion is empty, just as physiology without intentionality is blind.

Dispassionate intentionality is what makes "artificial intelligence" artificial, inhuman. Books and movies such as *Invasion of the Body Snatchers* present us with inhuman humanoids who have intentionality but no emotion, and the fact that they also feel pain and presumably have sensations does not salvage them. The philosophical image of the mind consisting of unfeeling propositions and propositional attitudes towards them on the one hand and simple sensations on the other sets up a dichotomy in which emotions cannot be taken seriously and the nature of the human mind is grossly dehumanized. The flurry of worries about the possible place of the Self in artificial intelligence in functionalist theories of mind are thus somewhat beside the point. It is the place of the emotions that should be the real worry, and the locus of the self—though not the Cartesian self—will follow in course.

In this traditional dichotomy, emotions get interpreted, accordingly, as a deviant species of sensation—hard to localize, impossible to pin down, with elements of intentionality that might best be attributed, perhaps grudgingly, to component or presupposed beliefs. (Thus

Robert Kraut, in his essay in Myers and Irani, *Emotions*, attributes the whole motivation of the cognitivist theory to this need to account for intentionality.) Or, when I argue that emotions are a species of judgment and attack the importance of feeling, it is too easily assumed that I am thereby denying the "felt" character of emotions, which I clearly do not want to do. But judgment is quite different from belief: it is not a state or a construct; it does take place at a particular time; it does have a specifiable experiential content. And there are many kinds of feeling besides crude Jamesian cramps in the viscera and obscure appeals to "affective tone." Indeed, it has become clear to many authors that even such standard phenomena as perception and imagination render the distinction between sensation and intention problematic. (See for example, the extended debate between Ned Block and Dan Dennett on the nature of visual imagery.) Many philosophers have long given up on the notion of pure sensations or "sense data" as the basis of experience. Perhaps it is time too to give up on the notion of pure intentionality as an equally misleading construct for the understanding of mind.

One problem with current discussions of intentionality is that they typically focus on a single species of intentions: propositional attitudes, with belief as the most familiar illustration. In such examples it is misleadingly easy to separate the 'attitude' or the believing from the proposition, which has many distinctive attributes of its own (it can be believed by any number of people, it is either true or false; it can also be doubted, denied and otherwise "entertained"). But it is not at all clear that the objects of most emotions can be so treated. First of all, many emotions are not propositional attitudes. "John believes that P" or "John believes what Mary is saying" may be analyzable in terms of attitudes towards a proposition but "John loves Mary" and "Mary despises John" cannot be so analyzed. Dennett, among others, has argued persuasively that such statements cannot be translated into propositional language and the first person equivalents of those ("I love Mary," as expressed by John) are not propositional attitudes either. Here too one finds a more reasonable interpretation of the emotivist insistence that ethical judgments as well as emotions are more like "Hoorah!" than they are like beliefs, not because of the impossibility of confirming or denying them but rather because they do not always have the *form* of the standard propositional attitude. (So too one is hard put to translate "This is good" into proper propositional form.)

One recent philosophical ploy has been to convert traditional intentionality talk into the linguistic mode as intentionality talk, or talk about talk. Whether or not this is plausible in matters of belief and assertion, it surely will not do in talk about the intentionality of emotions. It is true, for example, that Soren Kierkegaard's father feared that God would strike him dead at any moment. One could analyze that fear in terms of an attitude toward a certain family of sentences and possible worlds, but it would not be unfair to say that such an analysis misses the emotion altogether. Adding a feverish jangle of unpleasant anxiety-like sensations won't save it either, for what emerges is a queer picture of sentence-mongering plus nonintentional sensations, hardly an accurate picture of a devastating and lifelong emotional experience.

c. Subject/Object

The subject/object distinction is one of the standard dichotomies of modern Western thinking—the personal subject on the one hand and a physical object or an "ideal" entity on the other. The phenomenological notion of intentionality only repeats this dichotomy; it does not question it. But against this distinction (and the more sophisticated phenomenological distinction between intentional act and intentional object) it has been objected, primarily by Heidegger but now too by a significant number of "holistic" analytic philosophers, that the distinction is illusory. But here too we can see how the traditional notion of the mind as divided into sensations and cognitions makes such a distinction so plausible. Consider, as an obvious paradigm of "subject-object", "John sees the ball." The independent physical existence of the ball makes it quite clear that seeing is one thing (however this is to be analyzed); the ball is something else—and this quite apart from any extravagant idealist theories of perception. And so, the analogy goes, if John gets mad at the ball, the analysis should look much the same, the "getting mad" on the one side (however this is to be analyzed) and the ball, exactly the same ball, on the other. In one sense, of course, it is "the same ball." The standard attributes of spatio-temporal existence and most primary and secondary qualities remain identical. But there is also a sense in which, when John is angry, it is not "the same ball" but something else, "that damn ball!", where this distinctively non-ontological property becomes the defining feature of the object in question. In other words, I want to say that the properties of the so-called intentional object are *not* identical for different substitutions of supposedly similar objects and descriptions. The properties of the intentional object are in part (possibly a large part) determined by the emotion itself. And, we might add, the properties of the emotion (not to be confused with various sensations) are to a large extent determined by the sort of object to which it is "directed." (This is why the "appropriateness" of emotional objects and emotion-labels has become so commanding a concept in recent philosophy and psychology. It is a logical, not a merely contingent feature of most emotions that they can be directed toward some sorts of objects (e.g. grief about a loss) and not others (grief about an unqualified gain).

Consider, similarly, "John believes that P", where the independence of the proposition *that P* makes it quite plausible to suggest that the model for intentionality should be the correlation of an attitude (believing) and its propositional object (*that P*). One might argue that the seeming independence of a proposition is only its detachability from any particular act of belief, assertion etc., just as one might qualify the notion of an intentional object such that the object-ball of seeing is in fact an *aspect* of the ball rather than the ball as such (Searle, *Intentionality*, 1982). Nevertheless the plausibility of the subject/act–object distinction has much to do with the obviousness of the distinguishability of physical objects from acts (mental or physical) directed to them and the similar obviousness of the distinguishability of propositions from propositional attitudes.

Once we get past belief and perception and turn to the emotions this distinction is none too obvious. In his classic book, *Action, Emotion and Will*, Anthony Kenny tries to maintain this scholastic distinction in emotions by explaining that, on the one hand, there is the feeling, on the other hand, the object. He never explains how it is that certain feelings should have intentionality, nor does he consider any but what he calls the "formal" properties of the object. But when we do pursue these topics, what we find is surprising. The supposed "feeling" disappears as we try to pry it away from the object, and the object itself becomes less of an independent entity to which the feeling is "directed" and far more the creation of the feeling itself. Consider: "John hates Mary for humiliating him." In fact John doesn't know much about Mary at all, and it would be simply false to say that he hates MARY. He hates a certain person defined by the parameters of his hatred. This is the person who cut him to the quick at the office Christmas party. She is not the person who has three sisters and won Merit Scholarship in high school. It's not that he doesn't hate MARY (though one might well say, as Mary's friend, that he doesn't hate "the real Mary"—which is very different from not really hating Mary, which he does). Students often capture this peculiar feature of emotional intentionality by calling it 'subjective' or, in the case of rage or romantic love, 'blind'. But this isn't quite right. It's not as if one has a feeling about something which or someone who already has determinate characteristics, and thus distorts his or her perception. A person who is in love does not "distort" the lover but rather creates a lover by virtue of a special kind of vision, a vision that idealizes (which is very different from distortion), a vision which "crystallizes" virtues out of ordinary traits, as Stendhal so delicately suggested. It would be a cynicism of the worst sort to insist that such a vision is a distortion, or that the person thus envisioned is not "really" so wonderful after all. Given a choice between the bland "thing in itself" of some objective viewpoint (which is still a viewpoint) and the celebratory vision of romantic love, it would be hard to defend the former. But so it is too with less positive emotions, and in every case, the object of the emotion is in this sense defined by the emotion. To what extent is classical ontology—in modelling itself after science instead of after art—an intentional "graying" of the world?

In his masterwork *Being and Time,* Heidegger chose moods as his weapon against the subject-object distinction, precisely because moods, unlike knowledge, make any sense of the independence of the object— or the subject—impossible. Heidegger's infamous pun on moods as "being tuned" (*Stimmung, Gestimmtsein*) is a bit weak to make this point, which is often underappreciated by scholars seeking to see Heidegger as a merely ontological antagonist to Husserl. Heidegger's aim is not just epistemological holism but a reorientation of the philosophical perspective as such. By making moods the key to "being-in-the-world" Heidegger not only by-passes the epistemological problems that have defined modern philosophy since Descartes; he also limits the importance of knowledge as such, to leave room for an affective world that really matters. Hans Georg Gadamer tells a revealing story about his own relationship with Heidegger and "hermeneutics" at mid-century. Their shift from "fundamental ontology" consisted, in part, of their shared concern that philosophy should compete with (if not exactly take the place of) art and poetry. Anyone with even a scant sense of the history of German Romanticism will recognize here the continuing saga of the *Romantik* against the "scientism" of Kant's (first *Critique*) influence. But like beauty, the object of most emotions is both in the object and in the eye of the beholder, and both eyes and behold-ers can be educated (or numbed) through philosophical reflection. This is not a problem so much as it is an opportunity for philosophical understanding. It is the over-emphasis on perception, belief and ontol-ogy that makes the subject-object distinction so seemingly obvious. A balanced emphasis on emotions and moods would require a revisioning or, perhaps, a new sensitivity for philosophy.

3. The Importance of Emotion in Philosophy

I have argued that some fields in philosophy might be considerably advanced by virtue of some attention to the nature and importance of emotion, but I expect that many readers rightly suspect that I have something else in mind by my title and by my emphasis on emotion, not by way of subject matter but rather by way of style. And indeed I want to make the point, above all, that philosophy must not only include the passions; it must be impassioned. We have too long prided ourselves on what Iris Murdoch has called the "dryness" of our subject, which we, of course, tend to describe in more flattering terms. But the ideals as well as the popular image of our profession as detached and disengaged is not just another consequence of "professionalism"; it is also part of our historical self-image, which is, I would argue, a tragic misinterpretation of our own traditions.

My own allegiances tend toward the more emotionally extravagant existentialists—Kierkegaard, Nietzsche, Camus and Sartre—whose sense of impassioned engagement often serves as a means of discrediting passion in philosophy today. But even a brief look at our definitive philosophical heroes should be enough to tell us that philosophy is something more than detached analysis and argument. Socrates, our ultimate model, entered into philosophy with wit, passion and a mission almost unimaginable in most professionalized philosophy today. Even Hume and Kant, hardly Kierkegaardian existentialists, display a passion and a mission—they called it "enlightenment" (*Aufklarung*)—in their works and in their lives that one would be hard pressed to find in the Journal of Philosophy. The idea of philosophy as a profession, a protected society for disengaged intellectuals working through problems and puzzles and proving their technical competence "just for its own sake," without getting excited about it, without doing anything with it and indifferent to the significance of ideas. The most professional philosopher is the most rigorous, careful, cautious, technical, "dry"; there is certainly a place for such accomplishment, but should we define our lives in its terms?

In a rather different context, Israel Scheffler has discussed the breach between emotions and reason as utterly destructive of education. ("In Praise of the Cognitive Emotions," *Columbia Educational Review*, December 1977, Vol. 79, no. 2.) He caricatures the standard view of emotion "as commotion—an unruly inner disturbance." The "hostile opposition of cognition and emotion," he says, "distorts everything it touches: mechanizing science, it sentimentalizes art, while portraying ethics and religion as twin swamps of feeling and unreasoned commitment." Education, he goes on to say, "is split into two grotesque parts—unfeeling knowledge and mindless arousal." So too the lives of philosophers seem aimed at perpetuating that educational tragedy. We teach dispassion, not just argumentation. How many philosophers still respond to a lecture on emotion with the announcement that such subjects, while interesting, have no place in serious philosophy? And how many times have I heard the tired witticism, before or after a lecture on love, "I prefer the practice to the theory." I do not say, "what ever happened to praxis?"

Philosophy is a passion, and as a passion it tends to infect whatever it touches with passion. Philosophy of science is perhaps exemplary in that it has almost always tended to begin with and encourage excitement about science. Aesthetics without enthusiasm for art or philosophy of religion without faith or feeling can be the most pointless of philosophical subjects. But it is ethics and social philosophy that provide us with our most embarrassing examples; how could these subjects of human behavior—which in the form of folk legends, plays and novels move and engage us far more than anything else in the world—have turned out to be so uninvolved in and unexcited by real human behavior, preferring far more to discuss the dry business of methodology and the abstract nature of "moral judgment"? It is often said, in debates about abortion and public policy, for example, that emotion should be avoided at all costs, but what emerges instead is indifference and irrelevance. Taking a stand does not preclude making an intelligent case; it rather motivates it. To mention a positive case, I remember the accusations of "fanaticism" that greeted Peter Singer's well-argued but also very personally moved and moving charge for "animal liberation." We need more such fanatics. It is an embarrassment to hear so many papers in philosophy begin, "I do not want to talk about so-and-so's conclusion, but I only want to point out a fallacy in the argument...." This is a canon of rationality we can live without, and while I have no objection to those who do this under the honorific title "philosophy", I think that we have had more than enough of the dogmatic definition of defining philosophy as such as nothing more than this. Philosophy is more than the analysis of arguments; philosophy is the engagement of arguments in the effort to take a stand for something.

We have put so much emphasis on logic, as opposed to its much discredited complement (not, antagonist) rhetoric that we find ourselves all but incapable of getting excited, or getting other people excited; indeed we tend to look at excitement as a sign of charlatanism. I think that it is safe to say that few lives are changed through logic, even (especially) irrefutable logic. One of our favorite topics—the famous ontological argument—has become of primary philosophical significance because it admits of unending variations in modal logic each more formally tantalizing than the last. In Saint Anselm's famous "proof", however, the point is quite clearly an expression of faith, indeed even a passionate expression—not only in the style of the writing (which we philosophers disdainfully strip away in search of the basic argument) but even in the premises themselves. The "proof" is more of a rhetorical celebration of the Most Perfect Being, in the terms of logic, than it is a logical argument which happens, in fact, to be about God. (Cf. our favorite counter-examples: "consider the most perfect imaginable unicorn...")

None of this is to demean the accomplishments that have been made in the formal side of philosophy. It is only to say that there is something else, something now missing, the other side of philosophy: metaphors, visions and sheer enthusiasm. It is simply appalling that some of the major introductory textbooks can say to students who are seriously trying to like our subject that philosophy is nothing but the evaluation of arguments, and then proceed to discuss such topics as the free will question or the possibility of justification in ethics—burning questions for a great many undergraduates—as if these were nothing but exercises in argument, convenient clashes of position which supply a rich fund of arguments, counter-arguments, far-fetched examples and even more far-fetched counter-examples.

It is essential that we put emotion back in philosophy. This is not incompatible with, but part of, making philosophy once again witty, entertaining, clever in a non-logical sort of way and, not an extraneous consideration—attractive and appealing to the students who parade by the hundreds of thousands through our doors every semester. They are not so impressed by technical wizardry as they are by passion and it is worth asking ourselves how we have come to take just the opposite view.

Shouldn't we be pleased by the new emphasis on emotion as a legitimate topic in philosophy? There has been more serious research on the philosophy of emotion in the past ten years than in the past ten decades of Anglo-American philosophy. But beware: rather than the influx of passion-invigorating philosophy, philosophy has too often eviscerated the passions. Current discussion of emotion too often tends to treat emotion only as an excuse for the same old discussions of intentionality or functionalism. Talk of emotion gets formalized and turned into epistemology in style if not also in content. Philosophical seminars on emotion tend to be all but devoid of real emotional concern. For example, one of my colleagues has written a rather tough-minded paper on sexual attraction, and he begins not with a familiar example— or even a dirty joke, which would be preferable— but with a formulation of the problem: "What does it mean to say that S wants O?" Now philosophically it should be obvious that this formulation already blocks some of the most important questions about the nature of sexual attraction and loads the case toward the traditional misunderstanding of the lustee as a mere "object." And in terms of style, it should be obvious that this formulation immediately removes this most exciting of subjects from the realm of all possible excitement. So too all of those "theories of emotion" that read more and more like the now tired analyses of the necessary and sufficient conditions for "S knows that P." There is now a legion of philosophers who write learned essays on why "there are no emotions" but it is hard to find a professional philosopher who will talk about the awful pain of jealousy, the insidiousness of envy and resentment, the voluptuousness of lust and the irresponsible joys of moral indignation. The introduction of emotion in philosophy is not just the rediscovery of a neglected topic. It is also the recognition that something has gone dreadfully wrong with the narrow way that we define and do philosophy.

This is not a defense of hystrionics in philosophy, and it is not to suggest that we should leap to the podium red-faced and throw stones. It is rather to reject the now fixed expectation that competent philosophy should be couched in that same dry, detached and dispassionate prose. Speakers no longer take a position so much as they "come to the conclusion," which they are quite rationally willing to change if anyone can come up with a better argument. To reject this mode of philosophizing is not to endorse deconstructivist violence in philosophy. It is a defense of those "calm" and constructive passions clearly displayed as well as discussed by Hume. No matter how formally formidable a philosophy may be, it must have a heart as well—think of Spinoza's *Ethics*. The philosophers who defined philosophy as the *love* of wisdom weren't kidding, even if it is a phrase that we now present only out of entymological obligation to our undergraduates. (They may not have much wisdom but they are certainly looking for love—in all the wrong places, one might add.) There is plenty of room for emotion in the idealized life of reason, and we have too long tried to do without it.

Daring Witness:
The Recovery of Female Time

Susan Griffin

A few months ago I told the organizers of this conference that the title of my lecture would be "Bearing Witness," but the telephone must have distorted the sound because it is printed in your programs as "Daring Witness." Though this is also an appropriate title. In order to bear witness in these times you must often dare witness.

I would like to begin by reading you a quotation from Dante's *Inferno:* "It is perhaps your anguish which snatches you out of my memory so that it seems I have never seen you." I hope the relevance of these words will become clear as I speak today. I am going to talk about a dangerous kind of forgetting that we are in the midst of today, and to render a philosophical and psychological examination of a particular lapse in memory through which we have lost a part of ourselves. This lapse has profound political implications and explains in some measure why it is that we are unable to acknowledge the depth of the environmental and nuclear crises we face today. I know that all of you know the dangers of acid rain, and of the danger of nuclear weapons. You must be very aware at this moment of the terrible effects of radioactive contamination from nuclear wastes, which will affect not only this generation but countless generations to come. We are also facing the diminishment all over the world of arable land which will mean famine for an increasing number of people, the death of the rain forests which provide oxygen for all of us, and the continual extinction of various kinds of plant and animal species.

Years ago, when my daughter was very small (I tend to measure things by her growth on the planet—which is a very female measurement of time) I remember watching a conference on ecology that was broadcast on television. My heart opened and lifted with a feeling that, *Oh, finally, here is an issue that can bring us all together. All of us are dependent on the earth for our survival. Now we will join forces to save the earth.* As you know, that combination of hope and vision I had twenty years ago has proven to be naive. In the interest of someday seeing that vision come into being, my aim here today is to discuss why in this Western Civilization we are divided against ourselves.

This state of dividedness is far more fundamental to our way of life than the transitory conflicts on which wars are based, including the Cold War. Despite almost frenetic activity and "busyness", when it comes to a reasonable response to real ecological crises, we are as a culture in a state of paralysis. In individual psychology, hysterical paralysis of this kind is often caused by an unconscious and seemingly irresolvable conflict. One part of the self is divided against the other.

Certainly this is the case with the shared mind of Western Civilization. For seen from one point of view, a point of view that might be very broadly defined as holistic, the languages, philosophical premises and even scientific paradigms of our culture are all based on a series of formally conceived dualities. And in studying these dualities one discovers that they fall into two categories: the categories Matter and Spirit. The divisions look like this:

Matter	*Spirit*
Nature	Culture
Body	Mind
Emotions/Senses	Intellect
Feminine	Masculine

In general in this culture, the spiritual realm, both in discourse and institution, is empowered, and the material realm is disempowered. Art, too, is in the disempowered realm and science is in the empowered realm. Of course this is all only a construct. Mind and body, culture and nature, matter and spirit are not in actuality separate. The biologically male and female are not the same as the social constructs of masculinity and femininity. But this construct has an aspect of reality because it is such a powerful belief system.

You may recognize this fundamental split between matter and spirit as belonging to Christian theology. In this case of course I am speaking of Christian theology as it emerged from the Holy Roman Empire and took on the values of Empire, not primitive Christianity nor the teachings of Christ. In this theology the spirit belongs to Heaven. It is pure and good and above the earth, unaffected by pleasure or pain, by desire, or death. The earthly realm, the province of matter, is also the region of the Devil, or evil. Hell is under your feet. Sensuality, sexuality, and all that is of this earth is corrupt, and must be distrusted.

An unexamined assumption of the modern age is that we are somehow, in our "scientific" thought, beyond this theology. But science began, in fact, as a theological discipline. Many of the questions that science still pursues today began as theological inquiries. For example, the question, *What is the nature of light?* which through the Michelson-Morley experiments eventually led to the theory of relativity and which certainly shaped quantum physics, was a religious question.

What is even more important, the fundamental duality between heaven and earth was preserved in scientific discourse. Only the vocabulary shifted. Instead of matter and spirit, scientists spoke about matter and energy. (In effect, the word "spirit" in both Hebrew and Greek referred to physical forms of energy.) To a large degree, the idea that the material and spiritual are separate realms must have, until the twentieth century, obscured all evidence for the continuum between energy and matter that we now understand exists.

In our age, science has taken on the mantle of authority that once belonged to the church. To the lay mind, and even to some technical scientists, the pronouncements of science on the nature of the universe remain as unassailable as Papal Bulls. But in fact, as Gaston Bachelard writes, even scientific materialism is an abstraction. Science does not speak with the authority of Nature. It constructs an idea of matter. And scientific ideas are not above history. Even the famous method of experimentation has been continually subject to historical influence.

A theology which derogated both matter and women came to bear on Francis Bacon's rhetoric, as he recommended the experimental method with these words, "We should put nature on the rack and examine her." Metaphors of the witch trials run throughout his works. This is perhaps not surprising. He was at one point chief justice in the Star Chamber which examined witches in England.

This is not an extraordinary historical coincidence, but part of a larger pattern. William Harvey, the doctor who discovered the circulation of the blood, was also an examiner of witches. The scientific revolution itself took place during the most intense period of witch burning. I am not suggesting a causal relationship here, but rather one of mutual influence. Beginning in the fourteenth century scientific views of the world began to challenge the old order. The earth was no longer the center of the universe. A structure of thought was being dismantled. In a culture that believes in the primacy of spirit and intellect, and which attempts to master nature with knowledge, a paradigmatic shift of this kind can be threatening. Moreover, these were the plague years. Witches believed to have occult powers—old women for the most part— provided a scapegoat for the fears of death and change which were part of these times. Woman, and indeed the entire realm of the feminine, has functioned as a categorical container for unacknowledged and unresolved fears for centuries.

The witch burnings also had an effect on scientific inquiry itself, beyond providing lurid metaphors. The burning of Bruno and the imprisonment and trial of Galileo had to have had a chastening influence. The philosophical shift which might have taken place as the result of new scientific understandings was truncated. Instead, new discoveries were interpreted within the old theological structures. Newton's discovery of the refractory properties of light—in which it was understood that color is not a property of an object being seen but is created by angles of light as they are interpreted by the eye—was taken as further evidence for the Christian belief that the senses are deceptive.

One can trace that attitude back to pre-Christian thought, to the Greek philosopher Democritus who said that sensual understandings are *bastard* understandings. I hope you can hear the sexual overtones of that metaphor. Embedded in this language is the assertion that sensual knowledge lies outside patriarchical structures of knowledge, outside, as it were, patriarchically authorized wedlock. By this metaphor sensual knowledge is made implicitly equivalent to illicit or unbounded sexuality. And these are not casual associations, but lie instead at the heart of our continued alienation from nature.

There is, however, another way in which Newton's discoveries about the nature of color can be interpreted. This approach does not denigrate sensual knowledge. Let me take as an example the color of the flowers here on the stage. They are yellow. Understanding that this color derives from something that happens between the flower, light and my eye, or our eyes, we can say that all of us and the light and the flowers are in a kind of communion through which we create something—something we feel and name and recognize—and this is the color yellow. The existence of color in this way of thinking becomes a symbol not of alienation but of union with the earth.

A sense of alienation from the earth, and by association, from the entire category of the feminine—sensuality, emotions, bodily states of consciousness—underlies one of the most fundamental tenets of modern science. And that is the idea of "objectivity." I am not speaking here of the attempt to be openminded, nor of the desire to examine one's assumptions and move beyond them. These are commendable goals. I am speaking rather of the illusion of "objectivity," of a dislocated, disassociated superiority to life itself, which is in fact an impossibility. This illusion of "objectivity" actually undermines the realistic effort to be openminded, because underneath the assertion of this disembodied superiority is an unconscious and inflexible desire to dominate reality, rather than to truly understand.

This illusion of objectivity derives in part from the idea of the Great Chain of Being that was part of Elizabethan Christianity. In an ascending hierarchy, the earth itself is at the bottom, then come plants and animals, then human beings, then angels and then God. In this scheme of things heaven is the most pure, or rather the only pure vantage point. All other locations are somewhat corrupt. But the human point of view can partake of divine consciousness, and is superior to all other material existence, especially insofar as sensual experience is "overcome." The material, bodily, sensual experience of human beings corrupts vision, just as the spiritual, intellectual aspect of humanity enlightens vision.

In fact, all perception, especially scientific perception, is embodied. There is no objective location. And as the Theory of Relativity has taught us, location affects even instruments of measurement. Moreover, as Heisenberg's Principle of Uncertainty shows us, what we measure is affected by our measurements. And I might add, those who see are affected by what they see. There is no safe "objective" vantage point from which to perceive the world purely. We are all material beings, enmeshed in a matrix of perception.

It is not irrelevant to say that "objectivity" in science has a social and political analogue in the attitude of empires toward their colonies—the attitude, for instance, of the Holy Roman Empire to Europe, or the attitude now of the United States toward nations it has colonized economically. The Empire believes that what is asserted within its boundaries is a superior point of view. It "knows best" not only for itself but for others. In this process the needs or desires of the Empire are conflated with the imagined needs of others. The same structure of dominance exists in the masculine definition of the female. The female point of view, like sensual data, is by definition an illegitimate source of knowledge. The testimony of women is regarded as suspect and deceitful.

From this perceptual hierarchy, a portrait of the other emerges as a being who is not only unreliable as a witness, but who is volatile, unpredictable, and above all unreasonable. The "other" is the subject who is studied—nature, the women, the "native", or, in the tradition of European anti-Semitism, the Jew. Though the descriptions of the other vary in detail, all are described as being more material (or "materialistic"), more sensual, more sexual, less spiritual, less intelligent (or in the case of Jews, having a mainly "canny" intelligence). Because of this supposed nature which is closer to *nature*, the dominant one in the hierarchical dyad (whether this one is male, or white, or part of an Empire) argues that control of the other is necessary.

But just under the skin of this prejudicial view of the other is an unconscious and deeply alienating self-hatred. We are all physical, material beings, sexually and sensually alive, and our consciousness, including all the processes of intellection, especially language, cannot be separated from material existence. The very word for "culture" derives etymologically from the word for agricultural cultivation. Cultivation of the soil. Language itself is produced by the shape of the mouth and the tongue, follows the cadence of the breath, resonates with the shape and acoustical range of the ear. Perception is an act of sensual participation in the world. We cannot separate one part of our nature from another. Our denigration of the flesh rebounds to reflect on the very core of our consciousness.

Moreover, the body, with its earthly needs and desires, is always present, always reminding us through hunger or tiredness or even pleasure of this part of ourselves we would try to deny. And I believe that if consciousness has any essential properties, one of these properties is the wish to reflect the wholeness of felt existence. Therefore, our own bodies halt us, in dreams, fantasies, unconscious symbols, and through distortions of desire, and projections. This civilization has accommodated this process of unconscious reclamation through mass structures of projection. The woman, the black, the Jew, the homosexual, become containers, vessels for the denied self. We are defined as having all those qualities which are hated and cast away. Black people are described, thus, as more sexual; it is part of the racist ideology that they sing and dance better. Women are called more emotional. Jews are supposed to be more materialistic. And in fact, the structures of society actually work to shape us to these stereotypes. Within the family system women are the ones who "carry" the emotions and look after the feelings of others. In the development of Capitalism, usury was supposed to be sinful. But it was also necessary. Jews were allowed to perform this task, since it was not defined as sinful in Judaism. At the same time, Jews were not allowed to own land or join the trade guilds; so, very few other avenues were left open besides trade and banking. What is also revealing in the history of racism and anti-Semitism is that both Jewish men and African men have been described pejoratively by white anthropologists and scholars as "feminine." What is feminine belongs to the realm of matter, and it is also disempowered, that is, to be dominated by the spirit.

But of course if matter and energy or matter and spirit are indivisible and part of a continuum, one cannot dominate the other. The philosophical assumptions and traditions of our civilization may succeed in creating the illusion that we are separate from nature, above the matrix of interdependency which is the biosphere, impervious to natural vulnerability, even aging and death. One born to a certain gender and class can, through the social institutions of marriage and domestic servitude, remain insulated even from the regular primacy of physical needs. Others grow and purchase and prepare food, others clean the toilets, others are responsible for material existence. But this illusion cannot last for long. We all age. We all face death. And even through the simple act of drawing breath, minute by minute the fact of our earthly existence returns to consciousness. We may, through nuclear fission, succeed in the illusion that we have separated energy from matter. But radiation exists, a ghostly reminder of the failure of our old way of thinking. Does our rigid belief in the separation between matter and spirit contribute to our denial in the face of the lethal effects of radiation on both the human cell and the environment?

In the twentieth century, the theological idea of heaven has been replaced with a technological dream of perfection. We imagine that somehow every woe has its technological solution. There is, of course, nothing wrong with human ingenuity. But just behind the technological dream, another less conscious dream shapes our behavior. That is the dream of escape from earthly existence. I am going to read you a passage from my book, *Woman and Nature*, which explores this dream of escape. It begins with an epigram from the Italian futurist poet, F.T. Marinetti. It may not surprise you that later he became part of the Italian Fascist movement. The second epigram, of a quite different character, is from Einstein.

Speed

The *Futurist Morality* will defend man from the decay caused by slowness, by memory, by analysis, by repose and habit. Human energy centupled by speed will master time and space....The intoxication of great speeds in cars is nothing but the joy of feeling oneself fused with the divinity.

F. T. Martinetti, "The New Religion Morality of Speed"

No material body can move faster than the speed of light.

Albert Einstein and Leopold Infeld,
The Evolution of Physics

The race-car driver is fearless. He speeds past death. In his speed is endless virility. As a lover he amazes flesh. Women fall. He is like lightning in his gestures. His will pervades all matter. He sees no boundaries. He tolerates no entanglements. Nothing must slow him down. Slowness is his enemy. If he engenders children, he does not remember them. Memory is his enemy. He does not stay in one place. He never spends time. Time is his executor. In his quest for greater and greater speed, he casts away whatever gives him weight. Weight is his enemy. He seeks weightlessness. He casts away excess. He does not tolerate the superfluous. He wants only the essential. His life is reduced to the essential. At the speed of light, which he longs for, he would shed even his body. But still he would have weight, still gravity would determine his path, still he would curve toward the earth. He glides as quickly as he can over surfaces. He does not want to touch the earth. Friction is his enemy. The smell of friction is the smell of burning is the smell of death. He cannot afford to think of death. Death is the commander of his enemies. He sheds his knowledge of death; he cannot afford to fear. The air is filled with anxiety. Space is filled with longing. He must traverse space instantly. (He must not give in to longing.) He must take the air by surprise. (He must not give in to terror.) As his speed increases, so does his power. He takes everything. Everything yields to him. He never waits. His hands move with infinite speed. What he steals vanishes. He keeps no records. He has no time. No memory. He moves. Motion is all he knows. He does not know what he moves through. The world is a blur to him. We are a blur to him.

To the world he says that clear outlines and separate existences are illusion. Only I exist, he says. The sides of your bodies, he states, wash into nothingness. Every irrelevant detail disappears from his sight. The line of his movement alone is clear. He worships the straight line. He abhors change of direction. Change of direction is his enemy. Curves are his enemy. He wants to be more than light, more than an electromagnetic wave, which has weight, which curves. He wants to be pure number, proceeding without the passage of time infinitely forward. This is his dream. Nothing will distract him. He will dream only of the future. He will escape gravity. He will escape his enemies. In his solitary world of speed nothing enters to disturb this dream. He is like a sleeper rapidly vanishing. *We cannot imagine his destiny. His destiny terrifies us.*

The attempt to maintain an Olympian hegemony over life has many casualties. Disowning our own earthly nature, and projecting what we deny in ourselves onto others, we have created categories of disempowerment and dispossession. In this way, the issue of social justice is inextricably intertwined with the issue of ecology. And with the issue of peace. Let me give you a literal example of this association from history. In the Harz Mountains, near a town called Nordhausen, there was a concentration camp known as Nordhuasen-Dora. This camp was built inside an abandoned mine shaft, hidden in the side of a Mountain. In concentration camp Dora, prisoners worked sixteen hours a day on the production of V-2 rockets. They were forced to sleep in the dirt in the mine shafts, in the midst of the whining noise of production, glaring electric lights, fetid air and filth. The death toll was so high that a stack of bodies habitually formed outside the entrance to the shaft more quickly than the bodies could be carried away.

Looking back on this terrible event, we can study it as if it were both a self-portrait and a frightening augury of a possible future. I am saying "we" in this case, because Germany is not alone in the tradition of racism and self-hatred that has shadowed this civilization. One might say that just as other more positive aspects of our culture reach their pinnacle in Germany in the midcentury, so did this tradition of hatred.

If we look deeply into this self-portrait, we can see a soul divided against itself, hating its own materiality which it projects outward onto the other—the Jew, or the women, or the black. For the hatred of the other, whether it be the Cold War enemy, or a racist scapegoat (in the language of the Third Reich, "the internal enemy") is fundamentally an expression of self-hatred. Is it any surprise then that the V-2 rocket manufactured by slave labor becomes the precursor for the ICBM missiles capable of carrying nuclear warheads which at this moment threaten all our lives? Underneath the desire to annihilate the other, is a wish to annihilate nature, the natural part of ourselves. In a word, to commit suicide.

This is a strange suicide, though, as oddly disconnected from conscious awareness as from its motivation. The Pentagon devises scenarios for waging nuclear war, and they call these staged rehearsals SIOP plans. According to one of these plans, the President dies in a nuclear attack, but the Vice-President survives; he flies in an especially equipped airplane that allows him to continue to wage nuclear war through computer. Symbolically then, the earthly self dies but a heavenly self, a sky self, continues to live and to control events on earth. At the core of our military plan for suicide is the illusion that we are above the things of this earth, and therefore we will be untouched by the death we are planning.

But of course we will be touched; we are touched even now. The low level radiation to which we are all daily exposed has a damaging effect on the cell's immunity. We are seeing a rise in the incidence of cancer, an increase in immunological diseases such as Lupus, and the advent of several new immunological disorders. In Europe, with the explosion at Chernobyl, you have experienced the devastating effects of nuclear power. Our bodies and this planet which we share are already suffering from a Third World War that knows no boundaries, and takes all life as a target.

And even if we were not facing our own cataclysmic or slow death, isn't it true that through our alienation from the earth we are losing a precious part of ourselves? According to Nazi ideology, Jews were accused of stealing from Germany. What is in fact true is that we in this civilization who have projected our materiality on others have lost the realization of our own physical participation in the universe. If it is true that the earth is beautiful and wondrous, and that the human body is beautiful and wondrous, it is also true that the human experience of physical existence is marvelous. It is a birthright, a part of the education of our souls which we have cast away.

What happens to human consciousness when we truly begin to understand that cells are not simply objects to be studied under a microscope, but filled with intelligence, a material intelligence that is our own? And if we truly begin to recognize ourselves again, and to know ourselves, might not our view of the earth begin to change, to deepen and broaden into wisdom?

Incipient in each new scientific discovery is the possibility of changing our approach to the world. To begin to respect nature, to see spirit and intelligence in nature, to see something whole and inviolable, something sacred in the earth, to begin to regard our bodies as more than mechanisms for production, but as sources of the most profound knowledge. We are being invited through insight to move out of an imprisoning set of assumptions which have separated us from our own existence. What I have called "Female Time" is really human time. It is earthly time; it is experience unfrozen from abstraction, the time it takes for a life to be lived. Yes, in this step, we give up our dominion over the earth. But we regain nothing less than the wonderful complexity of existence, and, at the deepest level, a reunion with our prodigal and deepest selves.

Who is that Masked Woman? Reflections on Power, Privilege, and Home-ophobia

Naomi Scheman

> *Be patient to all that is unsolved*
> *in your heart*
> *And try to love the questions themselves*
> *Do not seek the answers*
> *that cannot be given you*
> *Because you wouldn't be able to live them*
> *And the point is to live everything*
> *Live the questions now*
> *Perhaps you will gradually without noticing it*
> *live along some distant day into the answers*
> Rainer Maria Rilke

In the summer of 1987 I gave a talk to a symposium of mostly European mostly literary theorists in Dubrovnik. I had been invited by one of the conveners, Hans Ulrich Gumbrecht (then at the University of Siegen in the Federal Republic of Germany), whom I had met at a literary theory conference at Indiana University and who had become excited by the challenge of feminist theory as an accepted and institutionalized part of the academy, a development much farther along in the U.S. than in Europe. My talk was entitled "The Body Politic/The Impolitic Body/Bodily Politics," and it had to do with the different representations of the body in pre-modern, modern, and post-modern European and Euro-American thought and with how those representations were inflected by race and gender. Afterwards I wrote it up, and it was translated into German by the other convener, Ludwig Pfeiffer, also at Siegen, and published in a collection of papers from the symposium.[1] I have never read the translation all the way through, something it would be quite hard for me to do.

The paper was written for strangers. It is meant to stand alone, presupposing no on-going conversation. I wrote it knowing it was to be translated into German, and it reads to me as though it had started in German and been translated into English (except for the title, which in German is clumsy and awkward). While writing it I felt as though I had broken into a cathedral and was pounding out Buxtehude on the organ (or so I said: I can't play the organ, and I couldn't recognize a piece of music as Buxtehude's). I felt freed of the expectations of my more domestic audiences: for (analytical) philosophical rigor and concision and for (American) feminist grounding in experience and connection to practice.

I subsequently read the paper (in English) to several different audiences made up mostly of strangers and of non-philosophers. Then, with some anxiety, in the fall of 1988, I read the paper at a meeting of Midwest SWIP (the Society for Women in Philosophy) in Northfield, Minnesota.

Bringing the paper home, although frightening, was something I needed to do. Most of what I write begins life as a talk at some distant place, in response to invitations to address audiences made up entirely or nearly entirely of strangers. I enjoy traveling, and I especially like being places where I'm responsible for nothing except my end of lots of conversations, and where I'm the center of attention for a fixed period of time, fussed over, and then left alone in a comfortable, anonymous hotel room. Writing happens later, when I'm pleasurably alone with my Macintosh. But, as much as I like it (or, precisely because I like it), I have become increasingly suspicious of the effect on my work of such a combination of solitude and life among strangers.

[1] "Der Körper des Gemeinwesens/Der unpolitische Körper/Körperpolitik" ("Body Politic/Impolitic Body/Bodily Politics," translated by Ludwig Pfeiffer) in *Materialität der Kommunikation,* selected papers from 1987 Dubrovnik colloquium, "Materialities of Communication," edited by Hans Ulrich Gumbrecht and Ludwig Pfeiffer, Suhrkamp, 1988, forthcoming in English in selected essays from that volume, Harvard University Press.

Most of my life, however, is spent neither alone nor with strangers. Most of the time I am teaching and interacting with friends and colleagues. From 1986 to 1989 I was chairing the Women's Studies Department, and I have been the Vice President of the Board of Directors of a feminist theater company, At the Foot of the Mountain, since 1980. For the past several years we have been struggling to transform the theater from an essentially white women's theater to a genuinely multi-cultural arena, while in Women's Studies we've been involved in analogous efforts involving hiring, the curriculum, alliances with ethnic studies departments, and, in 1987, working in an academic/community, multi-cultural coalition to host the National Women's Studies Association annual meeting. What was troubling me was the contrast between what I thought I believed—in theorizing not only from but in these interactions with students, friends, and colleagues and my work in the community—and what I actually did, which was to theorize alone or as a stranger.

When I read the "Body" paper at SWIP, I asked for help in bringing what I did back home, in exploring how it fit with what others closer to me were doing. In a long conversation afterwards María Lugones, a philosopher at Carleton College and a friend, challenged me in ways I hadn't quite anticipated. She pointed out that, although ostensibly concerned with the conditions for constructing a politically usable and non-imperialist first person plural in which to theorize, I had in the paper kept the role of theorist to my solitary self. I appealed to the "experiences" of people of color to provide the raw material for a more adequate theory, which it would remain the prerogative of people like me to create and authorize.

The other side of that arrogance was my elision of the specificities of my own actual life. Although the paper began on what seemed to be an autobiographical note, placing myself in what I argued was the oxymoronic position of a woman philosopher, I said nothing of how I came to be in that position, how I came to do theory, why it mattered to me, to whom I felt myself to be connected, and so on. Just as only those like me were really theorists, apparently only those unlike me had experiences worth noting: theorists learn from experiences (whoever's they were); they are not shaped by them.

There is little point in saying that, of course, I don't want or mean to do any of these things, that I am, in fact, committed to deploring them in my own and others' work. The point is that I do, usually, write from an insufficiently examined place, in an insufficiently examined voice, and, most importantly, in insufficiently examined relation to several audiences and communities. I write most easily and fluently from the academy, as a theorist, and for strangers. I want to try to examine some of what I have thereby obscured or elided, some of the voices other than my own, as well as some of my own voices, that I have silenced or (mis)interpreted. I am assuming that my experiences are not wholly idiosyncratic (although I know them not to be shared even by many who are demographically similar to me: white, Jewish, female, middle-class, academically successful and rewarded, heterosexual) and I hope that the exploration will reveal things others will find useful, whether they are prone to theorizing as I do or have found themselves angry at others who do, or both.

I start with the recognition that I am in many ways more comfortable among strangers or acquaintances or relatively distant colleagues than among those to whom I am more closely related. I find it comforting to be expected to perform, to jump through some set of hoops, to earn approval. It is obviously relevant to my comfort that those around me with the power to grant or withhold approval have mostly set me tasks I could perform, and they have not withheld the approval I earned. Among the tasks I am best at are those associated with theorizing: seeing connections among apparently disparate things, explaining those connections imaginatively and clearly, and speculating on what holds it all together. I learned to theorize as a student of philosophy and, before that, as my father's daughter, both of which I was very good at and for which I earned a great deal of approval. What it is to theorize as a feminist and as my mother's daughter is both less clear to me and more frightening, and something more important than approval is at stake. Thus, my "home-ophobia": pun, of course, fully intended.

The preceding four paragraphs are a slight revision of a proposal I sent to the organizers of a conference on "Feminisms and Cultural Imperialism: Politics of Difference" at Cornell in the spring of 1989. Although the people at the conference were predominately strangers, there was a difference that unsettled my usual ease: most of those on the program and many of the audience were people of color, and things infinitely more important than being clever or even profound were at stake. And I had decided to talk as the very specific person I am, in particular, as a Jew.

As I went on to say in the proposal, an important piece of the puzzle has to do with power and privilege and the ways I have learned, as a daughter and as a theorist, both to identify with the privileged and to fight them, usually in the name of some oppressed others. (I came of age on the edges of the civil rights movement and later the antiwar movement.) I have rarely had to fight for myself, and I need to examine the consequences of my fighting for others from a position of ease with their oppressors. And I need to examine my fear of and uneasiness with those whose causes (as I understand them) I champion. One obvious piece of the fear is that of losing my voice.

If the position that I have doesn't distinctively well equip me with the tools and talents for theorizing—that is, if I recognize that others (e.g., women of color) can speak for themselves, and theorize for themselves—then my own theorizing seems privileged neither in the way of the old Archimedean point from which reality appears as it really is, nor in the way of the vantage point of the oppressed. For many feminist theorists the recognition of the nonexistence of any Archimedean point was compensated for by the (originally Marxist) idea that the standpoint of the oppressed was one of epistemic privilege, and that, as women, we occupied such a standpoint. But, as we reluctantly learned, there is no such standpoint that all women share, and, for many of us, myself included, the place where we stand is shaped more deeply by privilege than by oppression, and consequently seems to partake of the epistemic liabilities we so clearly pointed out in the case of men.[2]

While trying to find the time and the courage to figure out how and why to theorize neither as the universal synthesizer nor as a representative of the oppressed, but as the particular person I am and with the particular others I am variously connected to, I continued to travel. In the spring and summer of 1989, before and after the Cornell conference, I went to a meeting of the Revisioning Philosophy Program on gender and philosophy at Esalen, then back to Dubrovnik, and then to the Program's conference on Philosophy and the Human Future at Cambridge. The Dubrovnik talk, "Your Ground Is My Body: The Politics of Anti-Foundationalism," is, like its predecessor, being translated into German by Ludwig Pfeiffer. My talk at Cambridge was entitled "If Your Ground Were Not My Body, What Might Our Ground Be?". It's never been written, and the present essay can be taken as its translation, not into a language I can barely read, but into my native tongue, what in Yiddish is called the "mame-loshn," the mother tongue. (I do not really know Yiddish. To the consternation of my elderly relatives, what I understand of it comes mainly from what I understand of German. But Yiddish feels natural to me: it sounds like home.)

There has been a recent rich conversation about the meanings of home to feminists of different races and ethnicities. In 1983 Barbara

---

[2] For a critical account of feminist standpoint epistemologies, see Sandra Harding, *The Science Question in Feminism* (Ithaca: Cornell University Press, 1986), and for a critique of the effects of unexamined privilege on feminist theorizing, including the assumption that privileged women can articulate universal female experience, see Elizabeth V. Spelman, *Inessential Woman: Problems of Exclusion in Feminist Thought* (Boston: Beacon Press, 1988).

Smith edited *Home Girls: A Black Feminist Anthology*,[3] with an introduction in which she discusses her choice of the title, the resonance of "home" for Black women: "Home has always meant a lot to people who are ostracized as racial outsiders in the public sphere. It is above all a place to be ourselves."(p.li) Bernice Johnson Reagon in her essay in that volume, "Coalition Politics: Turning the Century," stresses the importance of not confusing the comfort of home with the frequently uncomfortable work of coalition-building. Too often, she argues, white feminists have taken the women's movement to be their home, and wondered why more women of color didn't want to join them in it, not noticing that, like all homes, it bore the marks of its proprietary occupants. White feminists have not left behind as much of our original homes as we have often wanted to think we have, nor have most women of color been eager to follow suit: even if the new feminist homes were not so recognizably white, the detachment from family and community that can feel like a liberating gesture for a woman of privilege is likely to be both a loss and a betrayal for a woman of color.

For Barbara Smith home is not necessarily comfortable: being oneself there may at times be a struggle. But even if it is not always the place of refuge and sustenance Reagon writes of, home as an arena of struggle is markedly different from a coalition. The difference is one of history and its connection to identity: the decision not to sever one's ties with home is a decision—or a recognition—that who one is is not detachable from that place or those people. One of the arguments women of color have made to white women is that we need to acknowledge those ties, the ways in which homes we may think we have left have shaped us, and we need to take responsibility for where we have come from.

In thinking about how to do that in my own life, I turned to Minnie Bruce Pratt's autobiographical narrative "Identity: Skin Blood Heart"[4] and an essay on it called "Feminist Politics: What's Home Got to Do with It?" by Biddy Martin and Chandra Talpade Mohanty[5] (both of whom were at the Cornell conference). Martin and Mohanty trace Pratt's journey from a Southern girlhood, marriage, and motherhood to an explicitly anti-racist lesbian feminism, noting how her narrative of the journey problematizes her relation to the various homes she has

[3] Barbara Smith, ed., *Home Girls: A Black Feminist Anthology* (New York: Kitchen Table Women of Color Press, 1983)

[4] Ellie Bulkin, Minnie Bruce Pratt, and Barbara Smith, *Yours in Struggle: Three Feminist Perspectives on Anti-Semitism and Racism* (Brooklyn, N.Y.: Long Haul Press, 1984)

[5] Biddy Martin and Chandra Talpade Mohanty, "Feminist Politics: What's Home Got to Do with It?" in Teresa de Lauretis, ed. *Feminist Studies/Critical Studies* (Bloomington: Indiana University Press, 1986)

had and made. Far from abandoning who she had been, by "leaving home" (becoming the feminist version of that American icon, the self-made man) according to Martin and Mohanty, "Pratt...succeeds in carefully taking apart the bases of her own privilege by resituating herself again and again in the social, by constantly referring to the materiality of the situation in which she finds herself." (p.194)

In thinking about the issues of home and privilege, I began as a white woman, but the specificities of Pratt's narrative made it clear to me that among the many differences between her life and mine, a particularly salient one for exploring the meanings of home was my Jewishness. I was born in 1946 of parents born in New York. Although the Holocaust barely preceded my birth, I was brought up in a suburban world that was carefully constructed to feel safe: at Passover seders Hitler merged in my mind with the Pharaoh as a vanquished oppressor who had been forced finally to "let my people go." But, despite the safety, it's become clear to me that home for me is not the stable place from which one sets out into the world, secure that, whatever else changes, it will still be there. Home is where, if you can't flee from it fast enough, they will kill you or take you away. Home is where pogroms happen; like most American Jews, I have only the vaguest idea of where my grandparents were born, and there are surely no relatives still to be found there.

Jewish "cosmopolitanism" needs, of course, to be seen in this light: our survival as a people has depended on our individual and communal ability to survive in diaspora, finding ways of making a living and making a life in a strange land, on the margins. (The stubborn brutality of Israel's response to the Palestinian people and to the Intifada is, I think, an indication of the extent to which the moral integrity of Jewish identity was tied to the conditions of diaspora and marginality and has not been sufficiently reconfigured to fit the conditions of being at home and the different sorts of responsibility that come with that.) In my own life, although I never feared being chased from the home I grew up in, it never occurred to me to remain there, certainly not in the Long Island suburb that felt like a nursery, a place designed to be grown out of, and which I barely remember, though I lived there from when I was two until I started college.

For the past fifteen years I have lived in places that are foreign to me, first in Canada, then in the Midwest. I like Minneapolis and have no desire to leave, but I cannot imagine thinking of it as home, as where I am from, no matter how long I live here. Part of what I like about it is precisely that it is not and never will be home. Before I could feel comfortable, though, I had to drive between here and the East coast. Until I'd done that (a couple of years after I moved here), I had attacks of a sort of agoraphobia: there was far too much continent all around. I needed to know where the nearest ocean was, not because I like oceans (which I do), but because I needed to know where to flee to. Just in case.

There is, of course, more than a little romantic posturing in all this. But I do see in my own life and in my sense of myself in the world the influence of the position of privileged marginality of many contemporary American Jews (a position that a significant number of German Jews enjoyed before the ascendancy of Nazism and that made it difficult for them to acknowledge the murderousness of their countrymen's intentions towards them). In feminist theory marginality has most often been contrasted with privilege; the position on the margin is precisely the position not shaped and limited by the myopias of privilege. But much Jewish experience, including my own, questions this association. Not all positions on the margin are the same. The place of usury in premodern Europe is an example: being forbidden to Christians, it was taken up by Jews, who came to play a vital and necessarily well-remunerated role in economic life, while being, precisely because they played this role, even more marginalized to core conceptions of privileged European identity.

Philosophers are, I think, in an interestingly analogous position. As I have argued elsewhere,[6] philosophical problems, notably the core epistemological problems of scepticism, can be seen as the residue of the construction of privileged subjectivity. Insofar as authority rests in one's ability to lay claim to a self essentially detached from bodily needs and desires, from emotions, from defining connections to other people, and from manual labor, one will find it problematic whether and how one can ever really know, for example, if one actually has a body, whether there is any world out there at all, whether other people have minds like one's own. The detachments that constitute authority are from everything culturally assigned to women, to the working class, and to those of races other than white. Thus, racism, classism, and gynophobic misogyny are at the heart of the subjectivity whose construction gives rise to the problems of philosophy.

The serious work of actually exercising that authority—in science, politics, or business—is hardly compatible with worrying about such notoriously intractable questions, so they are shunted off onto philoso-

---

[6] In addition to "Your Ground Is My Body," which will be published by Suhrkamp in German in a volume edited by Hans Ulrich Gumbrecht and Ludwig Pfeiffer, see "The Unavoidability of Gender," forthcoming in the *Journal of Social Philosophy* (Winter 1991); and "Though This Be Method, Yet There Is Madness in It: Paranoia and Liberal Epistemology," forthcoming in Louise Antony and Charlotte Witt, ed., *Feminism and Reason* (Boulder, Colorado: Westview Press).

phers, hopelessly impractical, abstracted eggheads, who serve as cultural scapegoats for the neuroses of privilege. Such a position is certainly marginal (necessarily so, since the questions that trouble philosophers can't be taken seriously), but it is not lacking in privilege.

It is a position I took to with an ease that now, as a feminist, I find troubling. The problems of philosophy seemed wholly natural to me. I said when I discovered philosophy, my first year in college, that I felt immediately at home with it, as though I was hearing my native tongue spoken for the first time. But it wasn't, of course, my mother tongue, and its naturalness to me is a reflection of the extent to which I was then my father's daughter. I was at Barnard, a women's college, and my teachers were women, which certainly made it much easier to feel that I could be a philosopher, but being a woman was not taken to mark any important difference, certainly not in one's relation to philosophical problems and methods. In a logic class at Columbia, much was made of my being a woman; at Barnard it seemed irrelevant.

I don't now think it is irrelevant, since I no longer believe (and am trying to stop acting as though I do believe) that theorists are essentially disembodied and ahistorical. My choice to inhabit problems that arise from the construction of privilege signified my willingness to disaffiliate with other women, that is, not to identify with those who rejected or were never offered the privilege of being treated like (privileged) men. It was a choice to identify with my father and with others who offered me approval if I learned my lessons well. It was, for reasons I do not yet fully understand, a less frightening choice than that of identifying with my mother.

It is too easy to say (though it is true) that my choice is understandable, that is, looks wholly rational, given the greater power associated with the world of men. What that explanation leaves out is the fear, which was—and is—not just the fear of (relative) powerlessness. It was—and is—the fear of home, the fear of women: home-ophobia. It is connected to my attitudes about the seasons, in particular, to the transition between winter and spring. April, for me, is the cruelest month[7] (except in Minnesota, where we still have blizzards then; here it's May). The "mixing [of] memory and desire," the re-emergence of what has been safely frozen, is frightening. In the winter boundaries are well-marked; things and people know their places. Spring brings thaw, the blurring of the boundary between inside and outside, a generally promiscuous mingling. I can tough out the winter: it makes demands on me, there are rules to follow, clear things to succeed at; it calls for

[7] T.S. Eliot, "The Waste Land," in *Collected Poems 1909-1962* (New York: Harcourt, Brace and World, 1970, p.53

hardness and rigor. Spring is another matter. It doesn't make demands at all, but it has hopes and expectations; it won't punish those who aren't up to its promises, as winter will punish those who aren't up to its threats, but it will be disappointed, saddened by those who can't or won't rise to its occasion. You can't tough out spring.

Heterosexuality is, for me, like winter. There is a lot I straightforwardly like about both, moments of intensest pleasure, and certainly desire. But there is also little I fear. I know what the challenges are, and I enjoy them, and if worse comes to worst, I know how to survive. With respect both to winter and to heterosexuality, my fearlessness is, of course, born of privilege: there are many for whom one or the other can be literally deadly, and in both cases there is no guarantee that my privilege will continue, or that it will be enough. But I feel safe.

As I don't in the spring, or with women. Where, objectively, I am, and know myself to be, safer, I feel frightened, because none of the tricks I have learned will do me any good. They're unnecessary, but without them I feel defenseless, and it does no good to say there's nothing for me to defend myself from. That's just the problem. I don't need the mask, but I'm seized with anxiety that underneath it, there's no face. Politically, personally, and as a theorist I am most comfortable when I feel least at home, when being myself is the last thing I have to worry about.

I remember a talk I gave soon after coming to Minnesota. In the front rows sat my new, senior colleagues, the people who would in a few years decide whether or not I got to keep my job. In the back were students and faculty from Women's Studies, my friends, people with no power over my future in the University. I spoke with ease, even bravado, certainly no fear, as long as I focused on the front rows. When my eyes went toward the back, my pulse raced and my throat grew dry: they— my friends, the people who I knew really cared about me—could, I was sure, see through the cleverness, would want more from me than that. With no power to make or enforce demands, they needed and expected me to speak honestly, to say things that mattered. It's a lot easier to be clever.

Among the things that matter: in the midst of increasing tension between Blacks and Jews some people are trying to make two groups and to heal the rifts. As part of this attempt, there are Black and Jewish Women in Dialogue groups, and I belong to one in the Twin Cities. One of the things we have tried is to reach some common understanding of the alliances between Blacks and Jews during the forties, fifties, and sixties, alliances that Jews typically remember far more fondly than Blacks do. For many Blacks, the memory is mixed: the support given to the civil rights movement by Jews is acknowledged and appreciated, but it didn't feel like an alliance between equals. Jews were too often in the role of the masked woman (or man)—the benefactor, riding into and out of town, doing good from behind a mask and atop a horse.

Jewish cosmopolitanism translated into marginality, not as on the edges but as at the interstices, strategically located socially, economically, residentially, between more privileged whites and Blacks. While recognizing the moral courage of chosen solidarity with those more oppressed, we need to acknowledge that many Jews, even among those truly committed to the civil rights agenda, compromised that solidarity by turning toward the greater safety of privilege. (Rumor has it that some have even become Republicans.) The movement of many Jews from major cities to the suburbs was in the name of safety, a resonant term for post-Holocaust parents. But, as Lata Mani pointed out to me when I discussed these issues at the Cornell conference, the "danger" Jews were fleeing was not Nazis, but the changing face of the inner city, too often summed up by the movement into Jewish neighborhoods of Blacks, the very people with whom they were supposedly allied.

Privilege is a very tricky thing. It allows one to do things that are genuinely valuable (like living in neighborhoods where children can go out to play without risking their lives and where the schools are well-equipped and not over-crowded): only those who have always had it are in a position to think it's worthless. But it is systematically distorting, of our perspective and of our values: it demands our loyalty to the unjust structures that grant it.[8] An understandable response to discovering that we have it at the expense of others, on whose backs it rests, is to try to use it on their behalf, to take advantage, for them, of our ability to move with relative ease among the oppressors. As a strategy, that may have its place, but as a way of life, it doesn't work. No one out there knows us well enough to keep us honest.

Bernice Reagon urges us not to think we are at home when we are in coalition; equally important, as she also notes, we have to be at home somewhere, not only for our own mental health, but precisely, as Barbara Smith puts it, "to be ourselves," which for some of us may be the hardest thing of all to be.

---

[8] See Adrienne Rich, "Disloyal to Civilization: Feminism, Racism, Gynephobia" in *On Lies, Secrets, and Silence* (New York: W.W. Norton & Co., 1979).

The Evolution of Embodied Consciousness

Michael Murphy

To the founders of most contemplative schools, the world was not an arena in which livelier, more conscious forms appeared in the course of time, but a place marked essentially by suffering and death. For early Buddhists, the world apprehended through the ordinary senses was *samsara*, a grinding wheel of death and rebirth. For Platonists and Neoplatonists, it was the lowest level on the great chain of being. For most Christian mystics, it was separated twice from God, by Creation and by the Fall.[1] Though all religious traditions have supremely life-affirming aspects, they have also produced powerful language about the world's uncertainty, its essential misery, its basic immunity to progress. Viewing the manifest world as a place to escape from, various mystics have helped orient religious practice away from the psychophysical transformation I am proposing here. "The body is a dung heap," wrote Thomas Kempis. An illumined soul in the flesh, said Sri Ramakrishna, is like "an elephant breaking out of a flimsy hut." For many ascetics to whom the body exemplified the earth's transience and

---

[1]Some thinkers of Greek antiquity, however, did entertain ideas of general progress, but they did not influence most Platonists, Neoplatonists or early Christian mystics. See: Nisbet, R. (1980) *The History of the Idea of Progress*. New York: Basic Books.

suffering (instead of its potential for numinous life), it seemed logical to seek deliverance from embodiment, and sensible to think that the extraordinary physical and mental powers produced by religious life had no more value finally than any worldly capacity that supports our inferior state.

Such attitudes need not rule our thinking, however, for the discoveries of modern biology and physics have given us new perspectives on the world and our human abilities. Our planet has been revealed in a new light, not as a static or cyclical world, but as an arena in which graduation upon graduation of species have occurred for several hundred million years. This stupendous advance suggests that humans might develop further. Evolution to date is a supreme inescapable gesture, pointing toward a mysterious future for living forms, leading us inevitably to suppose it could continue through further aeons producing a play of bodies beyond our present capacities to imagine. Indeed, it has shown that it can even exceed its established laws and patterns. Because evolution has gone beyond its own bounds before, and because there is evidence that superior kinds of life are latent in the human race, it is not unreasonable to think that in spite of our many liabilities further progress, even a new kind of evolution, might be available to us.

The vast development of life upon earth makes a further unfolding of humankind more plausible than it would be in a cosmos that appeared to be going nowhere. The universe itself, as it has been revealed to us by modern science, invites us to open our imagination and correlate our sense of human possibilities with evolution's dynamic advance. A vision of spiritual life embedded in the facts of cosmic, organic and psychosocial development gives new perspective to phenomena associated with religious practices including the many extraordinary powers it produces. For if it is indeed the case that we can realize a richer existence upon earth, we would develop capacities for creative interaction and engagement with the world. "We need not shun [extraordinary powers] and cannot shun them," wrote the Indian philosopher Sri Aurobindo:

> ...there is a stage reached by the yogin, when, unless he avoids all action in the world, he can no more avoid the use of the siddhis of power and knowledge than an ordinary man can avoid eating and breathing; for these things are the natural action of the consciousness to which he is rising, just as mental activity and physical motion are the natural action of man's ordinary life. All the ancient *rishis* used these powers, all great yogins have used them, nor is there any great man...who does not use them con-

tinually in an imperfect form, without knowing clearly what are these supreme faculties that he is enjoying.[2]

But to repeat: our world-engaging capacities, the "siddhis of power and knowledge" Aurobindo referred to, have often been neglected or suppressed by the very traditions in which they have most dramatically arisen. In following the time-tested wisdom that a purging of egocentricity is necessary to realize enlightenment or union with God, many ascetics have spurned many capacities which their discipline opened to them. Indeed, nearly every religious tradition has pronounced severe prohibitions against certain normal as well as extranormal capacities. Ascetic excesses of some Christian desert fathers, for example, were widely emulated in the fourth and fifth centuries and into medieval times.[3] Sri Chaitanya (b. 1485), one of India's most renowned saints, spent the last years of his life in nearly continuous trance, setting an example that countless devotees have tried to imitate since.[4]

Though such extremes have not been the rule in religious life, they have existed in nearly every tradition, along with more balanced practices. Indeed, there is a spectrum of transformative activities embedded in or related to the great religions, running from those that drastically suppress mind and flesh to Zen-inspired martial arts or the earthly and joyous expressions of Hasidism.

To best appreciate our possibilities for further development, we must draw upon both the facts of evolution revealed by modern science and the witness of spiritual traditions East and West. To do this, one must confront two fundamental realities: a universal development of (inorganic and living) forms that has lasted for several billion years, and transcendent orders of existence conceived or experienced for several millennia by people all over the earth. The possibility of integrating these two aspects of existence is fundamental to my inquiries here.

[2]Sri Aurobindo (1972) Sapta-Chatusthaya. In *The Collected Works*. Volume 27. Pondicherry, India: Sri Aurobindo Ashram Trust, p. 366. For a longer discussion of the siddhis, see Volume 27, pp. 366-374, and index reference in Volume 30 of *The Collected Works*.

[3]Duchesne, L. (1933) *Early History of the Christian Church*. Volume II. London: John Murray, p. 391. Lecky, W.E. (1975) *History of European Morals*. Volumes I ~ II. New York-Arno.

[4]In Pondicherry, India, I watched a yogi in trance being fed by his followers. His eyeballs were rolled back so that only the whites of his eyes could be seen; he sat erect in the lotus position; and his face reflected ecstatic absorption. According to the people around him, he had achieved *nirvikalpha samadhi*, and "would never return to this world."

In this essay, I shall first review some philosophical ideas regarding progress, evolution, and the history of consciousness. I will then discuss possibilities for further human development, and conclude with cautionary notes: first, against uncritical enthusiasm for some brave new *Übermensch;* and second, against gullible acceptance of every testimonial for extraordinary human abilities. In order to steer a path between ignoring or denying metanormal phenomena on the one hand, or gullibility on the other, I shall suggest an approach I call *synoptic empiricism.*

I. The Evolution of Embodied Consciousness

During the two centuries since "progress" became a prominent idea in the West, the philosophers Fichte, Schelling, Hegel, Bergson, Solovyev, Berdyaev, Whitehead, Samuel Alexander, C. Lloyd Morgan, Jean Gebser, Charles Hartshorne, Teilhard de Chardin and Sri Aurobindo, among others, have tried to comprehend or explain the evolutionary universe in relation to something ultimate, eternal, or everlasting. In various ways, each of them provides lines of support for a simultaneous embrace of nature and supernature by linking the world's progress to *Geist,* Deity, "the ever-present Origin," *Satchitananda,* or some other version of a world-transcending (yet immanent) Reality. The richness of their speculations shows what a fertile cross-matrix, what a promising field for philosophic inquiry appears when universal development is considered together with intuitions and experiences of a Supreme Principle or Divinity. Furthermore, their insights often illumine particular processes and specific human conditions that inhibit or facilitate metanormal development. Many insights of these philosophers suggest that the links between superordinary dimensions of existence and this world's developmental processes are ripe for new understanding.

Looking away from either aspect of existence, it seems to me, constitutes a supreme philosophic avoidance. Philosophers of ancient and medieval times should not be faulted because they did not know about evolution, but anyone now who attempts to build a comprehensive understanding of this world without contemplating its stupendous history is a self-blinded explorer. And conversely, no general theory of human development should overlook the enormous witness to mystical knowing and superordinary abilities revealed by modern religious studies, psychical research, anthropological studies of shamanism, and other kinds of systematic inquiry into extranormal capacities. The evolving universe and "supernature", however named, stand before us now as two inescapable facts. It is telling, I think, that so many great philosophers since the late 18th century have explored the relations between them.

This essay draws upon several sets of ideas about evolution's relation to metanormal realities. Here I will describe four of them: notions of emergent evolution; concepts of evolutionary "subsumption"; proposals that new types of consciousness have developed at various times and places in the human race; and doctrines of "involution-evolution." I do not subscribe to all the concepts related to or derived from these particular sets of ideas, but each of them provides insight, language, or a philosophic stance that strongly resonates with my proposals about human development.

A.

Samuel Alexander, C. Lloyd Morgan, C.D. Broad, Joseph Needham, Michael Polanyi and others have developed the idea that evolution produces "emergent" structures, processes and laws (or "habits") which had not previously existed.[5] According to most versions of this thesis, emergent items in the world cannot be explained or predicted from the conditions, events, or patterns that they grew out of. They are fundamentally novel, not rearrangements of pre-existing elements. They are qualitatively—not merely quantitatively—different from anything that existed before them. The concept of emergence implies the existence of "levels", that is, portions of the world marked by qualities, forms and regularities peculiar to them and emergent from other domains. Emergent evolutionists have disagreed, however, about the number of levels existing in this universe. Morgan, for example, lists four—psychophysical events, life, mind, and Spirit (or God); and Alexander five—space, time, matter, life, and Deity; while others have objected to such definite enumerations because countless gradations exist between inorganic matter, plant or animal species, and humankind. But in spite of their differences, philosophers who have emphasized emergence and novelty in the world's development have lent support to the notion of "evolutionary transcendence." With

[5]Alexander, Samuel (1920 & 1979) *Space, Time and Deity*. Gloucester, MA: Peter Smith. Morgan, C. Lloyd (1923) *Emergent Evolution*. New York: Henry Holt. Broad, C.D. (1925 & 1980) *The Mind and Its Place in Nature*. London: Routledge & Regan Paul. Needham, Joseph (1937) *Integrative Levels: A Revaluation of the Idea of Progress*. London: Oxford University Press. Polanyi, Michael (1964) *Personal Rnowledge*. New York: Harper Torchbook .

biologists such as Dobzhansky and Ayala, they have helped to elucidate the fact that matter, life and mind each operate with distinctive patterns. Doctrines of emergence help us view metanormal phenomena on their own terms, not in a reductionistic manner that distorts or obscures their significance for human development. Emergent evolutionists encourage us to oppose reductionisms that inhibit understanding of those scientifically anomalous events that might signal a new evolutionary order.[6]

B.

In the course of evolution, new levels build upon those that precede them, appropriating earlier processes in their unique activity. Thus life takes up inorganic elements, using them for its distinctive ends; and humans depend upon biological processes for a functioning more complex than their animal ancestors'. Hegel saw an analogous process at work in human development, and used the German word "*aufheben*"—which suggests both annihilation and preservation—to describe the frequent subsumptions of cultural forms by their successors. In the dialectic of history, he claimed, earlier kinds of human behavior and consciousness (*Gestalten des Bewusstseins*) have been "lifted up" to higher levels.[7]

The Indian philosopher Sri Aurobindo also emphasized this aspect of evolutionary change.

> ...one by one there appear material forms and forces, vegetable life, animals and half-animal man, developed human beings, imperfectly evolved or more evolved spiritual beings: but because of the continuity of the evolutionary process there is no rigid separation between them, and each new advance or formation takes up what was before. The animal takes up into himself living and inanimate Matter; man takes up both along with the

[6]Doctrines of emergence have been developed by numerous scientists who have not subscribed to evolutionary philosophies such as Alexander's or Morgan's. "[The] evolutionary version of the emergence doctrine," wrote Ernest Nagel, "is not entailed by the conception of emergence as irreducible hierarchical organization, and the two forms of the doctrine must be distinguished." See: Nagel, Ernest (1979) *The Structure of Science.* Indianapolis: Hackett, pp. 366-379.

[7]Solomon, Robert C. (1983) *In the Spirit of Hegel: A Study of G.W.F. Hegel's Phenomenology of Spirit.* New York: Oxford University Press. Miller, A.V. (trans.) (1977) *Phenomenology of Spirit by G.W.F. Hegel.* With an analysis of the text and forward by J.N. Findlay. New York: Oxford University Press. Baillie, J.B. (trans.) (1910) *Phenomenology of Mind.* New York: Harper (1967 Reprint).

animal existence...by whatever means, the Consciousness secretly indwelling in matter is able thus to make its way upward from the lower to the higher gradations, taking up what it was into what it is and preparing to take up both into what it will be.[8]

Emerging consciousness, which in Aurobindo's philosophy is essentially Divine, takes up the life form it inhabits

...to raise it up to a higher level, to give it higher values, to bring out of it higher potentialities. And this [it] does because evidently [it] does not intend to kill or destroy it, but, delight of existence being [its] eternal business and a harmony of various strains, not a sweet but monotonous melody the method of [its] music, [it] wishes to include the lower notes also and, by surcharging them with a deeper and finer significance, get more delight out of them than was possible in the cruder formulation.

In Aurobindo's view, since our goal is a numinous life upon earth instead of release from embodiment, a life in which the "delight of existence is our eternal business," we must draw upon our diverse inheritance, including our biological processes and the inorganic elements that comprise them, our emotions, cognitions, and spiritual impulses to realize our full capabilities. Therapeutic and religious disciplines, however, often fail to appropriate the richness evolution has left us—neglecting our imagination or intellect, doing violence to our feelings, or dampening our physical energies by one-sided disciplines. But by seeing that we can integrate the many dimensions of our lives in a "harmony of various strains," as Aurobindo put it, rather than "a sweet but monotonous melody," and by appreciating the fact that such synthesis is analogous to the subsumptions evident in earlier stages of evolutionary progress, we can embrace our stupendous heritage and take first steps toward realizing our potentials more fully.

C.

The idea that consciousness has advanced in the human race, giving rise to new types of awareness, has been developed by Hegel, Bergson, Aurobindo and other philosophers during the last two hundred years. The notion that mind is multi-leveled preceded Hegel,

[8]Sri Aurobindo (1972) "The Evolutionary Process—Ascent & Integration." Chapter XVIII. *The Life Divine*. Volume 18. Book I. In *The Collected Works*, Pondicherry, India: Sri Aurobindo Ashram.

of course, having appeared for example in Plato's metaphor of the divided line (*The Republic* VI:509-11); in Plotinus's distinction between *nous*, and *dianoia*; and among Hindu, Buddhist, Jewist, Christian, and Moslem thinkers since antiquity. Modern philosophers such as Hegel and Bergson, however, have emphasized the idea that new levels of mind appear in the course of human history, like other emergent properties of the universe. Even if they have roots in eternal or pre-existing orders of existence, new kinds of consciousness have become manifest for the first time *on earth* in particular societies and individuals, then spread to others by education or example.

According to Hegel, each stage of human development is canceled and preserved in the dialectical progress of history. In his *Phenomenology of Spirit* he traced this ongoing process from the slave of antiquity, who struggled successfully against nature's difficulties, to the stoic's establishment of freedom within himself independent of nature's demands, to the skeptic's increase of freedom by dissipating restrictive categories of thought, to the Christian believer's discovery of freedom in a transcendent God, to the modern intellectual's appropriation of reason's highest principles. In this dialectic, each successive form of consciousness subsumed the forms that preceded it in extending its repertoire of thought and volition.

D.

Hegel, and Sri Aurobindo, among others, advanced the idea that this world's unfoldment is based upon the implicit action, "descent", or "involution" of a Supreme Principle or Divinity. Unlike the emergent evolutionists I have mentioned, these philosophers accounted for the progressive expression of higher forms or qualities by positing their secret existence or immanence in nature. In Hegel's conception, *Geist* gradually reveals itself to itself through the long dialectic of history, recovering its fundamental completeness by a series of dialectical syntheses in which one aspect of itself after another was subsumed (*aufgehoben*) in a higher fulfillment.

Henry James Sr., a thinker overshadowed by his famous sons William and Henry, developed a synthesis of ethical, social and metaphysical speculation based largely upon Swedenborgian and Neo-Platonic ideas. For him, evolution was preceded by the involution of Divinity in the world.

> Whatsoever creates a thing [he wrote] gives it being, *in*-volves the thing, not the thing it. The Creator involves the creature; the creature *e*volves the Creator...[9]

> Let us clearly understand then that the Divine operation in creation is made up of two movements: one...creative, which is a movement of humiliation consisting in giving us natural being or identity; the other...redemptive, which is a movement of glorification consisting in giving us the amplest individual or spiritual expansion out of that base root. The prior movement, the descending, statical, the properly creative one—gives us natural selfhood or consciousness, a consciousness of separation from God, of a power inhering in ourselves and independent of Him. The posterior movement—the ascending, dynamical, and properly redemptive one—gives us spiritual consciousness, a consciousness of union with God.[10]

Writing several decades later, Aurobindo articulated a doctrine of involution-evolution that resembles James's.

> The animal is a living laboratory in which Nature has, it is said, worked out man. Man himself may well be a thinking and living laboratory in whom and with whose conscious co-operation she wills to manifest God. For if evolution is the progressive manifestation by Nature of that which slept or worked in her, involved, it is also the overt realization of that which she secretly is. We cannot, then, bid her pause at a given stage of her evolution, nor have we the right to condemn with the religionist as perverse and presumptuous or with the Rationalist as a disease or hallucination any intention she may evince or effort she may make to go beyond. If it be true that Spirit is involved in Matter and apparent Nature is secret God, then the manifestation of the divine in himself and the realization of God

---

[9]James, Henry (1853) "The Works of Sir William Hamilton," *Putnam's Magazine,*Volume II, (November) p. 479.
[10]James, Henry (1863) *Substance and Shadow.* Boston:Ticknor and Fields, pp. 396-397, 425-526.

within and without are the highest and most legitimate aim
possible to man upon earth.[11]

Though there are significant differences between their philosophies, both Aurobindo and James saw universal evolution arising from a
previous involution of Divinity in nature. Both of them might be called
"evolutionary emanationists" in that they regarded the manifest world
to be an emanation of Divinity (or the One) like Neo-Platonism and
some schools of Vedanta, but at the same time conceived it to be a
dynamic process creatively seeking to express its Source, rather than a
static structure from which some individual souls might ascend to
enlightenment or union with God. James's biographer Frederic Young
wrote: "To read Aurobindo's masterpiece, *The Life Divine*, is, to one who
has read the senior James's works, to experience an indescribable feeling that Aurobindo and James must have corresponded and conversed
with each other; so much spiritual kinship is there between the
philosophies of these two thinkers!"[12] Both of them regarded
"apparent Nature" to be "secret God," and saw the Supreme Reality
emerging more fully in this world through the vicissitudes of time. Like
philosophers since the late 18th century such as Hegel and Bergson,
they "temporalized the great chain of being," to use the historian
Arthur Lovejoy's phrase, conceiving the manifest world "not as the
inventory but as the program of nature...carried out gradually and
exceedingly slowly in the cosmic history."[13]

[11]Sri Aurobindo (1972) *The Life Divine.* In *The Collected Works*, Volume 18, Book I.
Chapter 1. Pondicherry, India:Sri Aurobindo Ashram.

[12]Young, Frederic (1951) *The Philosophy of Henry James, Sr.* New York:Bookman, pp.
167-169.

[13]Lovejoy, Arthur (1936) *The Great Chain of Being.* New York: Harper Torchbooks, p.
244. In describing this "temporalizing", Lovejoy wrote:

> ...an important group of the ruling ideas of the early eighteenth century—
> the conception of the Chain of Being, the principles of plenitude and
> continuity on which it rested, the optimism which it served to justify, the
> generally accepted biology—all were in accord with the supposedly Solominic
> dictum...there not only is not, but there never will be, anything new under
> the sun. The process of time brings no enrichment of the world's diversity; in
> a world which is the manifestation of eternal rationality, it could not
> conceivably do so. Yet it was in precisely the period when this implication of
> the old conception became most apparent that there began a reaction
> against it. For one of the principal happenings in eighteenth-century thought
> was the temporalizing of the Chain of Being. The *plenum formarum* came to be
> conceived by some, not as the inventory but as the program of nature, which
> is being carried out gradually and exceedingly slowly in the cosmic history.
> While all the possibles demand realization, they are not accorded it all at
> once. Some have attained it in the past and have apparently since lost it;
> many are embodied in the kind of creatures which now exist; doubtless

Until progress and evolution became prominent ideas in the West, the idea of emanation and return was usually embedded in world views that regarded the world to be a static (or cyclical) existence to which time adds nothing new.[14] That the emanationist vision has been wedded to both evolutionary and non-evolutionary cosmologies indicates its lasting appeal to the metaphysical imagination, its resonance with an intuition prevalent in different eras and cultures. The idea of "divine emanation" economically and beautifully reflects a realization reported by countless people since antiquity that they enjoy a secret contact, kinship, or identity with the founding Principle or Ground of this universe. Such realization, which gives philosophical doctrines of emanation-return (or involution-evolution) compelling justification and support, may be brief or long-lasting, spontaneous or the result of transformative practice. Philosophers and mystics of virtually every religious tradition have expressed versions of it through parables, aphorisms, or metaphysical formulations, while contemporary studies of ecstatic experience have shown that people with diverse religious beliefs report similar experiences. Thus:

- "Before your parents were," asks a famous Zen *koan,* "what is your original face?" This celebrated line suggests that we enjoy an essential "personhood" that preceded our birth and will outlast death.
- In a famous Hindu parable, a tiger separated since birth from its mother is raised by sheep, believing itself to be one of them until another tiger shows it its own reflection in a river. We are all tigers, the parable implies, all secretly God (or Brahman) though we think we are something else.

infinitely many more are destined to receive the gift of actual existence in the ages that are to come. It is only of the universe in its entire temporal span that the principle of plenitude holds good. The Demiurgus is not in a hurry; and his goodness is sufficiently exhibited if, soon or late, every Idea finds its manifestation in the sensible order.

The causes of this change were of several sorts; but the one which is most pertinent to our subject lay in the difficulties to which the principle of plenitude itself, as it had traditionally been interpreted, gave rise, when its implications were fully drawn out and seriously considered. Those implications were, on the one hand, intolerable to the religious feelings of many minds; and, on the other hand, it became increasingly apparent that they were hard to reconcile with the facts known about nature. The static and permanently complete Chain of Being broke down largely from its own weight. (*Ibid.,* pp. 244-245).

[14]Arthur Lovejoy's *The Great Chain of Being* presents a classic review of emanationist doctrine as it developed in Western culture from Plato's dialogues to the writings of Novalis, Schelling and other writers of the late 18th and early 19th centuries.

- The Platonic doctrine of *anamnesis*, or "recollection", which asserts that we can remember the Divine Ideas underlying sense impressions, is based upon the belief that humans have immortal souls that communed with those Ideas before assuming a mortal body. Though scholars have debated the extent to which Plato himself enjoyed mystical illumination, Platonist and Neo-Platonist thinkers have traditionally asserted that humans are secretly rooted in Divinity, and can realize that fact through the practice of virtue, the pursuit of beauty, and philosophic inquiry (or dialectic). "God," wrote Plotinus, "is outside of none, present unperceived to all; we break away from Him, or rather from ourselves; what we turn from we cannot reach; astray ourselves, we cannot go in search of another; a child distraught will not recognize its father; to find ourselves is to know our source."[15] The metaphor of "homecoming" in this passage is expressed by the German poet Novalis in his famous line *immer nach hause*, "always homeward" to our secret Source.

- Though according to Christian dogma the human soul could not enjoy identity with God, the Dominican priest Meister Eckhart wrote: "To gauge the soul we must gauge it with God, for the Ground of God and the Ground of the Soul are one and the same." And in another passage he asserted: "The knower and the known are one. Simple people imagine that they should see God, as if He stood there and they here. This is not so. God and I, we are one in knowledge." In similar fashion, St. Catherine of Genoa claimed: "My Me is God, nor do I recognize any other Me except my God Himself."[16]

- And the Sufi Saint Bayazid of Bistun wrote: "I went from God to God, until they cried from me in me, 'O thou I'!"

These lines from Buddhist, Hindu, Neo-Platonist, Christian, and Islamic traditions reflect an enduring realization, shared by countless people since ancient times, of a Principle ordinarily hidden but immediately recognized as our "original face," our true identity (as a tiger among sheep), our immortal soul, our shared Ground with God, our secret at-oneness "with all the Gods."[17] Such realization strongly supports (and gives rise to) doctrines of emanation and return. In its light,

[15]Plontinus. *Enneads.* VI.9.7. Stephen MacKenna translation.

[16]Cited in: Huxley, Aldous (1970) *The Perennial Philosophy.* New York: Harper Colophon Books, pp. 11-12.

[17]For a review of metaphors regarding our human "return to the Source," see: Metzner, Ralph (1986) *Opening to Inner Light.* Chapter 8. Los Angeles: Jeremy Tarcher.

it is natural to see the manifest world either as a stage for the individual soul's return to its Source, or (like Aurobindo and James) a universal evolutionary process by stages expressing its secret Divinity.

The involution-evolution idea helps account for certain longings, illuminations, and apparent remembrances of a primordial Super-existence; and helps explain the profound resonance between human volition, imagery, emotion, and flesh through which psychophysical transformations appear to be mediated. Our cells, by this account, respond to our thoughts and intentions (and to superordinary agencies) because they arise from the same eternal or primordial Source. The involution-evolution idea resonates with my proposals here that transformative practice (like evolution) can progressively embody our latent supernature. According to this formulation, human nature can realize unitive awareness and metanormal powers because that is its secret predisposition. Because the Creator has descended into the creature, as the elder James put it, the redemptive movement of nature "gives us a consciousness of union with God." Or as Aurobindo wrote, "If apparent Nature is secret God, then...the realization of God within and without are the highest and most legitimate aim possible to man upon earth."

In summary, these four sets of ideas, each of them developed in modern times by philosophers who tried to reconcile evolution with ultimate or eternal principles, strongly resonate with my proposals here: first, anti-reductionist doctrines of "emergence", with their emphasis upon novelty and emergent levels of existence, because they provide insight and a philosophic stance to support the proposition that superordinary functioning is part of the world's creative advance; second, the notion of subsumption, because it illuminates a central aspect of development in the cosmic, biological, and psychosocial domains, and because it supports the idea that transformative practice can take up all our parts in a higher integration; third, the conception that consciousness has advanced by stages in the human race, because it relates our understanding of individual growth to the long process of human history; and fourth, the involution-evolution idea because it so powerfully unifies evidence that we humans have multiple roots in our animal-hominid ancestry and in our latent supernature.

Each of these ideas, it seems to me, can be developed to illumine our possibilities for growth. But let me emphasize the word "develop." To serve practical life, including the transformative disciplines proposed in this book, conceptual schemes must be refined in the light of our unfolding experience. Though they provide orientation for our various activities, we must remember that philosophic maps are not the territories they represent, that they often hide or obscure many features of the things they are meant to depict, and that they sometimes need to be supplemented by other maps and metaphors. Indeed, successful functioning sometimes requires willingness to entertain principles that might seem at first to be contradictory. Thus, for example, religious disciplines are assisted at times by notions of self-exceeding (and the heroic metaphors they inspire) while at other times they require ideas of "non-attainment", "surrender to grace", or self-acceptance.

II. Possibilities for Further Human Development

It is my hope that a survey of extraordinary functioning will help some people see possibilities for growth they would not otherwise recognize. Such an inventory suggests there is potential creativity in certain human activities which at first sight seem strange or perverse, and in doing so opens up ways of growth that are closed by philosophies insensitive to our more radical capacities for change and the wilder ranges of superordinary experience. That some metanormalities emerge first as sickness or high eccentricity is undoubtedly true. Psychogenic physical changes demonstrate our great capacity for bodily transformation, while certain experiences that are frequently deemed to be pathological are the first stages of healing vitality or cognition. If we take a strictly materialistic view of human nature, we are not likely to see that certain upsetting or perverse-looking episodes have a *telos*, or tendency toward the expression of extraordinary capacities that can support activity for the sake of our fellows. To know that "kundalini-type" excitement, loss of boundaries between oneself and others, even visions of "other worlds" might be first signs of life-giving powers can help us embrace them. The involution-evolution idea supports openness to emergent supernormalities, then, but it does more than that. By alerting us to the immanence of a supreme goodness in the world at large, it can, without overlooking evil or suffering, promote a general sense of hope, a faith in life, a readiness to see goodness in others. These virtues can help us to be creative and loving people, and thus better able to serve our fellows.

The view of human possibility developed here, with its involution-evolutionist perspective, also points us toward great adventures. For if it is indeed the case that we can transform our thinking, feelings, and flesh, that we can develop a more luminous embodiment, we stand at the edge of an immense frontier. This frontier, conceivably, could attract our love of exploration, our need for new territories, our drive to exceed ourselves, and in so doing help reduce certain evils caused by lack of creative outlet. I don't think it far-fetched to suggest that much of our over-consumption (and consequent degradation of the environment), drug addiction, and need for deadly conflict result from energies that could be re-channelled. Balanced transformative practices can, I believe, give us new substitutes for violence, drugs and delinquency. Cultivation of extraordinary capacities can make us more capable of enriching the world. By helping to promote such activity, the ideas reviewed in this essay serve compassionate ends rather than the detached contemplation of life against which many sensitive thinkers protest.

Though mystical experience illumines our understanding of both this world and ultimate Reality, it reinforces or gives birth to various world-views, some of them laden with beliefs unwarranted by the experience itself. Though they "in general assert a pretty distinct theoretic drift," wrote William James, mystical insights are "capable of forming matrimonial alliances with material furnished by the most diverse philosophies and theologies."[18] Most people, it seems, are prone to accept ideas associated with the conditions that produce such experience, those "over-beliefs"—to use another James formulation connected to the moral admonitions, practices, or social circumstances that catalyze its occurrence. "Here the prophets of all the different religions come," James wrote, "with their visions, voices, raptures, and other openings, supposed by each to authenticate his own peculiar faith."[19] Metanormal cognition, in short, like all extraordinary capacities, is subject to cultural shaping, and can also be clouded by various pathologies. Given our general fallibility, such knowing must be incorporated by degrees (though sometimes large degrees) into our developing consciousness. Because it can be colored by unexamined motives, needs, and beliefs, it has to be disciplined. It "must be sifted and tested, and run the gauntlet of confrontation with the total context of experience," James wrote.[20] Like data from other domains of experience, mystical insight needs to be confirmed by our own tests and by the witness of others.

[18]James, William (1902) *Varieties of Religious Experience.* New York: Random House Modern Library, pp. 407, 417.

[19]*Ibid.,* 503-504.

[20]*Ibid.,* 418.

III. The Need for a Synoptic Empiricism

In this final section I take up two of the most prevalent criticisms leveled against lofty aspirations: first, the political, second, the epistemological. I want to discuss two sets of ideas that impede discussion of high level human change, namely notions of the *Übermensch* stemming from Nietzsche, and, second, the question of evidence in the area of supernormal or paranormal functioning.

Nietzsche's *Übermensch*, in philosopher Walter Kaufman's words, "made his public appearance" in *Thus Spoke Zarathustra*. The term itself had been used by Heinrich Muller (*Geistliche Erquickungestunden*, 1664) and Goethe (in a poem *Zueignung* and in *Faust*, Part I, line 490)[21]; but Nietzsche gave it new meaning, which the English "superman" does not convey. The *Übermensch* is not a muscleman, of course, nor a tyrant, nor produced by natural selection. Nietzsche wrote in *Ecce Homo* (III.I) that only "scholarly oxen" could interpret his idea Darwinistically. The Overman, according to Kaufman, "has overcome his animal nature, organized the chaos of his passions, sublimated his impulses, and given style to his character."[22] The Overman's "power" comes from self-mastery, not dominance over others. His joy arises from a transcendent dimension of personhood (his "true self"), not from satisfaction of ordinary appetites. Nevertheless, various aspects and distortions of Nietzsche's proposals about the *Übermensch* have hindered discourse about human self-exceeding. The Nazi's appropriation of certain Nietzschean passages to justify their claims for a master race are foremost among these.

Commenting upon this misappropriation, Walter Kaufman described Nietsche's lifelong opposition to anti-Semitism, his strong advocacy of racial *mixture* (to promote cultural vitality), his reverence for the Old Testament, his scorn for German nationalism, his disgust with most political functionaries, his belief that human advance depended upon self-cultivation rather than selective breeding, and his scorn for mass enthusiasms such as those Nazism would inspire. Nazi apologists such as Richard Oehler systematically misquoted Nietzsche

---

[21]Kaufman, Walter (1974) *Nietzsche*. Princeton: Princeton University Press, pp. 307-308.

[22]*Ibid.*, 316.

or took some of his words out of context to support their contention that he anticipated Nazi claim's about a German master race.[23]

> ...Nietzsche's views are quite unequivocally opposed to those of the Nazis [Kaufman wrote] more so than those of almost any other prominent German of his time or before him...and these views are not temperamental antitheses but corollaries of his philosophy. Nietzsche was not more ambiguous in this respect than is the statement that the Nazis' way of citing him represents one of the darkest pages in the history of literary unscrupulousness.[24]

But clarifications of Nietzsche's views on race won't dispel a tendency among some people to associate conceptions of further human development with a power-hungry superman. Indeed, such an equation has hindered some peoples' ability to think boldly about high level change at all. Our thinking, however, does not have to be limited in this way. We are not obliged to equate extraordinary functioning with a master race or narcissistic Overman. For it seems to be the case that metanormal capacities flower best in conjunction with a unitive awareness of the world, with a developing empathy and love for one's fellows. There is a volition beyond ordinary drives for dominance, a self-transcending identity based upon solidarity with others, a superabundant vitality that overflows to those in need. And furthermore, the cultivation of metanormal capacities requires a disciplined surrender of ego-centered activity through practices informed by fellow aspirants, friends and mentors.

Still, it is good, I believe, that worries about metanormality are part of our intellectual climate today, given the many dangers of high level change. Evolution might meander in the metanormal domain as it has everywhere else, giving rise to perverse or monstrous behaviors; and metanormal capacities can support our destructive impulses. Suspicions about metanormality, then, can help us balance our theories and practice. The *Übermensch*, by his vivid presence in contemporary thought, reminds us that visions of human growth must be framed with wisdom and care.

Likewise, visions of extraordinary capacities exhibited by human beings, from athletes to mystic sages, must be regarded with a careful balance of open-mindedness and skepticism—a stance I call *synoptic empiricism*. Each field of inquiry that informs my research into extraordi-

---

[23]Kaufman cited some of these misquotations and compared them to their original version. See: *Ibid.* Chapter 10: The Master Race.

[24]*Ibid.*, 303-304.

nary human functioning has its own ways of providing evidence for human transformative capacity. Some, such as medical science, depend heavily upon controlled experiments and elaborate instruments. Others, such as anthropology, rely primarily upon field observations and the elicitation of subjective reports (as well as subsequent checking of those among different investigators). And still others, such as comparative religious studies and psychical research, depend upon reliable testimonies to experiences or events that are not always repeatable upon command, and the systematic comparison of such testimonies with those of witnesses to similar phenomena. Each of these fields has developed unique methods of inquiry in response to its distinctive subject matter. Each is empirical, in the sense that it depends upon disciplined acquaintance with (or experience of) its data, whether that acquaintance is established through controlled experiment, observation of naturally occuring events, or comparisons of subjective reports and reliable testimonies to unusual phenomena.

Science, psychical research, and comparative religious studies give us many ways to explore both normal and extraordinary human functioning. Improved experimental devices, observational methods, rules of testimony, and introspective techniques developed in modern times provide us with increasing knowledge about human nature, including more information about bodily structures and processes than any culture had before. Indeed, some of the phenomena studied today could not have been known in previous eras. With all their wisdom about healing and growth, for example, physicians of former times could not measure alterations in white cell count produced by placebos, or recognize the neuropeptides that mediate mood changes induced by transformative practices. Furthermore, contemporary scholarship has given us unprecedented access to esoteric lore of shamanism and the religious traditions. The *Tibetan Book of the Dead*, a document once reserved for a restricted group of Buddhists, is available now in paperback editions. The upanishads, once transmitted orally in Hindu culture, have been published in many translations. Secrets about dervish practices previously reserved for Sufi initiates are discussed in popular books. Though this publicizing of the esoteric has had some unfortunate results—helping to create a climate, for example, in which destructive cults have flourished—it has also helped broaden many people's perspectives about religious experience. While we have lost much once known within the sacred traditions, it is arguable that no single culture has possessed so much publicly accessible lore about shamanic and contemplative capacities as we do today.

Contemporary science and scholarship, then, give us many ways to explore human nature, often providing information about our functioning unavailable in previous times. Unfortunately, however, professional specialization, divergent (or conflicting) conceptual systems, and the information explosion make it difficult to bring the varieties of evidence for human transformative capacity into a single purview. Like the unassembled pieces of a great jigsaw puzzle, discoveries about human physiology, psychodynamics, and extraordinary capacities are scattered across the intellectual landscape, isolated from each other in separate domains. Nevertheless, they can be viewed together so that we can find connections among them. A synoptic acquisition of soundly verified data that draws upon science, psychical research, religious studies, and other fields is the general method I use in my research.

But let me emphasize the term "soundly verified". Because accounts of extraordinary human experience have various degrees of plausibility, we must approach them with both openness and critical distance. Whether any Tibetan lama has in fact levitated is far less certain, obviously, than the evidence that brain waves can be slowed through meditation. Whether any Catholic saint has lit up a dark room through prayer is less certain than our knowledge that hypnosis helps some people control pain during surgery. To explore the further reaches of human nature, in short, we must be open-minded with an eye for confabulation. Amid innumerable reports of extraordinary human feats, we need both prudence and imagination, both discrimination and willingness to suspend judgment. For an inquiry into the further realms of human potential, we must be bold while employing the critical spirit that characterizes good science. At the same time, we may be limited in such exploration because certain kinds of understanding available to previous cultures have been lost. Many insights arising from religious experience have almost certainly disappeared. Once fertile schools of contemplation have vanished, so that it is difficult now to observe or participate in ecstatic practices prominent in times past. But our loss of sacred tradition is partly compensated for by modern studies of mystical states and paranormal phenomena. Frederic Myers, William James, Herbert Thurston, and other scholars have compared observations and introspective reports regarding metanormal functioning, stimulating subsequent research and suggesting lines of further inquiry. They have helped to create a new kind of natural history, as it were, showing that specimens of extraordinary awareness and behavior can be collected for comparative analysis. Like naturalists who by gathering biological specimens helped reveal the fact of evolution, these researchers have prepared the way for new understandings of our human potential. But here, too, we find broken lineages. Few people now appreciate Myers' work, though he was a principal founder of modern psychical research (and invented the word "telepathy"); and few students of religious experience read Herbert Thurston, even among Roman Catholics, though he was perhaps the leading Catholic expert on paranormal phenomena in the first half of the 20th century.

In discussing paranormal and mystical events, I realize that many scientists and academic philosophers today are suspicious about them. I share some of this skepticism, for many accounts and explanations of such events are enveloped in superstitious belief, unwarranted philosophic generalization, and incoherent speculation. Nevertheless, there is considerable evidence for such phenomena, much of it soundly verified or provided by reliable witnesses. Numerous stories about scientifically inexplicable healing and saintly powers from Roman Catholic sources such as the Medical Bureau at Lourdes and the *Acta Sanctorum* are persuasive, for instance, because they have been critically scrutinized by churchpeople concerned to dispel pious delusion. Respected anthropologists have carefully studied shamanic abilities and checked their observations against those of fellow anthropologists. Psychical research has produced many descriptions of extrasensory and psychokinetic events provided by competent witnesses. And a wide range of metanormal cognitions have been subjected to verification procedures developed in the religious traditions to help contemplative aspirants discriminate between illusory and valid experience. Roman Catholic churchmen and scholars, anthropologists, psychical researchers, and contemplatives have shared the empirical spirit in that they have acquired data—whether testimonies to spiritual healing and saintly powers, observations of shamanic acts, or their own paranormal and mystical experiences—which they have then submitted to verification procedures. Today we possess a great range of evidence for metanormal capacities because people in these different fields have winnowed accurate from distorted perceptions of extraordinary phenomena, and have worked to discriminate good data from bad. As I have said, in gathering this evidence, people in different fields have needed different methods of data acquisition and verification. Roman Catholic ecclesiastics and scholars, in their assessment of healing and saintly powers, have relied upon testimony which they have checked through cross-examination of witnesses and comparisons with third-party reports of the same phenomena. Psychical researchers have supplemented reliable accounts of paranormal events with many kinds of experiment. And contemplative aspirants have tested their mystical insights against the experience of their peers and teachers.

The contemplative traditions, for example, have claimed that objects of mystical insight such as Buddha Nature, God or Brahman are realities that exist independently of any human experience, and have held that these objective realities can be apprehended through particular practices that produce experiences (or data) which can be confirmed by the contemplative's mentors or fellow seekers. In this they are—broadly speaking—empirical. Philosopher Stephen Phillips has called this position "mystic empiricism," and has argued that a parallelism exists between the evidentiality of sensory and mystical experience.[25] Granting this general parallelism, we must acknowledge two more similarities between scientific and contemplative "empiricisms": first, that both can be distorted by bad practice; and second, that both are subject to inhibitions of discovery caused by strict adherence to particular (scientific or religious) beliefs. Just as some laboratories perform bad science, certain religious communities have breakdowns in their disciplines. And just as potentially significant data are sometimes rejected because they cannot be accounted for by a conceptual system currently dominant in a particular science, metanormal events that deviate from a particular religious model are sometimes suppressed. St Teresa of Avila's struggles with her confessors over the nature of her mystical experiences exemplify this sort of exclusion.[26]

Science, psychical research, and contemplative practice share a recognition that knowledge is processed—and potentially distorted—in complex ways. They all have procedures for data accumulation and confirmation such as those noted above because they all must deal with their practitioners' faulty mediations of knowledge. Because we suffer perceptual distortions caused by fatigue, sensory malfunctions, or unexamined needs and motive; because our grasp of any data may be hampered by limiting beliefs and expectations; and for other reasons, we need help in clarifying our apprehensions of data in any domain of experience. Our mediations of knowledge—whether sensory, rational or metanormal—have to be freed from their distorting tendencies. The natural and human sciences, psychical research and religious practice all include procedures for this, including peer-review and replication of results in science, experimental laboratory procedures and cross-checking of anecdotal accounts in psychical research, and scrutiny by fellow seekers and religious masters in the contemplative life. All of these disciplines try to identify and reduce the distorting impact of various

[25]Phillips, Stephen H. (1986) *Aurobindo's Philosophy of Brahman*. Leiden, The Netherlands: E.J. Brill, pp. 5-53. In a preface to Phillips's book, philosopher Robert Nozick writes:

> Aurobindo is a mystic empiricist in that he builds upon his mystic experiences, offering us descriptions of them, hypotheses that stick rather closely to them, and also bold speculations which reach far beyond the experiences themselves in order to place them in a coherent world picture. [*Ibid.*, p. viii] .

[26]St. Teresa of Avila. *Autobiography*. See for example Chapters 27, 28 & 29.

mediations upon their participants, disengaging them (hopefully) from illusions and blind spots, broadening their apprehension of sensory, psychological, or spiritual data.

But despite the disciplined tests of experience provided by psychical research and the contemplative traditions, many scientists and philosophers today reject mystical truth claims and the evidence for paranormal phenomena. Such rejection may be prompted by lack of acquaintance with the data of psychical research and the enduring testimony to mystical experience, or by automatic associations of extranormal experience with outmoded and superstitious beliefs, or because such experience appears to violate current assumptions of mainstream science.[27] However, given the abundance of evidence for telepathy, clairvoyance, psychokinesis and related phenomena that we now possess, and the long, robust history of contemplative activity East and West, it is a great mistake to exclude extranormal phenomena from our accounts of human nature. Indeed, that is why many, if not most great thinkers since antiquity have either placed paranormal and mystical experience in the center of their philosophies or at least given them serious consideration. With his metaphor of the divided line in Book Six of *The Republic*, for example, Plato explored the relations between *eikasia*, image-making, *pistis*, opinion, *dianoia*, discursive reason, and *noesis*, contemplative insight (or direct apprehension of the Good). Plotinus related sense-data, discursive intellect, and mystical illumination in his encompassing view of God and the world, and like Plato discussed occult connections between humans and supraphysical entities. Kant and Hegel emphasized two kinds of knowing, *Verstand*, ordinary rational understanding, and *Vernunft*, a more intuitive form of reason; while Bergson characterized "intuition" and "intellect" as two fundamental modes of human cognition, and regarded mystics to be forerunners of human evolution. And numerous Eastern philosophies have integrated sensory, rational, and contemplative knowledge in their metaphysical systems. According to Advaita Vedanta, for example, sense

---

[27]Describing such assumptions, the British philosopher C.D. Broad wrote:

There are certain limiting principles which we unhesitatingly take for granted as the framework within which all our practical activities and our scientific theories are confined. Some of these seem to be self-evident. Others are so overwhelmingly supported by all the empirical facts which fall within the range of ordinary experience and the scientific elaborations of it (including under this heading orthodox psychology) that it hardly enters our heads to question them. Let us call these *Basic Limiting Principles*. Now psychical research is concerned with alleged events which seem *prima facie* to conflict with one or more of these principles [Broad, C.D. (1953) *Religion, Philosophy and Psychical Research*. New York: Harcourt, Brace, p.7].

perception, rational inference, and yogic illumination are all *pramanas*, "sources or means of acquiring new knowledge", and all are deemed to be "instrinsically valid."[28] In the words of British philosopher C.D. Broad:

> ...if we can judge what philosophy *is* by what great philosophers have *done* in the past, its business is by no means confined to accepting without question, and trying to analyze, the beliefs held in common by contemporary European and North American plain men. Judged by that criterion, philosophy involves at least two other closely connected activities, which I call *Synopsis* and *Synthesis*. Synopsis is the deliberate viewing together of aspects of human experience which, for one reason or another, are generally kept apart by the plain man and even by the professional scientist or scholar. The object of synopsis is to try to find out how these various aspects are inter-related. Synthesis is the attempt to supply a coherent set of concepts and principles which cover satisfactorily all the regions of fact which have been viewed synoptically.[29]

This essay is written in the spirit of Broad's "synopsis" and "synthesis", as it joins different fields and kinds of human experience, and attempts to specify certain relations among them. Without data from many domains of inquiry, without various *kinds* of knowing, our understanding of human development will be incomplete. Without a deliberate viewing together of our physiological, emotional, and cognitive processes, without a coherent set of concepts to relate our normal and metanormal functioning, we cannot comprehend many possibilities for further human advance.

Courage without prudence, honesty without kindness, or high-intentioned confrontation without empathy can be destructive to personal relations. Stoic philosophers of ancient Greece had a term for this insight: *antakolouthia*, "mutual entailment of the virtues." An analogous interdependence exists, I propose, among the various kinds of knowing. There is a mutual entailment, too, among scientific, moral, parapsychological, and contemplative discovery if we want to understand

---

[28]Smart, Ninian (1964) *Doctrine and Argument in Indian Philosophy*. London, p. 220. Deutsch, Eliot (1969) *Advaita Vedanta, a Philosophical Reconstruction*. Honolulu: University of Hawaii Press, pp. 86-90.

[29]Broad, C.D. (1953) *Religion, Philosophy and Psychical Research*. New York: Harcourt, Brace & Co., p. 8.

human nature in its many dimensions. If scientific discovery depends upon instruments appropriate to the particular domain under investigation, then a world view that includes more than one domain depends upon the various instrumentalities used to investigate them. If we only have a telescope, we cannot specify blood changes that accompany meditation, but if we only accept evidence provided by medical instruments in studying the results of meditation, we will never comprehend the experience of mystics. Every competent scientist knows that his or her science depends upon methods appropriate to the data at hand and further, that sub-specialties of a given science have distinctive approaches (witness the different procedures employed by different branches of physics). Does not the same rule hold for separate domains of experience? We must be *adequate* to the data of a given object-domain, whether provided by sensory experience or mystical cognition.

In summary, then, to conceive and pursue a balanced development of our metanormal capacities, we need many fields of experience and various kinds of data-acquisition. If we need a term for this approach, we might call it a "synoptic, multi-disciplinary, multi-dimensional, or integrative empiricism" (remembering of course that "empiricism" usually refers to data-acquisition and verification limited to sensory experience).

Making it Concrete:
Before, During and After
Breakdowns

Francisco J. Varela

1. The Disenchantment of the Abstract

1.1 Shifts in cognitive science

'Rationalistic', 'Cartesian' or 'objectivist': these are some terms used to characterize the dominant tradition within which we have grown in recent times. Yet when it comes to a re-understanding of knowledge and cognition I find that the best expression to use for our tradition is *abstract:* nothing characterizes better the units of knowledge which are deemed most 'natural'. It is this tendency to find our way towards the rarified atmosphere of the general and the formal, the logical and the well-defined, the represented and the planned-ahead, which makes our western world so distinctly familiar.

The main thesis I want to pursue here is that there are strong indications that the loose federation of sciences dealing with knowledge and cognition—the cognitive sciences—are slowly growing in the conviction that this picture is upside down and that a radical paradigmatic or epistemic shift is rapidly developing. At the very center of this emerging view is that the proper units of knowledge are primarily *concrete*, embodied, lived. This uniqueness of knowledge, its historicity and context, is not a "noise" that occludes the brighter pattern to be captured in its true essence, an abstraction. The concrete is not a step towards anything: it is how we arrive and where we stay.

Perhaps nothing illustrates better this tendency than to sketch briefly the gradual transformation of ideas and research program in the very pragmatic field of artificial intelligence. Research in its first two decades (1950-1970) was based on the computationalist paradigm according to which knowledge operates by logic-like rules for symbolic manipulation, an idea which takes its full expression in modern computers. Initially efforts were directed at solving the most general problems, such as natural language translation or devising a "general problem solver." These attempts, which tried to match the intelligence of a person who is a highly trained expert, were seen as tackling the interesting, hard issues of cognition. As the attempts for such tasks consistently failed, the only way to make some headway was to became more modest and local in the task demanded. The most ordinary tasks, even those performed by tiny insects, are simply impossible to achieve with a computational strategy. The culmination of these years can best be expressed by noting a conviction which gradually has grown among the community of researchers: it is necessary to invert the expert and the child in the scale of performances. It became apparent that the deeper and more fundamental kind of intelligence is that of a baby who can acquire language from dispersed daily utterances, or can constitute meaningful objects from a previously unspecified world.

Let me unfold this emerging view which revitalizes the role of the concrete by focusing on its proper scale: the cognitive activity as it happens in a very special space that we may call the hinges of the *immediate present*. For it is in the immediate present that the concrete actually lives. But before this unfolding we need to revise some entrenched assumptions inherited from the computationalist orthodoxy.

1.2 Minds and disunited subjects

If we turn away from AI to consider the living, there is considerable support for the view that brains are not logical machines, but highly cooperative, inhomogeneous and distributed networks. The entire system resembles a *patchwork* of sub-networks assembled by a complicated history of tinkering, rather than an optimized system that results from some clean unified design. This kind of architecture also suggests that instead of looking for grand unified models for all network behaviors, one should study networks whose abilities are restricted to specific, concrete cognitive activities which interact with each other.

This view of cognitive architecture has begun to be taken seriously by cognitive scientists in various ways. For example, Minsky[1] presents a view in which minds consist of many "agents" whose abilities are quite circumscribed: each agent taken individually operates only in a small-scale or "toy" problems. The problems must be of a small scale because they become unmanageable for a single network when they are scaled-up. This last point has not been obvious to cognitive scientists for a long time, as we said in reference to AI. The task, then, is to organize the "agents" who operate in these specific domains into effective larger systems or "agencies," and then to turn these agencies into higher-level systems. In doing so, mind emerges as a kind of "society."

It is important to remember here that, although inspired by a fresh look at the brain, this is a model of the mind. In other words, it is not a model of neural networks or societies; it is a model of the cognitive architecture that abstracts (again!) from neurological detail and hence from the web of the living and of lived experience. Agents and agencies are not, therefore, entities, nor material processes; they are abstract processes or functions. The point bears emphasizing, especially since Minsky sometimes writes as if he were talking about cognition at the level of the brain.[2] As I will emphasize in what follows what is missing here is the detailed link between such agents and the incarnated coupling, by sensing and acting, which is essential to living cognition. But let us pause for the moment to follow some of the implications of the notions of fragmented and local cognitive sub-networks.

The model of the mind as a society of numerous agents is intended to encompass a multiplicity of approaches to the study of cognition, ranging from distributed, self-organizing networks even up to the classical, cognitivist conception of symbolic processing. This encompassing view challenges a centralized or unified model of the mind, whether in the form of distributed networks, at one extreme, or symbolic processes, at the other extreme. This move is apparent for example when Minsky argues that there are virtues not only in distribution, but in insulation, i.e. in mechanisms that

---

[1]Marvin Minsky, *The Society of Mind* (New York: Simon and Schuster, 1986).

[2] For example, in their Epilogue to the new edition of *Perceptrons*, (MIT Press, Cambridge, 1987), Minsky and Papert write: "How, then, could networks support symbolic forms of activities? We conjecture that, inside the brain, agencies with different jobs are usually constrained to communicate with one another only through *neurological* [our emphasis] bottlenecks (i.e., connections between relatively small numbers of units that are specialized to serve as symbolic recognizers and memorizers)." But if these bottlenecks are essential for symbolic activities, they would, presumably, have to exist for artificial minds too, thus it is not clear why they are neurological instead of being features of the abstract, cognitive architecture.

keep various processes apart.[3] The agents within an agency may be connected in the form of a distributed network, but if the agencies were themselves connected in the same way they would, in effect, constitute one large network whose functions were uniformly distributed. Such uniformity, however, would restrict the ability to combine the operations of individual agencies in a productive way. The more distributed these operations are, the harder it is to have many of them active at the same time without interfering with each other. These problems do not arise, however, if there are mechanisms to keep various agencies *insulated* from each other. These agencies would still interact, but through more limited connections.

The details of such a programmatic view are, of course debatable. But the overall picture that it suggests—and which is not unique to Minsky's formulation through agent and agencies—is that of mind not as a unified, homogenous entity, nor even as a collection of entities, but rather as a *disunified, heterogenous, collection of processes.* Such a disunified assembly can obviously be considered at more than one level. What counts as an agency, i.e., as a collection of agents, could if we change our focus, be considered as merely one agent in a larger agency. And conversely, what counts as an agent could, if we resolve our focus in greater detail, be seen to be an agency made up of many agents. In the same way, what counts as a society will depend too on our chosen level of focus.

Having thus set the stage for this key issue in contemporary cognitive science, I want to develop its implications for the question at hand: the present-centeredness of the concrete.

2. On Being There: During Breakdowns

2.1 Readiness-to-Action in the Present

Our present concern is with one of the many consequences of this view of the disunity of the subject, understood as a cognitive agent. The question I have in mind can be formulated thus: given that there is a myriad of contending sub-processes in every cognitive act, how are we to understand the moment of negotiation and emergence when one of them takes the lead and constitutes a definite behavior? In more evocative terms: How are we to understand the very moment of being-there when something concrete and specific shows up?

---

[3] This idea has also been extensively explored, though in a somewhat different context, by Jerry Fodor, *The Modularity of Mind* (Cambridge, Mass.: Bradford Books/MIT Press, 1983).

Picture yourself walking down the street, perhaps going to meet somebody. It is the end of the day and there is nothing very special in your mind. You are in a relaxed mood, in what we may call the readiness of the walker who is simply strolling. You put your hand into your pocket and suddenly you don't find your wallet where it usually is. Breakdown: you stop, your mind setting is unclear, your emotional tonality shifts. Before you know it a new world emerges: you see clearly that you left your wallet in the store where you just bought cigarettes. Your mood shifts now to one of concern for losing documents and money, your readiness-to-action is now to quickly go back to the store. There is little attention to the the surrounding trees and passersby; all attention is directed to avoiding further delays.

Situations like this are the very stuff of our lives. We always operate in some kind of immediacy of a given situation: our lived world is so ready-at-hand that we don't have any deliberateness about what is and how we inhabit it. When we sit at the table to eat with a relative or friend, the entire complex know-how of handling table utensils, the body postures and pauses in the conversation, are all present without deliberation. Our having-lunch-self is transparent.[4] You finish lunch, return to the office and enter into a new readiness with a different mode of speaking, postural tone, and assessments. We have a readiness-to-action which is proper to every specific lived situation. New modes of behaving and the transitions or punctuations between them correspond to mini (or macro) breakdowns we experience constantly.

I will refer to any such readiness for action as *microidentities* and their corresponding *microworlds*. Thus, the way we show up *as* is the way things and others show up *to* us. We could go through some elementary phenomenology and identify some typical microworlds within which we move during a normal day. The point is not to catalogue them but rather to notice their *recurrence:* being capable of appropriate action is, in some important sense, a way in which we embody a stream of recurrent microworld transitions. I am not saying that there aren't situations where recurrence does *not* apply. For example when I arrive for the first time in a foreign country there is an enormous lack of readiness-to-hand and recurrent microworlds. Many simple actions such as social talk or eating have to be learned and done deliberately. In other words microworlds/identities are historically constituted. But the pervasive mode of living consists of the *already* constituted microworlds which compose our identities. Clearly there is a lot more that

---

[4]I borrow this use of the notion of transparency from an unpublished manuscript by F.Flores and M.Graves, (Logonet, Berkeley, 1990). I am grateful to F.Flores for letting me read this ongoing work. My own ideas, and this text, have greatly benefitted from it.

should be explored and said about the phenomenology of ordinary experience—not enough has been done.[5] My intention here is more modest: merely to point to a realm of phenomena, which is intimately close to our ordinary experience.

When we leave the realm of our lived human experience and shift to animals the same kind of analysis applies as an external account. The extreme case is illustrative: biologists have known for some time that invertebrates have a rather small repertoire of behavior patterns. For example the locomotion of a cockroach has only a few fundamental modes: standing, slow walking, fast walking, and running. Nevertheless this basic behavioral repertoire makes it possible for these animals to navigate appropriately in *any* possible environment known on the planet, natural or artificial. The question for the biologist is then: How does the animal decide which motor action to take in a given circumstance? How does its behavioral selection operate so that the action is appropriate? How does the animal have the commonsense to assess a given situation and interpret it as requiring running as opposed to slow walking?

In the two extreme cases, human experience during breakdowns, and animal behaviors at moments of behavioral transitions, we are confronted—in vastly different manners to be sure—with a common issue: at each such breakdown the manner in which the cognitive agent will next be constituted is neither externally decided nor simply planned ahead. It is a matter of *commonsensical emergence*, of autonomous configurations of an appropriate stance. Once a behavioral stance is selected or a microworld is brought forth, we can more clearly analyze its mode of operation and its optimal strategy. In fact, the key to autonomy is that a living system, out of its own resources, finds its way into the next moment by acting appropriately. And it is the breakdowns, the hinges that articulate microworlds, that are at the source of the autonomous and creative side of living cognition. Such commonsense, then, needs to be examined at a microscale: at the moments where it actualizes *during breakdowns*, the birthplace of the concrete.

2.2. Knowledge as Enaction

Let me now explain what I mean by the word "embodied" highlighting two points: (1) that cognition depends upon the kinds of experience that come from having a body with various sensory-motor capacities; and (2) that these individual sensory-motor capacities are themselves embedded in a more encompassing biological and cultural *context*. These two points were already introduced above when discussing breakdown and commonsense, but

---

[5]I am specially thinking of Heidegger's *Sein und Zeit* and Merleau-Ponty's *Phenomenology of Perception* as prime examples.

here I wish to explore further their corporeal specificity, to emphasize once again that sensory and motor processes, perception and action, are fundamentally inseparable in lived cognition, and not merely contingently linked in individuals.

In order to make my ideas more precise let me now give a preliminary formulation of what I mean by an *enactive approach to cognition*[6]. In a nutshell, the enactive approach consists of two points: (1) that perception consists in perceptually guided action, (2) that cognitive structures emerge from the recurrent sensory-motor patterns that enable action to be perceptually guided. These two statements will become more transparent as we proceed.

Let us begin with the notion of perceptually guided action. For the dominant computationalist tradition, the point of departure for understanding perception is typically abstract: the information-processing problem of recovering pre-given properties of the world. In contrast, the point of departure for the enactive approach is the study of how the perceiver can guide its actions in its local situation. Since these local situations constantly change as a result of the perceiver's activity, the reference point for understanding perception is no longer a pre-given, perceiver-independent world, but rather the sensory-motor structure of the cognitive agent, the way in which the nervous system links sensory and motor surfaces. It is this structure—the manner in which the perceiver is embodied—rather than some pre-given world, that determines how the perceiver can act and be modulated by environmental events. Thus the overall concern of an enactive approach to perception is not to determine how some perceiver-independent world is to be recovered; it is, rather, to determine the common principles or lawful linkages between sensory and motor systems that explain how action can be *perceptually guided* in a *perceiver-dependent* world.[7]

This approach to perception was in fact one of the central insights of the analysis undertaken by Merleau-Ponty in his early work. It is worthwhile to quote one of his more visionary passages in full:

> The organism cannot properly be compared to a keyboard on which the external stimuli would play and in which their proper form would be delineated for the simple reason that the organism contributes to the constitution of that form..."...The properties of the object and the intentions of the subject...are not only intermingled; they also constitute a new whole." When

the eye and the ear follow an animal in flight, it is impossible to say "which started first" in the exchange of stimuli and responses. Since all the movements of the organism are always conditioned by external influences, one can, if one wishes, readily treat behavior as an effect of the milieu. But in the same way, since all the stimulations which the organism receives have in turn been possible only by its preceding movements which have culminated in exposing the receptor organ to external influences, one could also say that *behavior is the first cause of all the stimulations*.

Thus the form of the excitant is *created by* the organism itself, by its proper manner of offering itself to actions from the outside. Doubtless, in order to be able to subsist, it must encounter a certain number of physical and chemical agents in its surroundings. But it is the organism itself—according to the proper nature of its receptors, the thresholds of its nerve centers and the movements of the organs—*which chooses the stimuli in the physical world to which it will be sensitive.* "The environment (*Umwelt*) emerges from the world through the actualization or the being of the organism—[granted that] an organism can exist only if it succeeds in finding in the world an adequate environment." This would be a keyboard which moves itself in such a way as to offer—and according to variable rhythms—such or such of its keys to the in itself monotonous action of an external hammer" [our emphasis].[8]

In such an approach, then, perception is not simply embedded within and constrained by the surrounding world; it also contributes to the *enactment* of this surrounding world. Thus as Merleau-Ponty notes, the organism both initiates and is shaped by the environment. Merleau-Ponty clearly recognized, then, that we must see the organism and environment as bound together in reciprocal specification and selection—a point which we need to constantly remind ourselves of since it is quite contrary to received views familiar to us from the Cartesian tradition.

A classical illustration of the perceptual guidance of action is the study of Held and Hein who raised kittens in the dark and exposed them to light only under controlled conditions.[9] A first group of animals was allowed to move around normally, but they

[8] Maurice Merleau-Ponty, *The Structure of Behavior*, trans. Alden Fisher (Boston: Beacon Press, 1963), p. 13.

[9] R. Held and A. Hein, Adaptation of Disarranged Hand-eye Coordination Contingent upon Re-afferent Stimulation, *Perceptual-Motor Skills* 8 (1958): 87-90.

were harnessed to a simple carriage and basket that contained the second group of animals. The two groups therefore shared the same visual experience, but the second group was entirely passive. When the animals were released after a few weeks of this treatment, the first group of kittens behaved normally, but those who had been carried around behaved as if they were blind: They bumped into objects and fell over edges. This beautiful study supports the—enactive—view that objects are not seen by the visual extraction of features, but rather by the visual guidance of action. Similar results have been obtained under other diverse circumstances and studied even at the single cell level.[10]

Lest the reader feel that this example is fine for cats, but removed from human experience, consider another case. Bach y Rita designed a video camera for blind persons that can stimulate multiple points in the skin by electrically activated vibration.[11] Using this technique, images formed with the camera were made to correspond to patterns of skin stimulation, thereby substituting for the visual loss. Patterns projected on to the skin have no "visual" content unless the individual is behaviorally active by directing the video camera using head, hand or body movements. When the blind person does actively behave in this way, after a few hours of experience a remarkable emergence takes place: The person no longer interprets the skin sensations as body-related, but rather as images projected into the space being explored by the bodily directed "gaze" of the video camera. Thus in order to experience "real objects out there" the person must actively direct the camera (by head or hand).

2.3 The Fine Structure of the Present

I have now situated the emergence of the concrete within the enactive framework for cognition, where it can really make sense. We can now return to the problem we started with: How can emergent microworlds arise out of a turmoil of many cognitive agents and sub-networks? The answer I wish to propose here is that within the gap during a breakdown there is a rich *dynamics* involving the concurrent sub-identities and agents. This rapid dialogue, invisible to introspection, has recently been revealed in brain studies.

This idea was introduced by Walter Freeman who, over many years of research, managed to insert an array of electrodes into the olfactory bulb of a rabbit so that a small portion of the global activ-

---

[10]See for example the elegant studies by P. Buisseret and his colleagues on the relation between eye movements and the visual world.

[11]P. Bach y Rita *Brain Mechanisms in Sensory Substitution* (New York: Academic Press, 1962), as described in B. Livingstone, *Sensory Processing, Perception, and Behavior* (New York: Raven Press, 1978).

ity can be measured while the animal behaves freely.[12] He found
that there is no clear pattern of global activity in the bulb unless the
animal is exposed to one specific odor several times. Furthermore,
he found for the first time that such emergent patterns of activity
are created out of a background of incoherent or chaotic activity by
fast oscillations (i.e. with periods of about 5-10 msec) until the cortex settles into pattern, which lasts until the end of the sniffing
behavior and then dissolves back into the chaotic background.[13]
Smell appears in this light not as a mapping of external features,
but rather as a creative form of enacting significance on the basis of
the animal's embodied history. What's most pertinent here is that
this enaction happens at the hinge between one behavioral
moment and the next, via fast oscillations between cell populations
that can give rise to coherent patterns.

There is growing evidence that this kind of fast dynamics can
underlie the configuration of neuronal ensembles. It has been
reported in the visual cortex in cats and monkeys linked to visual
stimulation; it has also been found in radically different neural
structures such as bird's brain, and even the ganglia of an inverte-
brate, *Hermissenda*.[14] This universality is important for it points to
the fundamental nature of this mechanism for the enaction of sensori-motor couplings. Had it been a very species-specific process,
typical say of mammalian cortex, it would be far less convincing as a
working hypothesis.

It is important to note here that this fast dynamics is not
restricted to a sensorial trigger: the oscillations appear and disappear quickly and quite spontaneously in various places of the brain.
This suggests that such fast dynamics involve all of those sub-networks which give rise to the entire readiness-to-hand in the next
moment. They don't just involve sensory interpretation and motor
action but also the entire gamut of cognitive expectations and emotional tonality which are central to the shaping of a microworld.
Between breakdown these oscillations are the symptoms of—very
rapid!—reciprocal cooperation and competition between distinct

[12]Walter Freeman, *Mass Action in the Nervous System* (New York: Academic Press,
1975).

[13]Walter Freeman and Christine Skarda, Spatial EEG Patterns, Nonlinear
Dynamics, and Perception: The Neo-Sherringtonian View, *Brain Research Reviews* 10
(1985): 145-175.

[14]For a recent review see Bressler,S., The gamma wave: A cortical information
carrier, *Trends Neurosc.* 13:161-162, 1990; the work of C.Gray and W.Singer, Stimulus-
specific neuronal oscillations in orientation columns in cat visual cortex,
Proc.Natl.Acad.Sci. (USA) 86:1698-1702, 1989 has been largely responsible for the
wider acceptance of this hypothesis; for Hermissenda see A.Gelperin and D.Tank,
Odour-modulated collective network oscillations of olfactory interneurons in a
terrestrial mollusc, *Nature* 345:437-439, 1990; and for the results on the bird's brain
see S.Neuenschwander and F.Varela (1990), Sensori-triggered and spontaneous
oscillations in the avian brain, *Society Neuroscience Abstracts*, vol. 16.

agents which are activated by the current situation, vying with each other for differing modes of interpretation for a coherent cognitive framework and readiness for action. On the basis of this fast dynamics, as in an evolutionary process, one neuronal ensemble (one cognitive sub-network) finally becomes more prevalent and becomes the behavioral mode for the next cognitive moment. When I say "becomes prevalent" I do not mean to say that this is a process of optimization: it resembles more a consolidation out of a chaotic dynamics. It follows that such a cradle of autonomous action is forever lost to lived experience since by definition we can only inhabit a microidentity when it is already present, not in gestation. In other words, in the breakdown before the next microworld shows up there is a myriad of possibilities available until, out of the constraints of the situation and the recurrence of history, a single one is selected. This fast dynamics is the neural correlate of the autonomous constitution of a cognitive agent.

2.3 From Temporal Fine Structure to Cognitive Action

Let us now turn to the idea that cognitive structures emerge from the kinds of recurrent sensory-motor patterns that enable action to be perceptually guided. As we just said the fast dynamics of agent reciprocity provides the playground for the emergence of a microworld. What we need to examine now is some evidence as to how to link this sensori-motor coupling with other kinds of typically human cognitive performance. Otherwise we might be tempted to attribute no significance to the foregoing except for the "low" level event of sensing and acting, but not for the true "higher" cognitive levels.

In fact, this basic idea is at the very core of the Piagetian program, and has been argued for in various recent works, such as Lakoff and Johnson.[15] We will present the idea of embodied cognitive structures with special reference to their work. Once again we must move out of the abstract and emphasize an experientialist approach to cognition. As Lakoff says, the central claim of their approach is that meaningful conceptual structures arise from two sources: (1) from the structured nature of bodily and social experience and (2) from our capacity to imaginatively project from certain well-structured aspects of bodily and interactional experience to conceptual structures.

Rational and abstract thought is the application of very general cognitive processes—focusing, scanning, superimposition, figure-

---

[15] See George Lakoff, *Women, Fire and Dangerous Things*, (Chicago: U Chicago Press, 1983) and Mark Johnson, *The Body in the Mind* (Chicago: Univ.Chicago Press, 1989).

ground reversal, etc.—to such structures.[16] The basic ideas that embodied (sensory-motor) structures are the substance for experience, and that experiential structures "motivate" conceptual understanding and rational thought. Since I have emphasized that perception and action are embodied in sensory-motor processes that are self-organizing, it is natural to see how cognitive structures *emerge* from recurrent patterns of sensory-motor activity. In either case, the point is not, as Lakoff notes, that experience strictly determines conceptual structures and modes of thought; it is, rather, that experience both makes possible and constrains conceptual understanding across the multitude of cognitive domains.[17]

Lakoff and Johnson provide numerous examples of cognitive structures that are generated from experiential processes. To review all of these examples here would take us too far afield. Let me discuss briefly only one of the most significant kinds: basic-level categories. Consider most of the middle-sized things with which we continually interact: tables, chairs, dogs, cats, forks, knives, cups, etc. These things belong to a level of categorization that is intermediate between lower (subordinate) and higher (superordinate) levels. If we take a chair, for example, at the lower level it might belong to the category "rocking chair," whereas at the higher level it belongs to the category "furniture." Rosch and others have showed that this intermediate level of categorization (table, chair, etc.) is psychologically the most fundamental or *basic*.[18] Among the reasons why these basic-level categories are considered to be psychologically the most fundamental are: (1) the basic-level is the most general level where category members have similar overall *perceived shapes;* (2) it is the most general level where a person uses similar *motor actions* for interacting with category members; and (3) it is the level where clusters of correlated attributes are most *apparent*. It would seem, therefore, that what determines whether a category belongs to the basic level depends not on how things are arranged in some pre-given world, but rather on the sensory-motor structure of our bodies and the kinds of perceptually guided interactions this structure makes possible. Basic-level categories are both experiential and embodied. A similar argument can be made for image-schemas emerging from certain basic forms of sensory-motor activities and interactions.

---

[16]George Lakoff, "Cognitive Semantics," in Umberto Eco et, al., eds, *Meaning and Mental Representations* (Indiana University Press, 1988), p. 121. This article provides a concise overview of Lakoff and Johnson's experientialist approach.

[17]*Ibid.*, p. 120.

[18] E. Rosch, C.B. Mervis, W.D. Gray, D.M. Johnson, and P. Boyes-Braem, Basic Objects in Natural Categories, *Cognitive Psychology* 8 (1976): 382-439.

3. Conclusion

Let me conclude by considering where the ideas sketched here have taken us. I have argued that perception does not consist in the recovery of a pre-given world, but rather in the perceptual guidance of action in a world that is inseparable from our sensory-motor capacities. I have also argued that cognitive structures emerge from recurrent patterns of perceptually guided action. We can summarize our discussion, then, by saying that cognition consists not in representation, but in *embodied action*. Correlatively, we can say that the world we know is not pre-given; it is, rather, *enacted* through our history of structural coupling. Furthermore we have also seen that the hinge that articulates enaction consists of fast non-cognitive dynamics wherein a number of alternative microworlds are activated. These hinges are the source of both common sense and creativity in cognition.

It is, therefore, the very contemporary quest for the understanding of understanding in cognitive science, which points in a direction we can consider post-cartesian in two important aspects. First, knowledge appears more and more as being built from small domains, microworlds and microidentities. Such basic modes of readiness-to-hand are variable throughout the animal kingdom. But what all living cognitive beings seem to have in common is that knowledge is always a know-how constituted on the basis of the concrete; what we call the general and the abstract are aggregates of readiness-for-action.

The second post-cartesian aspect: such micro-worlds are not coherent or integrated into some enormous totality which regulates the veracity of the smaller pieces. It is more like an unruly conversational interaction. It is the very presence of this unruliness which allows for the constitution of a cognitive moment according to the system's constitution and history. The very heart of this autonomy, the fast time of the agent's behavior selection, is forever lost to the cognitive system itself. Thus what we call traditionally the 'irrational' and the 'non-conscious' is not contradictory to what appears as rational and purposeful, but its very underpinning.

What is Moral Maturity? Towards a Phenomenology of Ethical Expertise[1]

Hubert L. Dreyfus
Stuart E. Dreyfus

Phenomenology has a great deal to contribute to the contemporary confrontation between those who demand a *detached* critical *morality* based on *principles* that tells us what is *right* and those who defend an *ethics* based on *involvement in a tradition* that defines what is *good*. This new debate between *Moralität* and *Sittlichkeit* has produced two camps which can be identified with Jurgen Habermas and John Rawls on the one hand, and Bernard Williams and Charles Taylor on the other. The same polarity appears in feminism where the Kohlberg scale, which defines the highest stage of moral maturity as the ability to stand outside the situation and justify one's actions in terms of universal moral principles, is attacked by Carol Gilligan in the name of an intuitive response to the concrete situation.

What one chooses to investigate as the relevant phenomena will prejudice from the start where one stands on these important issues. If one adopts the traditional philosophical approach one will focus on the rationality of moral judgments. For example, on the first page of his

[1]We would like to thank Drew Cross, David Greenbaum, Wayne Martin, Charles Spinosa, Charles Taylor and Kailey Vernallis for their helpful comments.

classic text, *The Moral Judgment of the Child,* Jean Piaget explicitly restricts ethics to judgments. He states at the start that "It is the moral judgment that we propose to investigate, not moral behavior ..."[2] Maurice Mandelbaum in his book, *The Phenomenology of Moral Experience,* a recent but unsuccessful attempt to introduce phenomenology into current ethical debate, makes the same move:

> The phenomenological approach's...essential method-ological conviction is that a solution to any of the problems of ethics must be educed from, and verified by, a careful and direct examination of individual moral judgments.[3]

Moreover, Mandelbaum does not seem to realize that he has already made a fateful exclusion. He claims that: "Such an approach...aims to discover the generic characteristics of *all* moral experience."[4]

But why equate moral experience with judgment, rather than with ethical comportment? Mandelbaum's answer to this question is symptomatic of the intellectualist prejudice embodied in this approach. He first gives a perceptive nod to spontaneous ethical comportment:

> I sense the embarrassment of a person, and turn the conversation aside; I see a child in danger and catch hold of its hand; I hear a crash and become alert to help.[5]

He then notes:

> Actions such as these (of which our daily lives are in no small measure composed) do not...seem to spring from the self: in such cases I am reacting directly and spontaneously to what confronts me....[I]t is appropriate to speak of "reactions" and "responses," for in them a sense of initiative or feeling of responsibility is present....[W]e can only say that we acted as we did because the situation extorted that from us.[6]

Mandelbaum next contrasts this unthinking and egoless response to the situation with deliberate action in which one experiences the causal power of the "I".

---

[2]Jean Piaget, *The Moral Judgment of the Child,* Glencoe, Ill. The Free Press, 1935, p. vii.

[3]Maurice Mandelbaum, *The Phenomenology of Moral Experience,* New York, N.Y., The Free Press, 1955, p. 31.

[4]*Ibid,* p. 36. (Our italics.)

[5]*Ibid,* p. 48.

[6]*Ibid,* pp. 48-49.

In "willed" action, on the other hand, the source of action is the self. I act in a specific manner because I wish, or will, to do so.... the "I" is experienced as being responsible for willed action.[7]

He continues:

To give a phenomenological account of this sense of responsibility is not difficult. It is grounded in the fact that every willed action aims at and espouses an envisioned goal. When we envision a goal which transcends what is immediately given, and when we set ourselves to realizing that goal, we feel the action to be ours.

And focusing on willed or deliberate action and its goal, we arrive at rationality. In willed actions...we can give *a reason:* we acted as we did because we aimed to achieve a particular goal. [W]hen asked to explain our action, we feel no hesitation in attributing it to the value of the goal which we aimed to achieve.[8]

Thus the phenomenology of moral experience comes to focus on judgment and justification. Granted that one aspect of the moral life and most of moral philosophy has been concerned with choice, responsibility, and justification, we should, nonetheless, take seriously what Mandelbaum sees and immediately dismisses, viz. that most of our everyday ethical comportment consists in unreflective, egoless responses to the current interpersonal situation. Why not begin on the level of this spontaneous coping?

Several methodological precautions must, then, be borne in mind in attempting a phenomenology of the ethical life.

1. We should begin by describing our everyday ongoing ethical coping. 2. We should determine under which conditions deliberation and choice appear. 3. We should beware of making the typical philosophical mistake of reading the structure of deliberation and choice back into our account of everyday coping. Since our everyday ethical skills seem to have been passed over and even covered up by moral philosophy, we had better begin with some morally neutral area of expertise and delineate its structure. To this end we will lay out a phenomenological description of five stages in the development of expertise, using driving and chess as examples. Only then will we turn to the much more difficult questions of the nature of ethical expertise, the

[7]*Ibid.*, p. 48.
[8]*Ibid.*, p. 48-49.

place and character of moral judgments, and the stages of moral maturity.

I. A Phenomenology of Skill Acquisition

Stage 1: Novice

Normally, the instruction process begins with the instructor decomposing the task environment into context-free features which the beginner can recognize without benefit of experience. The beginner is then given rules for determining actions on the basis of these features, like a computer following a program. The student automobile driver learns to recognize such interpretation-free features as speed (indicated by his speedometer). Timing of gear shifts is specified in terms of speed. The novice chess player learns a numerical value for each type of piece regardless of its position, and the rule: "Always exchange if the total value of pieces captured exceeds the value of pieces lost." But such rigid rules often fail to work. A loaded car stalls on a hill; a beginner in chess falls for every sacrifice.

Stage 2: Advanced beginner

As the novice gains experience actually coping with real situations, he begins to note, or an instructor points out, perspicuous examples of meaningful additional components of the situation. After seeing a sufficient number of examples, the student learns to recognize them. Instructional *maxims* now can refer to these new *situational aspects*. We use the terms maxims and *aspects* here to differentiate this form of instruction from the first, where strict *rules* were given as to how to respond to context-free *features*. Since maxims are phrased in terms of aspects they already presuppose experience in the skill domain.

The advanced beginner driver uses (situational) engine sounds as well as (non-situational) speed. He learns the maxim: shift up when the motor sounds like it is racing and down when its sounds like it is straining. No number of words can take the place of a few choice examples of racing and straining sounds.

Similarly, with experience, the chess student begins to recognize such situational aspects of positions as a weakened king's side or a strong pawn structure, despite the lack of precise definitional rules. He is then given maxims to follow, such as attack a weakened king side.

Stage 3: Competence

With increasing experience, the number of features and aspects to be taken account of becomes overwhelming. To cope with this information explosion, the performer learns to adopt a hierarchical view of decision-making. By first choosing a plan, goal or perspective which organizes the situation and by then examining only the small set of features and aspects that he has learned are relevant given that plan the performer can simplify and improve his performance.

A competent driver leaving the freeway on a curved off-ramp may, after taking into account speed, surface condition, criticality of time, etc., decide he is going too fast. He then has to decide whether to let up on the accelerator, remove his foot altogether, or step on the brake. He is relieved when he gets through the curve without mishap and shaken if he begins to go into a skid.

The class-A chess player, here classed as competent, may decide after studying a position that his opponent has weakened his king's defenses so that an attack against the king is a viable goal. If the attack is chosen, features involving weaknesses in his own position created by the attack are ignored as are losses of pieces inessential to the attack. Removing pieces defending the enemy king becomes salient. Successful plans induce euphoria and mistakes are felt in the pit of the stomach.

In both of these cases, we find a common pattern: detached planning, conscious assessment of elements that are salient with respect to the plan, and an analytical rule-guided choice of action, followed by an emotionally involved experience of the outcome. The experience is emotional because choosing a plan, goal or perspective is no simple matter for the competent performer. Nobody gives him any rules for how to choose a perspective, so he has to make up various rules which he then adopts or discards in various situations depending on how they work out. This procedure is frustrating, however, since each rule works on some occasions and fails on others, and no set of objective features and aspects correlates strongly with these successes and failures. Nonetheless, the choice is unavoidable. Familiar situations begin to be accompanied by emotions such as hope, fear, etc., but the competent performer strives to suppress these feelings during his detached choice of perspective.

Stage 4: Proficiency

As soon as the competent performer stops reflecting on problematic situations as a detached observer, and stops looking for principles to guide his actions, the gripping, holistic experiences from the competent stage become the basis of the next advance in skill.

Having experienced many emotion-laden situations, chosen plans in each, and having obtained vivid, emotional demonstrations of the adequacy or inadequacy of the plan, the performer involved in the world of the skill, "notices," or "is struck by" a certain plan, goal or perspective. No longer is the spell of involvement broken by detached conscious planning.

Since there are generally far fewer "ways of seeing" than "ways of acting," however, after understanding without conscious effort what is going on, the proficient performer will still have to think about what to do. During this thinking, elements that present themselves as salient are assessed and combined by rule and maxim to produce decisions.

On the basis of prior experience, a proficient driver fearfully approaching a curve on a rainy day may sense that he is traveling too fast. Then, on the basis of such salient elements as visibility, angle of road bank, criticalness of time, etc., he decides whether to let up on the gas, take his foot off the gas or to step on the brake. (These factors were used by the *competent* driver to *decide that* he was speeding.)

The proficient chess player, who is classed a master, can recognize a large repertoire of types of positions. Experiencing a situation as a field of conflicting forces and seeing almost immediately the sense of a position, he sets about calculating the move that best achieves his goal. He may, for example, know that he should attack, but he must deliberate about how best to do so.

Stage 5: Expertise

The proficient performer, immersed in the world of skillful activity, *sees* what needs to be done, but must *decide* how to do it. With enough experience with a variety of situations, all seen from the same perspective but requiring different tactical decisions, the proficient performer seems gradually to decompose this class of situations into subclasses, each of which share the same decision, single action, or tactic. This allows an immediate intuitive response to each situation.

The expert driver, generally without any attention, not only knows by feel and familiarity when an action such as slowing down is required; he knows how to perform the action without calculating and comparing alternatives. He shifts gears when appropriate with no awareness of his acts. On the off-ramp his foot just lifts off the accelerator. What must be done, simply is done.

The expert chess player, classed as an international master or grand master, in most situations experiences a compelling sense of the issue and the best move. Excellent chess players can play at the rate of 5-10 seconds a move and even faster without any serious degradation in performance. At this speed they must depend almost entirely on intuition and hardly at all on analysis and comparison of alternatives. We recently performed an experiment in which an international master, Julio Kaplan, was required rapidly to add numbers presented to him audibly at the rate of about one number per second, while at the same time playing five-second-a-move chess against a slightly weaker, but master level player. Even with his analytical mind completely occupied by adding numbers, Kaplan more than held his own against the master in a series of games. Deprived of the time necessary to solve problems or construct plans, Kaplan still produced fluid and strategic play.

It seems that beginners make judgments using strict rules and features, but that with talent and a great deal of involved experience the beginner develops into an expert who sees intuitively what to do without applying rules and making judgments at all. The intellectualist tradition has given an accurate description of the beginner and the expert facing an unfamiliar situation, but normally an expert does not *solve problems. He* does not *reason.* He does not even act deliberately. Rather, he spontaneously does what has normally worked and, naturally, it normally works.

We are all experts at many tasks, and our everyday coping skills usually function smoothly and transparently so as to free us to be aware of other aspects of our lives where we are not so skillful. That is why philosophers overlooked them for 2500 years, until pragmatism and phenomenology came along.

John Dewey introduced the distinction between knowing-how and knowing that to call attention to just such thoughtless mastery of the everyday:

> We may...be said to *know how* by means of our habits.... We walk and read aloud, we get off and on street cars, we dress and undress, and do a thousand useful acts without thinking of them. We know something, namely, how to do them.... [I]f we choose to call [this] knowledge...then other things also called knowledge, knowledge *of* and *about* things, knowledge *that* things are thus and so, knowledge that involves reflection and conscious appreciation, remains of a different sort ...[9]

---

[9]John Dewey, *Human Nature and Conduct: An Introduction to Social Psychology,* London, England, George Allen and Unwin, 1922, pp. 177-178.

We should try to impress on ourselves what a huge amount of our lives—working, getting around, talking, eating, driving, and responding to the needs of others—manifest know-how, and what a small part is spent in the deliberate, effortful, subject/object mode which requires knowing-that. Yet deliberate action, and its extreme form, deliberation are the ways of acting we tend to notice, and so are the only ones that have been studied in detail by philosophers.

II. Implications of the Phenomenology of Expertise for Ethical Experience

The rest of this paper is based on a conditional: *If* the skill model we have proposed is correct, then, in so far as ethical comportment is a form of expertise, we should expect it to exhibit a developmental structure similar to that which we have described above. On analogy with chess and driving it would seem that the budding ethical expert would learn at least some of the ethics of his community by following strict rules, would then go on to apply contextualized maxims, and, in the highest stage, would leave rules and principles behind and develop more and more refined spontaneous ethical responses.

To take a greatly oversimplified and dramatic example, a child at some point might learn the rule: never lie. Faced with the dilemma posed by Kant—an avowed killer asking the whereabouts of the child's friend—the child might tell the truth. After experiencing regret and guilt over the death of the friend, however, the child would move toward the realization that the rule, "Never lie," like the rule, "Shift at ten miles per hour," needs to be contextualized, and would seek maxims to turn to in different typical situations. Such a maxim might be, "Never lie except when someone might be seriously hurt by telling the truth." Of course, this maxim too would, under some circumstances, lead to regret. Finally, with enough experience, the ethical expert would learn to tell the truth or lie, depending upon the situation, without appeal to rules and maxims.[10]

Since we are assuming that such a spontaneous response exhibits ethical expertise, the parallel with chess and driving expertise raises two difficult questions: (1) What is *ethical* expertise? and (2) How does one learn it? In driving and chess there is a clear criterion of expertise. In chess one either wins or loses, in driving one makes it around a curve or skids off the road. But what, one may well ask, counts as success or

---

[10]This is not to deny that, as in driving, a great deal of background skill picked up by imitation and by trial and error is required before one can learn by testing rules.

failure in ethics? It seems that in ethics what counts as expert performance is doing what those who already are accepted as ethical experts do and approve. Aristotle tells us: "What is best is not evident except to the good man." (V1.12.) This is circular but not viciously so.

Learning exhibits the same circularity. To become an expert in any area of expertise one has to be able to respond to the same types of situations as similar as do those who are already expert. For example, to play master level chess one has to respond to the same similarities as masters. This basic ability is what one calls having talent in a given domain. In addition, the learner must experience the appropriate satisfaction or regret at the outcome of his response. To become an expert driver one should feel fear not elation as he skids around a curve. Likewise, to acquire ethical expertise one must have the talent to respond to those ethical situations as similar that ethical experts respond to as similar, and one must have the sensibility to experience the socially appropriate sense of satisfaction or regret at the outcome of one's action.[11]

Aristotle was the first to see that expert ethical comportment is spontaneous, and Dewey repeats his insight:

> As Aristotle pointed out...it takes a fine and well-grounded character to *react immediately* with the right approvals and condemnations.[12]

But, the tradition leads even the most careful to pass over ongoing coping. Thus even Dewey privileges problem solving. In *Theory of the Moral Life* he tells us:

> [E]ven the good man can trust for enlightenment to his direct responses...only in *simpler* situations, in those which are already upon the whole familiar. The better he is, the more likely he is to be perplexed as to what to do in *novel, complicated situations*.[13]

This, according to Dewey, arouses deliberation:

> We hesitate, and then hesitation becomes deliberation.... A preference emerges which is intentional and

---

[11]It is easy to see that if one enjoyed skidding one could never become an accepted member of the everyday driving community, (although one might well become an expert stunt driver). Similarly, without a shared ethical sensibility to what is laudable and what condemnable one would go on doing what the experts in the community found inappropriate, develop bad habits, and become what Aristotle calls an unjust person.

[12]John Dewey, *Theory of the Moral Life*, New York, N.Y., Holt, Rinehart and Winston, 1960, p. 131. (Our italics.)

which is based on consciousness of the values which deliberation has brought into view.[14]

Dewey seems here to be equating the simple with the familiar and
the novel with the complicated. But if our analogy with the chess grand
master can be trusted, Dewey, on this interpretation of the passage, is
making a traditional mistake. True, ethical persons can trust their practical wisdom only in familiar situations, but why should these be only
the "simple situations"? The chess grand master does, indeed, have a
more refined set of discriminations which makes him or her sensitive to
differences that fail to affect a merely proficient performer, but this
same refined set of distinctions, based on a wider range of familiar situations, is precisely what allows the expert to respond spontaneously to
complex situations without deliberation. As ethical skills increase one
would expect the expert to encounter fewer and fewer breakdowns.
Indeed, phenomenological description suggests that the greater the
experience, the *rarer* the need for deliberation. The basketball star,
Larry Bird, to switch to sports for a moment, is sensitive to more threats
and opportunities than his teammates, but this does not mean that he
has to deliberate more often. Indeed, he says just the opposite:

> [A lot of the] things I do on the court are just reac-
> tions to situations...I don't think about...the things I'm
> trying to do... A lot of times, I've passed the basketball and
> not realized I've passed it until a moment or so later.[15]

But the mistaken idea that when the situation becomes complex an
agent must deliberate—articulate his or her principles and draw conclusions as to how to act—only becomes dangerous when the philosopher reads the structure of deliberation back into the spontaneous response. This intellectualizes the phenomenon. One will then assume
that intentional content— what John Searle calls an intention in action,
and Kant calls the maxim of the act—underlies all moral comportment.

Even Aristotle, whom Heidegger lauded as "the last of the great
philosophers who had eyes to see and, what is still more decisive, the
energy and tenacity to continue to force inquiry back to the phenomena''[16] seems, in this area, to be corrupted by intellectualism. Like a
good phenomenologist dedicated to "saving the phenomena", Aristotle

[13]*Ibid.* (Our italics.)

[14]*Ibid.*, p. 149.

[15]Quoted in L.D. Levine, *Bird: The Making of an American Sports Legend*, New York,
N. Y., McGraw Hill, 1988.

[16]Martin Heidegger, *The Basic Problems of Phenomenology*, Bloomington, Ind., Indiana
University Press, 1982, p. 232.

stays close to normal everyday experience and sees the immediate, intuitive response, precisely as characteristic of an expert. "Know-how [*techné*] does not deliberate" he tells us in the *Physics,* (Bk. II, Ch. 8). But when it comes to ethics, he sometimes seems to overlook skillful coping for intentional content. In *The Nicomachean Ethics* he tells us that to act justly or temperately the agent "must choose the acts, and choose them *for their own* sakes".[17] "Choice" here could be given a non-intellectualist reading as meaning responding to the situation by doing one thing rather than another. But that still leaves the troubling claim that the action must be done for the right reason—"for its own sake." It seems that according to Aristotle we must know what the agent thought he was doing—what he was aiming at. This is like saying that good chess players, drivers, and basketball players should be praised or blamed not for their brilliant intuitive responses, but only for what they were trying to do. We must be prepared to face the disturbing fact that a person may be responsible for an action he was not intending to perform, and that therefore there may be no intentional content which determines under what aspect we are to judge the action. We can only tell if a person is courageous, for example, by seeing his spontaneous response in many different situations.

In most contexts Aristotle can be interpreted as having understood this, but many commentators seems to go out of their way to emphasize Aristotle's intellectualism. Alasdair MacIntyre, who is willing to correct Aristotle where necessary, tells us that, according to Aristotle: "The genuinely virtuous agent...acts on the basis of a true and rational judgment."[18] Indeed, in MacIntyre's account of the virtuous life, the moral agent is reduced to a competent performer deliberately choosing among maxims:

> In practical *reasoning* the possession of [an adequate sense of the tradition to which one belongs]...appears in the kind of capacity for *judgment* which the agent possesses in knowing how to *select* among the relevant stack of *maxims* and how to *apply them* in particular situations.[19]

Perhaps MacIntyre accepts this view, which would seem to undermine his own position, because he has not understood the nature of

---

[17]Aristotle, *The Nicomachean Ethics,* Book II, 4, Ross translation. (Our italics.)

[18]Alasdair MacIntyre, *After Virtue,* Notre Dame, Ind., University of Notre Dame Press, 1981, p. 140.

[19]*Ibid.,* pp. 207-208. (Our italics.)

intuitive skills. It may be no coincidence that his description of chess expertise sees it as "a certain highly particular kind of analytical skill".[20]

We have shown so far that the level of everyday intuitive ethical expertise, which Aristotle saw was formed by the sort of daily practice that produces good character, has, from Aristotle himself to Dewey, from Mandelbaum to MacIntyre, been passed over by philosophers, or, if recognized, distorted by reading back into it the mental content found in deliberation. It would be a mistake, however, to become so carried away with the wonder of spontaneous coping as to deny an important place to deliberative judgment. One should not conclude from the pervasiveness of egoless, situation-governed comportment, that thought is always disruptive and inferior. Getting deliberation right is half of what phenomenology has to contribute to the study of ethical expertise.

Expert deliberation is not inferior to intuition, but neither is it a self-sufficient mental activity that can dispense with intuition. It is *based upon* intuition. The intellectualist account of self-sufficient cognition fails to distinguish the *involved* deliberation of an intuitive expert facing a *familiar* but problematic situation from the *detached* deliberation of an expert facing a *novel* situation in which he has no intuition and so, like a beginner, must resort to abstract principles. A chess master confronted with a chess problem, constructed precisely so as not to resemble a position that would show up in a normal game, is reduced to using analysis. Likewise, an ethical expert when confronted with cases of "life-boat morality" may have to fall back on ethical principles. But since *principles* are unable to produce expert behavior, it should be no surprise if falling back on them produces inferior responses. The resulting decisions are necessarily crude since they have not been refined by the experience of the results of a variety of intuitive responses to emotion-laden situations and the learning that comes from subsequent satisfaction and regret. Therefore, in familiar but problematic situations, rather than standing back and applying abstract principles, the expert deliberates about the appropriateness of his *intuitions*. Common as this form of deliberation is, little has been written about such buttressing of intuitive understanding, probably because detached, principle-based, deliberation is often incorrectly seen as the only alternative to intuition.

Let us turn again to the phenomenon. Sometimes, but not often, an intuitive decision-maker finds himself torn between two equally compelling decisions. Presumably this occurs when the current situation lies near the boundary between two discriminable types of situations, each with its own associated action. Occasionally one can com-

---

[20] *Ibid.*, pp. 175-176.

promise between these actions, but often they are incompatible. Only a modified understanding of the current situation can break the tie, so the decision-maker will delay if possible and seek more information. If a decision-maker can afford the time, the decision will be put off until something is learned that leaves only one action intuitively compelling. As Dewey puts it:

> [T]he only way out [of perplexity] is through examination, inquiry, turning things over in [the] mind till something presents itself, perhaps after prolonged mental fermentation, to which [the good man] can directly react.[21]

Even when an intuitive decision seems obvious, it may not be the best. Dewey cautions:

> [An expert] is set in his ways, and his immediate appreciations travel in the grooves laid down by his unconsciously formed habits. Hence the spontaneous "intuitions" of value have to be entertained subject to correction, to confirmation and revision, by personal observation of consequences and cross-questioning of their quality and scope.[22]

Aware that his current clear perception may well be the result of a chain of perspectives with one or more questionable links and so might harbor the dangers of tunnel vision, the wise intuitive decision-maker will attempt to dislodge his current understanding. He will do so by attempting to re-experience the chain of events that led him to see things the way he does, and at each stage he will intentionally focus upon elements not originally seen as important to see if there is an alternative intuitive interpretation. If current understanding cannot be dislodged in this way, the wise decision-maker will enter into dialogue with those who have reached different conclusions. Each will recount a narrative that leads to seeing the current situation in his way and so as demanding his response. Each will try to see things the other's way. This may result in one or the other changing his mind and therefore in final agreement. But, since various experts have different past experiences, there is no reason why they should finally agree. In cases of ethical disagreement, the most that can be claimed is that, given the shared *Sittlichkeit* underlying their expertise, two experts, even when they do not agree, should be able to understand and appreciate each

---

[21]John Dewey, *Theory of the Moral Life*, p. 131.
[22]*Ibid.*, p. 132

other's decisions. This is as near as expert ethical judgments can or need come to impartiality and universality.

III. Current Relevance

But, one might well ask, so what? Transparent, spontaneous, ethical coping might, indeed, occur, but why not begin our philosophical analysis where the tradition has always begun—where there is something interesting to describe, viz., moral judgments, validity claims and justification? Still, before passing over everyday coping as philosophically irrelevant, we should remember that getting the story right about action and mind had huge consequences for the pretensions of a new discipline that calls itself cognitive science. Concentrating on representations, rules, reasoning and problem solving, cognitivists passed over but presupposed a more basic level of coping, and this blindness is now resulting in what more and more researchers are coming to recognize as the degeneration of their research program.[23] So it behooves us to ask: Does the passing over of ethical expertise have equally important practical implications?

We believe it does. The phenomenology of expertise allows us to sharpen up and take sides in an important contemporary debate. The debate centers on the ethical implications of Lawrence Kohlberg's Piagetian model of moral development. Kohlberg holds that the development of the capacity for moral judgment follows an invariant pattern. He distinguishes three levels. A Preconventional Level on which the agent tries to satisfy his needs and avoid punishment; a Conventional Level, during a first stage of which the agent conforms to stereotypical images of majority behavior, and at a second stage follows fixed rules and seeks to retain the given social order; and a Postconventional and Principled Level. The highest stage of this highest level is characterized as follows:

> Regarding what is right, Stage 6 is guided by universal ethical principles.... These are not merely values that are recognized, but are also principles used to generate particular decisions.[24]

Jurgen Habermas has taken up Kohlberg's findings and modified them on the basis of his own discourse ethics, adding a seventh stage—

---

[23]See H. Dreyfus and S. Dreyfus, "Making a Mind vs. Modeling the Brain: AI back at a Branchpoint," *The Artificial Intelligence Debate*, Cambridge, Mass., M.I.T. Press, 1988.
[24]*Ibid.*, p. 412.

acting upon universal procedural principles that make possible arriving at rational agreement through dialogue.

Habermas sees Kohlberg's work as evidence that moral consciousness begins with involved ethical comportment, but that the highest stages of moral consciousness require the willingness and the ability to "consider moral questions from the hypothetical and disinterested perspective."[25] Thus, according to Habermas, Kohlberg's research lends empirical support to his modified, but still recognizable, Kantian view that the highest level of moral maturity consists in judging actions according to abstract, universal principles. He tells us that "The normative reference point of the developmental path that Kohlberg analyzes empirically is a principled morality in which we can recognize the main features of discourse ethics."[26]

It follows for Habermas that our Western European morality of abstract justice is developmentally superior to the ethics of any culture lacking universal principles. Furthermore, when the Kohlberg developmental scale is tested in empirical studies of the moral judgments of young men and women, it turns out that men are generally morally more mature than women.

In her book, *In a Different Voice*, Carol Gilligan contests this second result, claiming that the data on which it is based incorporates a male bias. She rests her objection on her analyses of responses to a moral dilemma used in Kohlberg's studies. She explains as follows:

> The dilemma...was one in the series devised by Kohlberg to measure moral development in adolescence by presenting a conflict between moral norms and exploring the logic of its resolution.... [A] man named Heinz considers whether or not to steal a drug which he cannot afford to buy, in order to save the life of his wife.... [T]he description of the dilemma...is followed by the question, "Should Heinz steal the drug?"[27]

Kohlberg found that morally mature men, i.e., those who have reached stage 6, tended to answer that Heinz should steal the drug because the right to life is more basic than the right to private property. Women, however, seemed unable to deal with the dilemma in a mature, logical way. Here is Gilligan's analysis of a typical case:

[25]Jurgen Habermas, "A Reply to my Critics," *Habermas Critical Debates*, Cambridge, Mass., MIT Press. 198~, p. 253.

[26]J. Habermas, *Moral Consciousness and Communicative Action*, p.150.

[27]Carol Gilligan, *In a Different Voice: Psychological Theory and Women's Development*, Cambridge, Mass., Harvard University Press, 1982, p. 27.

Seeing in the dilemma not a math problem...but a narrative of relationships that extends over time, Amy envisions the wife's continuing need for her husband and the husband's continuing concern for his wife and seeks to respond to the druggist's need in a way that would sustain rather than sever connection....

Seen in this light, her understanding of morality as arising from the *recognition* of relationship, her *belief* in communication as the mode of conflict resolution, and her *conviction* that the solution to the dilemma will follow from its compelling *representation* seem far from naive or cognitively immature.[28]

The first point to note in responding to these interesting observations is that many women are "unable to verbalize or explain the rationale"[29] for their moral responses; they stay involved in the situation and trust their intuition. Many men, on the other hand, when faced with a moral problem, attempt to step back and articulate their principles as a way of deciding what to do. Yet as we have seen, principles can never capture the know-how an expert acquires by dealing with, and seeing the outcome of, a large number of concrete situations. Thus, when faced with a dilemma, the expert does not seek principles but, rather, reflects on and tries to sharpen his or her spontaneous intuitions by getting more information until one decision emerges as obvious. Gilligan finds the same phenomenon in her subjects's deliberations:

The proclivity of women to reconstruct hypothetical dilemmas in terms of the real, *to request or to supply missing information* about the nature of the people and the places where they live, shifts their judgment away from the hierarchical ordering of principles and the formal procedures of decision making.[30]

Gilligan, however, undermines what is radical and fascinating in her discoveries when she seeks her subjects' *solutions* to *problems,* and tries to help them articulate the *principles* underlying these solutions. "Amy's moral *judgment is grounded* in the belief that, 'if somebody has something that would keep somebody alive, then it's not right not to

---

[28] *Ibid.*, pp. 27-30. The cognitivist vocabulary we have italicized should warn us that, in spite of her critique, Gilligan may well have uncritically taken over the cognitivist assumptions underlying Kohlberg's research.

[29] *Ibid.*, p. 49.

[30] *Ibid.*, pp. 100-101. (Our italics.)

give it to them'",[31] she tells us. Yet, if the phenomenology of skillful coping we have presented is right, principles and theories serve only for early stages of learning; no principles or theory "grounds" an expert ethical response, any more than in chess there is a theory or rule that explains a master-level move.

As we would expect, Gilligan's intuitive subjects respond to philosophical questions concerning the principles justifying their actions with tautologies and banalities, e.g., that they try to act in such a way as to make the world a better place in which to live. They might as well say that their highest moral principle is "do something good." If Gilligan had not tried to get her intuitive subjects to formulate their principles for dealing with problems, but had rather investigated how frequently they *had* problems and how they deliberated about their spontaneous ethical comportment when they did, she might well have found evidence that moral maturity results in having fewer problems, and, when problems do arise, being able to act without detaching oneself from the concrete situation, thereby retaining one's ethical intuitions.

The second, and most important, point to consider is that Gilligan correctly detects in Amy's responses to the Heinz dilemma an entirely different approach to the ethical life than acting on universal principles. This is the different voice she is concerned to hear and to elaborate in her book. In answering her critics she makes clear that it is not the central point of her work that these two voices are gendered.

> The title of my book was deliberate, it reads, "in a *different* voice," not "in a *woman's* voice."...I caution the reader that "this association is not absolute, and the contrasts between male and female voices are presented here to highlight a distinction between two modes of thought...rather than to represent a generalization about either sex."[32]

She calls the two voices "the justice and care perspectives."[33] On one description to be good is to be *principled*, on the other, it is to be *unprincipled* i.e., without principles.

---

[31] *Ibid.*, p. 28. (Our italics.)

[32] C. Gilligan, "On *In a Different Voice:* An Interdisciplinary Forum," *Signs: Journal of Women in Culture and Society,* 1986, Vol 11, no. 2, p. 327.

[33] *Ibid.*, p. 330. For an early intuition that the two voices are, indeed, gendered, at least in our culture, see Nietzsche in *Human all too Human:*

Can women be just at all if they are so used to loving, to feeling immediately pro or con? For this reason they are also less often partial to causes, more often to people; but if to a cause, they immediately become partisan, therefore ruining its pure, innocent effect.... What would be more

Although Gilligan does not make the point, it should be obvious to philosophers that we inherit the justice tradition from the Greeks, especially Socrates and Plato. It presupposes that two situations can be the same in the relevant moral respects, and requires principles which treat the same types of situation in the same way. The principle of universalizability thus becomes, with Kant, definitive of the moral. All of us feel the pull of this philosophical position when we seek to be fair, and when we seek universal principles guaranteeing justice and fairness as the basis of our social and political decisions. Moreover, we must resort to universal principles when we seek to justify what we do as right, rather than simply doing what the wisest in our culture have shown us is appropriate.

The other voice carries the early Christian message that, as Saint Paul put it, "the law is fulfilled", so that henceforth to each situation we should respond with love. Proponents of this view sense that no two situations, and no two people, are ever exactly alike. Even a single individual is constantly changing for, as one acquires experience, one's responses become constantly more refined. Thus there is no final answer as to what the appropriate response in a particular situation should be. Since two abstractly identical situations will elicit different responses, caring comportment will look like injustice to the philosopher but will look like compassion or mercy to the Christian. We feel the pull of these Christian caring practices when we respond intuitively to the needs of those around us.

It is important to be clear, however, as Gilligan is not, that the care perspective does not entail any particular way of acting—for example, that one should promote intimate human relationships. The Christian command to love one's neighbor does not dictate how that love should be expressed. Caring in its purest form is not ordinary loving; it is doing spontaneously whatever the situation demands. As we have seen, even if two situations were identical in every respect, two ethical experts with different histories would not necessarily respond in the same way. Each person must simply respond as well as he or she can to each unique situation with nothing but experience-based intuition as guide. Heidegger captures this ethical skill in his notion of *authentic care* as a response to the *unique,* as opposed to the *general,* situation.[34] Authentic caring in this sense is common to *agape* and *phronesis.*

Responding to the general situation occurs when one follows ethical maxims and gives the standard acceptable response. This would correspond to the last stage of Kohlberg's Conventional Level. For Kohlberg and Habermas, on the next Level the learner seeks princi-

---

[34]Martin Heidegger, *Being & Time*, New York, N.Y., Harper & Row, 1962, p. 346.

pled justification. On our model, however, reaching the Postconventional Level would amount to acting with authentic care. When an individual becomes a master of the *Sittlichkeit* he or she no longer tries to do what *one* normally does, but rather responds to the unique situation out of a fund of experience in the culture.

This gets us back to the debate over which is more mature, acting upon rational judgments of rightness, or intuitively doing what the culture deems good. On the one hand, we have Kohlberg's Stage 6 and Habermas' Stage 7 both of which define moral maturity in terms of the ability to detach oneself from the concrete ethical situation and to act on abstract, universal, moral principles. On the other hand, we have Gilligan (with John Murphy, who views the "transition to maturity as a shift from 'the moral environment to the ethical, from the formal to the existential'.")[35] According to this view the mature subject accepts "contextual relativism."[36] Murphy and Gilligan state the issue as follows:

> There are...people who are fully formal in their logical thinking and fully principled in their moral judgments; and yet...are not fully mature in their moral understanding. Conversely, those people whose thinking becomes more relativistic in the sense of being more open to the contextual properties of moral judgments and moral dilemmas frequently fail to be scored at the highest stages of Kohlberg's sequence. Instead, the relativising of their thinking over time is construed as regression or moral equivocation, rather than as a developmental advance.[37]

Habermas recognizes that "the controversy [raised by Gilligan] has drawn attention to problems which, in the language of the philosophical tradition, pertain to the relation of *morality* to ethical life *(Sittlichkeit).*"[38] He, of course, continues to contend that rational morality is developmentally superior to *Sittlichkeit*. And, indeed, if, like Habermas, one thinks of morality exclusively in terms of *judgments* which are generated by *principles*, the ability to stand back from personal involvement in the situation so as to insure reciprocity and universality becomes a sign of maturity. But if being good means being able to learn from experience and use what one has learned so as to

[35]W. B. Perry, *Forms of Intellectual and Ethical Development in the College Years: A Scheme*, Holt, Rinehart & Winston, 1968, p. 205, as quoted in .John M. Murphy and Carol Gilligan, "Moral Development in Late adolescence and Adulthood: a Critique and Reconstruction of Kohlberg's Theory," *Human Development*, 1980, p. 79.

[36]John M. Murphy and Carol Gilligan, op. cit., p. 79.

[37]*Ibid.*, p. 80. (Again note the cognitivist vocabulary: thinking, judgment, dilemmas.)

[38]J. Habermas, *Moral Consciousness and Communicative Action, p.* 223.

respond more appropriately to the demands of others in the concrete situation, the highest form of ethical comportment consists in being able to stay involved and to refine one's intuitions. Habermas needs to supply an argument why the development of ethical expertise should follow a different course than the development of expertise in other domains. Otherwise, it looks like we should follow Murphy and Gilligan in recognizing that at the Postconventional Level the learner accepts his intuitive responses, thus reaching a stage of maturity that leaves behind the rules of conventional morality for a new contextualization.

It is important to see that the above in no way shows that questioning the justice or rightness of aspects of our *Sittlichkeit is* illegitimate or immature. But the demand for fairness and justice in social decision making and for a rational critique of ethical judgments has to exhibit its own developmental stages and requires an independent source of justification. Our skill model is meant neither to contribute to finding grounds for such rightness claims nor to call into question Habermas's important contribution in this area. What we are arguing here is that even if there are claims on us as rational moral agents, acting on such claims cannot be shown to be superior to involved ethical comportment by asserting that such claims are the outcome of a development that makes explicit the abstract rationality implicit in context-dependent ethical comportment. Like any skill, ethical comportment has its *telos* in involved intuitive expertise.

When one measures Gilligan's two types of morality—her two voices—against a phenomenology of expertise, the traditional Western and male belief in the superiority of critical detachment to intuitive involvement is reversed. If, in the name of a cognitivist account of development, one puts ethics and morality on one single developmental scale, the claims of justice, which requires judging that two situations are equivalent so as to be able to apply universal principles, looks like regression to a competent understanding of the ethical domain while the caring response to the unique situation stands out as mature practical wisdom.[39] In this case the phenomenology of

[39]If one accepts the view of expertise presented here, one must accept the superiority of the involved caring self. But our skill model does not support Gilligan's Piagetian claim that the *development* of the self requires crises. Skill learning, and that would seem to be *any* skill learning, requires learning from *mistakes* but not necessarily from *crises*. A crisis would occur when one had to alter one's criterion for what counted as success. Aristotle surely thought that in his culture, the men at least, could develop character without going through crises. The idea of the necessity of moral crises for development goes with an intellectualist view of theory change that may well be true for science but which has nothing to do with selves. This is not to deny that in our pluralistic culture, and especially for those who are given contradictory and distorting roles to play,

expertise would not be just an academic corrective to Aristotle, Kant, Piaget and Habermas. It would be a step towards righting a wrong to involvement, intuition, and care that traditional philosophy, by passing over skillful coping, has maintained for 2500 years.

crises may be necessary. It may well be that women are led into traps concerning success and need crises to get out of them. Thus Gilligan may well be right that crises *in fact* play a crucial role in modern Western women's moral development, even if they are not *necessary*.

Why Business is Talking About Ethics: Reflections on Foreign Conversations

Joanne B. Ciulla

Introduction

In October of 1986 London's Lord Mayor invited 100 representatives from industry and the professions to a conference on company philosophy and codes of business ethics. A year later, a group of European managers and academics formed the European Business Ethics Network. In 1988 the first European business ethics journal, *Ethica Degli Affari,* was published in Milan, Italy. That same year, the Japanese government gave the Hitachi Institute funding for a large cross-cultural study on corporate responsibility. Similar events took place in the southern part of the world. Monterrey University in Mexico and the Catholic University Madre y Maestra in the Dominican Republic both developed ethics programs for their professional schools in 1988, and a wealthy Venezuelan business man donated a chair in business ethics to Instituto De Estudios Superiores De Administracio in Caracas. What is going on here?

Nine years ago, Peter Drucker said that business ethics was a fad. He called it "ethical chic."[1] Foreigners regarded the subject as a typically American form of self-righteousness—the U.S. kept the world safe for democracy and now it was on a mission to save it from unscrupulous business practices. Today things are different. Questions about the social and ethical responsibilities of business are not just the concern of a few well-meaning individuals, nor are they the invention of bored academics or muck-raking journalists. In this paper I argue that recent ideological changes in the social, political and economic environment have compelled businesses to rethink their social role and their moral obligations. The subject of business ethics is as much about social, political and economic ideology as it is about morality. Hence, it is a topic that business leaders cannot avoid discussing in today's business environment.

Over the the past three years, I have had the opportunity to talk to a variety of managers and academics from England, Europe, Japan, the Dominican Republic and Venezuela about business ethics. These conversations have helped me formulate a sketch of why ethics is a pressing topic of discussion in the current business environment. As a philosopher, I am most interested in the following questions: Why are business people talking about ethics? What does the current discussion of business ethics mean? This working paper marks the beginning of a long-term research project on the cross-cultural convergence of ethical principles in business.

For some business people "ethics" is rather like Oscar Wilde's "love that dare not speak its name." They are very concerned with ethical issues, but they are uncomfortable talking about them.[2] Many people

---

[1]Peter Drucker, "What is Business Ethics?," *The Public Interest*, (No. 63, Spring 1981).

[2]Some European managers are not altogether comfortable with the subject of business ethics. My most fruitful conversations were at a Ditchley Foundation conference called, "Maintaining Cultural & Ethical Values in a Free Market," (Enstone, England, June 24-26, 1988). Unfortunately, proceedings of Ditchley meetings are not for attribution. Initially, I thought that this would be an empirical study based on interview data; however, due to the fact that most of the managers with whom I spoke preferred not to be quoted, I decided not to carry out such a project, because I thought that I could learn more from a more casual conversation. Also, since some managers had a difficult time answering the basic question, "Why are business people concerned about ethics today?," I felt that a broader interpretive paper might be useful.

Portions of this paper were delivered at the following Universities:

St. Gallen University, Switzerland, May 3, 1990

Nijenrode Business School, The Netherlands, April 26, 1990

IESA, Caracas, Venezuala, March 12-16, 1990

St. Johns College, Cambridge University, Aug. 8, 1989

Green College, Oxford University, May 3, 1989

The Stockholm School of Economics, April 16, 1989

object to the term "business ethics" and prefer to characterize ethical problems as managerial problems. In the U.S. the subject has been referred to as social responsibility, business and the external environment, corporate responsibility, and business and ethics. The Germans and the German speaking Swiss, prefer to call it "*Wirtschaftsethik,*" which loosely translated means the ethics of relationships between economics and society. Meanwhile bankers in France coined the word *deontologie,* (duty) for their statement on ethics. In Latin America people tend to refer to business ethics in the negative. When they talk about ethical issues in business, they usually use the word "corruption."

In this paper I will use the term business ethics as a general term to refer to a subject that covers the broad range of issues related to the social and ethical responsibilities and norms of business. I will also use it to refer to the category of issues related to good and evil, and right and wrong in business. When I discuss particular relationships between business and society, I will use the term social responsibility. I shall begin by looking at how the political and social changes have necessitated discussion of business ethics in the U.S. and the U.K.. I then talk about how similar phenomena affect the European dialogue. Finally, I focus on the major themes of discussions about business ethics in four countries and speculate on the role that these themes play in the international conversation.

The Reagan/Thatcher Ideology

Conservative politics and liberal economics can be a burden and a blessing to business. Both Ronald Reagan and Margaret Thatcher began a process of shifting public responsibilities to the private sector. Reagan promised to shrink government and to get it off citizens' backs. He encouraged business to support the arts and social programs and then cut government spending on welfare. President Bush continued with Reagan's theme. In his inaugural speech Bush evoked the old barn-raising ideal of volunteerism. He asked everyone to pitch in and create "a thousand points of light." Thatcher held a similar philosophy. Like her friend Reagan, she had an enormous faith in the ability of the free market to create wealth and the "trickle down effect" to distribute it. Both leaders lionized the entrepreneur as the national savior who would put the country back on its feet and make it a contender.

The Reagan/Thatcher ideology focused on creating wealth, not distributing it. They repeatedly told the public that the private sector

I am most grateful for the comments and insights of those in attendance.

could deliver better goods and services than the government. Their public philosophy gave business more power, but it also had the curious consequence of giving business more social obligations. This is ironic because in the past, social critics feared that without tight restrictions, businesses would exploit the labor force and destroy the social, moral and aesthetic fabric of society. This world view was particularly strong during the Victorian era and was expressed by many of the great British writers such as Dickens, Ruskin, and Carlyle. For the most part their concerns were justified and legislation, such as child labor laws, zoning restrictions, liability laws and anti-trust laws, were enacted to moderate the seamy side of capitalism.

It's not surprising that business ethics blossomed in an era of con-servative political ideology that favored a freer market and self-regula-tion over government intervention. Labor and the political left in the U.S., U.K. and Europe have shown little interest in the subject and are rarely represented in public forums or conferences on business ethics. The British labour party's new slogan "business where appropriate, government where necessary" begs the real question facing democra-cies today—i.e. How do we determine the appropriate roles for busi-ness and government? I was told by a labour M.P. that "the labour party is not concerned with problems in business ethics and it does not have any interest in the subject." There is a curious tension between the interests of organized labor and the whole idea of making business more ethical. Because of the adversarial stance of labor in the U.S. and the U.K., labor owes its power and moral authority to the unethical behavior of business. Unions provide external regulation of business, they protect workers from the potential of management to misuse its power. By acting ethically, employers can thwart union organizing. They do this by providing fair wages and benefits, and by improving the quality of worklife. Like unions, the democratic party has traditionally played a critical role towards business and favors protective legislation to self-regulation. There is a role for labor and the political left to play in discussions of business ethics. Improving the moral standards of business is not incompatible with external regulations.

Public and Private Responsibility

Since business was held up by Reagan and Thatcher as the knight in shining armor, the public began to expect more benefits from business and less from the government. In the U.S. these expectations have been growing for years. Large firms not only provide for pensions and health care, but they are also branching off into social services like daycare. Some managers in the U.K. are perplexed by the new role of business. British management consultant Charles Handy observes:

> It's been made increasingly clear, in Britain at least, that it is the organization's job to deliver; it is not its job to be everyone's alternative community, providing meaning and work for all for life; nor is it its job to be another arm of the state, collecting its taxes, paying the pensions, employing the handicapped and the disadvantaged, administering an implicit incomes policy or collaborating with an exchange rate policy.[3]

Handy believes that this extended role of business may get in the way of its real function which is to deliver quality goods and services. As one British chief executive complained, "My social objectives add five per cent to my costs." Professor Jack Mahoney, director of the Business Ethics Research Center at Kings College, adds a different twist to the Handy statement. Mahoney believes that business is as powerful a social agent as the state, and the churches. However, he wonders whether the streamlined business of the future will be able to carry its social burden and at the same time get on with business.[4] Mahoney may be right, especially if industry continues in its quest to produce more from less, while government continues to produce less service at a greater cost.

While the public expects more from the private sector, companies may soon realize how much they had depended on government. Ironically, the current *laissez-faire* political and economic environment may be letting business *do* more than it bargained for. Most firms cannot operate without a physical infrastructure, i.e. roads, water, electricity, etc.. They also require a social infrastructure that includes things like police protection, a competent civil service, public education, social services and a healthcare system. When the government of a developing country cannot provide the required infrastructures, businesses usually take up the slack. In spite of the influence of Reagan/Thatcher type ideology on other European countries, public spending in the EEC has grown from 29% of the GDP in 1960 to 39% today, but the quality and quantity of public services seem to be eroding.[5] In an era of indebted and overburdened governments, the prosperous private sector will eventually have to compensate for the erosion

---

[3]Charles Handy, *The Age of Unreason*, (London: Hutchenson, 1989) p.71.

[4]Jack Mahoney, "The Role of Business in Society," (Gresham College Public Lecture, April 19, 1989).

[5]"Capitalism's Visible Hand," *The Economist*, (May 19, 1990), p. 11.

of the social infrastructure (and perhaps the physical infrastructure) in order to function.

For example, in the U.S. and the U.K. the government funded education system is in a state of crisis. This means that a growing portion of the work force may not graduate with the basic skills needed by industry. So it is not uncommon to find companies donating funds, staff and equipment to education. In the U.S. one often reads news items about companies "adopting" schools or supplying staff and equipment to them. Corporate leaders point to the shrinking labor supply and the need for specialized skills as a justification for these social commitments. Motorola Inc., for example, offers a six month remedial education program to improve the basic skills of poorly educated employees. Its education director complained that "We spent $5 million on this training last year, and that came right out of the profits. The public schools should handle this task."[6]

In England, "Industry Matters," a subgroup of the Royal Society for the Encouragement of Arts and Manufacturers, established a program to improve the image of business and to encourage the entrepreneurial spirit in young children. Supported by private industries, this program set up mock businesses in elementary schools so that children could learn about running a business. One elementary school was given a miniature McDonalds so that the children could play at working. In another school, students started a small crafts shop. The Industry Matters program aims not only at developing business skills, but it also hopes to instill pro-business attitudes in young people.

Private Influence on Public Policy

Social activism by business is laudable. However, it does raise some serious questions about the responsibilities of government and the proper role of business in a democracy. Corporate leaders find themselves thinking carefully about the delicate lines between helping society, serving its own interests, and shaping public policy. It is one thing for a company to donate computers to a school and quite another for it to determine the curriculum of that school. Does one lead to another?

Questions about the line between public and private responsibility seem to be asked more by corporate leaders than by American politicians. Look, for example, at the dilemma AT&T faced. Pro-Life groups recently threatened to boycott AT&T because they objected to the

[6]Louis Uchitelle, "Surplus of College Graduates Dims Job Outlook for Others," *New York Times,* (June 18, 1990), p.1.

company's donations to Planned Parenthood. The AT&T foundation rescinded its $50,000 grant to Planned Parenthood. Many of AT&T's employees and stockholders reacted in anger and disappointment at its decision. In a letter to all AT&T employees, the AT&T foundation said "We don't think a corporation should take a position on abortion, one way or another. It's not a corporate issue."[7] The letter went on to argue that AT&T gave Planned Parenthood money for its educational programs, but since Planned Parenthood had taken the lead in the political fight over abortion, customers, shareholders and employees on both sides viewed the grant as taking a side on the debate.

AT&T set boundaries in the letter. It wouldn't take a position on an individual ethical issue, nor would it take sides on a political debate. However, it was willing to take a stand on a social problem because it could justify its position by appealing to corporate interests. The letter went on to announce that AT&T launched a $2.25 million program for prevention of teen pregnancy and teen parenting. The program targeted 10 cities where AT&T had the most employees. Clearly, the corporation realized that there is no such thing as value free corporate giving. Their response takes corporate interests into account and shows a sensitivity to what is a publicly acceptable way for them to affect society. But nagging questions remain. How much influence does the funding agency have on the recipient? Is Planned Parenthood being "punished" for taking a stand? What were the conditions of the funding?

Business Values as Social Values

The British seem less concerned about the charities that a company supports than they are about the influence of business and market values on public services. Public discussion about business ethics in England centers on two issues. The first is political. How do we delineate the social responsibilities of the public and private sectors? This will become a particularly important question for the Northern European welfare states, especially if they are forced to cut taxes and government services in order to be competitive. England, like the other welfare states, has a deep concern for the common good. For example, last year there was a tremendous public outcry when Thatcher suggested that business build a private toll road to ease the traffic around London. A far more passionate debate occurred as the Thatcher government attempted to make the public health service more "efficient."

---

[7]AT&T in-house letter, April 9, 1990.

Many interpreted this to mean that cutting costs and streamlining procedures would diminish the quality of public healthcare.

The concept of stewardship and service to society with its shared values and traditions is very important to the British. Its roots lie in the ideas of the Scottish enlightenment. Adam Smith believed that civil society was a precious and precarious creation. Adam Ferguson called it "a gift." He said civil society protected the individual from the state, but at the same time kept him from being at the mercy of nature.[8] Individualism hung in the balance with the obligation to care for the common good. Hence, Mrs.Thatcher ruffled a lot of feathers with her quip "there is no such thing as society."

The second issue that is distinctive to the British public discussion of business ethics is their concern for the effect of market values like consumerism, instrumentalism, efficiency, and profits, on human or moral values—i.e. Is it wise to let economic considerations dominate all facets of our lives? This debate is a throwback to the 19th century worries about the moral and aesthetic vacuity of capitalism. It also reflects the traditional root values of the British aristocracy, which are basically agricultural, anti-industrialist and anti-capitalist—the social ideal here is the land-owning gentleman.[9] While editorials in the 1980's complained about greed on Wall Street, America's pragmatist tradition is not uncomfortable with economic values such as utility and efficiency. However, if one looks closely at pragmatists such as Josiah Royce, John Dewey and Charles Sanders Pierce, one sees that the American pragmatists, like the thinkers of the Scottish enlightenment, tempered practical concerns with commitment to civic ideals. All of these philosophers believed that democracy demanded social responsibility.

The British are uneasy with applying business values to society. For example, an editorial in the *Sunday Observer* complains that the language of the market has come to dominate all institutions, including education. The author, an educator named Peter Abbs, says the government regards education as "a giant industrial process whose products have to be managed, promoted and sold, and brought into line with adjacent industrial processes, manufacturing and marketing and mass produced commodities." He quotes the education secretary of State who referred to teachers as "the main agents for the delivery of the curriculum."[10]

---

[8]Adam Ferguson, *An Essay on the History of Civil Society,* (Philadelphia: Wm. Fry, 1819), p. 32.

[9]William Pfaff, *Barbarian Sentiments,* (New York: Hill and Wang, 1989), p. 34.

[10]Peter Abbs, "Victorian Values v Tabloid Glitz," *The Sunday Observer,* (Oct. 15, 1989).

The editorial also objects to the values that are established when business interacts with education. To illustrate, Abbs points to a student computer dating project in which students were "successfully" matched. The winners were given a free dinner, donated by McDonalds, and a ride in a Rolls Royce that was provided by a local car hire firm. According to Abbs, all of the values that the contest encouraged were wrong, from the transactional nature of the personal relationship to a reward that encouraged conspicuous consumption.

Deregulation

Deregulation stimulated discussion of business ethics inside companies. It was supposed to unleash market forces, get rid of the dead wood, and make everything more efficient. The financial industries greeted it with with joy, expansive growth, and then a sobering crash. For some deregulation meant "what is no longer prohibited is permitted." The scandals and the subsequent disgrace of companies like Guinness and Drexel Burnham Lambert, compelled managers to think about the ethics of their employees. There also emerged questions about the social impact of hostile takeovers and leveraged buyouts on the economy.

Deregulation is often justified by the assumption that the market will discipline business and/or companies and industries can regulate themselves. If they didn't regulate themselves, then new laws would be created. Prudent firms began to think about their operations from a moral point of view. Just as the Reagan/Thatcher ideology in effect gave business more social responsibility, deregulation had the effect of giving it more ethical responsibility. During the regulated days many companies worked under the assumption that they were ethical if they followed the law. Most businesses were in favor of deregulation. That meant that in order to keep from being re-regulated, they had to find ways to insure the legal and ethical integrity of their employees, and their industry. This is one of the reasons why businesses in the U.S. began to put pressure on business schools to teach ethics.

Corporate restructuring and fear of takeovers indirectly led managers to think more about the ethical environment inside the firm. One way to lower operating costs is to get rid of expensive middle managers. Flattening the traditional pyramid-shaped hierarchy means that there are fewer managers to direct and police workers. Employees further down in the hierarchy are given more decision-making responsibility. This cuts red tape and can make an operation more efficient, but it also requires managers to trust their employees to make good business decisions without big brother looking over their shoulder. Large companies in particular have begun special training programs to communicate their ethical standards on such issues as accepting gifts and conflicts of interest. These programs are also designed to improve skills at making ethical judgements.

Codes of Ethics

Because of the dominance of law in American culture, it is difficult for some to think about ethics except in terms of laws. For example, when President Bush entered office, he appointed a lawyer to be his ethics czar. The basic job of the czar was to revise the rules on government ethics. However, the scandals that took place involving White House employees had far less to do with rules than they had to do with the idea that individuals had lost sight of what it meant to be a public servant. While laws shape formal notions of right and wrong, the values that are imbedded in roles and social practices also mold social and personal morality.

Yet, the most common ways that firms respond to ethical concerns is by drafting a code of ethics. As of 1986, seventy-five percent of all Fortune 500 companies in the U.S. had one. Sometimes these codes resemble a mission statement, sometimes they state a very general set of values, while other codes look more like operating policies. Ethics codes are often drawn up by the legal compliance department of American companies and are considered a first line of defense against illegal activities. Codes of ethics are the easiest way for companies to address ethical issues. Good codes are not just rules of conduct, but statements about what it means to be in that particular company and business. On their own, codes don't do much and are sometimes ignored. However, they can serve an important function if they introduce constructive dialogue about ethical issues into the organization.

British companies are less enthusiastic about codes of ethics. Some U.K. companies regard corporate codes of ethics as nothing more than the latest import from Wall Street and of little use to British industry. One executive said, "Our American counterparts may need ethics codes, but we don't." She wasn't implying that the British were more ethical, but rather that they, unlike the Americans, shared a common set of values. In a more homogeneous society with a stronger class consciousness, ethical behavior tends to be embedded in roles and articulated in virtues related to those roles. As one company official explained, "Who can afford the time and money to write something that normal people will carry out automatically and the bad guys will only ignore?"[11] Nonetheless, the Institute of Business Ethics (IBE) surveyed 300 of the largest British Companies. They received 100 usable replies and discovered that 55 of the companies had a code of ethics and 20 of them contained instructions on how to react to a moral dilemma faced in the course of doing business (for example what to do when offered an inducement to recommend a particular product or service).[12]

A study of the top 200 French, 200 German and 200 British firms, indicates that ethics codes are mostly an American practice that traveled to Europe via American subsidiaries.[13] Out of the 184 replies, the authors, Catherine Langlois and Bodo Schlegelmilch, found that 78 companies had adopted codes of ethics. Thirty-five percent of these companies had non-local parents and 19% of them had American parents. Out of the European companies without codes, the researchers discovered that 22% of them did not have any U.S. connection. The French had the least amount of companies with codes (30%), the German had the most (51%) and the British fell in the middle at 41%. The German and British companies had stronger U.S. connections than the French and they were also larger. The Langlois/Schlegelmilch report confirmed an earlier study that noted a positive correlation between the size of the company and the adoption of an ethics code.[14]

Comparisons of the content of ethics codes in the Langlois/Schlegelmilch study show that there are national differences in the priority given to certain values. For example, all European codes address employee conduct, whereas only 55% of the U.S. companies do. Over 80% of the U.S. companies mention the customer, while only 67% of the British and German codes do. French companies show the greatest concern for the customer—93% of their codes refer to customer relations. In contrast to the French, the British codes don't talk much about relations with customers or shareholders. Most U.S. codes discuss business government relations and 86% mention relationships with suppliers. Less than 20% of the European codes discuss either of these issues. The German codes were distinctive for their tendency to

[11]Michael Skapinker, "Clarifying the Ground Rules," *Financial Times,* (July 22, 1988).

[12]Simon Webley, *Company Philosophies and Codes of Business Ethics* (London: The Institute for Business Ethics, 1988).

[13]Catherine Langlois, and Bodo Schlegelmilch, "Do Corporate Codes of Ethics Reflect National Character?," unpublished paper.

[14]J. Melrose-Woodman, and I. Kvernda, "Towards Social Responsibility: Company Codes of Ethics and Practice," *British Institute of Management Survey Reports,* (No. 28., 1976).

emphasize a moral obligation to innovate and improve technology. Sixty percent of their codes mention it, compared to 20% in France, 6% in the U.K. and 15% in the U.S..

The codes are all very similar in terms of the general headings—employee conduct, community and environment, customers, shareholders, suppliers and contractors, political interests, and innovation and technology. But the similarities in codes may not be as significant as the differences. Companies often research other corporate codes before writing their own. Organizations such as The Ethics Resource Center in Washington and the Institute of Business Ethics in London serve as repositories for corporate codes. They also offer assistance to companies who want to write one. This may account for why the codes resemble each other. However, the important things to compare in codes are the ways in which a company differentiates itself through a statement of its values and priorities.

The Langlois/Schlegelmilch study also shows that in Europe ethics codes are very new and appear to be a growing phenomenon. The proportion of European companies with codes rose from 14% in 1984 to 41% in 1988, with most codes adopted in 1986. Fifty-six percent of the respondents from companies without codes indicated that they were "likely" or "very likely" to adopt a code by 1990. This study provokes the question, Why have European companies all of a sudden felt the need to adopt a formal code ethics? Is this just a new convention adopted from American management theory, analogous to things like matrix organizations or MBO's? Does this trend mark a change in the perception that managers have about the morality of their employees and the business environment in general?

Pluralism and Moral Strangers

Several general factors account for changes in the ethical environment of European businesses. The first factor is related to size. As companies become larger they require more formalized communication networks. Larger companies, and obviously ones with foreign operations, are likely to have workers, suppliers and customers from different backgrounds and different value systems. Hence they might feel the need to clarify the company values. Also changes from family owned conglomerates to public companies may require a firm to reassert its identity and values.

Growing pressure from environmental groups, consumer groups, anti-apartheid groups—all acting under the ever watchful eye of the press—compel some companies to stipulate their policies on ethical issues or risk being caught off guard and put in a potentially damaging position. Mass communication, growing media interest in business and the increase in public ownership of businesses makes it difficult for a company to keep its actions secret. In other words, private property isn't as private as it used to be.

The upcoming unification of the European market has inspired some European companies to formally articulate their values. Within firms of all sizes and within most industries, there are new players. At a number of levels, the European business environment has become more pluralistic and now consists of people who have different sets of values. The free market, which is ideally a meritocracy, tends to break down traditional class barriers, but it also creates new classes. For example in the City of London the old boy network of brokers from the same class and the same school has been eroded by the intense competition that was unleashed by the Big Bang when face-to-face trading on the floor of the exchange was replaced by electronic trading. After the Big Bang, old timers in the financial industry bitterly complained about the class of street-smart kids who were making a fortune in the City. This new breed of business person is as much of a moral stranger as someone from a different culture. Their values are different, they don't know about the unspoken customs.

I would argue that the main reason why European companies have started to adopt ethics codes is because the social and political environment of business became more like America's in respect to the assumptions that managers must make about the pluralism of values within their firms and among their business associates. The pluralist nature of a liberal democracy makes discussions about ethics mandatory. American society guarantees people the right to determine their moral values and obligations, but it doesn't really offer guidelines on how to fulfill them. Thus it depends less on roles and traditions and more on laws and formal statements of ethics. Since institutions cannot depend on moral consensus, they must make sure that they articulate a moral point of view. Organizations that operate in liberal societies need to guard against the danger of becoming nothing more than areas where people act out their preferences. They must create a moral environment that tolerates an individualist and a collectivist vision of morality. Both of these moral visions are problematic. As political scientist Amy Gutmann points out, "Most conservative moralists set their sights too low, inviting blind obedience to authority; most liberal moralists set them too high, inviting disillusionment with morality."[15]

Many of the British managers complained about the demise of traditional values and the need for formal rules. It's not uncommon for people to worry about the values of the younger generation. But one feature that seems particularly prevalent in the young people in the U.S. and the U.K. is their lack of faith in the future—they have an underlying sense that things are going to get worse. As a result of this fear, they feel that they have to get as much as they can before it runs out. This generation grew up on an economic roller coaster. Oil shock, recession, inflation, high unemployment and potential of environmental disaster bred a short-term world view, which is not limited to the younger generation. Ethical action is difficult for those who do not believe that some good will come of it, if not now, then in the future.

Some British managers worried about the impact of intense competition on the values of people in their firm and their industry. One manager said that the business world had become too complex for ad hoc ethical decisions and the company needed to give guidance to its employees. Others seemed to feel a need to reestablish what it was that their company stood for. Some British and European businesses seemed to be going through crises of identity and trust. There was a sense that their employees and other business associates had become moral strangers who were undependable.

The Global Economy & Moral Obligations to Strangers

Perhaps the most obvious reason why ethics is on the business agenda is because few businesses are insulated from forces in the global economy. The interdependencies of business cross national boundaries, which means that the modern firm depends on and has obligations to strangers all over the world. This requires a very sophisticated way of thinking about morality. It is far more difficult to think about the moral obligations that we have to strangers than it is to think about our obligations to friends, family, and countrymen. Sociologist Alan Wolfe has observed that the less we live in tightly bound communities organized by strong ties, the greater our need to recognize dependence on perfect strangers. He says, "To be modern in short, requires that we extend the 'inward' moral rules of civil society 'outward' to the realm of

---

[15]Amy Gutmann, *Democratic Education* (Princeton: Princeton University Press, 1987), p.61.

non-intimate and distant social relations."[16] Many business people and politicians have asserted that we need to return to traditional values, which usually means things like honesty, integrity, promise-keeping, etc.. But that is different from the idea of returning to a traditional model of morality.

Another reason why business ethics has emerged as a distinct subject is because the model of morality found in traditional societies is not adequate to make decisions about right and wrong in an interdependent world. Traditional morality rests on the assumptions of a small scale society with authority that is passed down through many generations. Moral obligation is tightly inscribed and limited in scope. Rules are expected to be followed, but the number of people to whom the rules apply are limited, by family, class, geography, ethnicity or political boundaries. Moral obligation is easy because individuals are not called on to act as moral agents who must choose from a wide variety of options. Authorities define the rules of social interaction. People know who they are tied to and to whom they have obligations.[17] Italy and Japan present good examples of societies with traditional moral structures. In both countries discussions about business ethics focus on broadening the notion of moral obligation.

Mario Unnia, founder of the Italian Business Ethics Network, commented, "Italians are not unethical, they just have a low ethical temperature."[18] Italians lack a strong sense of the state. They operate under the Catholic tradition of law—they believe in making laws, but not enforcing them (there are more lawyers in Rome than in all of France). Yet, Unnia says that Italians don't like formal regulations and they prefer self-regulatory mechanisms. The only authority structure that Italians readily accept is that of the family.

On a local level, Italian business can be characterized by parochial values. Unnia thinks that Italy is still a country of "amoral familism," which the sociologist Edward Banfield described as "the inability to concert activity beyond the immediate family."[19] One fascinating Italian study compares the way that morality functions in business, government and the mafia. It shows how each system is ethical in itself, but unethical as soon as it interacts with other larger moral systems.[20]

[16]Alan Wolfe, *Whose Keeper?*, (Berkeley: University of California Press, 1989), p. 20.

[17]*Ibid.*, p.2

[18]Mario Unnia, "Business Ethics in Italy: The State of the Art," unpublished remarks delivered at the Society of Business Ethics, (Washington, D.C., Aug. 11, 1989).

[19]Edward C. Banfield, *The Moral Basis of a Backward Society*, (New York: Free Press, 1958), p. 10.

[20]P. Arlacchi, D. Forte, A. Martinelli, M. Unnia, "Tecnostruttura, Lobbystruttura, Mafiostruttura," unpublished paper from Prospecta, (Milano, June 1986).

Unnia believes that the business community in Italy has to address two threats, both related to morality based on small spheres of loyalty and affiliation. First they face the threat of organized crime (the mafia) and second, the threats posed by a corrupt and inefficient political system. As Unnia points out "few understand that the internationalization of the economy runs parallel with the process of sharing the values of the international business community." In Italy the concept of moral responsibility to strangers at home is a key problem that discussions of business ethics must address.

The Japanese have also struggled to understand their new roles and responsibilities to other cultures. In 1988 the Japanese National Institute for Research Advancement sponsored a study done by the Hitachi Institute called "Future Stage of Corporate Social Responsibility in the Era of Overseas Production." The authors begin by arguing that because of the rising value of the yen, increasing labor costs, and complaints about the trade imbalance, it will be necessary to move more production overseas. In order to avoid friction in these operations the report says, "It has therefore become necessary to grasp the corporate social responsibility not merely from a domestic level, but also from the international viewpoint."[21]

The Hitachi report points out that Japan lags behind the U.S. and Europe in overseas production. So in order to compete, Japanese companies will have to adopt a level of social responsibility "at a level no lower than that of the U.S. and the European enterprises, the firstcomers." This raises some interesting questions about whose values will form the moral minimum in international business. History tells us that the ideology of the most powerful tends to dominate.

To a Westerner, the Japanese concern about social responsibility does not appear to stem from a "good will," or a moral impulse. It is based on decreasing friction between overseas operations and their host country. Strikingly absent from the report is the desire to assert any Japanese values except for the social value of harmony. The report tells us that in Japan, corporate responsibility includes such things as job security, import promotion and price stability. It says that soon companies may add to this list the obligation to have "countermeasures toward decreasing political friction." The Hitachi Report offers three guidelines, two of which are relativist in nature, "Think globally, and act locally," and "When in Rome, do as the Romans do" (but the report

---

[21]T. Hatchoji, T. Nishikawa, Y. Ohinata, G. Ichihari, S. Takahashi, *Future Stage of Corporate Social Responsibility in the Era of Overseas Production*, (Tokyo: Hitachi Research Institute, 1988), p.1.

adds that you sometimes have to do more). The third asserts the need to act with "enlightened self-interest."[22]

Basically, "enlightened self-interest" comes down to working with other cultures' values and expectations, so that Japanese companies can fulfill their corporate responsibility at home. The Hitachi Report attempts to understand how other cultures think about social responsibility, not how Japanese companies should think of it. It observes that U.S. companies tend to contribute to community projects. (In February of 1990, the Japanese government began offering tax breaks to companies who give money to philanthropic organizations in the U.S..) Individuals in British firms take the lead in charity activities. In West Germany projects geared towards the construction and maintenance of society are usually led by the government. According to the study, the major emphasis of social responsibility in Asia is not on contribution to local projects, but on projects that contribute to the country's economic growth such as training and technology transfer.

It is interesting to compare the task of Japanese business ethics with that of Italy, the U.S. and Europe. If Italian business suffers from familial amoralism, the Japanese might be said to suffer from national amoralism. Both business cultures need to expand their notion of moral responsibility to strangers. For the Italians this means that they need to develop a stronger concept of the common good within their national business community. The Japanese seek to understand how their common good is related to caring for the common good of other cultures. Americans, on the other hand, are sometimes charged with being ethical imperialists. They need to sort out which values to keep and which ones to reconsider when doing business abroad. The Europeans, faced with the prospect of 1992, are caught somewhere in between all of these. Internally, there seems to be less consensus on what is right and wrong in business and externally, there is a desire to maintain their identity and traditional values in a unified European market and a global economy.

Conclusion

So far I have talked about how political philosophy, public opinion, deregulation, organizational structure, greater pluralism in the workforce, organizational restructuring, scandals, the media, and the globalization of business have inspired discussion about business ethics. If the above phenomena have made Western and Japanese business people

[22]*Ibid.*, p. 2.

wax philosophic about ethics, one wonders how the Eastern European nations and the Soviet Union will treat the ethical issues related to the changes in their political and economic system. Some people wonder whether discussions of business ethics are the luxury of affluent societies and prosperous businesses. They argue that developing countries and struggling firms are more interested in survival than the niceties of ethics.

The historian Karl Polanyi observed that in preindustrial societies economic relations tend to be embedded in the social sphere, in industrialized societies social relations tend to be embedded in the economic sphere.[23] One way to understand the meaning of the current conversation about business ethics is that we are attempting to discover the kinds of social, moral and legal arrangements that are necessary for a free market to function. This is particularly true in developing countries.

But most American and European managers usually don't talk about business ethics in these terms. On the level of everyday life, business managers worry that they can no longer depend on a workforce with similar moral values. Today, managerial problems often center on issues related to trust and loyalty. In liberal societies social institutions like church, family, education, and the state are less effective at shaping a coherent set of moral values in citizens. Thus organizations have to create norms to guide employees, while at the same time tolerating a variety of individual values.

Businesses in Europe and the U.S. now play a more visible and active social role. They are celebrated and condemned for their effect on the environment and they are encouraged to take ethical and political stands on issues like South Africa. This puts the corporation into the role of a moral agent and requires business leaders to develop sophisticated positions on a variety of social and ethical issues. The obligation of business to take on more social responsibilities seems to grow as governments become either less able or less willing to shoulder them. Where business is perceived to be more capable than government, the public has begun to expect action.

In industrialized and developing countries, discussions about business ethics express a need to expand traditional notions of morality from family, company and country to a variety of strangers. This is not because businesses have some new moral mission, but because they are learning some painful lessons about what happens when they don't coordinate their own interests with those of other stakeholders. The emerging interdependence of economies may require all participants

[23]See, Karl Polanyi, *The Great Transformation*, (Boston: Beacon Press, 1944).

to adopt certain ethical understandings about business. Interesting questions for the future research are, Who will set the standards? What will the standards be? And most importantly, How will those standards be determined? On a formal level, the framework for ethical norms will be set by regulations, trade agreements and at talks such as the Uruguay round on the GATT. But the actual standards of ethics and social responsibility will be established by the daily policies and practices of local and multinational companies. This is why the current international discussion of business ethics is so complex and so important. More and more, business leaders find themselves facing problems that require them to choose between actions that are based on existing ethical norms, or those that are based on a stricter ethical standard. The latter course of action requires bold leadership, because as we all know, ethical behavior doesn't always pay, and even when it does, it often pays late.

II.

Democracy, Individualism
and Pluralism

Autonomy and Responsibility: The Social Basis of Ethical Individualism

Robert N. Bellah

My remarks this morning have been stimulated by a paper of Jay Ogilvy's entitled "Beyond Individualism and Collectivism,"[*] that I imagine a number of you have read. In that paper he gives a sketch of the philosophical pedigree of American liberal individualism and Soviet Marxist collectivism and suggests not an eclectic fusion of the two but some new starting points from which to look at our problems that might provide us with common ground, even while each side works through a critical appropriation of its own tradition. I agree with most of what Jay says about Western liberal individualism, but I have some problems with his analysis of Soviet Marxist collectivism. Since I want to use most of my precious minutes to talk about where we go from here, let me simply indicate what my problems are, rather than fully argue them, and leave the matter for further discussion.

I believe Hegel and Marx belong within the tradition of modern Western individualism, even though they criticized aspects of it. Neither

---

[*]This essay is included at the conclusion of this section, *Beyond Individualism and Collectivism*, pp.217-233.

of them was a thoroughgoing collectivist or "wholist." Indeed I believe Hegel has much to teach both Western liberals and Eastern Marxists because he saw better than either usually have that the real problem of modernity is what Charles Taylor has called "situated freedom." Hegel was the theorist of a modern *Sittlichkeit*, an institutionalized life-form within which freedom of the individual would be realized in a concrete society, as opposed to the more purely liberal emphasis on *Moralitat*, the structure of abstract justice concerned largely with individual rights and morality. Marx was suspicious of Hegel's ideas about *Sittlichkeit* and felt that on the one hand existing institutions were so involved in the capitalist exploitative system that they could not be saved, but that on the other the actual regime of freedom that would occur after the capitalists were expropriated could not be described in advance. This left a large gap when the revolution actually did succeed. That actual Communism turned out to be statist was not foreseen or desired by Marx nor by the Lenin who predicted the withering away of the state. Both seemed to believe that a modern economy, once the exploiters were removed, would virtually run by itself leaving free individuals to cooperate non-coercively with one another. Thus if we mean by Soviet collectivism the state authoritarianism that is now crumbling in the Soviet Union and Eastern Europe, it was an ironic outcome of inadequacies in Marxist theory combined with particular social circumstances, not the inevitable outcome of a collectivist philosophical tradition.

In the Western world and the United States in particular there have been similar ironies, that we overlook at our peril. Our founders were certainly devoted to the idea of the freedom of the individual, but they linked that freedom to an understanding of economic life that would have consequences they did not expect. It was a commonplace among them that political economy was a branch of political ethics and its practice an exercise in public morality. The primary teacher of that public morality was John Locke. It is remarkable how much of our current understanding of social reality flows from the original institutionalization at the end of the 18th century (the "founding") and how much of that was dependent on the thought of John Locke. Locke's teaching is one of the most powerful, if not the most powerful, ideologies ever invented. Indeed I suspect it is proving to be more enduring and influential, which is not to say truer, than Marxism. It promises an unheard of degree of individual freedom, an unlimited opportunity to compete for material well-being, and an unprecedented limitation on the arbitrary powers of government to interfere with individual initiative.

Locke exemplifies the right to life, liberty and the pursuit of happiness in the act of appropriation by the solitary individual of property from the state of nature. Government is then instituted for the protection of that property. Once men agree to accept money as the medium of exchange, the accumulation of property is in principle without any moral limit. Locke rejects all limits on the freedom and autonomy of individuals other than those they freely consent to in entering the (quite limited) social contract. He specifically attacks the patriarchal family, arguing implicitly for the rights of women and explicitly for the lack of obligation of children to parents. Limited government exists to provide a minimum of order for individuals to accumulate property. All traditional restraints are rejected and nothing is taken for granted that is not voluntarily agreed to on the basis of reason. That is an overly condensed but not unfair statement of Locke's position. All of this is possible, according to Locke, because of the assumption that the "natural harmony of interests" (an assumption not shared by Locke's predecessor, Hobbes), will lead to the creation of a free and tolerant good society. In many respects this vision has turned out to be as utopian as Marx's realm of freedom.

In Lockean America we may comfort ourselves that we have long been aware of the dangers of the state and that we have protected our society from the state through constitutional provisions such as the Bill of Rights and many legal restrictions on arbitrary state action. We can certainly see today that the Marxists' dismissal of bourgeois liberal freedoms was a catastrophic mistake. Still it would be unwise ever to forget that over the last two centuries we have developed, for a variety of reasons not least having to do with our dynamic economy, a most unLockean state, and that today Americans, too, are threatened by the arbitrary actions of the state. Recently the *San Francisco Chronicle* reported that a fifteen-year-old boy was apprehended in his home by INS officers and taken to Mexico, without a chance to call his father or a lawyer, even though his father is in this country legally. We know about such cases and we express our outrage, but they continue, and will continue until we manage to put the proper legal restraints on such governmental agencies as the INS.

A far more serious example is the way in which Lyndon Johnson manipulated congress into passing the Gulf of Tonkin resolution, which was a critical step in involving the United States in a terrible war, planned and executed by a small group of high administrative officials, without either public approval or adequate congressional oversight. The cost of that war in damage to the life of our communities, to our life-world, was enormous and we are still paying for the consequences.

But this morning I want to concentrate on another danger to the survival of a free society in America, one we are much less aware of than the danger from the state because it comes from a direction that the

Lockean tradition did not fear. That is the danger from the economy. Czeslaw Milosz has spoken of the state eating up the substance of society. I want to suggest that the economy can also "eat up the substance of society." Jurgen Habermas puts the danger in another striking phrase. He says that the administrative state and the market economy can "colonize the lifeworld." Like some 19th century imperialists they can invade the life-world as though it were a primitive society and subject its moral life to the constraints of money and power.

The danger that I want to focus on today is particularly pernicious just because of what is going on behind the iron curtain. We may be blinded to what really threatens us by the phenomenon that Robert Heilbroner has recently called "The Triumph of Capitalism." In a February Issue of *The New Yorker* Heilbroner wrote:

> Less than seventy-five years after it officially began, the contest between capitalism and socialism is over: capitalism has won. The Soviet Union, China and Eastern Europe have given us the clearest possible proof that capitalism organizes the material affairs of humankind more satisfactorily than socialism: that however inequitably or irresponsibly the marketplace may distribute goods, it does so better than the queues of a planned economy; however mindless the culture of commercialism, it is more attractive than state moralism; and however deceptive the ideology of a business civilization, it is more believable than that of a socialist one. Indeed, it is difficult to observe the changes taking place in the world today and not conclude that the nose of the capitalist camel has been pushed so far under the socialist tent that the great question now seems how rapid will be the transformation of socialism into capitalism, and not the other way around, as things looked only a half century ago.

One of the consequences of this remarkable change is a new opportunity for world community because of the lessening of the military competition between the United States and the Soviet Union. That is one of the most hopeful aspects of the world situation today.

But we in America are tempted to emphasize not just that the cold war is over, or almost over, but that we won it. There will be a McDonald's in Moscow. What more tangible evidence of our victory? And the lesson we draw is not that society has resisted the state but that capitalism is the answer to all our problems: the free market works, all we need is individualism, a minimal state and entrepreneurial energy. As Walter Russell Mead has pointed out this is only the current euphoric version of an old utopia: "All markets are free, all competition fair, all unions dead, all workers contented. Credit is cheap; government small. The bureaucrats—corporate, governmental and academic—collapse under the weight of their own incompetence, leaving a free field for the innovative and progressive entrepreneurs."

But Heilbroner in his second paragraph, a paragraph that begins ominously with the word "yet," indicates clearly that that is the wrong lesson to draw:

> Yet I doubt whether the historic drama will conclude, like a great morality play, in the unequivocal victory of one side and the ignominious defeat of the other. The economic enemy of capitalism has always been its own self-generated dynamics, not the presence of an alternative economic system. Socialism, in its embodiments in the Soviet Union and, to a lesser degree, China, has been a military and political competitor but never an economic threat. Thus, despite the rout of centralized planning—to judge by the stories coming from Moscow, it has the proportions of a rout—one would have to be very incautious to assume that capitalism will now find itself rid of its propensity to generate both inflation and recession, cured of its intermittent speculative fevers, or free of threatening international economic problems. Nevertheless, in one very important respect the triumph of capitalism alters the manner in which we must assess its prospects. The old question "Can capitalism work?," to which endless doubting answers have been given by its critics, becomes "Can capitalism work well enough?," which is quite another thing.

So I will take the unpopular position that the triumph of capitalism should lead us not to triumphalism but to self-reflection. Indeed I will argue that the greatest threat to our genuine human happiness, to real community and to the creation of a good society comes not *only* from a state whose power becomes too coercive (we can never underestimate that danger), but from an economy that becomes too coercive, that invades our private and group lives and tempts us to a shallow competitive individualism that undermines all our connections to other people. Let me say at once that we need a good government and a good economy. It is not a question of abolishing them, but of putting the proper limits on them. We know that we need to limit the state. I want to argue that we need to limit the economy as well when it becomes imperialistic and threatens to dominate our lives. Indeed I would argue that there is such a thing as market totalitarianism that parallels state totalitarianism and is a real threat to us in America today.

My point, then, is that both East and West, both Soviets and Americans, have similar problems. We both need to reinvigorate or create as the case may be those institutions that can provide us with a real socially situated freedom and protect us from a coercive state that Marx did not foresee and a coercive economy that Locke did not foresee. The key for both societies, though the institutional changes we need will be different, is democracy, which, in its genuine form is, I believe, as much on the American agenda as on the Russian.

Freedom, for most Americans, is an essential ingredient in a definition of a good society but, as with all the great moral terms, we need to probe more deeply what freedom really means. For many of us, freedom still has the old meaning of the right to be left alone. In an older America where one could spend most of one's life on one's own homestead that kind of freedom had a certain plausibility. But in the great society of today freedom cannot mean simply getting away from other people. Freedom must exist within and be guaranteed by institutions, such as the right to participate in the economic and political decisions that affect our lives. Indeed I believe that the great classic criteria of a good society—peace, prosperity, freedom, justice—all depend today on a new experiment in democracy, a newly extended and enhanced set of democratic institutions, within which we as citizens can learn to discern better what we really want and what we ought to want if we are to sustain a good life on this planet for ourselves and the generations to come. Such an understanding would show us that our identity as persons is constituted through our participation in a variety of communities and that we are fulfilled as persons only in and through the institutions that link us to others.

I know that talking about "institutions" will raise doubts in the minds of many of you. The very idea of institutions is intimidating to Americans. We need to understand why that is the case and why it is so important for us to overcome our anxiety and think creatively about institutions. By institutions I mean patterns of expected action to which we must conform or be prepared to face social sanctions. For example, institutions may be such simple customs as the handshake in a social situation where the refusal to respond to an outstretched hand will cause embarrassment and some need for an explanation of one's uncivil behavior or they may be highly formal institutions such as taxation where refusal to pay what is required may result in fines and imprisonment.

The problem with institutions for individualistic Americans is that they appear to impinge on our freedom. In the case of the handshake this impingement may give rise only to a very occasional qualm. More powerful institutions seem more directly to threaten our freedom. The classical liberal view for just this reason held that institutions ought to be as far as possible neutral mechanisms that individuals can use to attain their separate ends. This view has been so persuasive that most Americans take it for granted. They share the classical liberal fear that institutions that are not properly limited and neutral may become oppressive and deprive us of our freedom. This set of beliefs leads us to think of institutions as efficient or inefficient mechanisms, like the Department of Motor Vehicles, that we learn to use for our own purposes, or as malevolent "bureaucracies" that may crush us under their impersonal wheels. It is not that either of these beliefs is wholly mistaken. In modern society we do indeed need to learn how to manipulate institutions. And all of us, particularly but not only the poor and the powerless, find ourselves at the mercy of institutions that control our lives often in ways we do not fully understand. Yet if these are our only conceptions of institutions we are left with a very impoverished idea of our common life, an idea which cannot effectively deal with our contemporary problems but only makes them worse.

What is missing in the classical liberal view of society? Just the idea that in our life with other people we are engaged continuously through our words and actions in the creation and re-creation of the institutions that make our life possible. This process is never neutral but is always ethical and political in that institutions, even such an intimate institution as the family, live or die by ideas of right and wrong and conceptions of the good. And conversely, while we in concert with others create institutions, they also create us: they educate us and form us through the socially enacted metaphors they give us, metaphors which provide normative interpretations of situations and actions. Such metaphors may be appropriate or inappropriate, but they are inescapable. A local congregation may think of itself as a "family." A corporate CEO may draw from the institution of sports in order to speak of the necessity of management and workers all being "team-players." "Democracy" is not so much a specific institution as a metaphoric way of speaking about an aspect of many institutions.

In short, we are not self-created atoms manipulating or being manipulated by "objective" institutions. We form institutions and they form us every time we engage in a conversation that matters, and certainly every time we act as parent or child, student or teacher, citizen or official, in each case calling on models and metaphors for the rightness and wrongness of action. So what the liberal idea tends to forget is that institutions are not only constraining but also enabling. They are not just neutral mechanisms but the substantial forms through which we understand our own identity and the identity of others as we seek cooperatively to achieve a decent society. Indeed, institutions are the social embodiment of what we called moral ecology in *Habits of the Heart.* Only by reforming our institutions can we strengthen our moral ecology.

The idea that institutions are objective mechanisms that are essentially separate from the lives of the individuals that inhabit them is not only mistaken: it is an ideology which, to the extent that we believe it, exacts a high moral and political price. The classical liberal view has elevated one virtue, autonomy, as almost the only good, but it has failed to recognize that even its vaunted individual autonomy is dependent on a particular kind of institutional structure rather than an escape from institutions altogether. Furthermore, by imagining a world in which individuals can be autonomous not only from institutions, but from each other, it has forgotten that autonomy, valuable as it is in itself, is only one virtue among others and that without such virtues as responsibility and care, which can only be exercised through institutions, autonomy itself becomes, as we argued in *Habits of the Heart,* an empty form without substance.

David Kirp in his book *Learning by Heart* (Rutgers U. P., 1989) gives some moving examples of a richer conception of institutions. He and his associates studied a number of instances where public school systems were faced with the challenge of admitting children with AIDS. In a situation of extraordinary anxiety superintendents, principals, teachers, and parents were called upon to decide what kind of school and what kind of community they wanted to have. The speech and example of the representatives of institutional authority took on an enormous importance, as did the capacity of the parents to respond. Doctors could explain that the risks were exceedingly small but administrators and parents had to decide whether to take any risk at all in order to extend the moral community to include a child in great need. In this situation finding the right metaphor, seeing the child primarily as a human being in need of special compassion, or primarily as a source of dangerous contamination, would be critical in the outcome.

These stories illustrate the truth that Mary Douglas expressed in these words: "The most profound decisions about justice are not made by individuals as such, but by individuals thinking within and on behalf of institutions." (*How Institutions Think,* Syracuse U.P., 1986, p. 124) We can extend her insight by saying that responsibility, so centrally important in our social life today, is something we exercise as individuals but within and on behalf of institutions. The character of individuals, particularly superintendents and principals, was of great significance in influencing outcomes. But that very character was in part a reflection of the history and moral resources of the community as a whole. By how they responded to a major challenge, administrators and parents changed the institutional definition of their schools and their communities. Those for whom the virtues of responsibility and care determined their action, and it is important for us to see that those virtues were not only located in the character of individuals but in their sense of themselves as representatives of institutions, had a sense not only that they had done the right thing but that they had taught their children a lesson more valuable than most of what goes on in the classroom. Those who, led only by a desire to protect what was theirs, opted to reject the stigmatized child, remained closed, bitter and defensive long after the event. Their children too had learned a lesson. Indeed the process Kirp describes is one of institutional learning for all concerned. It is not just that some school systems acted better than others. It is that some school systems learned to understand what a good school system would really look like, and then they endeavored to make their actual system embody that more deeply understood institutional model.

But many of the institutions that are most important in our lives are, on the face of it at least, much less accessible to understanding and participation than the patterns of decision making in local school boards. We know that we are affected by changes in the national and international economy, the policies of the federal government and its relations with other nations, the industrial and agricultural developments that threaten the global environment, and the way in which information is controlled by the mass media, but we feel overwhelmed by the problem of understanding these complex aspects of the Great Society and helpless to do much about changing them.

In spite of the complexities and the difficulties, these large-scale institutions too can be better understood and they are indeed amenable to citizen action and the influence of a global public opinion. To imagine them as largely autonomous systems that operate on their own mysterious internal logic or can be fine-tuned only by experts is to opt for some kind of modern gnosticism which sees the world as controlled by the powers of darkness and leads us to look only to our private survival. The modern ideal of a democracy governed by intelligent public opinion and participation, though severely challenged by the developments of the last two centuries, is not only worth redeeming in our own society, but, so far as possible, requires extension to the human community as a whole. If I had time to give this argument an adequate philosophical basis I would attempt to renew and extend earlier efforts to create an American public philosophy that would be less trapped in the cliches of rugged individualism and more open to an invigorating and fulfilling sense of social responsibility. I would draw on the radically democratic philosophy of Pierce, Royce, Mead and Dewey and the sobering theological reflections of H. Richard and Reinhold Niebuhr. But that is work for another day.

For Tocqueville, democracy was the key to the understanding of American life, but he saw it as a movement with world-historical implications. Today when the term is asserted hopefully or defiantly in Moscow, Warsaw, Budapest or Beijing, as well as reiterated in a thousand contexts in the Western world, Tocqueville's prediction appears to be coming true. But it is all too easy for us to imagine that democracy refers to the future in presently or recently authoritarian societies but is comfortably and securely established in our own. One of the features of the concept of democracy is that it cannot be easily pinned down, or comfortably confined to a single set of features. It does not mean simply the assembly of all the citizens in the ancient polis. It does not mean simply the regime of individual rights and representative government established since the eighteenth century in America. The participation, dignity and equality of all, which are the very essence of the democratic process, restlessly call into question every set of institutions, including our own.

We have learned that when the Marxists thought they could bring social justice and ameliorate economic exploitation without bothering with "bourgeois democratic institutions" they made a catastrophic blunder, a blunder that has cost the world much in blood and suffering. It is for just such institutions that the populations of the Communist nations are everywhere clamoring. But the dramatic loss in legitimacy of the authoritarian Communist regimes can be taken not simply as cause for self-congratulation on the part of Western democracies, but as an opportunity to think anew about the very real inequalities that gave Marxism a chance in the first place. Our individual rights and constitutional government are a precious heritage that we must constantly defend, but they are not the total fulfillment of the democratic vision. As long as there are homeless on the streets, a grotesque and growing inequality of income distribution and an even more grotesque inequality of property distribution, exploited and marginalized communities at home and abroad, we have not redeemed the hope of participation, dignity and equality. As long as our more affluent citizens see themselves locked in a private competitive struggle for the good things in life, with little sense of responsible citizenship in a good society, the work of democracy still needs to be done.

We face serious problems at every level of our institutional life. The most immediate source of our problems comes from the economy and the administrative state, both of which continue to expand rapidly in their scope and the degree to which they penetrate our lives. However different the form, the essential problems of the Soviet Union and the United States today are the same. The dynamism and scale of the power emerging from these super-institutions in both societies tempts us to view them as natural phenomena to which we can merely adapt but which we cannot control. If that were true they would not be institutions at all, for institutions are human creations. It is above all these institutions that must face the challenge of democracy today.

The citizens of the ancient polis were determined to govern themselves rather than be ordered around by an oligarchy. The founders of the American republic established a regime that guarded individual rights while insuring that citizens could choose their own representative rulers. Today the question is whether we can penetrate the modern economy and the administrative state with genuine democratic institutions. If we cannot, then whether our heritage is Lockean or Marxist we will be crushed by impersonal structures that will leave us as isolated and helpless individuals. If we can, and I deeply believe we can, recreate a genuinely democratic institutional structure in the heart of the economy and the state, then we will realize ourselves as ethical individuals, able to combine autonomy and responsibility, because we have created the institutions that both express and enable that kind of democratic personhood to appear.

John Dewey, Spiritual Democracy, and the Human Future

Steven C. Rockefeller

The human race faces the urgent challenge of creating a global community marked by economic opportunity, equal justice, freedom and respect for nature, or its survival as a species is in doubt. The obstacles to achieving community locally as well as internationally are great, for almost everywhere peoples suffer from moral confusion, bitter social conflicts, fragmentation of experience and knowledge, and the deterioration of the environment. In the poet's words, the center no longer holds. There is, then, an urgent need for ideas with integrating spiritual power, for a unifying moral and social faith that is able to affirm the value of cultural pluralism in the process of liberating and harmonizing the self and society on a national, regional and global basis. Such a faith must be comprehensive enough to integrate the technological, economic, social, environmental, moral, and religious dimensions of experience; it cannot otherwise bring the wholeness and harmony that we need.

This essay focuses on an idea that has roots in the moral vision of the Hebrew prophets and in the social ideals of ancient Athens. It concerns an idea that has steadily grown in influence over the centuries and has had extraordinary transformative power throughout the world for over two hundred years. In short, it is the purpose of this essay to

explore the global moral, social, environmental, and religious significance of democracy. As symbolized by the construction of the Statue of
Liberty in Tiananmen Square last spring and the appearance of glas-
nost in the Soviet Union, it is probably already the most widely shared
moral value in the world today. Reflecting on the widespread disillusionment with communism in the Soviet bloc and China, Francis
Fukuyama has even gone so far as to argue in a widely debated essay
that western liberal democracy, which is based on the ideas of freedom,
equality, and the consent of the governed, has already won "an una-
bashed victory" over Marxist-Leninism and all other ideological rivals.
Democracy as a mode of political and economic organization has deci-
sively established itself, declares Fukuyama, as "the ideal that will govern
the material world in the long run."[1] These developments are cited, not
to enter the debate over the correctness of Fukuyama's thesis about
current history, but as a way of calling attention to the world-wide
potential that lies in the democratic ideal. Also, it is not being implied
that the word democracy always possesses a consistent meaning in
international discourse, and it may well be that the full significance of
democracy as a social ideal is yet to be revealed as different peoples
throughout the world explore experimentally its possibilities and
meaning in their own social and spiritual contexts.

The question at issue can be stated briefly: Is there a distinctively
democratic way of liberation and community, and does it involve an
ideal possibility for the future development of the social, economic,
moral and religious life of the human species worthy of humanity's
shared faith and devotion? This essay argues that the democratic ideal
may be understood in such a way as to justify the claim that it does possess this broad significance. Sustaining this argument involves demon-
strating that the idea of democracy has, at least in some quarters, historically involved a depth and fullness of meaning that is not commonly
appreciated and that it has a potential for acquiring even greater meaning as democratic societies adjust to the challenge of the environmental
crisis.

In reflecting on the significance of the democratic ideal, it is helpful to turn back to earlier American intellectual traditions, and especially the thought of John Dewey. Dewey's philosophy of "creative
democracy" took form in the late nineteenth century under the influence of Hegel, the St. Louis Hegelians, T. H. Green, and Walt
Whitman. Hegel had taught that universal freedom is the goal of the
world historical process. Developing Hegel's prophecy that America is

---

[1]Francis Fukuyama, "The End of History?" *The National Interest,* 16 (Summer
1989), 4.

"the land of the future," Whitman called for realization in America of "a sublime and serious Religious Democracy."[2] For Whitman the democratic ideal is a "fervid and tremendous idea" of "vast, and indefinite, spiritual and emotional power" that gives to American life its moral purpose and underlying unity. He called for the emergence of "a cluster of poets, artists, teachers fit for us, national expressers, comprehending and effusing for men and women" the meaning and values associated with this great idea.[3]

Having learned to respect democratic values as a youth in Vermont, John Dewey was deeply moved early in his philosophical career by Whitman's vision, and he aspired to be one of those "poets, artists, teachers" interpreting for the people the profound spiritual meaning of the democratic ideal. Starting with Protestant Christian social values and the Neo-Hegelian philosophy of the organic unity of the spiritual and the material, the ideal and the real, he set out to construct his own philosophy of individual liberation, social transformation, and harmony with the divine. As he reconstructed his early Neo-Hegelian ethical idealism and developed a new brand of humanistic naturalism, which charts a middle way between a tough-minded and tender-minded world view, the idea of democracy remained of central importance.[4]

As has been suggested, thinkers like Whitman and Dewey understand the idea of democracy to involve much more than a theory of political organization and economic opportunity, important as this is. It is more fundamentally a great moral and social ideal that comprehends all human relations and has important implications also for humanity's relations with nature and the divine. Understood in this more comprehensive sense, the democratic ideal embraces for Dewey both a philosophy of ongoing social reconstruction and a philosophy of "a personal way of individual life." It was his conviction that democracy as a mode of social, political and economic life could be sustained and perfected only if democracy also became a personal philosophy and faith, a unifying way of ethical life and spiritual growth. Democracy as an individual way "signifies the possession and continued use of certain attitudes, forming personal character and determining desire and purpose in all

[2]G.W.F. Hegel, "America is Therefore the Land of the Future," in *The American Hegelians*, ed. W.H. Goetzmann (New York: Alfred A. Knopf, 1973), p. 20. Walt Whitman, *Democratic Vistas*, in *Walt Whitman*, ed. Mark Van Doren (New York: Viking Press, 1945), p. 365.

[3]*Ibid.*, pp. 323-324.

[4]See Steven C. Rockefeller, "John Dewey: The Evolution of a Faith," in *History, Religion, and Spiritual Democracy, Essays in Honor of Joseph L. Blau*, ed. Maurice Wohlgelernter (New York: Columbia University Press, 1980), pp. 5-35.

the relations of life."[5] As a comprehensive moral ideal, Dewey argues that it should govern human relations in family life, the school, the church, business and industry as well as in government. Moreover, the democratic way becomes an individual path of moral and spiritual growth, a personal way of liberation and transformation. It involves, in other words, a form of spiritual practice in the sense of a way to grow and realize the enduring meaning of life and to find peace, wholeness, and harmony with the world and the divine. In his mid-thirties, Dewey broke with the Congregational church, in which he had been an active member since boyhood, and thereafter had little interest in institutional religion. He never ceased to believe, however, that his work was consistent with the Christian spirit, and was convinced that if the Christian tradition with its gospel of freedom and hope had ongoing relevance and meaning in the contemporary world, it was to be found in the thoroughgoing democratic reconstruction of experience and all social institutions and interactions.

In what follows, I will explore Dewey's vision of the democratic ideal. In conclusion, the essay will briefly consider the possibilities of a further environmental reconstruction of the idea of democracy and discuss the democratic reconstruction of the religions.

1. Christianity and Democracy: Equality, Freedom, and Shared Experience

In Dewey's view, the American democratic ideal has roots in Christian ideals, and he arrived at his own philosophy of "creative democracy" by undertaking a radical reconstruction of the Protestant Christian tradition in the eighteen eighties and nineties. It is important, however, to make clear in this regard that as a mature thinker, Dewey did not believe that faith in democracy necessarily requires any particular metaphysical or theological foundation for its validation. As one of the founders of American pragmatism, he looked for confirmation of the meaning and value of the democratic life in the consequences that flowed from it as revealed by human experience. It is nevertheless illuminating to consider Dewey's understanding of the interconnection between Christian and democratic values.

In 1894, in his last major religious statement before leaving the institutional church, Dewey summarized what he viewed as the three

---

[5]John Dewey, "Creative Democracy–The Task Before Us," in LW 14:226. EW, MW, LW refer to the Early, Middle and Later *Works of John Dewey* edited by JoAnn Boydston and published by Southern Illinois University Press, Carbondale, Ill.

most fundamental Christian ideals or values. First he mentions the idea of "the absolute, immeasurable value of the self" or human personality. Second, he cites the notion of a kingdom of God, that is, the idea of a community of free persons bound together in all their relations by mutual love and support and by shared values, that is, devotion to the common good. Third, he cites the idea of the revelation of liberating truth to humanity, and he has in mind primarily practical truth sufficient for the guidance of life.[6] Even after Dewey abandoned traditional theism and neo-Hegelian idealism, he continued to associate God or the divine with practical wisdom, especially unifying social ideals, and all those cosmic processes that support realization of the ideal. The reality of the divine is found for Dewey chiefly in the animating spirit of authentic community and is experienced as a living reality in and through all relations informed by sympathy, moral wisdom, and affection.[7]

Dewey goes on to point out that at the time Christianity emerged, these three basic ideas found little opportunity for realization in the everyday world, because politically and industrially society to a large extent treated the mass of people not as persons but as things, means to ends external to themselves. The church justifiably existed as an institution where these ideals could be nurtured separate from society. Given the social situation, the faithful understandably hoped for realization of these values by supernatural means in some future eschatological event. A spirit of world denial and other-worldliness was pervasive. However, over time the gradual spread of basic Christian values caused a transformation of society, and democracy as a social reality was born. The emergence of democracy was coupled with the industrial revolution and the rise of the middle class causing a major shift in human orientation and aspiration. These social, political and economic forces generated a new spirit of world affirmation and created unheard of possibilities for earthly liberation and fulfillment. As a result, Dewey argues, it became possible for the first time to appreciate fully "the direct, natural sense" of Christian teaching, which calls for liberation of all persons regardless of race, class or gender, in and through the revelation and incarnation of the truth, or, in other words, realization of a kingdom of God that embraces all and finds expression in all social relations.[8]

Given the vast changes in the social situation caused by science and democracy and in the light of their transformative potential, the objective of Christianity and religious persons everywhere should be, Dewey

---

[6]John Dewey, "Reconstruction," in EW 4:98-102.
[7]John Dewey, *A Common Faith,* in LW 9: 29-37.
[8]John Dewey, "Christianity and Democracy," in EW 4:7-8.

contends, "a society in which the distinction between the spiritual and the secular has ceased, and as in the Greek theory, as in the Christian theory of the Kingdom of God, the church and the state, the divine and the human organization of society are one."[9] The practice of democracy in the context of a technological age makes this a real ideal possibility, Dewey argues. "Democracy, the crucial expression of modern life, is not so much an addition to the scientific and industrial tendencies [of contemporary culture] as it is the perception of their social or spiritual meaning."[10]

In 1892 Dewey stated clearly the momentous social and spiritual meaning that is for him the promise of democracy.

> The next religious prophet who will have a permanent and real influence on men's lives will be the man who succeeds in pointing out the religious meaning of democracy, the ultimate religious value to be found in the normal flow of life itself. It is the question of doing what Jesus did for his time.[11]

Dewey acquired from the Neo-Hegelians the belief that there is no fundamental dualism of God and the world, the ideal and the real, the spiritual and the material, and he retained the conviction as a naturalist that everyday life is inherently full of positive meaning and value. His later thought as well as his early thought is inspired by a passion for unification, or more specifically, for unification of the ideal and the real. He labored as a philosopher to develop a way of living, working, thinking and interacting with the world so as to realize in experience the ideal meaning in life. Democracy as a mode of social organization and a way of personal life has momentous import according to Dewey, because it provides for the first time in human history an opportunity for all persons regardless of race, class, ethnic origin, or gender to realize "the ultimate religious value to be found in the normal flow of life itself," that is, in nature and in everyday life in the secular world. Democracy so understood is, then, the great spiritual challenge and opportunity of the new age.

These convictions make it clear why Dewey does not view the death of the god of supernaturalism as in the final analysis a spiritual catastrophe. Though undeniably painful for many people, it involves a critical transformation in the evolution of human consciousness that opens

---

[9]John Dewey, *The Ethics of Democracy*, in EW 1:248-249.
[10]John Dewey, "Intelligence and Morals," in MW 4:39.
[11]John Dewey, "The Relation of Philosophy to Theology," in EW 4:367.

the door to a deeper and fuller ideal possibility in the religious and moral life of humanity. In the midst of the secularized world, which the atheist and religious conservative alike view as godless and devoid of ultimate meaning, Dewey finds a situation that has made it possible for religious meaning and value to emerge in new vital freer forms. His vision is something much more profound than a liberal dream of ongoing material progress, and he lamented the excessive materialism and externalism in American life. To dramatize the point, one might say, using a Mahayana philosophical vocabulary, that democracy for Dewey promises a way of life that offers all persons the opportunity to awaken to the identity of *nirvana* and *samsara*. Furthermore, he understood as few others have that, if men and women in contemporary civilization are to find the wholeness, inner peace and meaning that are the fruit of a healthy religious life, and, if the terror and suffering of modern history are to be overcome in the social sphere, then religious life and social life must not only be reconstructed, but they must also be fully integrated. Part of the power and ongoing relevance of Dewey's thought is to be found in the way that he seeks to address the social, moral and religious problems of the age by holding them together and thinking them through as interrelated aspects of a single whole.

Dewey argues that the fundamental link between Christianity and democracy is to be found in the emphasis on equality, freedom and shared experience in the ethics of democracy. The social ideal of equality recognizes the absolute worth of human personality and the individual person. It requires that all persons be treated as ends and not as a means only. It implies most fundamentally, according to Dewey, guaranteeing to every man, woman and child the opportunity "to become a person," to realize his or her distinctive capacities.[12] Realization of personality, or ongoing human growth (to use the language of his later thought), becomes in Dewey's philosophy the most fundamental social objective and a supreme moral good.

Dewey considers freedom a basic democratic value because it is necessary to realization of personality and the pursuit of happiness. The self, he argues, is essentially a self-determining will, and if personality is to be perfected "the choice to develop it, must proceed from the individual." Hence, the development of the self is thwarted in authoritarian social structures where power and control are centralized in the hands of the few. Dewey points out that self-realization requires the development of moral will, moral responsibility, the capacity for moral choice. The self becomes and is the self it chooses to be in its concrete activities. In Dewey's view persons are genuinely free only insofar as they

---

[12]Dewey, *The Ethics of Democracy*, pp. 244-248.

have developed a capacity for intelligent judgment and choice. People are not born with this capacity. It must be developed, and the achievement of positive freedom is conditioned by the quality of the social institutions in which an individual lives, learns and works.

Democracy as a social ideal also means a community of free persons in which all are bound together by shared experience and a commitment to the common good. "Since democracies forbid, by their very nature, highly centralized governments working by coercion," Dewey points out, "they depend upon shared interests and experiences for their unity..."[13] Freedom of inquiry, assembly and speech become essential, for "free and open communication...is the heart and strength of the American democratic way of living." Class divisions, religious or racial prejudices, and discrimination on the basis of sex, "imperil democracy because they set up barriers to communication, or deflect and distort its operation." The democratic spirit is antithetical, then, to all social barriers that estrange human beings from one another and limit the potential for shared experience. "Democracy is a name for a life of free and enriching communion."[14]

Free communication and the sharing of experience characterize both the internal and external relations of a democratic institution or society. Any social group imbued with the democratic spirit seeks a free give and take with its neighbors. In this way the sharing of experience, the discovering of common values, and the building of community expand. Such is the democratic strategy for the progressive enlargement of authentic community until it embraces all of humanity. In Dewey's world community, the primary social entities would not be nation states, but those voluntary associations formed by men and women from around the world to pursue their shared interests in education, the arts, the sciences, the humanities, business, athletics. The chief task of government is to protect and facilitate the "life of free and enriching communion" which is the very life of democracy.

"If democracy has a moral and ideal meaning," Dewey writes in *Democracy and Education*, "it is that a social return be demanded from all and that opportunity for development of distinctive capacities be afforded to all."[15] In other words, as he points out elsewhere, in a democratic community every person is both a "sustaining and sustained" member of the whole.[16] In this regard, the question may be

[13] John Dewey, "The Need of an Industrial Education in an Industrial Democracy," in MW 10:137-138.

[14] John Dewey, *The Public and Its Problems*, in LW 2:350.

[15] John Dewey, *Democracy and Education*, in MW 9:129.

[16] John Dewey, *Individualism Old and New*, in LW 5:68.

asked: What makes Dewey think that educating people, developing their capacities for freedom of choice, and creating opportunities for free communication will result in commitment to the common good and an attitude of social service?

In the final analysis, Dewey believes that human beings educated in a genuinely liberating environment will act in a socially responsible fashion because it offers them a path to the deepest and richest fulfillment possible. He rejects the idea of a fundamental dualism between the individual and society, self and world, as the product of a false psychology. The individual person is not an atomic entity that can develop itself and find satisfaction as an isolated self. Humans are social beings interconnected with their environment, and the communities in which they choose to live shape their character, habits and beliefs. They have a basic need to feel that they belong to the larger whole and find enduring meaning in life by achieving a deep-seated adjustment with their world. According to Dewey's psychology and theory of education, developing one's distinctive capacities in and through responding to the needs of the community is the soundest approach to self-realization. A person best serves the common good by devotion to the capacities with which he or she is endowed and by loyalty to the needs of the social environment. "There is something absolutely worthwhile, something 'divine' in the demands imposed by one's actual situation and powers."[17] The ideal towards which a democratic society should work, then, is creation of a community in which all individuals are provided with the opportunity to develop and employ their special abilities. The individual in this way finds realization of self and the community is sustained.

In developing these ideas about equal opportunity, freedom and community, Dewey sought a way of humanizing the industrial sphere, of making industrial relations subordinate to human relations. This endeavor led him to embrace the concept of "industrial democracy," which is central to his social philosophy. In brief, Dewey's point is that all social institutions—business, industry and government as well as the family, school and religious bodies—are responsible for providing an environment that makes it possible for the people working in these institutions to grow as persons and to develop their distinctive capacities. Social institutions exist first and foremost, not as means of producing things, but as "means of *creating* individuals," as agencies for developing responsible, self-motivated, resourceful and creative

---

[17]John Dewey, "Outlines of a Critical Theory of Ethics," in EW 3:321.

persons.[18] In other words, all social organizations have an educational task to perform:

> ...the test of all the institutions of adult life is their effect in furthering continued education. Government, business, art, religion, all social institutions have a meaning, a purpose. That purpose is to set free and to develop the capacities of human individuals without respect to race, sex, class or economic status. And this is all one with saying that the test of their value is the extent to which they educate every individual into the full stature of his possibility. Democracy has many meanings, but if it has a moral meaning, it is found in resolving that the supreme test of all political institutions and industrial arrangements shall be the contribution they make to the all-around growth of every member of society.[19]

Dewey further explains what this entails: "Full education comes only when there is a responsible share on the part of each person, in proportion to capacity, in shaping the aims and policies of the social groups to which he belongs."[20] Emancipation from external oppression and social welfare programs cannot set a people free unless their living and working environment develops in them the powers of initiative, inventiveness, deliberation and intelligent choice.

In an effort to facilitate the development of industrial democracy, Dewey as a philosopher labors persistently to break down the long standing western dualisms between the spiritual and the material, the ideal and the natural, and means and ends. These dualisms, he argues, have the effect of degrading the material or natural by stripping it of inherent moral and spiritual meaning. This in turn has a dehumanizing and dispiriting effect on the life of the mass of people whose lives are largely bound up with material and industrial concerns. Dewey's point is that the material and spiritual, means and ends, are organically connected so that the ideal values that illuminate human life are realized and made manifest only in and through the natural and material. In other words, true ideals are properly understood as possibilities of nature. Ends are constituted by means so that properly understood means have all of the meaning and value attributed to ends. Industrial democracy means realizing the inherent meaning and value of

[18]John Dewey, *Reconstruction in Philosophy*, in MW 12:191.
[19]*Ibid.*, p. 186.
[20]*Ibid.*, p. 199.

industrial work and reconstructing the industrial sphere so that they are actualized for those involved in it.

Dewey's ideal of industrial democracy has been criticized as impractical and utopian. Its realization does involve overcoming complex educational, social, and economic problems. Nevertheless it remains a valid definition of a genuinely liberated society and an ideal by which a democratic culture should be guided. It is furthermore an ideal that gives concreteness to the idea of integrating the spiritual and the secular and to the notion of "the religious meaning of democracy."

2. Democracy as a Personal Way of Life

To appreciate Dewey's idea of democracy fully, it is necessary to explore further some of the fundamental attitudes that he associates with the democratic spirit. First of all, the democratic way of life is animated by a faith in human nature, a "faith in the potentialities of human nature as that nature is exhibited in every human being irrespective of race, color, sex, birth and family, of material or cultural wealth."[21] Dewey adds "that this faith may be enacted in statutes, but it is only on paper unless it is put in force in the attitudes which human beings display to one another in all the incidents and relations of daily life." Dewey has often been criticized for maintaining a faith in human nature that is naive and unduly optimistic. In response he explains his position:

> Democracy is a way of personal life controlled not merely by faith in human nature in general but by faith in the capacity of human beings for intelligent judgement and action if proper conditions are furnished. I have been accused more than once and from opposed quarters of an undue, a utopian, faith in the possibilities of intelligence and in education as a correlate of intelligence. At all events, I did not invent this faith. I acquired it from my surroundings as far as those surroundings were animated by the democratic spirit. For what is the faith of democracy in the role of consultation, of conference, of persuasion, of discussion, in formation of public opinion, which in the long run is self-corrective, except faith in the capacity of the intelligence of the common man to respond with common sense to the free play of facts and ideas which are secured by effective guarantees of free inquiry, free assem-

---

[21]Dewey, "Creative Democracy," p. 226.

bly, and free communication? I am willing to leave to upholders of totalitarian states of the right and the left the view that faith in the capacities of intelligence is utopian.[22]

Reinhold Niebuhr, who in the 1930s was a harsh critic of Dewey's liberal optimism, conceded in 1944 that a consistent pessimism regarding human nature leads invariably to "tyrannical political strategies." Niebuhr concluded: "Man's capacity for justice makes democracy possible; but man's inclination to injustice makes democracy necessary."[23] Dewey would agree.

Second, Dewey gives special attention to what he calls "intelligent sympathy" as an essential democratic virtue. "Sympathy as a desirable quality is something more than feeling. It is a cultivated imagination for what men have in common and a rebellion at whatever unnecessarily divides them."[24] It involves the will "to join freely and fully in shared or common activities." More specifically sympathy is sensitive responsiveness to the interests, sufferings, and rights of others. He finds sympathy "the animating mold of moral judgment...because it furnishes the most efficacious intellectual standpoint."[25] "Sympathy...carries thought out beyond the self," "renders vivid the interests of others," and "humbles...our own pretensions" encouraging the development of impartial moral judgments. Sympathy "is the tool, par excellence, for resolving complex situations." Dewey, however, did not believe that feelings of compassion by themselves are an adequate guide in the moral life. He urged development of what he calls "intelligent sympathy," that is, a union of benevolent impulses and experimental inquiry into conditions and consequences.

Third, Dewey argues that the democratic way of life involves an attitude of cooperation and peace that includes a commitment to non-violent methods of resolving conflicts whenever possible.

> ...democracy as a way of life is controlled by personal faith in personal day-by-day working together with others. Democracy is the belief that even when needs and ends or consequences are different for each individual, the habit of amicable co-operation—which may include, as in sport, rivalry and competition—is itself a priceless addition to life. To take as far as possible every conflict which arises—and

[22] *Ibid.*, p. 227.

[23] Reinhold Niebuhr, *The Children of Light and the Children of Darkness* (New York: Charles Scribner's Sons, 1944), pp. xii-xv.

[24] Dewey, *Democracy and Education*, pp. 127-128, 130.

they are bound to arise—out of the atmosphere and medium of force, of violence as a means of settlement, into that of discussion and of intelligence, is to treat those who disagree—even profoundly—with us as those from whom we may learn, and in so far, as friends. A genuinely democratic faith in peace is faith in the possibility of conducting disputes, controversies, and conflicts as co-operative undertakings in which both parties learn by giving the other a chance to express itself, instead of having one party conquer by forceful suppression of the other—a suppression which is none the less one of violence when it takes place by psychological means of ridicule, abuse, intimidation, instead of by overt imprisonment or in concentration camps. To co-operate by giving differences a chance to show themselves because of the belief that the expression of difference is not only a right of the other person but is a means of enriching one's own life-experience, is inherent in the democratic personal way of life.[26]

The depth of good will demanded by Dewey's idea of the democratic spirit is revealed in his counsel "to treat those who disagree—even profoundly—with us as those from whom one may learn, and in so far, as friends." Regarding Dewey's attitude toward non-violence, he was led to support World War I, but the consequences of the war left him deeply disillusioned. During the 1920s and 1930s he worked tirelessly in support of the international movement to outlaw war and consistently attacked the communist advocacy of class war as the means of social progress.

3. Experimentalism and the Ethics of Democracy

The democratic way of life, Dewey teaches, is an ethical way guided by "intelligent sympathy" and concern for the common good. Such a way of life fosters ongoing growth in the individual and transforms and sustains the community. At this juncture it is useful to seek clarification of Dewey's democratic ethics of intelligent sympathy and social reconstruction. Here one finds him working out his interpretation of the "direct, natural sense" of Christian belief in the revelation of liberating practical truth.

[25]John Dewey, *Ethics*, in LW 7:251-252, 270, 299-300.
[26]Dewey, "Creative Democracy," p. 228.

As a philosopher of democracy, Dewey seeks in his approach to ethics a middle way between absolutism and subjectivism, just as in his metaphysics he seeks a middle way between supernaturalism and an atheistic scientific materialism. Moral absolutism has the advantage of affirming the objective validity of moral values. However, it also involves ideas of an external authority and a fixed hierarchy of ends and goods that reflect aristocratic social values and feudal class divisions, Dewey asserts. It frequently is an obstacle to progressive social change. It may be used to obstruct the development of independent thought and has all too often in human history fostered fanaticism and the gross abuse of power. Subjectivism respects the freedom of the individual and the authority of direct personal experience, but it leaves society and the individual at the mercy of whim, prejudice, passion, uncriticized habit and narrow self-interest.

Dewey argues that the democratic spirit in ethics charts a course between the extremes of absolutism and subjectivism by looking for guidance to experience and intelligence, or, more specifically, to the experimental method of knowledge. By giving authority in matters of knowledge, including moral values, to experimental intelligence rather than to something external to experience, Dewey seeks to develop a method of moral knowledge consistent with the democratic faith in human nature, education, free inquiry, and public debate. By adapting the experimental method of the sciences to the process of moral valuation, he endeavors to overcome the split between science and moral and religious values and to give moral judgments an empirical foundation and objective validity. Moreover, Dewey's larger theory of the moral life becomes a theory of the unification of the spiritual and the material and pursues the full integration of the moral good with ordinary life. In his democratic reconstruction of Christianity, then, the experimental method becomes the instrument for the ongoing revelation of practical truth, and the authentic moral life becomes the incarnation of liberating truth in everyday existence.

Dewey's pragmatism and democratic experimental ethics reflects the marked influence of Darwinian biology and William James' functional psychology and instrumentalist view of mind. The mind according to James and Dewey is chiefly an organ designed to assist the human being in adapting to its environment. They view ideas and beliefs first and foremost as guides to action. Knowledge may possess for thinkers a certain inherent aesthetic meaning, but it has a fundamentally instrumental function. Ideas are to be evaluated according to their effectiveness as guides to ongoing growth and to well-being in the fullest sense. Ideas, like the tools of a craftsman, are not only to be respected and prized but also to be refined and reconstructed so as to better meet the demands of the situation. As an evolutionary naturalist, Dewey emphasizes the pervasive presence of change and rejects all ideas of fixed final causes. There are no absolute fixities in nature. Even species come to be and pass away. Moral and religious values, he reasons, may and should change in response to the needs of a changing human situation.

Instead of seeking absolute ideals and offering ready-made solutions to moral problems, pragmatism adopts a genetic and experimental approach that focuses on developing a method for dealing with specific moral difficulties as they arise in concrete situations. It directs a person facing a moral dilemma to carefully clarify the nature of the problem and then to give attention to specific alternative values or ideal possibilities that might guide conduct in the situation, noting especially the conditions necessary to actualize them, that is, the means to their realization. With the aid of this knowledge of conditions or means, it studies the actual consequences that will flow from acting under guidance of the alternative values in question. In the light of a knowledge of consequences, it then evaluates these ideals taking into consideration the specific needs of the moral problem at hand. Pragmatism, then, evaluates moral values or ideals with reference to specific problematic situations and in the light of the means involved in their realization and the consequences that necessarily follow.

In Dewey's middle way, true moral values are relative to the situation, but since moral judgments are based on an examination of conditions and consequences, they possess objective validity. Much of the popular discussion of moral values today incorrectly assumes that the only alternative to absolutism is subjectivism, because it is thought that relativism inevitably means subjectivism. Dewey clearly demonstrates that this is not the case. It is also widely assumed that science and empirical methods of knowledge support moral subjectivism. Again, Dewey's ethical experimentalism shows that this is not necessarily true. The experimental method of knowledge cannot prove that the values of beauty and goodness are objectively real, but this Dewey the empirical naturalist and pragmatist asserts is hardly necessary and not its function. The reality of values—social, moral, aesthetic, religious—is disclosed in direct, immediate experience. One does not need philosophy and science—reflective experience—to reveal or demonstrate that values are real unless one adopts an "arbitrary intellectualism" and makes the unempirical assumption that "knowledge has a monopolistic claim to access to reality."[27] However, the experimental method of inquiry

---

[27]John Dewey, *Experience and Nature*, in LW 1:28; John Dewey, *The Quest for Certainty*, LW 4:20.

may become a way of evaluating and reconstructing the many goods and related purposes that are discovered in and through direct experience, that is, it may serve as an instrument for deepening and refining the human vision of the ideal possibilities of life. It also may help in the process of realizing these ideal possibilities by disclosing the means necessary to chosen ends. In this fashion Dewey seeks to overcome the division between science and human values and to develop a method of moral guidance adequate to the demands of a democratic and technological age.

Regarding the criteria for making moral decisions, Dewey points out that deliberation is called into play when a problematical situation arises, and the criteria for evaluating alternative courses of action are supplied by the situation itself. The end of action is judged good which overcomes the original problem and reestablishes a harmonious situation.[28] He also emphasizes "a plurality of changing, moving, individualized goods and ends."[29] His point is that the good will vary according to individual need and capacity and the situation. Each situation is unique having "its own irreplaceable good." It is the task of intelligence using the method of experimental empiricism to determine just what the good is in any particular situation. The supreme value at any one time varies with the situation, which is a further reason for rejecting the idea of a fixed hierarchy of goods.

> Every case where moral action is required becomes of equal importance and urgency with every other. If the need and deficiencies of a specific situation indicate improvement of health as the end and good, then for that situation health is the ultimate and supreme good.[30]

It is "a final and intrinsic value" and "the whole personality should be concerned with it." Dewey here broadens the idea of what constitutes moral action and again seeks to break down the dualism of spiritual and material. He would liberate people to live wholeheartedly in the present, realizing the inherent meaning and value of even the most ordinary everyday tasks. He seeks to locate the center of gravity and attention in the moral life within the process of living. It is the difference between what Paul calls living under the law and living in the spirit.[31]

---

[28]John Dewey, *Theory of Valuation*, in LW 13:231-233.
[29]Dewey, *Reconstruction in Philosophy*, p. 173.
[30]*Ibid.*, pp. 176, 180.
[31]Dewey, *Ethics*, p. 279.

As an evolutionary naturalist who views the universe as unfinished and open to novel creative possibilities, Dewey opposes any idea of a fixed supreme good, but he was not without his own general definition of the moral good and a comprehensive end of moral action. He argues in *Experience and Nature* (1925), for example, that to common sense "the better is that which will do more in the way of security, liberation and fecundity for other likings and values," because "the best, the richest and fullest experience possible" is "the common purpose of men."[32] Dewey assumes, then, that there is a common sense, common purpose generated by experience and shared by all, which is growth toward the richest and fullest experience possible. He has, however, abandoned the Hegelian idea of some pre-established notion of the universal self and every other idea of a fixed end. His thought shifts the emphasis from achievement of a pre-established goal to a concern with the process of growing itself, emphasizing the intrinsic value of the process as lived each day and its ongoing open-ended nature: "Not perfection as a final goal, but the ever-enduring process of perfecting, maturing, refining is the aim in living."[33]

In his discussion of moral virtue, Dewey returns to a classical Christian theme, asserting that love may be understood as the comprehensive moral virtue. He then proceeds to give his own democratic experimentalist's definition of love. By love he means wholehearted interest in those objects, ends, and ideals which the process of experimental moral evaluation recognizes as good. In other words, love is the whole self responding with complete interest and intelligent sympathy to the needs of the situation and the perfect union of subject and object, of self and activity—the activity dictated by the ideal possibilities of the situation. The good person "is his whole self in each of his acts," and "his whole self being in the act, the deed is solid and substantial, no matter how trivial the outer occasion."[34] "To find the self in the highest and fullest activity possible at the time and to perform the act in the consciousness of its complete identification with self," that is, its ultimate meaningfulness in this situation, is to live as a liberated and enlightened moral being. So defined, love realizes the full positive value of the present situation. It ensures responsibility. It also involves the classical Greek virtues of courage, self-discipline, justice and wisdom.[35] Love so defined is the way of freedom and growth for the individual

---

[32]Dewey, *Experience and Nature*, pp. 311, 321.

[33]Dewey, *Reconstruction in Philosophy*, p. 181.

[34]John Dewey, *The Study of Ethics*, in EW 4:245, 293.

[35]*Ibid.*, p. 361; Dewey, *Ethics*, p. 259.

and the community. It is the perfection of democracy as a creative way of personal life.

Dewey's experimental reconstruction of the moral life involving the ideas of sympathetic responsiveness, complete identification of self and activity, and wholehearted living in the present, reminds one of the spiritual practice of teachers as diverse as St. Francis of Assisi, Zen Master Dogen, and Martin Buber.[36] They all emphasize that a vital spiritual life involves being able to respond to a situation with the energy and attention of the whole self. In other words, one finds here in Dewey a theory of what might be called a secular democratic form of spiritual practice.

Dewey's democratic strategy for ongoing creative social change emphasizes the development of the social sciences, experimental ethical valuation, education, and communication. In this regard, he has been justly criticized for failing to appreciate fully the depth of the contradictions that divide social groups in the contemporary world and for not recognizing the necessity for "confrontational politics and agitational social struggle."[37] Nevertheless, Dewey's approach remains fundamental, for without experimental inquiry and evaluation confrontation will be without intelligent purpose, and without communication the peace of authentic community will never be more than a dream.

4. The Democratic Way and Religious Experience

In her essay on *Democracy and Social Ethics* (1902), Jane Addams, the founder of Hull House in Chicago, writes that the democratic way brings "a certain life giving power" and a sense "that we belong to the whole, that a certain basic well-being can never be taken away from us whatever the turn of fortune."[38] Dewey, who worked closely with Addams on many liberal social fronts and learned much from her about the meaning of democracy, shared these sentiments. In short, he found the democratic way of life to be a source of sustaining religious experience.

As a Hegelian idealist Dewey had embraced a certain ethical as well as aesthetic mysticism arguing that the democratic life leads to an expe-

[36]See for example, John C. Maraldo, "The Hermeneutics of Practice in Dogen and Francis of Assisi: An Exercise in Buddhist-Christian Dialogue," in *Eastern Buddhist*, 14 (1981), pp. 22-46.

[37]Cornel West, *The American Evasion of Philosophy: A Geneology of Pragmatism* (Madison: University of Wisconsin Press, 1989), pp. 101-107.

[38]Jane Addams, *Democracy and Social Ethics* (Cambridge, Mass.: Harvard University Press, 1964), p. 276.

rience of union with God, the Universal Self. As a naturalist, he ceased to think of God as in any sense a being. Nevertheless, in *A Common Faith* (1934), he asserts that, if a person wishes to use the term God, or the divine, it may quite properly be used to refer to all those conditions and processes in human nature, society and the universe at large that have a liberating and unifying effect on human life and contribute to the actualization of the ideal. So defined the divine includes the creative democratic life.

Furthermore, Dewey argues that the democratic faith and way of life have the power to give to experience a distinctly "religious quality." He identifies the religious quality of experience with a deep enduring sense of unification of self and of self and world.[39] It includes feelings of belonging to the larger whole, cosmic trust, and peace, and it involves a sustaining sense of the meaning and value of life. Reflecting on the religious significance of the democratic life in 1920, he borrows some imagery from Wordsworth and writes: "When the emotional force, the mystic force one might say, of communication, of the miracle of shared life and shared experience is spontaneously felt, the hardness and crudeness of contemporary life will be bathed in the light that never was on land or sea."[40] Even in the midst of failure and tragedy a person committed to the ethics of democracy may be "sustained and expanded...by the sense of an enveloping whole."[41] Given the unifying and sustaining effects of a moral faith in democracy, Dewey argues that it may properly be called a form of religious faith.

He also points out that philosophical reflection and aesthetic intuitions of a mystical nature may reinforce and deepen the religious quality of experience generated by a faith in democracy. In short, there is divine grace flowing in the democratic life and natural experience as Dewey understands it. One could even argue that his account of the religious quality of experience implies more about the nature of the divine than is expressed in his philosophy, but that is not a matter which can be explored in this essay.

5. Respect for Nature and the Ethics of Democracy

Today the human race faces a major environmental crisis which will make the planet uninhabitable unless there are major changes in humanity's moral values and behavior in relation to nature. Dewey's philo-

---

[39]Dewey, *A Common Faith*, pp. 8-17.
[40]Dewey, *Reconstruction in Philosophy*, p. 201.
[41]John Dewey, *Human Nature and Conduct*, in MW 14:181.

sophy lays the foundation for such a development by rejecting all dualisms of spirit and nature and of mind and body and by proposing an ecological world view. As a philosophical naturalist, Dewey identifies nature as the all-encompassing whole of which humanity is a part interrelated with all other parts. Nature is the primal matrix out of which the human spirit has evolved, and humanity's creativity and spiritual life are viewed as expressions of possibilities resident in nature and as dependent on nature as well as human effort for full realization. Having a keen sense of the interrelation of culture and nature, Dewey counselled "piety toward nature," and he expressed appreciation of the Taoist spirit of living in harmony with nature.[42] He conceived the democratic community to be intimately interrelated with all those aspects of nature which support and help to make possible the flowering of human civilization, but he did not explore the idea of extending the ethics of democracy to encompass the rights of nature outside the human sphere. Today this further step is imperative. Some thinkers have already proposed such a development.

In recent decades animal rights activists and environmentalists have been working to extend the liberal tradition of natural rights to embrace plant species, animals and eco-systems as well as human beings. This has resulted in an expansion of the idea of the democratic community. The first to make the connection with democracy explicit was an Englishman and champion of animal rights, a contemporary of John Dewey's named Henry J. Salt. As early as 1894 Salt is found calling for the perfection of democracy by including "all living things within its scope."[43] More recently, the American theologian and medieval historian Lynn White, working in the tradition of St. Francis of Assisi, has advocated a new spiritual democracy that recognizes all living things as possessing intrinsic value and ethical rights.[44] In a Pulitzer prize-winning book of poetry, Gary Snyder, who has been influenced by Zen Buddhism and Native American traditions, calls for a new definition of democracy that conceives it to involve a social order in which plants and animals are given legal rights and represented in the councils of

---

[42]Dewey, *A Common Faith*, pp. 18, 36; John Dewey, "As the Chinese Think," in MW 13:222-224.

[43]Henry S. Salt, *Animals' Rights Considered in Relation to Social Progress* (New York, 1894) as quoted in Roderick Frazier Nash, *The Rights of Nature* (Madison: The University of Wisconsin Press, 1989), p. 28.

[44]Lynn White, Jr., "Continuing the Conversation," in Ian G. Barbour, ed., *Western Man and Environmental Ethics* (Reading, Mass., 1973), p. 61 and Lynn White, Jr., "The Future of Compassion," *Ecumenical Review* 30 (April 1978), p. 107. See Nash, *The Rights of Nature*, Chapter 4.

government.[45] There is, of course, already legislation in many nations forbidding certain kinds of animal abuse and protecting endangered species and wilderness areas.

The expansion and deepening of the idea of the democratic community proposed by Salt, White, and Snyder involve constructive proposals for giving the democratic ideal a necessary added dimension of ethical meaning. In an age that is learning how to think ecologically, the ethics of creative democracy must integrate the values of economic well-being and equal rights for humans with respect for the needs and rights of other life forms and ecosystems.[46]

6. The Democratic Reconstruction of the Religions

Fukuyama in his essay on the triumph of western liberal democracy sees the future as "a very sad time," because he identifies liberal democracy with consumerism and finds it suffering from "impersonality and spiritual vacuity...at the core."[47] Dewey, who arrived at his idea of the democratic ideal by reconstructing Christian ethics, would argue that, even if Fukuyama is correct about the current spiritual condition of liberal democratic societies, his assessment suffers from a failure to appreciate the full ethical meaning of the idea. Democracy as Dewey conceives it offers liberal democratic societies an opportunity to recover their spiritual center and to become profoundly ethical at the core. The democratic way involves a full integration of religious life and secular life. It offers the religious person a meaningful way to be religious in the contemporary world, and it offers society a way to find the meaning and value that consumerism cannot provide.

These observations raise questions about the relation of creative democracy, or what could also be called spiritual democracy, to the great world religions. The democratic faith can be practiced within the framework of a humanistic and naturalistic world view, and it does not necessarily require the support of traditional institutional religion. It is also quite capable of living peacefully in association with different religious faiths, provided they respect the ethics of democracy in living together. Furthermore, it can be actively supported by a variety of reli-

[45]Gary Snyder, "Energy is Eternal Delight" and "Wilderness" in *Turtle Island* (New York: New Directions Publishing Corporation, 1974), pp. 104, 106-110.

[46]I am particularly indebted to conversations with Professor J. Ronald Engel and his work on a world conservation ethic, which will soon be published, for first bringing to my attention the possibilities for integrating the ethics of democracy and environmental ethics.

[47]Fukuyama, "The End of History?" pp. 14, 18.

gious world views, and the democratic life can be deepened and enriched by this association. The religions in turn are developed in a positive fashion by undergoing a democratic reconstruction that brings their symbols, ideas and practices fully into harmony with democratic values.

Historically the world religions have been a mixed blessing for humanity. On the one hand, they have been treasure houses of faith, wisdom and compassion providing beneficial methods of spiritual growth and transformation. On the other hand, they have often suffered moral corruption, and they have been a source of superstition, fanaticism, persecution, and war. The greatest single moral failing of the religions has been their inability to instill in the mass of their followers an attitude of respect for the rights and dignity of all human beings including those of different religious faiths. Where the influence of democratic social change has been strong, many religious groups have endeavored to revise official doctrine and teaching in this regard. Wherever the spirit of religious absolutism and fundamentalism is strong, this issue can be a serious problem, and throughout the world social and political conflicts continue to be exacerbated by religious exclusivism and intolerance.

Another particularly pressing moral issue is the discrimination against women within many religious institutions, which has been unmasked by feminist theology in recent decades. The corrective to interfaith hostility, religious bias against women, and other forms of unjust religious discrimination is to be found in the ethics of democracy and the abandonment of those patriarchal, monarchical and imperialistic images of God that foster undemocratic attitudes and behavior. This is fundamental to what is meant by the democratic reconstruction of the religions. In line with a transformation of the democratic ideal into a vision of a community of all life, democratic reconstruction would also support those movements within the religions that are developing an environmental ethics and a supporting ecological world view.

The democratic spirit also works to break down completely the dualism of the sacred and the secular, and it focuses religious concern first and foremost in the life of relationship and intelligent sympathy. Wholehearted ethical action is the finest flower of the religious life, and the deepest mystical insight and union with the divine comes in and through its radiant energy. As Martin Buber has expressed it, turning inward and concentration by means of prayer and meditation are preparation for going forth, and the Eternal Thou is encountered in everyday life in and through relationship to persons—and also to dogs, trees, and stones—insofar as each is treated as a thou and not only as an it. In all the world religions there are traditions which emphasize some variation on this teaching. A democratic reformation of the religions would make it central and seek to clarify its implications for an understanding of God, the moral life, and spiritual practice in societies being transformed by ongoing technological change, democratic reform, and destruction of the natural environment.

Writing in 1946, Albert Schweitzer, who embraced an ethics of reverence for all life as essential to the survival of civilization, states the general issue using a Christian theological vocabulary:

> Belief in the Kingdom of God now takes a new lease of life. It no longer looks for its coming, self-determined, as an eschatological cosmic event, but regards it as something ethical and spiritual, not bound up with the last things, but to be realized with the cooperation of men....Mankind today must either realize the Kingdom of God or perish. The very tragedy of our present situation compels us to devote ourselves in faith to its realization.[48]

The growing nuclear threat only adds urgency to Schweitzer's words, which in the democratic spirit stress human responsibility and invention rather than divine control and intervention.

Devotion to the community of God in its democratic transformation means commitment to the creation of social institutions that would enable all human beings to develop fully their capacities for spiritual freedom, intelligent judgment, aesthetic enjoyment, creating, sharing, cooperating and loving. At its best, the democratic mind knows that none are truly free until all are free, and that the spiritual meaning of our time is to be found by working to build a world where freedom is universal. This is especially true at the end of the twentieth century, because advancement towards the goal of freedom is a possibility as never before, even if the complexities and difficulties are greater than ever. Also, as Schweitzer understood, the concept of liberation must be extended to the entire biosphere.

Ethical principles with democratic implications have been at work in a variety of traditions within the great world religions for centuries. Various forms of liberation theology have in the last two hundred years worked to overcome the dualism of the religious and the secular. The democratic reformation of the religions under the impact of democratic social change and interfaith dialogue is far advanced today in

---

[48]Albert Schweitzer, "The Conception of the Kingdom of God in the Transformation of Eschatology," in *Religion From Tolstoy to Camus,* ed. Walter Kaufmann (New York: Harper Torchbooks, 1961), pp. 420, 424.

some quarters. It remains to make men and women fully conscious of the meaning and potential of this process and to extend it. Space does not permit discussion of democratic change within specific traditions, but a few general comments are in order. What is being contemplated would respect the unique identity of each of the religions and of the many traditions within them. Many paths can be followed as ways into the democratic life. The objective is not to impose on the religions some moral ideal external to their traditions; that would be an undemocratic procedure. It is rather to encourage development from within each tradition of those ethical principles and images of the divine which have creative democratic and ecological implications and support freedom, human rights, equal opportunity, collective participation, peace in living together, and respect for nature. The democratic reformation of the religions will be accomplished only when they come to recognize in the democratic way the deeper practical meaning of their own spirituality.

This discussion would be incomplete without considering the contradiction between the democratic faith and authoritarianism and absolutism. Democracy rejects authoritarianism as the fundamental method of education and government, because it is inconsistent with the goal of a free self-governing individual. The defenders of authoritarianism, like Dostoevski's Grand Inquisitor, can at times mount strong arguments. Authoritarianism may have popular appeal: witness the rise of fascism in the 1930s and theocracy in Iran more recently. Respect for duly constituted, responsible authority has its place. Obedience to the moral truth is an important virtue, and a vow of obedience to a superior authority in a monastic situation may be an effective instrument for getting rid of ego.

However, the democratic faith opposes authoritarianism. In the final analysis it believes that the full meaning of human life is realized only in and through the challenge and risk of freedom. There are great risks, as the abuse of freedom in liberal democratic societies reveals again and again. There is much to be learned from a democratic social philosopher with a profound appreciation of the problem of evil in human nature such as Reinhold Niebuhr. Nevertheless, the central concern in a democratic environment is always the creating of free persons—persons with independent minds capable of intelligent responsible choice—not obedient persons whose minds and wills are subordinate to an external authority. Autonomy and direct personal realization of the truth constitute the critical issue.

Commitment to the liberation of the individual is the most fundamental aspect of the great spiritual significance of democracy. When a school system, an economic system, a religious community or a government lose sight of this ultimate objective, democracy begins to die. The democratic objective of a self-governing individual does not necessarily imply moral subjectivism. The democratic faith as outlined in this essay is identified with an ethical experimentalism that affirms the reality of objective moral truth and the critical social significance of an enlightened sense of moral responsibility. Autonomy is not an end in itself, but without it the individual cannot undertake the great social and religious challenges of life.

The problems with absolutism have already been discussed in connection with Dewey's theory of ethics. It remains to make clear that it is quite possible for the democratic spirit to embrace a faith in God, the Eternal One, while standing firmly opposed to absolutism in the sense of a belief that one particular revelation, creed or set of dogmas contains a fixed and final formulation of the absolute truth. The democratic faith may be harmonized with a trust that there is at work in the cosmos an ultimate meaning that transcends the threats of evil, time and death. However, such a faith when consistent with the democratic spirit would insist that by its very nature the Truth cannot be grasped by the discursive intellect alone and formulated in concepts once and for all. Socrates, who firmly believed in the reality of the Absolute Truth and may well have directly experienced it, makes the critical point when he asserts that the wisest human being is one who knows his or her own ignorance. The highest wisdom of the Buddha is expressed in a thunderous silence. One Christian mystic speaks of God as a dazzling obscurity.

A person may find a way to God in and through the symbols and beliefs of a particular religious tradition, but symbols and beliefs should not be confused with the reality of God itself. One may rightfully trust a particular religious tradition without adopting the arrogant and dangerous belief that one possesses the absolute truth and that other religious paths are necessarily inferior or wrong. Faith in God is consistent with democracy when it leads an individual to spiritual poverty and the humble effort to help others knowing always that, while the Truth may possess us as its instruments, we do not possess it. Such faith offers the deepest support to creative democracy as a unified way of social, economic, moral and religious life.

The task of criticizing and developing the democratic ideal can give post-analytic philosophy a coherent social purpose, and it offers liberation theology—especially in North America—the possibility of a more comprehensive and integrated vision than it has yet achieved. A thoroughgoing democratic reconstruction of the religions in a world experiencing democratic social transformation will breathe new life into the religions and fresh energy into democracy as a way of liberation. It will enable men and women in the midst of their everyday existence to look anew to the great religious traditions for guidance in wrestling with the deeper mysteries of life and death. It will unify social, moral and religious life, bringing a wholeness, peace and joy that many seek and few today are able to find.

Viewpoints

Don Hanlon Johnson

Isaiah Berlin, in an essay in which he attempts to define a pluralism that is distinct from both relativism and monism, writes:

> The very notion of a final solution is not only impracticable but, if I am right, and some values cannot but clash, incoherent also. The possibility of a final solution—even if we forget the terrible sense that these words acquired in Hitler's day—turns out to be an illusion; and a very dangerous one. For, if one really believes that such a solution is possible, then surely no cost would be too high to obtain it: to make mankind just and happy and creative and harmonious forever—what could be too high a price to pay for that? To make such an omelette, there is surely no limit to the number of eggs that should be broken—that was the faith of Lenin, of Trotsky, of Mao, for all I know, of Pol Pot. Since I know the only true path to the ultimate solution of the problems of society, I know which way to drive the human caravan; and since you are ignorant of what I know, you cannot be allowed to have liberty of choice even within the narrowest limits, if the goal is to be reached...and if there is resistance based on ignorance or malevolence, then it must be broken and hundreds of thousands may

> have to perish to make millions happy for all time. What
> choice have we, who have the knowledge, but to be willing
> to sacrifice them all?[1]

But a pluralistic worldview is not so easy to come by. It constantly falls prey to attacks from two sides. There is the argument that Truth cannot be many, and that one individual or community has happened upon its full articulation. All other viewpoints are, at best, faulty translations; at worst, seductions. The assaults on pluralism from this side are not confined to the power-seeking missionary religions and secular ideologies. They come also from a more sophisticated group of thinkers, cross-cultural, who identify themselves with the perennial philosophy. They argue that one fundamental structure of reality lies underneath what they consider to be a deceptive multiplicity of worldviews. (Usually, that structure is a version of the Platonic hierarchy with its various levels starting at body, through mind and soul, culminating in spirit.) In their view, all human religions and philosophies are partial manifestations of that single pattern of the true and the good, usually revealed to an esoteric few, mostly men, well schooled in the history of certain kinds of philosophy and mysticism.

From an opposite flank comes a nihilistic, relativistic assault. It asserts that no set of values has any more grounds for respect than any other; adherence to a particular world view is not a matter of evidence and intellectual method, but of taste or faith. This view makes it particularly difficult for people to consider pluralism as a respectable viewpoint, because they commonly associate it with relativism. After this bloodiest of centuries, it is difficult to argue with conviction that any belief system is as worthy as any other.

It goes without saying that the human world is de facto pluralistic. Some would argue that this condition should eventually be transcended in a utopian unity. Others, with a sigh of resignation, argue that we must shape ourselves to live in this situation because it is the best we can do, but it would be ideal if we could all come to agreement on a single worldview. This essay concerns the possibility of a view that would not just tolerate, but embrace a plurality of viewpoints as healthier than monistic alternatives. In such a view, the multiplicity of worldviews, like the multiplicity of plant and animal species, would be seen not as a necessary evil, but as contributing to the unique beauty of our planet.

I came to such a view through theoretical and practical studies of the human body. I had to resolve the two kinds of objections raised above by grasping the full implications of what it means that each of us

[1] "On the Pursuit of the Ideal," *The New York Review of Books* (March 17, 1988), p. 11.

has a literal viewpoint. That viewpoint is constituted by the virtually unlimited number of elements that constitute the differences between your and my sitting, standing, watching, speaking, listening, moving through life...on different buttocks and feet, with differently innervated eyes and ears.

Analysis of the literalness of viewpoint undercuts both assaults on pluralism. Against the arguments of the perennial philosophy and other monisms, it does not allow the possibility of a universal viewpoint: even if I could stand in the exact location from which you view the world, my bones and nervous system will be at least slightly different, giving me a different angle on the same material. Against relativism, it does not imply that all viewpoints are equal, but that they are different. It opens up the realization that you have a perspective on life from where you stand, which I can never have, and without which my perception of life would be less comprehensive.

A pluralism of literal viewpoints also provides an ethical measure. There are some world views that would obliterate the literal. The abusive parent and the political torturer would destroy the other person's standing, moving and speaking. The colonialist would uproot ancient communities from the lands which nourish their spiritualities and healing practices. Religious and philosophical ideologies would have people believe that the way they stand in their peculiar space is a source of error to be corrected by reliance on officially sanctioned authorities or mathematical logic.

A literal viewpoint is constituted by the fact that we are embodied. But saying it that way contains a host of hidden assumptions. What does it mean to have a body? Which of many bodies is one speaking of? Whose?

Which One?

Until the turn of the century, there was broad agreement in the West about the nature of "the body": it was defined either as the wild animal-to-be-tamed of the Graeco-Roman and Christian traditions, or the physical object-to-be-quantified of the modern era. Within several areas of human inquiry, those oversimplified paradigms have been whittled away to the point where one can no longer assign any simplistic meaning to "the body." Because it has become an explicit object of study in many disciplines and takes on different meanings in each, one must now ask "Which body are you talking about—the one defined by biomedicine, psychology, literary criticism, anthropology, sociology,

Tibetan buddhism, medieval Christian mystics or phenomenology, etc.?"

The Western deconstruction of "the body" to "which one?" took a major turn in the mid-16th Century with the work of Vesalius. In anatomical art before him, "the body" is that single thing defined by skin boundaries. One gets only modest peeks at bodily interiors: a fully dressed woman reclining on a couch modestly opens her belly to reveal hints of her intestines; a bare-chested man shows us a little of his heart. Suddenly Vesalius's sketches reveal bodies within bodies made of networks of muscles and bones, arteries and veins, brain and nerves.

I deliberately refer to the different sets of drawings as "bodies." The drawings of Vesalius and his successors give the impression that each system of the skin-bounded body is a world in itself, with its own internal laws, oblivious to other worlds, the cardiovascular world seemingly moving alongside the neural world like the Platonic and Cartesian bodies negotiating a kind of dance with the soul. This is not only a matter of aesthetic impressions. Each of these sets of visual bodies generated its own world of research and therapeutics—orthopedics, cardiology, neurology, gastroenterology—which has been developed in relative independence of other specialities. Those bodies gave birth to multiple disciplines, buildings, jobs, and enormous grants.

Vesalius's images of bodies were derived from his carving up corpses. Evolving biotechnologies revealed more details of those early bodies, and even more bodies. The invention of microscopes revealed the cellular body. X-rays opened up the possibility for the first time to map the interiors of the living body which turned out, strangely enough, to be very different from the dead. With such advanced technologies as photomicroscopy, magnetic resonance imaging, PET and CAT scans, one gets the impression, though illusory, that one can see directly into the interior of bodies. And there one finds what a century ago would have seemed to be a mystical vision of pulsing cells, clusters of fuzzily delineated organs, and fluid flows.

The relatively new biomedical field of psychoneuroimmunology has been capitalizing on this now widely recognized multiplicity of "bodies." Scientists who have been studying such phenomena as heart disease, cancer, and AIDS have been engaged in designing research paradigms based on networks of interaction between the biological world of T-cells, neuropeptides, hormonal activity and muscular stress, and the social world shaped by divorce, diet and listening to Mozart. Such research would have been unthinkable when "the body" was defined by skin, muscles, and bones.

Another major deconstruction of the body into "bodies" came from the work of a small group of anthropologists who argue that "the body" is the primal artifact of a particular culture, varying from "the body" in other cultures just as much as its music, pottery, dance, religion or cuisine. A seminal essay in this field, *"Les techniques du corps,"* was written by Marcel Mauss in 1934.[2] By "techniques of the body," Mauss meant the wide range of activities which shape the protean body of the infant into an adult, including styles of caring for infants, gender formation, styles of work, exercise, sexual postures, dance and ritual. He argued that such activities, which seem so "natural," are actually highly developed expressions of a culture's values. If you examine any particular technique, such as using a shovel, you will find that the technique, and the body it goes towards shaping, differ, sometimes radically, from culture to culture. During the past 60 years, the ramifications of his thesis have been investigated in the techniques of many different cultures.

Over several years, I have carried on my own research in this area. One person I interviewed is a rabbi in the contemporary Chasidic tradition. He writes of his shaping:

> In the Yeshiva school, being fat was considered a sign of overindulgence in 'this world.' I became thin. There was a concept of modesty, *'tznius'*, which required that men, and especially women, show as little skin as possible. Men were supposed to crack the benches—to study in a sitting position. The best men were those who were never without a book in their hand, even while traveling. Women were not expected to do this.
>
> When walking in the streets, when there was a possibility of looking at women's bodies with enjoyment (an avoidable evil) the ideal position was to walk slightly bowed over, so that you could just see three to five feet in front of yourself, not more.
>
> Overly careful grooming was considered effeminate. Male jewelry or perfume was not acceptable. Beards were required and hair length was short. Haircuts were defined by the number of degrees of the cutting edges of the clippers. A zero indicated extremely short, almost bald. I used to go for a three, and one went for a one. Sidelocks were kept long.
>
> When one followed all these customs, there was a feeling of living in the Bible itself.

[2]Trans. B. Brewer, *Economy and Society*, vol. 2, no. 1 (1973), pp. 70-88.

A particular culture's healing practices will have profound effects on how a child comes to experience and conceptualize "the body." An American who has been raised in a climate of surgery, drugs, and orthopedic devices will think about his or her body differently than will a Southeast Asian who has been raised to use meditation, movement postures, herbs, sensitive manipulation, and acupuncture for health. This person, whose shaping I studied, is an internationally known teacher of body movement, raised in a system of healing developed within the mid-Western working class during the 19th century:

> My father is a chiropractor and I was "adjusted" from the earliest age. I remember being in a car accident when I was 10 and having a whiplash. My father took me to another chiropractor because the insurance company wouldn't let him do the diagnosis. From hearing them talk I developed the impression that some of my thoracic vertebrae had been pushed too close together. I felt stiffness there for years. My neck was adjusted many times. This helped relieve the pain, but I never felt I knew where the right position for my head and neck were. Also, I felt that someone else had to adjust my spine using their hands in order for it to be ok. I could not do this on my own simply by walking, breathing, or feeling my weight. I didn't trust MD's to know anything about my back, but I didn't trust myself either. When I first started doing Chinese movement I remember being surprised whenever I felt my spine reposition itself. Later, after learning Sufi dancing, I remember being surprised when I just took a relaxed breath while standing, and my whole back realigned.

A striking contrast is the relation of body to self described by a Vietnamese philosopher who now works as a counselor for fellow refugees in the Bay Area:

> I remember my mother. Her way of taking care of the family's health had brought the cosmic and human dimension to my body. Thanks to her, my individual life embodied the cosmic life, not separated from it. And we lived a life that was not abstracted from the actual life that lived us.
>
> Living on a land where food was not abundant, I know how important the art of cooking is. Meal is medicine. In preparing food, my mother could use medical quality and tastefulness to compensate for deficiency in nutrient and

calorie. Everyday while walking on the market place, talking to people, or on the way home, my mother always diagnosed the rhythms of the environment so she could prescribe the appropriate meal for my family. Feeling 'the strange wind,' listening to the unusual bird's song, looking at the insect's activities, or seeing the unseasonal fruit, she could detect the change in the environment, and tried to cook the meal so that the health of the family could be protected properly. In the case of emergency, she knew where to get the medicine, even in the wilderness or in the neighbors' gardens. My mother could tell the story of any scar on her children's bodies. She remembered all the marks and spots that carried her hope and fear for the future of her children according to her belief in physiognomy.

His training in that physiognomy, a highly sophisticated system of mapping body structures based on ancient Vietnamese texts, began when he was 14 years old and his uncle diagnosed his future in terms of that system. "I learned to understand human characters and fortunes through all parts of the body. With that kind of learning, I never see the human body isolated from the whole context of life."

Another major deconstruction of "the body" into "bodies" is in the area of sociopolitical thought. Marx was the first to argue that a person's economic class affected his or her experience and definition of "the body." Alienation is primordially a physical reality, based on the shaping of muscle, bone and perception. The care-burdened man's experience of his body, he pointed out, is radically different from that of the man of leisure. The former learns to move, feel and think of his body as a beast of burden or as a machine; the private "soul" is his only place of freedom. For the man of leisure, the body is the source of maintaining status, and of great pleasure. Michel Foucault furthered Marx's seminal arguments in his analysis of the body as the focal point for struggles over the configurations of power. Population size, gender formation, the control of children, and of those thought to be deviant from the society's ethos are major concerns of political organization— and all concentrate on the definition and shaping of the body.

The contrasts between these two women, both having grown up within miles of each other in the same region of the South, illustrate how body-shaping reflects the sociopolitical order. The first, from the old upper-class, writes:

My body was blessed with easy access to medical, dental and orthodontic care. Being blessed with 'good genes' we were obliged to take care of our health and appearance. Posture was very important to all my formative influences: family, school, church, and country clubs. 'Stand up straight, sit up straight, keep your spine erect, chin up, hold in your stomach, tighten your fanny and pull your shoulders back.' Daddy's military school injunctions were the same as Miss Hutchison's School for girls. We stood when the teacher entered the room, were told to walk not run quietly through the halls, and neither spread our legs, nor cross them. Ballet and toe dance classes straightened us out even more. Ballroom dancing classes were another critical source of body training. Like the princesses in our fairy tales we were supposed to be regal, graceful, serene, elegant, demure, and of course slender, like Grace Kelly and Audrey Hepburn.

There was physical education at school and summer camp, at University Club and the country club. I learned volleyball, basketball, track, softball, soccer, archery, canoeing, sailing, English and Western riding, swimming, badmitton, croquet, water-skiing, golf and bowling. These were cultural necessities, not fun to do because they set up competitiveness about the way we looked and moved and scored.

The second woman was shaped by a life working on an Appalachian farm, being physically and sexually abused. In striking contrast to her upper-class contemporary, she learned to dance not through formal instruction but in weekly gatherings at the local gas station on Saturday nights. Her comments on how she learned that bodily activity show a very different notion of authority and community:

> I was never taught, nor needed to learn for social reasons (or able for economic reasons) ballroom dancing, ballet, or modern dance. I did learn folk dancing, rock and roll, and the traditional dance of the area 'cloggin.' I loved the folk dancing, the reels, squares, etc.—the clear sense of a communal form, the energy and groundedness of it. Everyone needed to participate fully and equally to complete the pattern, much like the pieces that come to complete the patchwork quilts.

Whose Body?

This question is provoked by a century of psychological research into body-image. Sir Henry Head, while treating wounded soldiers, found that a sense of one's body as something with two legs persisted even when a leg or two had been amputated. At the same time (around 1890), Sigmund Freud was struck by the case of a patient who, though manifesting no neurological damage, dragged his left leg as if it had been paralyzed. Their early research has been developed by such scientists as Paul Schilder and Seymour Fisher who have illuminated the vast differences among people's perceptions of their bodies depending upon their unique psychological and physical histories. When anyone says something about "my body," or "the body," we now know that what that person means and experiences may differ radically from what another means and experiences. One person may have learned to experience himself as a sophisticated computer, with a hard-edged sense of boundaries between himself and others, containing a collection of imaginatively well-defined "parts." Another may, by contrast, experience her body-boundaries as constantly in a state of flux, like the boundaries between a stream and its banks, and have very little sense of specific body parts but a general sense of different textures of internal energy. Their views of interpersonal relationships, health, values will reflect those profound differences in body-image.

Various psychotherapies have developed during this century that make use of these discoveries. They see that one's worldviews and emotional problems are embedded in physical symptoms, muscle tensions and spontaneous gestures.

The repeated asking of the two questions of any statements about the body—which one? whose?—is an emancipatory practice: like a meditation mantra, it loosens the bonds of dogma. (One might, with profit, raise the same questions when philosophers use the words "Mind," "Soul" or "Spirit.") When one becomes familiar with the enormous complexity and particularity of the neuromuscular substrate for abstract ideas, one finds it harder to justify any kind of absolute viewpoint: where would it be located? what kind of eyes would be looking? what would be the memories and images that mediated what the eyes saw?

At the same time, nihilism also falls by the boards because of the ancient patterns that exist in these various bodies: chemical, physical, biological, archetypal and psychodynamic. Though each of us is a different and rococo jungle, we are not without order. And as one can see in religious ecumenism or in psychological conferences, those orders are intelligible; they can be explained in great detail among people who still remain grounded in their different points of view, while profiting from humane dialogue.

Body and Spirit

Because debates about pluralism often involve questions about spirituality, something has to be said about the relation of bodily to spiritual viewpoints.

Despite repeated moves to divide the two realms, spiritual practices have always been radically experiential, bodily, having to do with birth, sex, work, disease, and death. The elaborate system of hatha yoga asanas, like Native American rituals, originated in attempts to gain a sense of unity with the different beings that make up the physical universe: lotuses, scorpions, lions, deer, buffalo, rainstorms, quiet breezes, imaginary demons. Jewish davvening, Christian kneeling and prostrating manifest physical experiences of awe in the presence of the sacred. Sufi whirling reconnects one with the movements of the stars and planets. Tai Chi Chuan imitates the movement of herons spreading their wings, engaging in combat. These ancient spiritual practices enable one fully to inhabit one's breathing, viscera, running, fear, and sexual excitement. They create a sense of a home from which one can journey into the wilderness of exotic states of consciousness and return to the safety of the familiar. A home that can endure the dislocations of war, disease and the death of loved ones.

Spirituality, in more ancient connotations, is abstract only in the sense that certain forms of music, painting and writing are abstract. Or that cognac is abstracted from grapes. It is about the immaterial only in the sense that vapors are immaterial compared to the liquids from which they are being distilled. Spiritual stories and practices are the most refined products of the collective viewpoints of a geographically situated culture. A people makes its characteristic liquors—Armagnac, slivovica, vodka, scotch—by subjecting its local grains or fruits to processes of distillation, whose methods have been evolved over centuries, passed down, often in secret, from generation to generation. In the same way, it selects from the infinite experiences which constitute its history certain key stories, and retells them from generation to generation— baby Moses being plucked from the rushes, Jesus battling Satan on the West Bank, Gautama sitting by the Ganges. Out of all the possibilities of gesture, posture and movement, it takes the barest few that it associates with desired states of peace or reverence, or that remind it of important experiences in its history, and forms those into rituals. It gradually weaves together its stories, songs, dances, architecture, cuisine, art, styles of work, and healing practices into the single cloth we call its spirituality. The vocabulary of that tradition will be taken from cycles of weather, shapes of the terrain, the surrounding animals and vegetation, the physical styles of work, healing, giving birth and cultivating visions.

The spiritual teachings recorded in such classic texts as the Bible, Koran, Upanishads and the Tao Te Ching, unlike the abstract commentaries written about them, are also experiential: the stories of peoples making sense of their journeys through different lands, their healing experiences, their modes of surviving attack. They are cast in the sensual imagery of how streams wear away stones, of lingam penetrating yoni, storms blowing through valleys, the sound of the lute played by a man weeping for his lost country.

Despite the arguments of perennial philosophy, there is no more universal spirituality than there is one kind of terrain common to every country, or one kind of liquor of which all others are variations. And yet, it is possible for someone from Texas to savor Norman Calvados.

In the United States, Eastern Europe, the Soviet Union, Israel and the Islamic world, many people are returning to the old spiritual stories. But there are serious problems with those stories as they stand.

The shared experiences of the original spiritual communities took place in a hierarchical context in which pluralistic values were not even a question. Those stories were often constructed on the assumption that one community had exclusive access to the Truth. And within each of those communities, only one or a few were thought to have the full access to the truth. They were the only ones with a truly authoritative voice; others were to submit to them.

Moreover, the classical stories, and particularly the theological commentaries that mediate those stories to us, are predominantly told by men, often men of a narrow class within society. As such, they leave out the experiences of women, children and men of marginal classes. In fact, the tales of the relations between "body" and "spirit" often take for granted the subjection of women, children, and slaves to men who were in positions of power.

The perennial philosophers are correct in their attempts to counter those deficiencies in classical religious stories by penetrating to the humanistic core that can be found in every tradition. But they err in trying to reduce all stories of humane behavior to one, when the point is to make a social world that honors a multiplicity of stories.

I want to make a final point in response to an objection to a pluralism of literal viewpoints. The notion that our worldviews are understood only by their connections to our different ways of standing with different neuromuscular physiologies is often taken to be solipsistic. The opposite is true. Solipsism comes from feeling and thinking of the self as embedded in a Cartesian coffin whose opacity prohibits an immediate contact with other selves. The deconstructions of "the body," like the deconstructions of the atom, open up the self to virtually unlimited avenues of connection with others and the world. When two people are walking along a path in the woods, there is an infinite amount that they can share: the fragrances, the feel of the cool breeze, the sound of the birds, the delight of tasting wild strawberries, the difficulty in breathing if they walk too fast, perhaps one with skill showing the neophyte how to carry a backpack to lessen the strain. That one is a male practicing Catholic and the other a woman secular scientist can recede into the background, matter for discussions over lunch, made easier by the walk.

The paradox is that the more I have become aware of the unique qualities of my perspective, rooted in the paths I have stumbled along to this particular vantage point, with my peculiar bones and hormonal arrangements, the more I have been able to listen in silence to the stories other people tell, without trying to translate them into versions of mine.

Resistance to Tolerance and Pluralism in World-Community: Otherness as Contamination

Bruce Wilshire

Little brown men [are only objects for us]. They are too remote from us to be realized as they exist in their inwardness.

William James

For the first time in history we are able to destroy the biosphere of the planet. Even much of Earth's inorganic material is threatened. As paradigmatic of solidity and reliability, Earth itself begins to shake, and we are goaded to think with unprecedented seriousness about who we are and what we ought to do. Where and what is our place in the whole? What ought one to do to contribute to the health and survival of the world? Is there any *reasonable* response to the novelty and gravity of our situation? It is not clear that there is, or that we can shoulder the responsibility of searching for one. The line of least resistance is a dazed automatism or paralysis. There are many difficulties, the most difficult one hidden, I believe. It is the human tendency to define one's being by brutally excluding certain others and other things from it, and then not to acknowledge what one has done.

In this paper I try to show that those who have done most to reconstruct our conception of reason and to maintain a life of reason—the American pragmatists—do perhaps their greatest service by opening our eyes to archaic impulses in our behavior that traditional conceptions of reason pave-over and hide. I mean, specifically, impulses to maintain a beleaguered identity in individual and group through tacit rites of purification in which members of other groups are treated as contaminating and polluting. "We are purely and certainly ourselves because wholly other from those unwashed others." This shunning includes animals, indeed, the whole living world. Traditional rationalistic or commonsensical conceptions of what counts as *one* of anything—conceptions of individuation and identity—are inadequate to account for the way otherness is directly experienced as contaminating, and for what we *are* as members of a group that counts itself elite.

ɞ

Space is more than a void, said John Dewey.[1] It is dynamic interplay and interchange. It bristles with the repulsive, magnetizes with the charismatic, numbs with the banal, throbs with vitality. It is dangerous or safe. As we are drawn through it to commanding positions or havens in it, these ends pull out the behavior which achieves them, as if by magic. Dewey criticises a conception of space since the 17th century: Space is a void, mere distance between any point and any other, measureable precisely—homogenous, isotropic, with every experiencer of space expunged from the basic picture of it, so space as colorless, odorless, purposeless, valueless. There are points on the coordinates set to measure space (and time), and units of physical reality corresponding to some of the points. We must suppose units of reality, for how else could we calculate and control trajectories of objects, and how else could Economic Man (for we must finally get humans in the picture) calculate his benefits and act accordingly?

Dewey's basic point had already been made by Kierkegaard: Though the above conception of the physical universe is adequate for the purposes of mechanistic physics, it is, philosophically speaking, a "lunatic postulate," for it abstracts from our immediate experience as beings in the world, and then forgets that it abstracts. It forgets the interplay, the emotional and dramatic reality, our vulnerability, ecstasy, and fear, our fragile and strange unity and identity preserved only through constant adjustment and readjustment to the world around us.

---

[1]John Dewey, *Art as Experience*, New York, 1980 [1934], p. 23.

It overlooks how each of us remains *one* being in *one* world, the gritty and obscure drama of everyday life.

The pragmatists' charge of unwitting abstractedness of mind is aimed at the whole tradition from Plato on. William James maintains that what secretly moves the tradition are needs of practice, not insight.[2] James pries behind the facade of Greek contemplativeness and finds crude needs to sort things out. He thinks the whole genus/differentia approach to logic and ontology is of very limited use. For example, to specify the essential characteristics of any human as genus animal, species rational, enables us to sort out one species from all others, and then to sort out each single instance of this species from every other (in modern parlance "human" is a "count noun"). This has great practical benefit in managing aspects of our behavior. But the price paid is tremendous. Particular pressing needs of the spectator or manager are met, but specificity and power are achieved through crude senses of identity and otherness. Things are herded together or divided in line with certain practical purposes, but these purposes are typically eclipsed in the glare of a presumptively detached *pure* intelligence, or a supposedly divine *logos* or *nous,* which is allegedly doing the classifying and dividing. Things divided tend to be definitively and simplistically cut off from what is *other* than they. Ignored is the full range of our actual first-person experience, and how our direct contact with otherness is subtly nuanced and deeply formative of who we are as organisms. That we are, for instance, so *close* to other *people* makes their otherness (if they are somehow alien) so much more oppressive than is the otherness of stones or stars.

James closed out his life with a sweeping indictment of the whole conceptualistic and rationalistic tradition, because it introduced artificial continuities as well as artificial divisions in our conception of experience, thereby deforming it. Secretly geared to needs to sort out, it must overemphasize what differentiates and obscure what is subtly shared and interfused. Though it gives the impression of enunciating a fundamental bond, and marking a fundamental division, the essence "rational animal" is so mentalistic, abstract, and indeterminate that it allows the thinker's deepest prejudices to insinuate themselves and limit the reference of the terms. It turns out that for most Greek thinkers women, slaves, children, and barbarians (those who "bar!" "bar!" bark like dogs) are not fully rational, so not fully human (and a

---

[2]William James, *A Pluralistic Universe,* Lecture VII, in B. Wilshire, *The Essential Writings of William James,* Albany, N.Y., 1985, p.365. All references to James, except the last, are found in this book.

distant echo can be heard very recently in Allan Bloom[3]). John Dewey kept insisting that the Greek emphasis on form was a misplaced aestheticism: to become rational (in specific senses) is perhaps the eventual result of arduous cultivation of self; it is an ideal. But a beautiful form "rational animal" should not be supposed to exist prior to and independent of the toils of human history, individual and corporate.[4]

James and Dewey would restore us to the concreteness of our actual situations, to the particularity of ourselves and the actual pressures, conformations, obstructions, releases, ecstatic inclusions, disgusted exclusions at work in our developing interactions in environments; and (following Charles Peirce in their different ways) they would restore us to the actual continuities that bind things together to some particular extent in habits of interaction—concrete universals. In his late Hibbert Lectures, published as *A Pluralistic Universe,* James lambasted the artificiality of rationalism's continuities and discontinuities. After herding us together under the facile rubric, "rational animal," the managerial mind then numbers us off, one, two, three—one body, one self. But are we really to think that our identity as individuals is carried around neatly and safely packaged within the envelope of the organism, as are our lungs, heart, guts? How about our lived sense of the other within the "circumpressure" of the surround, as James put it? Not until Hegel is a dialectical notion of concepts worked out. But his is a new rationalism—a maniacal abstractionism, James thinks—in which the unity of the universe consists in a super concept which, self-dynamic, becomes its own other. James deconstructs and radically appropriates this idea; he formulates "a pulverized identity-philosophy" in which each individual is, in its own way, "its own other."[5]

Ignoring lived experience, both lived continuity and lived otherness, rationalism sorts things out as well as binds them together in abstract conceptions, hence "internally" and necessarily. In its extreme form, absolute idealism, even our lived sense of possibility (that we can do a or b or c or n) is reduced to some truth for the Absolute Mind, which truth of course is locked into all other truths with internal necessity, undoubtedly beyond our comprehension, but dulling the edge of our impulses, faiths, energies, dangers, possibilities. Absolute idealism cannot allow real indeterminacy ("Or" names a genuine reality, James says).

[3]I am referring to the not so subtle racist and sexist prejudices in Bloom's *The Closing of the American Mind...*, New York, 1987.

[4]This is a recurrent theme in Dewey. For example, see his *Experience and Nature*, New York, 1958 [1929], p. 29 where he writes of *the* philosophic fallacy.

[5]*A Pluralistic Universe,* p. 363.

For James there is a kind of unity in the universe, but it is pluralistic: not essential characteristics of all Being which run through all things, a through and through unity which renders the universe a block for Thought; but a "concatenated unity" in which things grow together to some extent from next to next (an ontologizing of "family resemblance" relations), and in which some of the relations cannot be predicted by conceptual thought, for they are "external;" and there is room in the universe for individuals to "rattle around" in particularity and freedom. For James, his view held powerful ethical implications: tolerance, a respect for individuality, for "live and let live." For truth forms an "unstayed wilderness," more than any cognizer, however idealized, can take in, and the participant knows more while the abstract theorizer or mere manager knows less. We should be humble, on guard against "that certain blindness in human beings," a failure to empathize, and James spoke out vigorously against our incursions in the Philipines during the Spanish American War: "Little brown men" are only objects for us, not embodied subjects living forward in the light of their future. "They are too remote from us to be realized as they exist in their inwardness."[6]

꙳

But while James's mature forays in metaphysics are surely important in advancing our theme—tolerance, pluralism, the world community—we will miss the full force of his position if we do not penetrate beyond his critique of artificial rationalistic formulations of continuity and discontinuity and deeper into his own conception of self as body-self and its direct experience of otherness. For once we do this we see *other* massive obstructions and impediments to pluralism and tolerance *hidden* by all rationalisms. The superficial notions of identity and otherness conceal these other difficulties. *Why*, for example, do we feel such distance from—and more than likely aversion to—little *brown* men? Do we subliminally equate brown with dirty—or with dangerous, or base? Only when we confront ourselves as thinkers who are *body*-selves, intimately open to, but highly vulnerable to, not-self, can we begin to understand this. Both James and Dewey struggled to grasp our reality as animal organisms caught up in the life of mind.

Twenty years before *A Pluralistic Universe*, James was preparing its ground in *The Principles of Psychology*. In "The Consciousness of Self" chapter he maintains that the being we call our self not only experi-

[6]Quoted in R.B. Perry, *The Thought and Character of William James,* Boston, 1935, II, p. 311.

ences its own existence (as presumably any animal does), but experiences it *as* "mine," *as* "my own." Its being includes its owning of itself, "*my*self." But what *is* this owner? James tries to properly respect the traditional assumption that the owner is a transempirical, non-objectifiable, spiritual being distinct from the body which is "owned" by it—"an abstract numerical principle of identity," "my bare numerical distinction from other men," "number One," the "pure Ego." But his close descriptions of his own experience of self suggest that this assumption of Ego need not be made. He is left with the radical idea that the experiencing human *body is* the self.

But it is not a human body that neatly reflects itself within itself, a hermetically sealed container, but one which is fatefully open to the world around it, and which endures as itself through time because otherness which it concernfully makes its own involves a constant sort of excitement rooted in the enduring body. Identity of self is perilous, for modes of otherness can be incorporated that cannot be tolerated, thus personal identity contaminated, infected. This idea must be added to his later pluralistic metaphysics, something he did not live to do adequately, if we are to grasp the difficulties of achieving pluralism and tolerance in world community. As "things hang together from next to next," and we either *feel* the transitions and connections or we miss them entirely, there is a perilous element—a point also developed by Dewey, as we will see.

For James, the self includes *all* that I can call mine, and a startling vista opens. Others whose opinions of me matter to me are *my* others and form my "social self." As appropriated by me, *their* images of me belong in *my* body, says James![7] The directness of the connection is unsettling. For example, when reproved or condemned by the other, my feeling of shame "is simply my bodily person, in which your conduct immediately and without any reflection at all on my part works those muscular, glandular, and vascular changes which together make up the 'expression' of shame."

But surely, we hasten to point out, I retain a sense of myself as distinct from the other, and as having some ability to critically appraise what the other thinks. James concedes the general point. In addition to the "social self" he speaks of what he calls the "spiritual self," "the self of selves," that which can "disown" perhaps all of one's other "selves," but which cannot itself be disowned by itself, for it must own itself as its own if it would even try to disown itself.

But we are only half-way mollified by this allusion to our critical faculties. First, the "spiritual self" approximates to maturity only in

---

[7] *The Principles of Psychology*, p. 97.

adulthood, after much of the self is formed, and then only in moments. Second, when James tries to pin it down—its incessant discriminations, its acceptances or rejections of things around him—he finds only habitual small movements in the head, behind the eyes, or between the head and neck (or chest), e.g., the holding of the breath in response to something repugnant. Identity of self, he suggests strongly, is perilous: it is the body's continual process of excitement as it adjusts and readjusts to the shocks and enticements of the world, the otherness, so that a tolerable balance of otherness-in-this-body is maintained. He does not pretend, in his incipient phenomenology, to fully describe this process of interchange with the environment, but he opens our eyes to the troubling dimensions of our contamination phobias and purification fixations—archaic impulses running beneath the surface of our technologized and professionalized lives.

After James's death, Dewey developed the idea of the self as body, and its "uncanny precariousness." In a mid-life crisis, both personal and professional, Dewey retained the therapist F.M. Alexander.[8] Dewey's body hid itself from Dewey; the organic conditions of his consciousness hid themselves from his consciousness. It was only *after* Alexander moved Dewey's body into unaccustomed positions that Dewey could even imagine their *possibility*. Somehow the body must take the lead in *forming*, as well as testing, hypotheses about itself, for if consciousness cannot grasp its own conditions in the body, it must wait for the body to generate a new consciousness. If we do not imaginatively stretch scientific method to include the peculiar difficulties of the body-self's self-knowledge, then science with its technological accoutrements unguided by wisdom, and unaware that it is an art, will lie upon us oppressively—"like an incubus."[9] After nearly a decade of sessions with Alexander, Dewey formulated his own theory of the sub-conscious mind: "our immediate organic selections, rejections, welcomings, expulsions...of the most minute, vibratingly delicate nature. We are not aware of the qualities of most of these acts."[10] Not to get in touch with these organic discriminations is to fail to reveal the pollution phobias and purification fixations which rule and limit our intercourse with the world. It is to remain strangely, uncannily precarious, aggressive, perilous—ourselves the unknown enemy.

ᕼ

[8]See Frank P. Jones, *The Alexander Technique: Body Awareness in Action*, New York, 1976, pp. 94-105.

[9]*Experience and Nature*, p. 382.

[10]*Ibid.*, p. 299.

The work of the anthropologist, Mary Douglas, *Purity and Danger* (1966), began to break the silence about purification and taboo that prevails generally in the scholarly world today.[11] The topics of purification and taboo are themselves taboo, for professionals who strive to authorize themselves as pure minds are typically averse to intimately connecting body and self even in thought. But failing to face our archaic shunnings of unwashed bodies, people, and groups can only diminish our already slim chances of curbing our powers of total destruction—either suddenly catastrophic in the case of nuclear war, or more gradually in the irreversible poisoning and depletion of Earth's resources.

Douglas analyzes ancient Hebrews' purificational practices as embodying the belief, for example, that clean things live and locomote properly in their environments, and dirty things do not. Eels, for instance, locomote improperly in the water and hence are unclean.[12] It is particularly the eating of these unclean creatures which is polluting. There is dread that a disordered reality will enter the body and disorder the self. What is disordered outside the body must be kept outside. Likewise what is inestimably valuable if kept inside the body—saliva or blood for example—will be polluting if ejected improperly, particularly if it is recontacted or reincorporated in the body. Pollution involves mixing what ought to be kept separate, especially untoward mixing of the materials inside and those outside the body.

It is not just the *body—understood as a physiologist would objectify and numerate it*—which is disordered and polluted, but it is the body experiencing itself *as* itself, that is, the *self*. Here in particular James's analysis helps us understand what is happening. Though the self is a body, there is still personal self, privacy, inwardness. But now all this is reconfigured: it cannot be dissociated from the *inner* contents, cavities, fluids of the *body*. Since these are vulnerable to transgression, mixing, contamination, so is the self.

Edwyn Bevan notes trenchantly,

> Probably the great majority of people...would feel that water into which they had washed their teeth was unclean, not for others only, but for themselves; they would much rather put their hands into water which another man had washed his hands before them than into water into which they rinsed their mouths.[13]

[11]Mary Douglas, *Purity and Danger,* New York, 1980 [1966].
[12]*Ibid.*, pp. 55-56.
[13]Edwyn Bevan, *Hellenism and Christianity*, New York, 1922, Chapt. 8, "Dirt."

Allowing some room for individual and cultural differences, I think Bevan's account is true, and it points up the extreme importance of the inside of the body for the structure of self. The pre-reflective experiencing of the contents of our bodies must belong to the immediate sense of personal self, and to recontact or reincorporate one's own saliva, once ejected, must be experienced as reincorporating portions of one's person that are no longer personal, that have, as it were, died. If Bevan is right, it is even more alienating than contacting water in which *another* person has washed his *hands*. In any case, it is vastly, I think surprisingly, important. Its importance cannot be reduced to germ theory. If one's saliva is deposited on one's chin it is unlikely that the main cause of aversion is the idea that it might contain harmful bacteria.

I am this body, but I am also the being who identifies with *other* humans. When my own saliva is experienced by me as being in public space it is experienced by me as *experienceable* by *other* humans. Other humans must not be mixed with *this* one, myself, for that will tend to pollute and disintegrate the particularity of *this* human being. James spoke of the inner ("spiritual") and outer ("social") selves. My own saliva must not be recontacted or reincorporated by me, for that would be to mix a part of me that is no longer intimate and inner with what remains such.

Nevertheless, this "outer me," this social nexus of reciprocating recognitions, is not simply *not* me, either. It is the corporate body of humanity (at least local humanity) with which I deeply identify. That is why it affects me so profoundly and holds both immense promise at times and immense threat at others. Engulfment can be ecstatic joy or terrifying pollution and possession. Engulfment in compatible others in appropriate circumstances is consummating intimacy and ecstasy. Engulfment in incompatible others is self-alienation, disruption, or demonic possession. (Even in joyous erotic relationships, when lovers probe each other's mouths with their tongues, it is not clear that they would happily accept each other's saliva if it passed through space in the form of drool. It would be too public, too experienceable by *others*—even by *they themselves*, separated as they are in space and capable of objectifying themselves. The crudeness of the example is, of course, the point.)[14]

Note that it is fellow humans, not lampposts or dogs or cats, whose judgment of us is decisive. The "outer me" is the "social self." I am most

---

[14]The pollution hypothesis, particularly as it applies to exclusionary behavior practiced by academic professionals, is more fully developed in my *The Moral Collapse of the University: Professionalism, Purity, Alienation*, Albany, N.Y., 1990. This article overlaps with that book.

deeply threatened by others because, in a sense, I—as social self—am in a position to threaten myself. This is difficult to understand. We must wrench ourselves and pick out an unaccustomed topic, an unaccustomed *individual.* I identify with a *corporate* individual which is divided into sectors, levels, organs, each with its valence and value. To identify myself as a certain sort is to identify myself as belonging in a certain organ of the *social* body, and others already there can reject or accept me. Because I identify with them, their judgment of me is so decisive; in the sense of myself as social self I can reject myself.

But what does this mean, really, "the corporate individual" with its various "sectors, levels, organs"? The arch-foe of Cartesian psycho/physical dualism and atomism, Giambatista Vico, made a penetrating observation in his *Scienza Nuova* (1725): "Words are carried over from bodies and from properties of bodies to signify the institutions of mind and spirit"—and this is no merely verbal matter. In fact, so overwhelming is the shadowy and slippery mimetic interchange of this body as it exists with others in the surround, that the image of a single, huge, social or group-body pervades all that we do. I am trying to clarify Vico's insight that the sense and meaning of the particular body gets fused with the sense and meaning of "institutions of mind and spirit"—the corporate individual, the group, *that* body with its various corporate levels and organs. Mechanistic science fixes, objectifies, and isolates a particular human organism at a unique point in space and time before the "omniscient" observer, and analyzes this body into causal conditions, elements, functions. But the organism's archaic consciousness fuses this particular body with the bodies of others around us so that a *corporate* body, the outer self, is formed. (Even when threatened by others we may covertly mime their mode of attack even as we overtly shrink from them. There is no assurance that we will be "thrown back upon our own resources" and "find our individual center" when attacked by others; hence occurrences of masochism.)

Particularly evident in moments of stress, but not limited to these moments, each human organism is absorbed in the corporate body, posted at various parts and levels of it. (So how much does it matter that John Quincey Jones is counted as *one* being?) Intellectuals, for example, tend to identify with other intellectuals, and the intellectuality of all tends to be associated automatically with the head, the capital, the directive agency of both the corporate and the individual body. Heads associate with heads, arms with arms, feet with feet, etc. As we actually live the personal body, it is the microcosm of the corporate body, the social group and its values and valences. Those who are in *middle* management execute others' directives, and are the "right arms" of the *top* or *head.* Those who do the *lowest* work in society do that which pertains to the lowest functions of the corporate body, its pedal and eliminative functions, janitors, sewer workers, etc. It is no accident that typically those who perform the most menial or repulsive tasks are foreigners of color imported into the corporate organism at its lowest levels. We think of Blacks in the South, Mexicans and Chinese in California, as much earlier it was Spaniards and Moors in Rome.

How do we relate to others who occupy different zones of the corporate body? Our membranes are permeable to psychical pollution from untowardly adjacent parts and "organs" of the social "organism." Ernst Cassirer recounts the Hindu myth of Purusha who is sacrificed to the gods, cut up, and his various body parts become the essence of various castes of persons.[15] Presumably we academic intellectuals belong to the head. But what if we get too close to lower parts of the social organism—the *untouchables?* Like Cassirer, most of us are appalled by this archaism, and would like to believe that it belongs in the past. Yet if Mary Douglas is correct, we still live at this archaic level, along with more recent levels achieved.

So we are threatened by pollution not only by untoward transits of matter across the boundaries of the personal body. This occurs, of course, but we must amplify and enrich the context. We are polluted by untoward contacts between ourselves and others within the *social* organism. We dread to recontact or reincorporate our own saliva, for example, because we experience it as experienceable by others in public space. We dread our most intimate "mineness" to be mixed with the others' otherness because we dread being disrupted at the heart of our private and personal selves. We particularly dread the most significant others, significant *either* because they must authorize one's inclusion within a particular social caste, *or* because they are clearly beneath one. It seems to be the former who are most threatening, however, at least sometimes. If I, who identify myself as an intellectual, am excluded by other intellectuals, I cannot place myself in a segment of corporate identity, and my identity, my reality, is imperiled.

[15]Ernst Cassirer, *The Philosophy of Symbolic Forms,* Vol. II, *Mythical Thought,* New Haven and London, 1955, pp. 54-56. Some philosophers maintain that only literal statements, directly testable by science, can be true. So they reject all statements about corporate individuals or group minds as "merely metaphorical." The most extreme form of this position (in the work of the positivist Hans Kelsen, for example) reads like this: Beliefs are caused by events inside the individual's body, therefore only individuals have minds, not groups. But in response: The cause of a belief does not adequately characterize it, only what it is *of* does so. And when the believer belongs to a group, and the beliefs are *of* what the others' beliefs are *of,* he or she participates in the group's beliefs, the group's mind–and, I want to say, "body." Concerning initiation into "thought collectives," see Ludwik Fleck, *Genesis and Development of a Scientific Fact,* Chicago, 1979 [1935]. Initiation rituals as purification rituals are treated in my *The Moral Collapse of the University.*

Now, my writing of the organism which is corporate or social has been metaphorical. I know no literal language that discloses equally well how we relate to each other as individuals who are corporeal and socially constituted. In illuminating to some extent these relations and realities, the metaphor of the corporate organism is true *as* a metaphor. It is not a literal truth, but it does not follow that it is false. Also, just because it is not the complete truth about these matters it does not follow that it is false. Nor does it follow that great deviations from the metaphor must be false (as great deviations from literal truths must be false). For example, there might be circumstances in which we could achieve more illumination by referring to *two* corporate organisms. Perhaps there are times and places in which nation states meet in such basic antagonism and stress that they can subsist together in the same space for only a short time. In order to maintain minimal cohesion as a corporate body, one must anihilate the other, and spread over everything in the perceptible surround. Perhaps some light is thrown on recent events in China to say that the erection in Tiananmen Square of another nation's corporate symbol—the Statue of Liberty—was so incompatible when inserted in that corporate organism that the head of that government was convulsed; the statue was violently expelled and those who erected it massacred. Then the unthinkable event was indeed suppressed from consciousness—"it never occurred."

৯

I believe the dire warnings made by noted ecologists are justified. They observe technologists' hubris—and "advanced" nations' greedy exploitation of Earth's resources, the common store—and point out that our plundering of Nature threatens both our spiritual and eventually our physical existence. Some ecologists claim our irreversible wastage of top-soil, our poisoning of air, water, and remaining soil, and our expunging of untold species of plants and animals is bringing the Cenozoic age to a close—the last 65 million years which saw the evolution of the marvelous array of mammals and birds, of grasses, shrubs, and flowering plants.[16]

These ecologists point out that perhaps the deepest problem is that we are unable to imagine the magnitude of what we are doing. Again, I agree. We need a new mode of consciousness. But how do we get this? No doubt, just being apprised of some of the gross facts helps some. But I would return us to the lessons of James and Dewey. A radical and perhaps frightening change of consciousness is needed to confront a

---

[16]For example, Thomas Berry, *The Dream of the Earth,* San Francisco, 1988.

radically new and dangerous situation. Friction between peoples may spark the final blasts, or, more likely, our exploitation of resources and disregard for others' needs and rights threatens to deplete and disorder the planet beyond its ability to replenish itself.

But how is this new consciousness to be achieved? If no straining within the present consciousness can reveal some of the crucial conditions of this very consciousness, then this consciousess cannot radically change or enlarge itself. It cannot do what is needed, cannot alter its own conditions. The conditions I mean are those habitual, practically automatic discriminations by the body-self—its welcomings and rejectings, its routine or delighted ingestions of the compatible, and its disgusted expulsions of the foreign, novel, incompatible—discriminations by which the very identity of the self is maintained in its interfusion with otherness. I mean an unconscious purification ritual which is so basic that it cannot be questioned without disturbing the foundations of the self and provoking ontological anxiety.

We are told an important truth when we hear that never before has one animal gained dominion over all others, and that plants and animals in their proper balance contribute essentially to life. And it is true that we powerfully and blindly resist acknowledging that we are a species of animal. We believe we are so special and so cunning that we can have our greed, our egoism, our pride, and our planet—all four. But these truths will be of little avail if we are not effectively directed to the minute movements of our own animal bodies which keep us alienated from other forms of life and from the fuller development of our own selves. We are too often alienated from other forms of *human* life—black, brown, dark, hence "dirty, dangerous, evil"—not to mention the other animals whom we routinely treat execrably. An essential element of Dewey's notion of intelligence is raw courage, guts: the willingness and patience to let one's own body disclose itself. He writes in an introduction to one of Alexander's books that we must correct Pavlov.[17] Instead of thinking of conditioned reflexes exclusively as forces that determine us, we can recondition some of our reflexes. This is a new reach of *freedom* and a fuller development of consciousness and self.

ক

Truly, the difficulty of imagining the magnitude of our difficulties is awesome; probably we will not make it. But we must believe that we can, for if we do not we are *surely* lost—a self-fulfilling prophecy. We

[17]F.M. Alexander, *The Use of the Self,* New York, 1932.

cannot assume that our present institutions will bail us out. I do not mean merely long-established religions. I mean our highly profession-alized secular institutions replete with their technology and "rational management." *All* these institutions were formed on the basis of assumptions laid down long before we learned that we can destroy the planet. It is natural to go to intellectuals in universities, the "problem solvers." But our difficulties are greater than mere *problems,* and as Whitehead pointed out, the 20th century university is founded on the dualistic and atomistic principles of 17th century natural science. Most importantly, I think that in no other place is purification ritual more rife and more blind to itself than in universities. The "pure", profes-sionalized intellect forever disengages itself from the body, the "execrementitious stuff," as James put it, which is the sorry remainder of the dualized self. Academic departments and professional groups are typically secure seats of intellectual fastidiousness and evasive disregard of the mundane or disgusting underside of life. Many philosophers today, I believe, are the most professionally crippled of all, most completely and least excusably cut off from our own American philosophers and their alive awareness of body, environing Nature, and the cosmos.

I agree with James that the basis of the self is an organic excite-ment. We can only try to free and discipline this excitement, educate it, so that the scope of our identifications and sympathies is broadened and deepened. Failing this, the beautiful Chinese proverb, "The Heavens, the Earth, and I are one flesh" remains merely pretty words—"mere sylabub and flattery and spongecake" as James, again, put it.[18] Pragmatism is more than the genteel "conversation of mankind" carried on in pathetically few of the 100,000 learned journals. It is redolent not just of paper and of hotel corridors, but of the Earth and our daily lives.

[18]William James, *The Varieties of Religious Experience: A Study in Human Nature,* New York, 1902, p. 356.

Beyond Individualism and Collectivism

James Ogilvy

At the heart of the old ideological conflict between East and West lies the opposition between individualism and collectivism. The Marxist-Leninist tradition put the interests of society as a whole above the interests of the individual, while western democracies are willing to protect individual liberties even at the expense of the interests of the collective. The recent demise of Marxist-Leninism should not be taken as a simple victory for the rights of the individual over the interests of the collective. As Robert Bellah and his colleagues have shown, unrestrained individualism has its costs. Before hurling collectivism on the dust-bin of history, then, it may be worth taking a second look at the dialectical relationship between collectivism and individualism.

Each approach has obvious merits. Society cannot afford irresponsible acts by individuals whose selfish whims may harm others. Further, individuals are most free to achieve self-realization in the context of a healthy society. As for the merits of individualism, none is more evident than the products of innovation and creativity that flower when individuals are given free play for their imagination.

Toting up the possible benefits of individualism and collectivism doesn't settle the matter of their ultimate correctness, however. The differences between individualists and collectivists will not be settled by some utilitarian calculus that could tally the greatest good for the greatest number at the end of two histories guided by individualist or collectivist ideologies. For the differences between individualist and collectivist go beyond guesses about probable historical consequences of the two different approaches. The differences between individualists and collectivists are ontological. They touch the very root of what it is to be a human being.

In the individualist tradition, the individual is the fundamental ontological unit, the alpha and omega of social philosophy. Society supposedly begins with the coming together of individuals whose being as individuals is already assumed. The social contract theories of Locke, Hobbes, and Rousseau assume the existence of already constituted individuals who come together to form society. Without the benefits of civil society, these Robinson Crusoe-like individuals would run the danger of retreating to the jungle; they would fall back into that "state of nature" described by Hobbes as a hostile environment where life is "nasty, brutish, and short." Rather than submit to the war of each against all, these already constituted individuals enter into a social compact. Civil society and the mechanisms of the state are then constructed as means to protect the ends of individual rights. In the individualist creation myth, then, the earth was not without form and void prior to the emergence of the state. Instead, there were individuals ontologically given on the first day of creation. They shape the state as a means toward satisfying their own ends. So, on the last day of creation, it is the interests of individuals—their liberties and their rights—that define the final purposes and measure the success of the state apparatus. Individuals stand at the beginning and at the end of this ontological, cosmogonical creation myth.

In the collectivist tradition, the story, the ontological myth is very different. For Marx, as for Hegel before him, the individual is not the concrete beginning point but an abstraction from the whole interconnected web of existence. Whether the whole is viewed in the idealist tradition as *Geist*, or world spirit, or in the materialist tradition as *Gattungswesen* or the species-being of man, both Hegel and Marx saw the individual as a product of alienation from that prior whole. As Alexandre Kojeve puts it in his interpretation of Hegel, mankind comes on the scene as a herd, not as an accidental assemblage of pre-constituted individuals. Mankind is first social, at however primitive a level, and only after certain social dynamics have been played out do individuals emerge as a social product.

For Hegel the relevant dynamic is the life and death struggle that issues in the master-slave relationship. Hegel's genius consisted in seeing that it was the slave, not the master, who would gain the greater degree of individual self-consciousness by virtue of a sharper confrontation with death and nature that is more immediate than the master's, whose relationship with existence is forever mediated by the slave. Marx's genius consisted in articulating the different aspects and stages of the slave's alienation, particularly under the conditions of capitalist production. Both Hegel and Marx see history as the progressive overcoming of alienation. Individuality is a kind of necessary and inevitable mistake that the collective must make if it is to develop from an undifferentiated herd on the first day of creation to a well-functioning, classless society on the last—that seventh day after the revolution when the alienation of the individual from the collective shall be overcome. Just as the individual served as the alpha and omega of the individualist creation myth, so society stands at the beginning and at the end of the collectivist creation myth. Just as society served as a means to the end of individual gratification, so the stages of individual alienation appear like the labors of Hercules on an Odyssey which the collective human spirit must traverse before the individual can return to his true home at the bosom of the collective.

There, then, are the ontological creation myths at the heart of the ideological contradiction between the individualist and collectivist tradition. It is important to appreciate the depth of the difference, the degree to which each ontology can be cogently interpreted as delusional within the context of the opposing paradigm. Like the therapist who can interpret a patient's resistances to therapy as part of the problem to be overcome, the proponents of each paradigm can interpret the resistances of their opponents as founded on fundamental errors that will be overcome in the course of history. Collectivists can hope that individualists will overcome their regrettable alienation from society. Individualists can hope that collectivists will someday see the merits of liberating individuals from the yoke of the state. Each tradition becomes a regrettable if necessary chapter in the longer, more comprehensive story that the other tradition has to tell. And each tradition consistently rejects the story told by the other, not because the other story is heard, understood, and the calculus of benefits computed differently; rather, the calculations are fundamentally incommensurable because the units of measure differ at an ontological level. Social benefits that are seen as the end of the collectivist creation myth are mere means to the gratification of individuals in the individualist creation myth. Individual self-realization seen as the end of the individualist creation myth, is seen as a means to bringing about a healthy society in the collectivist creation myth. Given the dialectical symmetry of these opposed approaches to means and ends, there is little hope of these two paths converging at an omega point where the trade-offs between individualism and collectivism would balance, or better yet, achieve a synergistic or symbiotic relationship. Because the two ontological myths are so different in their appraisals of both the beginnings and the endings of their respective stories, there is little likelihood that their tellers could ever agree on what counts as a happy ending.

So much for social ontology and its expression in creation myths. The point of elaborating these myths is not to choose among them but to grasp the symmetry of their opposition and the consequent unlikelihood of either side convincing the other in a purely ideological debate. As long as each side holds on to its ontology, the argument of the other side can be deflected as the product of a delusional process, and each side has a fully cogent account for how and why its opponents have become so deluded. Until both sides appreciate the paradigmatic character of their opposition, that is, until both sides appreciate the fact that their arguments will be reinterpreted through the eyes of a different world view with a different social ontology, neither side will be truly heard by the other. Misinterpretation will persist, not because English and Russian are so different, but because the ontological vocabularies of individualism and collectivism describe different worlds. In the world and in the world view (or paradigm) of the collectivist, society or the whole is the fundamental unit of existence. In the world and world view of the individualist, the individual is the fundamental, ontological unit.

It is as if socialists see the individual as the intersection of two preexisting lines of relationship, and individualists see the lines of social relationship as coming after and connecting pre-existing points. The axioms of their respective social geometries differ accordingly—and like two parallel lines in Euclidian geometry, never the twain shall meet.

In order to get beyond the opposition between individualism and collectivism, philosophical debates along the lines just described will not succeed as an alternative to brute force. But brute force is obsolete in the era of nuclear weapons. So what hope do we have if neither force nor persuasion are available as means for mediating our differences?

I believe that there is hope in a dialogue that digs down to the ontological roots of these ideological differences. Each side must appreciate the degree to which not only the other but also itself is trapped in a so-called hermeneutic circle. Hermeneutics is the discipline of interpretation. The hermeneutic circle is the closed loop in which a world view interprets the world in ways that support its own paradigm. A given epistemology supports an ontology which in turn supports the original epistemology.

Just as flies knit together an integrated world view from many images coming through the hundreds of facets on their spherical eyes, and frogs see a world where flies appear more prominently than the background, so individualists and collectivists alike tend to see worlds that nourish and support their own respective predispositions. Where nature's ecology can support and sustain niches where frogs with their eyes for seeing individual points can co-exist with flies who see the whole as they look in all directions at once, the ecology of cultures and nation-states has reached a condition that can no longer support such differences of vision. It is as if the frog's tongue and the fly's bite had suddenly gained the power to obliterate the whole swamp if sufficiently provoked.

So the time has come to acknowledge not only the fact that we see the world fundamentally differently, but also, that we must each dig down to the roots of our respective visions of the world to see whether that seeing of the world is in fact based upon a fundamental ontology, or whether our fundamentally opposed ontologies are not in fact founded upon different ways of seeing. If we can break into both hermeneutic circles at the point of seeing rather than at the point of being, if we can examine our paradigms and epistemologies rather than persist in opposing our ontologies, then there is some hope of liberating ourselves from the ontological creation myths that underlie and perpetuate the stalemate of conflicting ideologies.

There is hope for a further revisioning of social relationships within and between East and West because the process has already begun. On both sides of the ideological divide, theorists have begun to question their own ontological creation myths. We are already in the midst of a process of demythologizing. In the West, several scholars have begun to question whether we haven't overdone individualism in the western tradition. At the same time, the costs of collectivism and the merits of individualism have now been acknowledged in the eastern bloc, as the remarkable turn in the Soviet Union and Eastern Europe have demonstrated.

In reviewing the evidence from both traditions, it will be helpful to attend to the time-honored distinction between theory and practice. Despite theoretical doubts about the status of individualism in the western tradition, there is evidence to indicate that in practice the West is becoming even more individualistic. In what follows I propose to devote most of my attention to (a) reviewing some of the evidence for increasing individualism in the United States; (b) interpreting that evidence in light of several different theories of individualism drawn from the western tradition; and (c) reinterpreting the same evidence as showing us several different versions of individualism.

While it is worth touching on developments in the Marxist tradition at least enough to indicate not only the symmetry of the original dialectical stand-off, but also the symmetry of responses that might overcome that stand-off, I will not presume to know the Marxist tradition as well as I know my own. Nor would it be appropriate to demythologize the ontological creation myths of another tradition. Demythologizing, like psychotherapy, is a practice that must be performed with the willing and enthusiastic participation of the analysand. My assumption is that most Soviets and East Europeans have already questioned the roots and merits of collectivism. The more urgent assignment at this time is a questioning of individualism before this perpetual dialectic tilts too far toward the rights and interests of individuals.

The Growth of Individualism in America

There can be little doubt that individualism is one of the cornerstones of the American tradition. The Founding Fathers of the Constitution were heavily influenced by individualist teachings in the philosophies of Locke and Rousseau. And early American philosophers and essayists added even more weight to the final authority of individual conscience as opposed to the laws of the state. "Why has every man a conscience, then?" asks Thoreau. "I think that we should be men first, and subjects afterward. It is not desirable to cultivate a respect for the law, so much as for the right. The only obligation which I have a right to assume is to do at any time what I think right." (Thoreau, "Civil Disobedience")

In his famous essay on "Self-Reliance," Emerson chimes in: "No law can be sacred to me but that of my nature. Good and bad are but names very readily transferable to that or this; the only right is what is after my constitution; the only wrong what is against it." In these and other similar statements, the founders of American individualism make it perfectly clear that the individual's appeal to his own conscience provides a higher court than the law of the land or the general will of the collective.

Individualism as construed by Thoreau and Emerson allowed for lofty defenses of civil disobedience in situations where the state condones injustices like slavery. But the dangers of such strong appeals to individualism were already apparent to Tocqueville. "Individualism is a calm and considered feeling which disposes each citizen to isolate himself from the mass of his fellows and withdraw into the circle of family and friends; with this little society formed to his taste, he gladly leaves the greater society to look after itself."[1] Not only is there danger to "the greater society" when individuals leave it to look after itself. Further,

---

[1] *Democracy in America,* ed. Mayer, p. 506.

there is the psychological risk of implosion. "Each man is forever thrown back on himself alone, and there is danger that he may be shut up in the solitude of his own heart."[2]

Throughout most of the 19th and 20th centuries, individualism has held the upper hand in this ongoing theoretical debate. There are exceptions. In his book, *Mind, Self, and Society* (1934), philosopher George Herbert Mead directly challenged the ontological priority of the individual self. "The process out of which the self arises is a social process which implies interaction of individuals in the group, implies the pre-existence of the group....[T]he origin and foundations of the self, like those of thinking, are social."

For the most part, however, claims for the primacy of society, or the collective, or the group were met by authoritative statements like David Riesman's in his essay (and book by the same title), "Individualism Reconsidered" (1951): "We must give every encouragement to people to develop their private selves—to escape from groupism—while realizing that, in many cases, they will use their freedom in unattractive or 'idle' ways.... I am insisting that no ideology, however noble, can justify the sacrifice of an individual to the needs of the group."[3]

Riesman finds it necessary to reconsider individualism because he realizes that its form is changing. He observes that the process of modernization freed people from external restraints imposed by religion or an hereditary aristocracy. But the individuals thus freed carried with them many of those same restraints, which they had *internalized*. "These men were bound by a character orientation I have termed 'inner-direction': they were guided by internalized goals and ideals which made them appear to be more individualistic than they actually were."[4] Only because one could assume that social restraints were still operative, in internalized form, was it possible to praise and pursue the virtues of individualism. "In sum, it proved possible in the West in early modern times to carry individualism to its limits of usefulness—and, in some cases, far beyond these limits—because a fair amount of social cohesiveness was taken for granted."[5]

It is precisely this assumption of social cohesiveness that has come into question since the 1950s. Social cohesiveness can no longer be taken for granted, largely because individualism has been pursued to its limits and beyond. Since the 1950s, individualism has in fact increased in the United States. And for the very reason that it has increased in

[2]*Ibid.*, p. 508.
[3]*Individualism Reconsidered*, Doubleday Anchor, 1955, pp. 26f.
[4]*Ibid.*, p. 13.
[5]*Ibid.*, p. 14.

practice, the theoretical questioning of its costs and benefits has also increased. Let us first consider some of the evidence for the factual increase of individualism in practice. Then I shall take up some alternative theoretical interpretations of the evidence for the growth of individualism.

In the Values and Lifestyles (VALS) Program at SRI International (formerly Stanford Research Institute), a number of us have engaged in empirical research on American values. Arnold Mitchell, the founder of the program, developed a typology to describe and track different lifestyle segments. Partly influenced by David Riesman, Mitchell chose as a fundamental dimension of differentiation the distinction between the "Inner-Directed" and the "Outer-Directed." The Outer-Directed are those who live their lives according to external restraints, overt or covert. They want to "keep up with the Joneses." They want to fit into the group by conforming to its norms. The Inner-Directed, on the other hand, listen to their inner voice for guidance.

Despite all the rhetoric in favor of individualism in America, most of the American population is more Outer-Directed than Inner-Directed, at least as these terms are operationally defined by responses to questions on the VALS questionnaire. Just as Riesman described the freed individuals of early modernity, so also in the America of the 1950s, most so-called individualists had in fact internalized the norms of society. Given the choice—which they were given by the rhetoric of individualistic free choice—most Americans tended to choose freely the very same values that had earlier been socially imposed. As Philip Slater put it in his trenchant critique of individualism, "Our society gives far more leeway to the individual to pursue his own ends, but, since *it* defines what is worthy and desirable, everyone tends, independently but monotonously, to pursue the same things in the same way."[6]

We can encapsulate the dialectical essence of what both Riesman and Slater are describing with the expression *conformist individualism.* This label threatens to be self-cancelling—an oxymoron. Aren't individualists the most likely to be non-conformists? So it would seem. But Riesman's talk of 'internalization' of external norms, and Slater's complaint that individuals abuse the leeway of individualism by choosing "independently but monotonously," are both intended to question the quick assumption that individualists will be non-conformists. They are both pointing to the fact that individualism, whether in early modern or late suburban forms, can be remarkably conformist in its actual expression.

---

[6]*The Pursuit of Loneliness,* Beacon Press, Boston, 1970, p. 9.

The 1960s introduced a major break in the tradition of *conformist individualism*. In the 1960s there arose, as if by a dialectical 'turning over into its opposite', a new kind of *non-conformist collectivism*. In the 1960s the youth rebelled *en masse*. The youth movement of the sixties was non-conformist—witness the importance of long hair and styles of dress—but remarkably collectivist. Solidarity among members of the counterculture was manifested in mass demonstrations and in communal lifestyles. Even in their non-conformity to mainstream styles, the blue denim on political activists and the tie-dyed costumes of hippies were as instantly recognizable as military uniforms.

The longer term effects of the 1960s were as complex and rich with internal dialectics as the reversal from conformist individualism in the 1950s to non-conformist collectivism in the 1960s. By the 1970s the Vietnam war was winding down, inflation was ratcheting up, and unemployment increased as the baby boom youth of the sixties entered a labor market constricted by oil-starved recessions. The rebelliousness of the 1960s had loosened the ties to old authorities. But the solidarity of "the Movement" disappeared as students graduated from college and faced the job market each on his or her own. With neither loyalty to the old establishment nor solidarity with their peers, many baby boomers slipped into what Tom Wolfe dubbed "the Me-decade."

The 1970s were experienced by many as individualistic to the point of rampant selfishness. Psychoanalytic literature became preoccupied with narcissism. Important testaments of the times include Christopher Lasch's book, *The Culture of Narcissism* (1979), Heinz Kohut's *The Analysis of the Self* (1971), and Richard Sennett's *The Fall of Public Man* (1977). In each of these books one finds a strong critique of the withdrawal of the individual into what Tocqueville called "the solitude of his own heart." But more important, one finds an acknowledgement of the historicity of that heart, its malleability under the influence of changing social and historical conditions.

Sennett is particularly acute on the difference between the new notion of personality as unique, and the Enlightenment ideal of a universal human nature. Lacking the Enlightenment belief in natural character, we no longer pursue a universal science of the sympathies and humors; yet, "We need to understand this alien notion of a natural realm of the self because we continue today to believe in notions of human rights which arose because of it."[7]

History has come full circle from Thoreau's call for individual civil disobedience against the state on behalf of the rights of slaves. What these modern critics are arguing is that the voice of individual con-

[7]Sennett, *The Fall of Public Man*, New York, 1977, p. 89.

science eventually defeats itself if that voice represents only one unique personality. If the voice of individual conscience has, as Riesman and Slater suggested, already internalized the rules of society, then that voice can be trusted not to deviate too radically from the collective will. Or if that voice of individual conscience speaks from the universal text of a fixed and timeless human nature, then all voices can be expected to speak as one. In either case, whether by internalization of social mores or by the assumption of a universal human nature, the defense of human rights can be justified by reference to a universally shared human condition. But once the social cohesion that had been taken for granted is shattered into shards of personalities whose uniqueness is more important than their commonality, then the defense of universal human rights is thrown into question. Suddenly it is every man for himself, and every woman for herself. Thus we entered the eighties.

During the late 1970s and the 1980s we have tracked an increase among the Inner-Directed from about 15% of the adult American population up to 21%. Other indicators also suggest an increase in individualism since the 1960s. Dan Yankelovich summarizes years of survey research in his book, *New Rules*. There he speaks of an increase in individual *self-expression* since the sixties. Other survey data from the National Opinion Research Center (NORC) at the University of Chicago show that between 1968 and 1976 the percentage of people willing to be bossed around on the job declined from 56% of the population to 36%. Each of these indicators—from VALS, from Yankelovich, and from NORC—suggests that individualism is on the increase *in fact*, even as the theorists I have quoted are becoming ever more critical of individualism *in theory*.

Since 1980 the most significant work on the factual spread as well as the theoretical critique of individualism has surely been Robert Bellah's *Habits of the Heart*. Bellah and his co-workers conducted in-depth interviews with over 200 people. What they found is very consistent with the dangers described by Tocqueville and Sennett: "If selves are defined by their preferences, but those preferences are arbitrary, then each self constitutes its own moral universe, and there is finally no way to reconcile conflicting claims about what is good in itself."[8]

One of the interviewees, to whom they give the name Brian, tries to explain his commitments: "Why is integrity important and lying bad? I don't know. It just is. It's just so basic. I don't want to be bothered with challenging that. It's part of me. I don't know where it came from, but

---

[8]*Habits of the Heart: Individualism and Commitment in American Life,* University of California Press, 1985, p. 76.

it's very important."[9] Bellah and his colleagues are sensitive to the loss
of a shared moral vocabulary, as is evident in Brian's inability to defend
or justify his values: "He lacks a language to explain what seem to be the
real commitments that define his life, and to that extent the
commitments themselves are precarious."[10] Brian seems to have values,
but he cannot explain how he got them or where they came from.
"'Values' turn out to be the incomprehensible, rationally indefensible
thing that the individual chooses when he or she has thrown off the last
vestige of external influence and reached pure, contentless freedom.
The ideal self in its absolute freedom is completely 'unencumbered'....The improvisational self chooses values to express itself;
but it is not constituted by them as from a pre-existing source. This
notion of an unencumbered self is derived not only from psychotherapy, but much more fundamentally from modern philosophy,
from Descartes, Locke, and Hume, who affect us more than we
imagine."[11]

Let me summarize this brief literature review of the debate over
individualism in America as follows: First, there is no question about
the fact that, from the writings of Emerson and Thoreau through to the
practices of people in the 1970s and 1980s, individualism is central to
the American tradition. But second, where the early theoretical critiques of individualism, from Tocqueville to Mead, took place against a
background of strong social cohesion, by the 1970s and 1980s one
could presuppose neither the pre-1950s social cohesion described by
Riesman, nor the social conformity that characterized the 1950s, nor
the solidarity in non-conformity that characterized the sixties. By the
1970s and 1980s individualism, both in theory and in practice, had
devolved from a defense of the individual's moral conscience to dia-
tribes against self-indulgence.

Bellah and his colleagues find themselves forced to level the following indictment: "We believe that much of the thinking about the self of
educated Americans, thinking that has become almost hegemonic in
our universities and much of the middle class, is based on inadequate
social science, impoverished philosophy, and vacuous theology."[12]

I believe that part of the "impoverished philosophy" that Bellah has
in mind is the individualist ontological creation myth. The notion of
the unencumbered self—as inherited "from Descartes, Locke, and
Hume, who affect us more than we imagine"—is precisely that alpha

[9]*Ibid.*, p.7.
[10]*Ibid.*, p.8.
[11]*Ibid.*, pp. 79f.
[12]*Ibid.*, p. 84.

and omega, that always already constituted individual who supposedly exists prior to and after all social and historical conditioning.

Writers like Philip Slater, Christopher Lasch, Richard Sennett and Robert Bellah are actively engaged in demythologizing the individualist ontological creation myth, even as opinion research and trends in popular culture suggest an increase in individualism in America. In the concluding section of this paper I would like to show how this demythologizing of American individualism points the way toward reframing the ideological conflict between Marxism and democracy.

Individualism Reconsidered Yet Again

Back in the fifties and early sixties, a great deal of social criticism was aimed at *alienation*. Then in the late sixties and seventies the lament shifted its focus to *narcissism*. There is a logic to this shift of emphasis. Much of the talk about alienation took the form of a tacit assumption that healthy persons were alienated from an impersonal, therefore unhealthy society. The shift in vocabulary from 'alienation' to 'narcissism' reflects a growing awareness that those who are alienated do not remain healthy. It is not the case that free and healthy individuals—unencumbered selves—simply choose whether to live independently when they feel alienated from society, or to form social contracts that overcome alienation by binding the individual back into solidarity with others. This scenario reflects faith in ontological individualism. The shift to talk about narcissism suggests a crumbling of that faith in the form of an acknowledgment that the alienated individual is *less* of an individual.

Rather than seeing healthy individuals alienated from an unhealthy society, the shift to talk about narcissism relocates the pathology in the individual, even though the authors I've mentioned are inclined to blame society for the individual's pathology. Rather than taking society to task for being too *im*personal, however, Slater, Lasch, Sennett and Bellah are all agreed that the greater danger lies in the invasion of the private realm by public institutions that are becoming *too personal*. The family planning clinic, the personnel office, the company psychotherapist, and the career guidance counselor all represent instances of what Jurgen Habermas has described as the "colonization" of the private realm of practical reason by the public realm with its instrumental reason.

If it is true, as these authors suggest, that institutional solutions to alienation and narcissism are likely to do more harm than good to the extent that they violate the very boundaries of privacy they were meant to shore up, then what hope is there for moving beyond pathological individualism? Can the bruised self of the narcissist be trusted to save itself? Can public institutions mend the tear of alienation without doing more harm than good?

I believe that there may be a way out, a third alternative that relies on neither the private self nor the public institutions of society or the state. I believe that part of the problem lies in the formulation of the problem in terms of a stark contrast between the public and the private realms. The starkness of that contrast is one more reflection of the dialectical contradiction between individualism and collectivism and their respective creation myths. I believe that the way out lies not with choosing one alternative or the other as savior, neither the private individual nor the public collective; rather, the way out lies in smoothing out the sharpness of the dichotomy between these dialectically opposed moments.

As long as the conflict between individualism and collectivism is conceived as a real conflict between two real opponents—The Individual vs. The Collective—I see no hope of resolution given the self-justifying nature of the symmetrically opposed hermeneutic circles. As long as both individualists and collectivists assume the ontological priority of either the individual or the collective, and are able to support that ontological priority with a corresponding epistemology or paradigm, then, as stated earlier, the twain shall never meet. There is no omega point of convergence that would constitute a happy ending for both individualists and collectivists because they *see* happiness as differently as the fly and the frog see the swamp.

The way out lies not with opting for one ontology or the other, but in appreciating the epistemological, paradigmatic character of the conflict. Once we appreciate the degree to which our paradigms support ontologies that are irreconcilable, then we are thrown back to questioning those paradigms and their corresponding ontologies. And once that questioning has begun, there opens up an opportunity for completely reframing the whole dialectic: *rather than seeing the individual and the collective as ontologically given and concrete, individuality and collectivity can be recast as equal and opposite abstractions from the concrete life of everyday communities.*

No individual is ever completely isolated. And no actual community has ever extended its reach to the entire species. Both individuality and species-being are abstractions from the concrete, day to day reality of life in limited communities. The concrete starting point of social theory should be neither the solitary individual—as much a fiction as Robinson Crusoe—nor the all-inclusive collective, which has never been concretely experienced by anyone. Not *one*, not *all*, but *some*. The concrete starting point of social theory should be those limited collectives we call communities, those groups of face to face others usually numbering somewhere between five people and five thousand people.

Once we reframe both individuality and collectivity as equal and opposite abstractions from concrete community, then both the individualist and the collectivist creation myths appear as instances of what Alfred North Whitehead called "the fallacy of misplaced concreteness."[13] To the naive observer, unbiased by either the individualist or collectivist tradition, nothing could be more obvious than the fact that real life as lived by real people always involves exchanges and interchanges among finite groups: language, commerce, work, play. It is only the very rare shepherd or lighthouse keeper who gets through a day without hearing a single human word from another. And even the daydreams of the solitary are shaped by what they have experienced of human interaction.

At the opposite extreme, it is only the rare astronaut or mystic who has had an opportunity to *experience* the human species as a single totality. The rest of us can speak the words, "the human species," and we can do our best to identify and empathize with people at great cultural and geographical distances. But the fact remains that the idea of all human beings remains an abstraction as compared with the concreteness of our face-to-face community.

It may be argued that we *ought* to experience an immediate fellow feeling with all human beings, that it is callous to be indifferent to the sufferings of others just because they happen to be half way around the world rather than next door. Such arguments are worth making. It may well be the case that the measure of one's psychological and spiritual development lies in the degree to which one identifies, as the Buddhists say, with all living creatures. Perhaps. But the point I am making has nothing to do with moral exhortation. The point I am making is epistemological and ontological rather than moral. I am suggesting that the universalist ideal of embracing the entire human species, whether it can or cannot, or ought or ought not to be *achieved* by dint of moral persuasion, is in any case not ontologically or epistemologically *given*. And consequently, the concept of the universal collective is an abstraction, an idea reached by various steps of extrapolation from the concrete experience of what are always very limited collectivities.

The same argument can and must be turned around against individualism. A long tradition from Emerson and Thoreau to Erik Erikson (inventor of the concept of the 'identity crisis') may well have some-

---

[13] *Science and the Modern World*

thing important to teach, namely, the need to become your own person, to be responsible, to think for yourself, to exercise a degree of subjectivity that is creative, to be more than a carbon copy of the influences that shaped you. All these exhortations can be put in ways that make a great deal of sense, even to the collectivist. How you, as an individual, *ought* to be is not at issue here. The point is that individual autonomy is *achieved*, not *given*. And consequently, the concept of the utterly isolated, self-sufficient individual is an abstraction, an idea reached by various steps of extrapolation from the concrete experience of life lived in a web of relationships with others.

There might seem to be a bit more concreteness and immediacy to individuality. After all, we are each visibly self-contained in our own bags of skin. As Heidegger stressed, I encounter my finitude in confronting the death that is my death and mine alone. But even this seemingly obvious point has been historically altered by our collective confrontation with nuclear holocaust, in which your death and my death are fused in the fireball of a shared collective fate. And even my capacity to entertain these thoughts is mediated by my use of a language that is not mine as an individual. As Wittgenstein definitively demonstrated in his critique of the idea of a private language, I cannot think thoughts with words without presupposing the community of language users who set the criteria for whether I am using my own words correctly. A world of difference separates Robinson Crusoe's articulate individuality from the solitude of the wolf-boy, who cannot speak and cannot share much of what it is to be human until he learns to speak and experience as a human.

Yes, there are individuals, and some who are more autonomous, idiosyncratic and creative than others. Yes, there are collectives, and some that are larger and more embracing than others. But neither The Individual nor The Collective is ontologically given as a privileged starting point for social philosophy. Both individuality and collectivity are biographical and historical achievements.

When individuality and collectivity are seen as possible achievements rather than as alternative ontological starting points, then the advantages of both individualism and collectivism appear as complementary rather than conflicting. The collective needs the spark of creativity and autonomy. The individual needs language, community and all the rest of the benefits of society.

When theory begins where practice begins, in the concrete, day to day life of groups, then it is perfectly clear that the group needs the strengths claimed by both individualism and collectivism. The group needs solidarity with other groups if it is not to feel isolated or threatened; at the same time that solidarity must not compromise the group's freedom to create, its liberty to improve upon tradition.

Groups can be autonomous agents, just as individuals can. Groups can also behave like collectives, providing the linguistic, cultural, social and economic support that individuals need to sustain their creativity. Both the strengths and weaknesses of individualism and collectivism are to be found in the concrete lives of groups. The advantage to finding the dynamics of individuality and collectivity in the concrete life of the group lies in the realization that neither individuality nor collectivity is either origin or end in itself. Nor does it make much sense to force the choice between individualism *or* collectivism. These theories based on abstractions are not like two teams, only one of which can win the championship, however much recent history may make us think of win/lose conflicts between ideological opponents. Starting with the concrete life of limited groups, it should be immediately apparent that the group needs to optimize the strengths of both individualism and collectivism, while at the same time minimizing the dangers of each extreme.

By reframing the dynamics of individuality and collectivity in terms of a series of concrete trade-offs—social cohesion at the price of some individual liberty, individual creativity at the expense of some exercise of authority—it should be clear that no magical solution to the real issues of social life has been achieved. Just because the strengths of both individualism and collectivism *can* be reframed in ways that cast them as complementary rather than sharply conflicting, it does not follow that all good things *will* always go together. There are real and abiding tensions between individual and collective interests.

The point of reframing the dialectic by seeing community as concrete and The Individual and The Collective as equal and opposite abstractions is not to pretend that individualists and collectivists have both made some sort of silly mistake. Rather the point is to dig down into each of these traditions to see how the real differences between them can be expressed in terms of trade-offs that must be made within every community rather than as irreconcilable differences that must lead to the definitive victory of one set of interests over the other.

Individualism in America has now reached the point of being recognized as too much of a good thing, or so the social critics I have reviewed would seem to be saying. Perhaps Americans could do with a little less individualism right now. Surely the Soviets could do with a little more individualism. Gorbachev's reforms confirm the view that the Soviet Union could do with less collectivism. And we in the United States could do with a bit more, again, *right now*. Timing is all important where dynamic balances among trade-offs are concerned.

The historian, Arthur Schlesinger, has suggested that there are cycles of public spiritedness and private spiritedness in American history. Since the sixties we have been on a swing toward private spiritedness in the West, which extends beyond the privacy of the individual to faith in the private sector as more capable than the public sector when it comes to solving many social problems. Witness the wave of privatization of education, healthcare, air travel, etc. in both Europe and the United States. If Schlesinger is right, then we can expect a return to more public spiritedness in the near future: less selfishness and more concern for the public interest.

This shift toward greater public spiritedness, if it occurs, should not be feared as tipping the scales of democracy toward collectivism. Nor should the granting of greater liberties in the Soviet Union and Eastern Europe be feared by Marxist conservatives as a capitulation to bourgeois subjectivism. Ideological purity at either extreme, pure individualism or pure collectivism, is built on what I hope to have unmasked as a fallacy of misplaced concreteness. The extremes are not concrete enough to be pure about. And the real concreteness of community is so complex and messy that purity would be a mistake to begin with.

The interests of liberty and creativity on the one hand, and social cohesion and tradition on the other, will always pull at the heart of each community. The point of this essay is hardly to resolve that tension once and for all, but to sustain that tension within the lives of all communities. Neither The Individual nor The Collective can win, because neither ever existed in the first place.

III.

Spiritual Traditions
and Philosophy

A Nonary of Priorities

Raimundo Panikkar

Philosophy and the Human Future was the title of an interesting Conference held at Cambridge, England from the 6th to the 11th of August 1989, convened by the Esalen Institute Revisioning Philosophy Program, which gathered some hundred participants, mainly philosophers from the United States of America.

This is not a report of the Conference, but just a reflection on the problematic.

Official Philosophy, like 'official churches' and 'official nation-states' are in crisis today. The unacademic attitude of having reduced the notion of Philosophy to what goes under that name in 'official academia' has led many philosophers to look for a wider and deeper philosophical activity outside 'Academia'. And, in fact, this Conference was prompted by the desire of offering an opportunity for a meeting of 'academic' and 'specialized' philosophers with thinkers in other professions. The 'trouble' is not with Philosophy, but with officialdom.

The interaction between philosophers and people of more immediate human concerns brought acutely to the fore three problems which I would like to mention.

I. The Need for a Universe of Shared Discourse

Because 'official' Philosophy has become a specialization it has, like Modern Science, a specialized language which is different from the parlance of the artist, the businessman, the worker, etc. One of the urgent tasks of Philosophy, it became obvious, is not the analysis of 'ordinary language' but to assist at the birth of a common language among a group of people engaged in the common concerns of living a fully human life. Philosophy is not just another discipline, but the critical link between the several human disciplines. Philosophy is *essentially* interdisciplinary. Philosophy cannot have a specialized language like the Modern Sciences. It has to foster a truly human language in each concrete situation. In fact the technical terms in philosophy were mostly ordinary words; a soup has *substantia*, a flower *essentia*, a tiger *natura*, Man *persona*,... Philosophy offers the matrix from which specialized disciplines may emerge. The old womb may be barren, but the human spirit is not dead.

II. The Crosscultural Imperative

Now, in our times, the rejuvenation of Philosophy cannot come from one single culture, and certainly not exclusively from the modern technoscientific world. *The task is today urgently crosscultural*—which does not mean transcultural or supercultural. Each Philosophy is rooted in a culture, and it is, in fact, its expression. As I have repeated time and again crosscultural studies do not mean to study other cultures, but to let some other cultures impregnate the very study of the problem which by this very fact has already been transformed. In this sense a crosscultural Philosophy does not study other philosophies but changes the very perception of what Philosophy is. Paraphrasing Marx I would say that it is not solely a question of how to change the world, but also how to love the world without ceasing to struggle how to understand it. It is a question of recovering the integral meaning of Philosophy. Philosophy, I submit, has a triple dimension. The triad is trinitarian, i.e. *intrinsically* threefold: no dimension is without the others. It is a triad of interdependent dimensions: Knowledge without love and action is not possible, and when the abstraction succeeds in 'isolating' knowledge like a chemical element, the result is not true knowledge. Similarly, action without love and knowledge is beating around the bush. Love without knowledge and action is sentimental and barren narcissism. Analogously it could be said regarding the relationship between each pair of the other elements.

In short, it is the task of Philosophy to know, to love, and to heal— all in one. It knows in as much as it loves and heals. It loves, only if it truly knows and heals. It heals if it loves and knows. But the relationship is not automatic. It is a kind of free wheeling. *Rota in rotae* said the Christian medievals quoting from the Bible. It is the function of Philosophy to understand, to be involved and to save. It is not foreign to the nature of Philosophy to act with wisdom, to love with discernment, and to perceive with detachment. It is not a question of blind action, selfish affection, or biased vision. All in one. And each dimension corrects the others. It cannot, in fact, subsist without the others.

It is this type of holistic Philosophy which makes us very sensitive to the state of the world today and constantly brings our philosophical discussion to the vital problems of our contemporary human predicament.

III. A List of Priorities

If something links "Philosophy" with "the Human Future," Philosophy has to take a stance and offer avenues of action for a more just and brighter "Human Future."

Here is the project of thought, action and compassion I propose. I formulate it in a *nonlogue* and submit it to further scrutiny without spelling out the meaning of each *sûtra*. In a simpler way it could be said that I am proposing the most urgent and important nonary of points for an enlightened, loving, and thus healing involvement. I am conscious of the utopian character of this *charter* and I do not elaborate now the intermediary steps or the required strategies to approach the goal. This is a communitarian task. Blueprints are out of place. I only underline that the seriousness of the hour demands the radicality of the points. Many of them overlap each other and some of them are of a more concrete character than others. Some are hierarchically related and all are mutually linked so that the change in one point depends on and effects the change of the others. Aristotle spoke of "political prudence," and I appeal to it for the implementation of the points. I have dealt elsewhere with most of the points. This is only a sort of memorandum.

1. Demonetization of Culture

Money has an important role to play in human interactions, but it has become a *totalitarian tyrant* in modern westernized culture. It has penetrated all spheres of human action: food, health, education, well-being, art, marriage,...all seem to depend on money. As geometry abstracts forms from physical perceptions, elaborates on the forms, and eventually applies those abstracted forms again to physical realities, money abstracts from human activities, 'abstracts' (extracts) money from them, and eventually makes those very activities dependent on money. The *real* world is not made of monetizable commodities like physical entities are not made of geometrical figures, fractals notwithstanding. And this is not only the case for spiritual values, but also for material realities. To have to pay for water, food—and soon air—is a sign of a sick culture.

The monetization of all cultural values is the natural outcome of the quantification of the human outlook. Money allows us to stick a quantitative tag to any human activity and makes it possible to measure that activity by its monetary coefficient. Even Modern Science begins today to surmise that physical entities may not be measurable, not only because of a factual Heisenbergian impossibility, but because of the theoretical incommensurability of any *real* thing. Reality is incommensurable to any intellect. This is why Reality is real and not only ideal. Once again Platonism is lurking from behind the western psyche.

2. Dismantling the Construction of the Tower of Babel

One of the most powerful symptoms of our times is the unbridled power of the world-market in a world economy where all goods are monetizable commodities on an abstract world scale. This global homogenization centralizes all goods in fewer and fewer agencies. In short, the centripetal tendency of our time is fruit of a mechanistic and quantitative conception of cultural values. Technocratic civilization kindles again the temptation of a World Empire. Technocentrism is the insidious temptation.

There is a paradox here. The material planet earth may not be the center of the universe, as the astronomic sun may not be the center of the milky Nay. Ethnocentrism may be obsolete, and anthropocentrism a weak substitute for a lost theocentrism which contradicts itself the moment it is interpreted by Men. Technocentrism claims to be unbiased (neither one race or even culture) and objective (neither Man nor God). This is not true, as I have argued elsewhere. But its power lies in the fact that Man needs a center, a point of reference, a place of convergence.

The difficulty lies with the geometrical interpretation of the metaphor projected into a mechanistic worldview. None of the mentioned things, none of us is the center of the universe. And yet, in a more holistic vision the center of the universe lies in each and every thing which constitutes precisely the *uni-versum*. Each Man and also each culture, (natural body of the individual), is a center of the entire Reality. Losing this vision of the center of Reality passing through our Self, we are condemned, more irresistibly than water precipitates down the torrents of the mountains, to fall into the precipices of fashion, power, profit, and, ultimately, despair. We are then atoms striving for survival at the cost of others. If life has a meaning only for the victors, only for those who 'make it', we create an artificial hell for all the others, and no amount of Redemption or Reincarnation can rescue them from it. The meaning of the life for the individual Irene cannot lie in her becoming the head of the Corporation where she works, having beaten the other 3.000 employees. The meaning of the people of Madagascar is not to pant after the 'model' of a rich and powerful USA.

Cultural pluralism means, among other things, that each culture has its own center, elusive, mobile and contingent as it may—and should—be. Without that self-confidence that in every one of us befalls the center of Reality, *homo sapiens* is reduced to *animal imitans*—to an aping animal (with all the connotations of the word).

We are the center of the universe, because as a microcosm we reflect the whole, but we are not the circumference of Reality. We can only be a center when we have no dimension of our own and are open to an ever greater circumference. The center stifles the moment it draws a circumference upon itself. This is the reason of the paradox that in order to decentralise culture we need more and more centered individuals and self-confident human societies. A self-reliant economy, for instance, means not self-sufficiency, but an equitable interdependent net of markets. Interdependence is not unilateral or unbalanced dependence. Bio-regions, as relatively complete ecosystems, offer here an appropriate paradigm.

3. Overcoming the Nation-States Ideology

The alternative is not to fall back into absolute feudalisms or 'primitive' tribalisms. The alternative has to be elaborated by fostering in an organic way the healthy tendency, noticeable everywhere, of increasing *ontonomies*, and working a network of multilateral—but not necessarily universal—relationships which allow for a fruitful coexistence. I am proposing neither a single gigantic Nation-State nor a proliferation of monadic and lilliputian nation-states.

It is not a question of shifting the notion of sovereignty from nation-states to peoples or even cultures. To overcome state-nationalisms does not mean to transpose the same ideology of self-sovereignty and absolute freedom to bigger units or even to the entire human race. There are no sovereign values on Earth. The ancients had the belief in a cosmic order, *ordo, rta, tao, dharma, kosmos,* or an upholder of it, God. Without an homeomorphic equivalent to those symbols the delicate balance between freedom and cohesion (let alone spontaneity and coercion) is not possible. The problem is not merely political. It is theological. Two given societies can be *ontonomically* related only if there is a third element co-ordinating them, only if they form part of a Whole which is more than its 'parts' but which requires the well-being of the 'parts' in order to be a harmonious Whole.

The Empire was a myth with a unifying force. Its demembration produced nation-states. The Empire could be sovereign because it was founded on a divine principle superior to it. Not so nation-states, but they retained the title (even against etymology—there cannot be many 'supremes'). The ideology of Empire has collapsed and, along with it, the absolute sovereignty of partial units. A new myth is required.

4. Reducing Modern Science to its proper Limits

The very grandeur of Modern Science is accountable for its unbounded success well beyond its proper boundaries. It has modified modern Man's ways of thinking in areas far distant from the domain of the scientific disciplines. It has influenced ways of living in almost all aspects of human civilization.

This reduction to its proper limits cannot be imposed from without. Modern scientific ideology is so wide-spread as to make any kind of heteronomous morality ineffective. We cannot bridle the intrinsic expansionist force of genetic engineering by legislation and artificial boundaries, for instance. It has to be by a discovery of the very *ontonomic* order of Reality. This discovery has to be fruit of an insight into the meaning of human life and the nature of Reality.

The limits of Modern Science are both epistemological and ontological, besides being objective and subjective. In spite of the sacred name of *scientia,* Modern Science is not identifiable with it. It is not *gnôsis, jñâna,* nor *hochma, chi, sapientia.* It has no intrinsic saving power. Not all epistemology is 'scientific'; not all cognition is measurable. Not all knowledge is covered by 'Science'. Modern Science cannot be equated with knowledge about the world, or insight into the nature of Reality.

Not all ontology is 'scientific'. Not even all being is necessarily reducible to the *logos*. Not all is object of Science and certainly the scientist as subject cannot be included in it.

5. Displacing Technocracy by Art

The direct result of modern techno-science is the technocratic complex of modern society. The old theocracies, monarchies, oligarchies, aristocracies, and even anarchies have given way today to modern technocracy. The *kratos*, the power, is not invested in God, in a special group of people, but in modern technology. Modern technology, like Modern Science, has borrowed a traditional word and invested it with a new meaning. 'Science' is not *scientia*, nor is modern technology synonymous with traditional techniques, *techné*, namely, arts, crafts, machines of first degree, arrangements of material artifacts without artificially induced accelerations,...There is the spirit—as inspiration—behind every *techné*. The craftsman has to be inspired. Modern technology has substituted the *Pneuma* by the *logos* in the sense of *ratio*. The 'scientist' needs information. This has given birth to technocracy.

Today the *kratos*, power, does not lie with the politicians. They have to obey the megamachine of the technocratic System. The power does not even lie with the experts. They need capital and political blessings; they can only work in an unilateral direction: increase of power, acceleration, miniaturization, efficiency, etc.

Unless we play demagogically with words, the *demos*, the people, cannot have *kratos*, power, unless it is not only entitled, but also able, to exert it. Technocracy makes it impossible for the people to steer its own destiny. The megamachine commands, and its experts of long and highly specialized years of training can just manipulate it, impotent also to direct it to other directions and uses than those allowed by the inner mechanisms of the technocratic system. Weapons, inflation, growth of megalopolies, agriculture converted into agribusiness, etc. are all fatal laws of the System, to cite just some examples.

The people can only recover its power if it can have dominion over its own destiny. Technocracy makes that impossible. It would require a highly specialized know-how which is impossible for the people to master. Technocracy makes children out of adults. The people cannot even know—and thus decide—what is good for them. The Computer surely knows! We have only to obey. Some feel that capitalism is incompatible with democracy. Technocracy is certainly contradictory to democracy. Protagoras had already seen it. While for all the other arts and crafts we can rely on qualified experts, the political art, the *politikê techné* cannot be delegated to other competent experts. (Plato, *Protagoras*, 222 b sq.) A new anthropology is required here.

The word art needs an explanation, so much are we accustomed to take this word for entertainment, folklore, and a somewhat marginal activity. Art is that which art-iculates life and brings it all together by the 'artistic' creation of the person. The meaning of life is to make a work of art of each of us. For this artistic creation we need the collaboration of the entire universe, from the Divine to Matter, and to our fellow-beings. Each one of us should be able to express oneself, to create one-self in positive symbiosis with the rest of Reality. Beauty and Love are paramount in most human traditions: the first attribute of God, the First of the Gods,... as so many traditions affirm.

6. Overcoming Democracy by Experiencing a Neo-Kosmology

The *demos* can have *kratos*, power, only if a people is more than the sum-total of more or less isolated individuals. Man is a person, a knot in a net of relationships, and not an autonomous individual. Man is an ontonomous being. We need a new anthropology. But a new anthro-pology requires a new notion of the cosmos. Concept is an inadequate word. For this reason I spell the word with k, literally transliterating from the original *kosmos* which has the stupendous connotations of world, order, and ornament. Kosmology then connotes not a new, probably 'scientific', concept of the universe, but the experience of how the cosmos manifests, reveals itself to us: our sense of the cosmos, our perception of Reality, our real world.

The cosmos we live in is not necessarily the astronomic, or the geo-logic, or even the geographic, or historiographic universe. Each culture has another sense of the cosmos. The main cause of our present day crisis is to be found in the latent conflict of kosmologies in and around us. *In* us, because our contemporary experience of Reality is ill at ease in the cosmos of a scientific vision of the world. *Around* us, because the mixing of people of different world-views cannot be peacefully handled if we compare only different texts and ignore the underlying contexts.

There are many voices today singing new tunes and mixing with the old, but we do not have (yet) a new sense of the real. We bother about miracles, feelings, and extrasensory perception, to cite some examples, because they are foreign and uncomfortable bodies in the overall prevalent 'scientific' cosmology.

We know, further, enough sociology, psychology and political science to ignore the fact that democracy is an indispensable tech-nique, but a very weak theory. We know not only that people are manipulable. We know also that the *demos* as the highest instance only works within a given and accepted *mythos* which gives a certain consensus to a particular people. The true *demos*, like the ancient *polis*, all need their temples, their Gods, their opening to a super-democratic power. We can only avoid tyranny if a new kosmology emerges. I have elsewhere spoken of the cosmotheandric insight.

7. Recovering Animism

Without quarreling about words, I understand by animism the experience of life as coextensive with nature. Every natural being is a living cell part of a whole, and mirroring the whole at the same time. Not only animals and plants are alive, also mountains and rocks, matter as well as spirit. "Who will deny that the elements earth and water are alive, since they give life to the creatures born from them?" says Marsilio Ficino in 1476 echoing an almost universal tradition. (*De amore*, VI, 3)

Philosophy has to do not only with the human future, but with the cosmic future and with the destiny of the entire universe. We are not only actors and spectators of the *Divine Commedia*. We are also authors of it—co-authors, to be sure.

Life is the time of being, said the ancients (*zoê chronos toû einai*). Anything temporal is alive by the very fact of being temporal. Time is not only, and not even mainly, a quantitative or 'scientific' parameter; it is the very life of the universe. Individual existence is the symbiosis of each entity with the Tree of Life, with the Being of beings.

The meaning of human life is, therefore, to share as fully as possible, the Life of the Universe. Christ came, says John the Evangelist, reporting Jesus's words, so that we may have Life and Life abundantly. Not all life is the same, to be sure. And the modern Gaia hypothesis is not the *anima mundi* of the neoplatonics, the *jîvâtman* jaina, Tylor's African animism, or Mach's philosophical vitalism.

Two features should be mentioned here, one negative and the other positive. Animism here stands for an overcoming of all mechanistic and rationalistic worldviews. There is a principle of freedom, of life in everything—as contemporary scientists seem to surmise also. Animism stands, further, for the relatedness of all reality according to one principle which is itself all relatedness and not univocal. To say all is alive is not to affirm that all is of one stuff or all alike. It affirms the moving, free, precisely living relationship of every brim of Reality. It connotes, further, that death is a real possibility.

8. Peace with the Earth

No ecological renewal of the world will ever succeed until and unless we consider the Earth as our own Body and the body as our own Self. This would be an aberration if the 'own' were to be understood as private and individual property.

Neither the Earth, nor the Body nor the Self is my (psychological) ego. We are sharers in the Word, as the Vedas say and the Gospel echoes—equating the Word with Divine Life, identifying Life with Light, and Light with God. The ecological problem is strictly theological—and vice versa!

The Jewish tradition reports about the Covenant of Noah. A Covenant with the Earth is one of our most urgent and important tasks. The ecological movement is not a technological new way of exploiting the earth more rationally and more lastingly. If there has to be an eco-philosophy worth of the name, it entails a different relationship with the Earth altogether. The Earth is neither an object of knowledge nor of desire. The Earth is part of ourselves—of our own Self.

Movements are underway to swear a human Covenant with the Earth. It is a covenant of fidelity towards ourselves. It is a question of sensitivity. It is this which has led me to describe the split of the atom—for whatever good intentions—as a cosmic abortion. We kill, and extract from the very womb of matter, the extra energy units which our greed needs because we have disrupted the rhythms of Nature. We do not only torture animals—and Men, if we include politics. We torture Matter as well.

Peace does not mean an idyllic or idealistic view of total passivity or the static idea of Life, as if positive and negative metabolisms were not required. The animal does not 'kill', but it eats. Man does not exploit when following Nature, it grows and evolves. The chain of being or the wheel of existence is a living thing. There is exchange, there is death. But there is also resurrection.

Peace with the Earth excludes victory over the Earth, submission or exploitation of the Earth to *our* exclusive needs. It requires collaboration, synergy, a new awareness.

9. Uncovering the Divine Dimension

Atheism, I submit, is another form of theism, although a negative one. Polytheisms, as well as monotheisms and deisms, belong already to a decaying kosmology. The old controversies about reason and faith, believers and unbelievers, are rapidly becoming obsolete. The divine

Mystery is not pigeonholed in neat philosophical categories. Pure transcendence is a contradiction in terms. It destroys itself the moment it is not only formulated but simply thought. Thought becomes then the bridge to transcendence and by this very fact transcendence is transcended (should I have said '*aufgehoben*'?) Pure immanence, on the other hand, becomes unnecessary. If the divine were purely immanent it would be identical with ourselves and thus, redundant.

To introduce the talk of the Divine implies accepting a 'something' irreducible and yet related to ourselves; a 'something' 'above' all our faculties (of loving, willing, knowing,...), and at the same time 'in' all of them. All too often 'God' has been envisaged as an x somewhat beyond the actual grasp of our faculties. This *x* recedes in the same measure that our knowledge advances, or our feelings deepen, or our will increases. This God is 'strategically' receding each time 'Science' advances. No wonder that most perceptive thinkers see this battle lost in advance. To cover our ignorance we do not need the Divine any longer. Pure potentiality would do.

The divine dimension is more than a plus in the aesthetical or intelligible *status quo*. It is 'more' than transcendence or immanence. The way to experience the divine can be a path of the *plus* or of the *minus*, fullness or emptiness, but in both cases the way is not the goal and yet the goal is nowhere behind or beyond the way. The divine dimension is a third dimension irreducible to but not independent from the other two, and thus not an 'object' of the senses or the intellect, i.e. matter and consciousness. And yet the divine is utterly meaningless without both. There is a dimension of freedom and infinitude which impregnates both matter and spirit, the senses and the intellect, the *aisthesis* and the *noesis*. The Greek tradition called it *ta mystika*, the 'space' in which we move and sense and think, in which we live and are.

Anthropomorphism is inadequate, and so is cosmomorphism when speaking about the Divine. And yet it is that *plus* and/or *minus* concerning both the experience of Man and Cosmos that opens up the very experience not of 'something Else' not of the other 'third' dimension of the trinitarian Whole. Reality is of cosmotheandric nature. The relation between the three dimensions is non-dualistic, trinitarian.

It is here, at this level, where we should situate the most upsetting and terrifying problem which no charter should eschew; the problem of evil.

There is disorder, suffering, hatred in this world, and on all levels. Blindness towards it or pure passivity would not do. A fight against it on the same level or with the same weapons only doubles the evil. Evil is—by definition—inexplicable. If we would explain it we would explain it away. It is certainly a 'privation', but also a privation of intelligibility.

Evil forces us to experience our contingency, our incapacity of having a neat and coherent picture of Reality. It opens us to the abyss of the Divine from the other side, as it were. It cures us from any superficiality and sense of self-sufficiency. It spurns us into our personal jump into Life and does not cover the risk. It is part of the Mystery.

"Philosophy and the Human Future" is more than the survival of the human species. To begin with, because Man *is* not a species. In the 'human' future the being of Being is at stake. And this is the burden of Philosophy—lest we make of Wisdom a farce, of Love a mockery, and of Man a robot.

Is There a Perennial Philosophy?

Huston Smith

Steven Katz's assertion that there is no perennial philosophy[1] has attracted considerable attention, and its categorical character raises in a pointed way two important questions. Formally, what is the perennial philosophy?—how is it to be defined?[2] And factually, does it exist? Do we find it everywhere, as the word "perennial" claims that we should?

Katz rules out the possibility of an ubiquitous philosophy because experience is socially conditioned and societies differ. "The single epistemological assumption that has exercised my thinking," he tells us, is that *"there are NO pure (i.e. unmediated) experiences.* Neither mystical experience nor more ordinary forms of experience give any indication, or any grounds for believing, that they are unmediated.... *All* experience is processed through, organized by, and makes itself available to us in extremely complex epistemological ways" (1978:26).

---

[1]"There is no *philosophia perennis*, Huxley and many others notwithstanding"(1978:24). Let us note right off that others, including others who do not accept the perennialist position, see things differently. Thus Owen Thomas has recently written that "the perennial philosophy...has been the dominant form of Western philosophy from Plato to Hegel" (63). Not Western philosophy only. "The 'perennial' philosophy [enlisted] most reputable philosophers of both Europe and Asia up to about A.D. 1450" (Conze, 25).

[2]Because "perennial" refers only to time, "primordial" (which includes space) is the better designator, but I shall stay with Katz's more prevalent nomenclature.

This bears on the perennial philosophy in two ways. First, it rules out the possibility of cross-cultural *experiences*, because "experience is contextual" (1978:56-57). And it renders cross-cultural *typologies* suspect, for these too are culture bound. Categories that purport to service multiple cultures slur differences that are important. Their generality insures that they are either vacuous or misleading in presuming more cross-cultural similarity than in fact pertains.

As these are the objections to the perennial philosophy that Katz argues I shall devote most of my space to them, but not without first pointing out that they focus on secondary issues. Katz's criticisms are the ones that perennialists most often hear, but the real issue lies elsewhere.

The Central, Neglected Claim of the Perennial Philosophy

The claim of the perennial philosophy is not that mystical experiences are cross-culturally identical. Its claims do not appeal to experience at all, save in the trivial sense that everything that enters our awareness can be said to be an experience of some sort. Nowhere in the thirty-odd books of Frithjof Schuon of the two perennial philosophers Katz mentions by name (1978:67)—do we find him undertaking a phenomenology of mystical states along the lines of Zaehner, Stace, and James. That he shuns this approach completely shows that the perennial philosophy he argues for does not turn on assessments of mystical phenomena at all; logically it doesn't even presuppose their existence. The other perennialist Katz names, Aldous Huxley, is less emphatic about this; he was, after all, an amateur rather than an exact philosopher. Yet no more than Schuon does he ground perennialism in experience. "The core of the Perennial Philosophy," he tells us, is "doctrines."[3]

The doctrines derive from metaphysical intuitions, and it is to these that the perennial philosophy appeals. To discern the truth of a metaphysical axiom one need not have an "experience." The ontological discernments of pure intellection, which must be distinguished from rational argumentation—*ratio* is not *intellectus*—have

[3]Introduction to Prabhavananda & Isherwood's translation of the *The Bhagavad-Gita*, p.13. The doctrines Huxley refers to are there listed as four. First: the phenomenal world is the manifestation of a Divine Ground. Second: human beings are capable of attaining immediate knowledge of that ground. Third: in addition to their phenomenal egos, human beings possess an eternal Self which is of the same or like nature with the divine Ground. Fourth: this identification is life's chief end or purpose.

nothing to do with mystical rapture or access to states of "pure consciousness." The legitimacy of a metaphysical truth, evident to the intellect, does not depend on *samadhi* or gifts of "infused grace." Nowhere does the *Brahma* Sutra, e.g., appeal to mystical experience to support its metaphysical claims and arguments. The drift is the opposite. Ontological discernments are enlisted to elucidate or validate the yogas and the experiences they deliver.

Like mystical theophanies, metaphysical intuitions are ultimately ineffable. No more than the former can they be adequately rationalized; strictly speaking, they can only be symbolized—not to objectify Brahman but to dispel ignorance is the *Shastras's* object, Vedantins tell us. The reasons for the ineffability in the two cases, however, are different. Infused or mystical graces, including the *samadhis* and *nirvakalpa* especially, bring into more or less direct view features of higher ontological orders. This does not happen in metaphysical discernment. There it is not *other* ontological realms, but principles that pervade them all that come to view. In both cases, analogy is the only final recourse for reporting, but the comprehension/experience distinction remains intact. To understand that 2+2=4 does not require access to higher realms of either consciousness or being.

Katz steers clear of metaphysics; his argument is phenomenological throughout. It seems safe to assume, though, that he would expect his "principle of no unmediated experience" to cover metaphysical discernments as fully as it does mystical states. As the latter coverage is the one he spells out, I proceed with it while re-emphasizing the point of this opening section. Only to the extent that Katz's arguments about mysticism can be read as applying *pari passu* to metaphysical intuitions do they bear on the perennial philosophy at all.

Is there a Universal Mystical Experience?

By his reading of it, Katz's unqualified premise—"there is NO unmediated experience"—suffices by itself to rule out the possibility that mystical experiences could be cross-culturally identical, but he adds induction to deduction by marshalling differences that turn up in mystical reports. His premise remains important, though, for he leans on it to argue that the differences are not confined to descriptions. The experiences that generate the descriptions are themselves different. Mystics in different traditions, and to some extent in different pockets of the same tradition, "see" different things.

This is overwhelmingly the case, of course. The question is whether, amidst these manifold differences, which no one disputes, there is one form of mystical experience that *is* cross-culturally identical—or better, indistinguishable, for it is impossible to determine whether even physical stimuli, such as the color red, are experienced identically. I am referring, of course, to what Stace calls the introspective type of mystical experience, which cannot be culturally pegged because no culturally-identifiable particulars turn up within it. It isn't culturally tinted because, as the pure white light of the void, it has no tint.

We can approach this question by way of developmental psychology's classification of the kinds of knowing that successively emerge as human beings learn to abstract. There is a charming story of a Tibetan refugee in Switzerland who, having been persuaded to turn over his hundred-franc note to a bank on the assurance that he could have it back on demand, returned the next day to prove that his informants had lied. The bank did not return his note, which for test purposes he had marked; it gave him a different note. To the bank, a hundred franc note was a hundred franc note. Not so to the Tibetan who had been reared in a barter economy wherein every item of exchange was unique.

To the perennialist this tells the whole story of the present controversy, but it cannot be assumed that others will agree, so its moral must be spelled out. To his ontological hierarchy of being, the perennialist aligns a noetic hierarchy that extends beyond Piaget's while resembling it. In infancy knowing hovers close to the physical senses, but in childhood it takes off into images. Adults go on from there to order their images with abstract concepts. Mystics in their introvertive moments invoke a fourth kind of knowing that rises above sensations, images, and concepts, all three. If those ingredients continue to operate, they do so subliminally—tacitly, as Polanyi would say. They are not in view.

Katz may not believe that this fourth mode of knowing occurs,[4] but nothing in his argument proves that it cannot. His formal point about experience being mediated no more rules it out than the diversely mediated experience of delegates to the World Health Organization prevents them from getting past Irish potatoes and Peking duck to talk about carbohydrates, nutrition, and (quite simply) food. As for his

---

[4]It seems clear that he doesn't. "There is no substantive evidence to suggest that there is any pure consciousness *per se*....The...contention that we can achieve a state of pure consciousness is...erroneous" (1978:57-58). For a reasoned argument to the contrary, see Merrell-Wolff.

empirical contention—that mystical accounts never report a culture-free experience—it is impossible of course to prove such a universal negative, but what is to the point is that Katz's handling of the data does not give him the edge over Stace who, sifting the same material (85-111), reaches the opposite conclusion; I mention Stace because he is the opponent Katz cites most often. Admittedly things get subtle here. For example, the longest account that Katz quotes to support his conclusion that mystics never rise above the particulars of their respective religious conditionings reads to my eyes as if it supports the opposite conclusion. I refer to Ruysbroeck's report (which Katz quotes on 1978:61) that at the apex of the mystical experience "the three Persons give place to...the bare Essence of the Godhead,...the Essential Unity...without distinction," which condition is "so onefold that no distinction can enter into it."

If there were such a thing as the introvertive mystical experience, Katz says in his final argument against it, it could not affect our understanding because the paradoxical and ineffable properties that are regularly ascribed to it "cancels [it] out of our language" and preclude "making any...intelligible claim for any mystical proposition" (1978:56).[5] Paradox and ineffability need to be uncoupled here. Far from saying nothing, a genuine paradox, such as matter being both wave and particle, can precipitate a noetic crisis, generating things not just to think about but to worry about. As for ineffable, far from its saying nothing, it too (in mystical context) makes a major claim: the claim that, poised on the rim of the human opportunity, the human mind can under exceptional conditions—the condition of infused grace it is sometimes called—see things too momentous to be fitted into language which on the whole serves quotidian ends. The claim may not be true, but only a crude positivism can deny that it is a *claim.*

Are Typologies Trustworthy?

Katz's second charge is directed against cross-cultural typologies, which he says are "reductive and inflexible, forcing multifarious and extremely variegated forms of mystical experience into improper interpretative categories which lose sight of the fundamentally important differences between the data studied" (1978:25). That typologies can and often do propose improper categories is again not

---

[5]By contrast, the protagonist in John Updike's latest novel, *Roger's Version,* attributes his passion for theology precisely to the way it "caresses and probes every crevice of the unknowable."

in dispute; the question is whether there can also be useful ones. Katz himself seems in the end to concede that there can be, for he closes his essay with a plea for "further fundamental epistemological research into the conditions of mystical experience...in order to lay bare the [presumably generic] skeleton of such experience" (66). If this is indeed the concession I take it to be, Katz's objection to the perennial philosophy on this second count cannot be that it *spins* a typology, but rather that the one it spins is "too reductive and inflexible." As he doesn't deliver on these charges,[6] the only way to respond is to present the perennial typology and let the reader assess it for himself. Does it make mincemeat of the religious corpus, cross-culturally examined, or does it (as the perennialist believes) cut where the joints are?

I shall summarize the perennialist typology, but before doing so I want to continue for a second stretch with Katz. Having responded to his criticisms of the perennial philosophy as he understands it, I wish (in the upcoming middle third of this essay) to show what there is about his project that causes it to misfire even when directed toward mystically defined perennialism.

Contra Katz

Katz tell us that his "entire paper is a 'plea for the recognition of differences'" (1978:25), but one difference he doesn't mention, and it proves to be the one that is crucial for the perennial philosophy. I refer to the difference between occasions on which (and contexts in which) differences are important, and other occasions and contexts in which similarities call for attention. Everything obviously both resembles and differs from every other thing: resembles it in that both exist; differs or there would not be two things but one. This being the case, when should we accent one pole, when the other? Claims for similarities or differences spin their wheels until they get down to *ways* and *degrees* in which things differ or are alike, and those variables shift with the problem we are working on. Does the fact that an Ethiopian's hunger is mediated by his African context cause it to differ from mine to the point where it throws international famine relief into question? If not, where are Katz's contexts and mediations relevant, and where are they not? Where, balancing his "plea for differences," is the place of Piaget's "decentration," the process of gradually becoming able to take a more and more universal standpoint, giving up a particular egocentric or

[6] Katz doesn't discuss the perennial philosophy's typology at all, so one must infer his criticisms of it from the general tenor of his argument.

sociocentric way of understanding and acting and moving towards the "universal communications community"? Overlooking this question, Katz bypasses most of the interesting and important issues in his topic. The neglect is particularly unfortunate in religion, where commissions to break through provincial contexts and conditionings—what Max Weber called "the fetters of the sib"—are half the story.

This distinction—to repeat, the distinction between occasions where differences need attention and ones where the flip side of the story becomes important—is so obvious that one wonders why Katz doesn't mention it. The Judaism from which he speaks may provide part of the answer, for it is especially important that that tradition retain its identity and distinctiveness. Insofar as this is an intended or unintended motive, the perennialist supports Katz completely in it.

Less acceptable to the perennialist is another influence I think I see at work. When I listen to Katz I don't hear him speaking for himself only, or even (if this pertains; I'm not sure) for Judaism. I hear him speaking for an important thrust in contemporary philosophy; indeed, the leading thrust, if Richard Rorty is right in reporting that twentieth century philosophy "is ending by returning to something reminiscent of Hegel's sense of humanity as an essentially historical being, one whose activities in all spheres are to be judged not by its relation to non-human reality but by comparison and contrast with its earlier achievement and with utopian futures" (748). "In all spheres" makes clear that by this view not even religion is to be judged by its relation to non-human reality—perhaps God for a starter? *Nothing* outside of socio-historical contexts may be legitimated or (are we to assume?) even meaningfully pondered.

Katz acknowledges in his closing paragraph that his thinking, too, is contextual. He doesn't identify its controlling context, but it seems clear that it is the socio-historical, or cultural-linguistic, holism just noted. As the adequacy of his critique of the perennial philosophy turns in the end on the adequacy of that holism, I devote the next short section to it. The way I caption that section is flippant, but I am willing to risk indignity for the sake of emphasis. In four short words, two of them abbreviated, it says exactly what I want the section to say. Katz is to be judged by the philosophical company he keeps, which company is limited.

By mid-century phenomenologists had persuaded philosophers that the Gestalt psychologists were right: the mind doesn't just add up the data that comes its way; it patterns that data, altering thereby the way the data appears. Introduced into the philosophy of science, this produced the realization that "all facts are theory-laden" (Hanson). Thomas Kuhn picked up that insight and ran with it; his *Structure of*

Scientific Revolutions has been the most cited book on college campuses for the last twenty-five years and turned "paradigm" into a household word. Already, though, Heidegger and Wittgenstein had deepened theoretical holism into practical holism.[7] Because thinking invariably proceeds in social contexts and against a backdrop of social practices, meaning derives from—roots down into and draws its life from—those backgrounds and contexts. This means that in considering an idea we must take into account not just the conceptual gestalt of which it is a part; we must also consider the social "forms of life" (Wittgenstein) whose "micro-practices" (Foucault) give noetic gestalts their final meaning. "In a real sense, the medium is...the content of truth" (Knitter:19). Wittgenstein insisted that "agreement in judgments means agreement in what people do and say, not what they believe" (Dreyfus: 235).

Katz's company is those who think that way.[8] Now for the way their thinking is limited. The social holism they belabor is insightful as a half-truth, but forced into the role of the whole truth it collapses under the weight of its own self-reference. Pushed to logical extreme, cultural conditioning becomes, first, cultural subjectivism, and finally cultural solipsism. It renders unintelligible the ways and degree to which we can and do communicate, understand, and yes, even experience cross-culturally. Underestimating these ways and degrees, it faces two unresolvable problems. First, it cannot adequately answer the problem of relativism. It can escape "cheap relativism" by appealing to underlying agreements or pragmatic outcomes, but relativism remains relativism, and to its expensive versions holism has no answer. Second, holism is unconvincing when it argues that meaning and truth are *generated* by society, never—not even in the case of arithmetic—

---

[7]On the difference between theoretical and practical holism, see Dreyfus.

[8]The way is not limited to philosophers; as the quotation from Knitter signals, it has moved solidly into religious studies. All of the contributors to the two volumes that Katz has edited on mysticism lean towards what George Lindbeck calls the "cultural-linguistic" approach which is challenging the "experiential-expressive" approach to religious experience, and noteables are buying into the view—Hans Kung for one, who acknowledges that Katz's views "fully confirm" his own on this issue (173). Whereas experiential-expressivism sees religions as expressions or objectifications of inner, preconceptual experiences of God, self and world, the cultural-linguistic approach insists that experience is shaped by its social context from the start. "Inner experiences are not prior to their linguistic exteriorization; rather, the symbol system is the pre-condition of the experiences—a sort of cultural public *a priori* for the very possibility of 'private' experience" (Wood, 236). That last sentence could have been written by Steven Katz.

apprehended by it.[9] Elsewhere I have argued these limitations of untempered holism.[10] Here I can only assert them.

The Perennial Philosophy Defined[11]

Let us be clear: the perennial philosophy is a philosophy, not a sociology or anthropology that would jump out of the empirical bushes if only we squinted hard enough. The perennialist arrives at the ubiquity of his/her outlook more deductively than inductively.[12] Having encountered a view of things s/he believes to be true, s/he concludes that it must be true universally, for truth has ubiquity built into its meaning. Not simple-mindedly. That "it is raining" is true in Berkeley doesn't make it true everywhere. But it does make it true everywhere that it is at this moment raining in Berkeley.[13]

Philosophy is not concerned with particulars such as what's happening in Berkeley; in the end it is concerned with the whole of things. The topic is too vast for individual minds. They need help, which help the perennialist finds in the world's enduring religious or wisdom traditions.[14] In theistic terminology these traditions stem from divine revelation, but if that way of speaking closes rather than opens doors, one can think of them as wisdom reservoirs. They are tanks, or in any case deposits. Distillations of the cumulative wisdom of the human race.

[9]According to Kripke, Wittgenstein so argued.

[10]In a forthcoming essay titled "Philosophy, Theology, and the Primordial Claim."

[11]Naturally I assume full responsibility for the definition here offered. My intent is to present the position I find in the writings of Rene Guenon, A.K. Coomaraswamy, Titus Burckhardt, Frithjof Schuon, Martin Lings, S.H. Nasr, and their like. *My Forgotten Truth* and two books by Nasr, one that he authored, the other he edited, present overviews of the position.

[12]In a later, 1985, essay, Katz seems to sense this but discounts the approach. The "hermeneutical procedure" of the perennialists, he says, is confessional: "as much by way of testimony as by way of analytic or historical scholarship.... [It] substitutes *a priori* and non-disconfirmable intuitions for reasoned, defendable theories or generalizations."(76) When this is contrasted with the hermeneutic Katz recommends, namely "restricting oneself to an independent and coolly distanced reading of the material," one wonders if part of Katz's objection to the perennial philosophy isn't disciplinary—an objection to philosophy itself. The final arbiter of truth, he seems to be saying, is the objective findings of the socio-historical sciences, or the sciences of man as they are coming to be called.

[13]Etienne Gilson's *Medieval Universalism* remains a classic defense of this point.

[14]Where else? Certainly not science, with which modernity displaced revelation; science registers only a fraction of the real. Shall it be, then, the autonomous reason of the Enlightenment? What defenders does it still have among frontline philosophers?

Some will protest their being lumped together this way. Is it immaterial that Hinduism and Buddhism teach reincarnation whereas Christianity rejected it; that Christianity and Islam affirm the soul whereas Buddhism negates it; that Christianity exalts the Trinity while Judaism and Islam repudiate it; that Judaism, Christianity, and Islam propound creation whereas Taoism and Neoplatonism prefer emanation? It's not immaterial at all, the perennialist replies; on the contrary, it is providential. Here, though, the relevant point is that, important as these differences are in respects that are about to be indicated, they are not ultimate. Red is not green, but the difference pales before the fact that both are light. No two waves are identical, but their differences are inconsequential when measured against the water that informs them all.

We are back with the point that arose earlier: people differ according to whether they incline towards similarities or differences. Perennialists are persons who are exceptionally sensitive to the commonalities that similarities disclose; they are drawn toward unity as moth to flame. Sensitized by its pull, they find tokens of unity profligate; they see similarities everywhere. It comes as something of a jolt, therefore, to find that others see their eye for resemblances as an optical defect—a far-sightedness that cannot read fine print.

As the world houses both correspondences *and* diversities, which come through most strongly must depend on the viewer. Enter the division between esoteric and exoteric personality types that invariably crops up in perennialist writings. The words "water" and "eau" differ in both sound and appearance, which is to say outwardly and exoterically. All the while, their meaning (hidden and therefore esoteric to the senses) is the same. At the elementary level of this example, everyone is an esoteric. What distinguishes the esoteric as a type is his aptitude, honed no doubt by desire, to press the distinction between form and content all the way. For him *all* particulars—things possessing distinguishing identities—are ultimately symbols. They are coverings or containers for inner essences which, being without final demarcations, prove in the end to be single.

With unity thus stressed, the theological story reads like this: there is one God. It is inconceivable that she not disclose her saving nature to her children, for she is benevolent: hence revelation. From her benevolence it follows, too, that her revelations must be impartial, which is to say equal; the deity cannot play favorites. Here for the first time, perhaps, empiricism enters the picture. Having moved this far largely deductively, the perennialist now opens his eyes to see if evidence supports the hypothesis that has come to view—does the theory check out? The great historical religions have survived for millenia, which is what we would expect if they are divinely powered. Stated negatively, God would not have permitted them to endure for such stretches had they been founded on error. Nor, conversely, would she have permitted multitudes to have been thrown into life's sea in oceans of desolation—ages and regions where there was no lifeline.

As for the manifest diversity in the traditions, neither equality nor the universality of truth requires that traditions be identical. We have already noted that the same thing can be said in different languages, but different things, too, can be said without violating parity or truth. It is as if the differences in revelations "flesh out" God's nature by seeing it from different angles. They supplement our view without compromising the fact that each angle is, in its own right, adequate, containing (in traditional locution) "truth sufficient unto salvation."

If we try to lift out the underlying truth that *makes* the several revelations internally sufficient, we must speak more abstractly, shifting from theology to metaphysics. There is an Absolute, which is likewise Infinite. This Infinite both includes and transcends everything else, which everything is (in categorical contrast) finite and relative. The way the Absolute transcends the relative is to integrate the relative into itself so completely that even the Absolute/relative distinction gets annulled: form is emptiness, emptiness form. (This separates perennialism from the monism it is sometimes (mis)taken for; it is, rather, *a-dvaita* or non-dual.) How the opposition is resolved we cannot, of course, imagine or even consistently conceive, which is one reason the Absolute is ineffable. Too vast for our logic not just in extent but in kind, it intersects with language to about the extent that a ball touches a tabletop. At the same time we are so (unwittingly) party to the Absolute that it constitutes the only finally authentic part of our being.

If all this sounds like playing with words, the charge takes us back to the distinction in spiritual personality types the perennialist finds inevitable. One man's mush is another man's meaning. Because not many can draw spiritual nourishment from—which is to say find *existential* truth in—abstractions on the order of the preceding paragraph's, more concrete formulations are required, which is where the historical religions come in. Not only for exoterics; esoterics, too, stand in need of them.[15] This is an aspect of the perennial philosophy that is often overlooked by critics who see it as setting loose to religions in the plural, patronizing if not bypassing their concreteness and particularity. Katz's two volumes perform a needed service in helping to correct the notion that "mysticism...is an autonomous realm of

[15]"Exoterism is the necessary basis of esoterism" (Frithjof Schuon, in Nasr 1986:121).

experience which only uneasily fits in with more traditional and widespread religious beliefs, practices, and communities" (1982: Introduction). What is unfortunate is that in countering that error the volumes muddy the waters by tarring the perennial philosophy, even its mature proponents, with the mistake. The charge that the transcendent unity of religions perceived by the perennialist fits "only uneasily" with the historical traditions is like charging that Chomsky's universal, deeplying linguistic structures ill-accord with actual languages. The perennialist finds the unity of religions in the religions in the way s/he finds beauty in paintings and song. A more esoteric thinker than Shankara cannot be imagined, but only theoretically can we separate his metaphysical discernments from the hymns to Shiva that he composed and that powered his *jnana*. On this point the perennialist agrees with the practical holist, Katz emphatically included. Holism presses its case too far when it claims that truth is *generated by* practices, but it is right in insisting that practice is essential to truth's effective assimilation.

So the unitary truth to which the perennial philosophy points does not depend on the world's religions, but from our side we are not likely to come upon it, much less keep it in place, save through them. Does that single truth constitute the essence of the enduring religions? Esoterics and exoterics will answer that question differently. Exoterics will be quick to point out that the perennial philosophy is the minority position everywhere, even in mystical India, to say nothing of the form-loving West. Esoterics admit this statistical point, but insist that profundity is not determined by headcount. Workmen can understand nature in ways that are fully adequate for practical purposes without knowing the Einsteinian (or even Newtonian) laws by which it works.

The standard consequential charges against the perennial philosophy are that it devalues matter, history, the human self (in both its individual and communal poles), and God's personal aspect. The esoteric disclaims these charges; after all, the dictum that "samsara is nirvana" pays the phenomenal world no small compliment. The esoteric sees nothing in his/her philosophy to prevent appreciation of the realities in question as much as his/her exoteric brothers and sisters, while at the same time recognizing that there are things that exceed those qualified and provisional realities. One does not need to be ignorant of things better than chocolate to enjoy chocolate as much as a four-year-old.

The Perennial Typology

I began by pointing out that in aiming his critique of the perennial philosophy at mystical identities, Katz sets out on the wrong foot. What is perennial (which is to say "no matter where or when") for that philosophy is, first, God (or the Godhead/Absolute if one prefers), and second, the generic human capacity to ascertain truths about Him/Her/It.

Of these truths, or discernments as I early spoke of them, the most important is God's ultimacy as compared with the world's lack thereof. The Real and the (comparatively) unreal, the Absolute and the relative, Infinite and finite, Noumena and phenomena, appearance and Reality everywhere we find this distinction emphatically drawn.

As all traditions consider the capitalized terms in the pairs to be ultimately ineffable, this seems to rule out the possibility of cross-cultural differences in characterizing them. To name names; is it possible, in the face of their unanimous countermand to all culturally mediated, conceptual, reified representations, to saddle the Kabbalah's *en-sof*, Eckhart's Godhead, Nirguna Brahman, Nirvana, and the Tao that cannot be spoken, with predicates that distinguish them from their counterparts?

Strictly speaking, this negative, apophatic, *neti—neti* aspect of the Absolute—metaphysically counterpart of the unmediated mystical experience that Katz goes after—is the only point where perennialists see the traditions converging indistinguishably. Thereafter revelation fractionates like light through a prism, and what the perennial typology spreads before us is correspondences. Whether one is more impressed by the similarities that underlie these correspondences (which at eventual levels of abstraction phase into archetypal identities) or by the different ways the archetypes are clothed in the various traditions, depends again on the esoteric/exoteric difference that was earlier introduced.

In any case, the correspondences factor out into a hierarchical ontology such as Arthur Lovejoy tells us "the greater number of subtler speculative minds and great religious teachers...through the Middle Ages and down to the late eighteenth century were to accept without question" (26, 59). Everywhere thoughtful people have sensed the presence of another, more fundamental world underlying our familiar, quotidian one. And each of these halves-of-being, immanent and transcendent, subdivides in turn, producing an embracing typology of four ontological levels. The phenomenal world divides into its visible and invisible sides, the former constituting nature and the latter the spirit world of folk religion. As for the noumenal world, it has regions the mind can grapple with theologically—the God of Abraham, Isaac and Jacob, Allah of the Ninety-nine Names, *Saguna Brahman,* the Buddha's *Sambhoga-kaya,* and the Tao that can be spoken—and abysmal depths, alluded to above, that baffle the mind's approach.

References

Conze, Edward
1967   *Buddhist Thought in India.* Ann Arbor: University of Michigan Press.

Dreyfus, Hubert
1985   "Holism and Hermeneutics," in *Hermeneutics and Praxis.*Ed. by Robert Hollinger. Notre Dame: University of Notre Dame Press.

Gilson, Etienne
1937   *Medieval Universalism.* New York: Sheed and Ward.

James, William
1902   *The Varieties of Religious Experience.* New York: Longmans, Green and Company.

Katz, Steven T.
1978   "Language, Epistemology, and Mysticism," in *Mysticism and Philosophical Analysis.* Ed. by Steven T. Katz. New York: Oxford University Press.
1982   ed.*Mysticism and Religious Traditions.* New York: Oxford University Press.
1985   "Recent Work on Mysticism," *History of Religions 25:76-*R6.

Knitter, Paul F.
1985   *No Other Name?* Mayknoll, NY: Orbis Books.

Kripke, Saul
1983   *Wittgenstein on Rules and Private Language.* Cambridge: Harvard University Press.

Kung, Hans
1986   *Christianity and the World Religions.* New York: Doubleday and Co.

Lindbeck, George A.
1984   *The Nature of Doctrine.* Philadelphia: The Westminster Press.

Lovejoy, Arthur O.
1936, 1964   *The Great Chain of Being.* Cambridge: Harvard University Press.

Merrell-Wolff, Franklin
1973   *The Philosophy of Consciousness without an Object.* New York: Julian Press.

Nasr, Seyyed Hossein
1981   *Knowledge and the Sacred.* New York: Crossroad.
1986 ed. *The Essential Writings of Frithjof Schuon.* Amity, NY: Amity House.

Prabhavananda, Swami, and Christopher Isherwood (trs.)
1944   *The Bhagavad-Gita.* New York: New American Library.

Rorty, Richard
1986   "From Logic to Language to Play," *Proceedings of the American Philosophical Association* 59:747-753.

Smith, Huston
1976   *Forgotten Truth.* New York: Harper and Row.

Stace, W.T.
1986   *Mysticism and Philosophy.* Los Angeles: Jeremy P. Tarcher, Inc.

Thomas, Owen C.
1986   "Christianity and the Perennial Philosophy," *Theology Today* 42:259-266.

Wood, Charles M.
1986   Review of Lindbeck in *Religious Studies Review* 11:235-240.

Zaehner, R.C.
1961   *Mysticism. Sacred and Profane.* New York: Oxford University Press.

Philosophy and Evolution of Consciousness[1]

Robert A. McDermott

Where there is no vision the people get out of hand.
Proverbs, 29:18

A man's vision is the single great fact about him.
William James, *Pluralistic Universe*

This paper aims to illumine the relationship between philosophy and the evolution of consciousness,[2] including a brief sketch of the his-

[1]This paper is a revised version of a talk, with the same title, delivered at the Esalen Conference, "Philosophy and the Human Future" (August 1989), which was a fitting climax of a three-year series of conferences entitled "Project for Revisioning Philosophy." All of the participants in these memorable and productive events hold in gratitude the generosity of their benefactor, Mr. Laurance S. Rockefeller, and conference organizers, particularly Jay Ogilvy.

A longer version of this paper was published under the same title in *Cross Currents* (Fall 1989). My gratitude to Joseph E. Cunneen and William Birmingham, co-editors of *Cross Currents,* for permission to republish this paper, and to William Birmingham for expert editorial improvements.

[2]Prior to my finding the writings of Rudolf Steiner in 1975, my understanding of the evolution of consciousness was influenced, successively, by the American process philosophers (particularly James, Dewey and Whitehead), by S. Radhakrishnan, Henri Bergson and Teilhard de Chardin, and then very substantially by the writings of Sri

tory of philosophy from its beginnings until its possible eclipse in our time,[3] and suggestions concerning ways in which philosophy can advance the evolution of consciousness. Such an advance can take place by means of a method and practice of philosophical imagination, particularly through applying this meditative philosophic discipline to the workings of philosophy in relation to the evolution of consciousness. When practiced as a spiritual discipline, as meditative thinking, philosophy can and should play a distinctive—perhaps decisive—role in showing the way out of the present crisis of consciousness.

To the extent that an account of the evolution of consciousness succeeds in describing the history of philosophy and its contemporary possibilities, it stands in contrast to the the philosophical position expressed by Huston Smith (above).[4,5,6] Because I also claim, however, that consciousness evolves by virtue of a spiritual source and goal, my position also lends itself to comparison and contrast with the philosophical position shared by several American pragmatists, particularly by William James. While this article focuses primarily on the relationship between my position and the perennialism of Huston Smith, I also present an account of the evolution of consciousness which falls approximately midway between perennialism and American pragmatism.

Aurobindo, for which see my *Essential Aurobindo* (West Stockbridge, MA: Lindisfarne Press, 1988; originally 1973). The version of the evolution of consciousness operative in this paper is based substantially on the writings of Rudolf Steiner, for which see my *Essential Steiner* (NY: Harper & Row, 1984), and the thought of Owen Barfield. Because Barfield's writings, by his own admission, are based on the thought of Steiner, they are included in the 85-page annotated bibliography in *The Essential Steiner*.

[3]For writings on the undoubtedly premature announcement of the death of philosophy, see especially: Kenneth Baynes, James Bohman and Thomas McCarthy, eds., *After Philosophy: End or Transformation?* (Cambridge, MA: MIT Press, 1987), and Avner Coher and Marcelo Dascal, eds., *The Institution of Philosophy: A Discipline in Crisis* (LaSalle, IL: Open Court, 1989).

[4]For the perennialist writings of Huston Smith, see especially *Forgotten Truth: The Primordial Tradition* (NY: Harper & Row, 1976); "Is There a Perennial Philosophy?" (*Journal of the American Academy of Religion*, LV:3, 553-66); "Is Onto-Theology Passe? or Can Religion Endure the Death of Metaphysics?" (*Religion & Intellectual Life*, Spring 1986, pp. 7-14); "Philosophy, Theology, and the Primordial Claim" (*Cross Currents*, Fall 1988, 276-88).

[5]For a critique of Huston Smith's metaphysics of unity, see Eugene Fontinell, "In Defense of Which Metaphysics? A Response to Huston Smith" (*Religion & Intellectual Life*, Spring 1986, 28-38); For Fontinell's own position, see "Faith and Metaphysics" (*Cross Currents*, Summer 1988, 129-45).

[6]In two recently published articles I discuss Huston Smith's perennial philosophy: "Philosophy as Spiritual Discipline," *Towards* (Winter 1989), and "Toward a Modern Spiritual Cognition," *Revision* (Fall 1989).

Readers of Huston Smith will be unsurprised by my suggestion that he would do well to modify his perennialist position in the light of evolutionary considerations. I will try to show, again, that Smith's claims for the timeless truth of esoteric, mystical, or perennialist intuition are not merely too broad, but unhelpful in relation to the present crisis in consciousness generally and in philosophy in particular.

Rudolf Steiner's account of the evolution of consciousness, articulated throughout several hundred volumes of writings and lectures[7] is more detailed and inclusive than the account of the evolution of consciousness developed accumulatively by classical American pragmatic thought from James to the present generation. Although it remains little known in the academic world, the account of the evolution of consciousness which Steiner revealed during the first quarter of this century remains the most comprehensive interpretation of its origin, principles of development, historical and scientific details and contemporary possibilities.

The position developed in this paper is daring in its unabashedly speculative reading—or, rather, in its acceptance and use of Steiner's reading—of the evolution of consciousness, and in its proposal to lift philosophy to Spiritual Science.[8] My middle-way affirms the mystical and the perennial, but not at the expense of the personal and cultural specificity evidenced in the evolution of consciousness; it also affirms a Jamesian tough-minded faith in the presence of a radically processive and pluralistic universe, but with a transformative epistemology. It insists that by means of meditation on our situation relative to the past and future, it is possible to work through (not around) relativistic pluralism to a mode of thinking which is at once individual and universal, temporal and spiritual, self-generated and revelatory.

Jamesian pragmatism, in both its classical and contemporary versions, and the perennialism developed by Titus Burkhardt, Rene Guenon, Frithjof Schuon and recently by Huston Smith, are important

---

[7]For Steiner's most systematic brief account of the evolution of consciousness, see his *Occult Science—An Outline* (London: Rudolf Steiner Press, 1969), ch. 4: "Man and the Evolution of the World," pp. 102-221; see also Steward C. Easton, *Man and World in the Light of Anthroposophy* (NY: Anthroposophic Press, 1975), ch. 2: "History and the Evolution of Consciousness," pp. 20-121.

[8]For Rudolf Steiner's effort to lead philosophy into Spiritual Science, see especially his works, *Philosophy of Spiritual Activity* (NY: Anthroposophic Press,1988; originally *Die Philosophie der Freiheit*, 1894; also translated as *The Philosophy of Freedom*); *The Riddles of Philosophy* (NY: Anthroposophic Press, 1973), *Individualism in Philosophy* (Spring Valley, NY: Mercury Press, 1989; originally published 1899); *Philosophy and Anthroposophy* (Spring Valley, NY: Mercury Press, 1988; originally published 1918); Owen Barfield, trans., ed., *The Case for Anthroposophy: Selections from Rudolf Steiner's VON SEELENRATSELN* (London: Rudolf Steiner Press, 1970).

philosophical positions because of their ability to bring greater intelligibility to the depth and varieties of religious experience. What they say about religious experience, however, diverges at the base: Jamesian pragmatism emphasizes the processive and the relational dimension of religious experience;[9] the perennialist position, particularly as systematized by Huston Smith, emphasizes the esoteric, mystical, ineffable and eternal.[10]

While a comprehensively articulated account of the place of philosophy in the evolution of consciousness clearly has more in common with a Jamesian pragmatic contextualism than with Smith's perennialism, Smith nevertheless offers a valuable critique of the various forms of relativism which issue from and help to sustain a shrunken view of knowledge.[11] His perennialism must count pragmatism as one of the relativist positions it seeks to expose and replace, but James' pragmatism is complemented and deepened by his life-long investigation of religious and psychical experience.

Both the perennialist and the process philosopher are working to establish a creative relationship between the relative, or contextual on the one hand, and a divine reality on the other, and both recognize the extent to which contemporary life and thought are threatened by chaos and despair. But whereas Smith puts his hope in the experience of an absolute reality as a way of transcending the relative, the Jamesian pragmatically affirms the relative and contextual.

---

[9]In addition to Eugene Fontinell, *Self, God and Immortality: A Jamesian Investigation* (Phila., PA: Temple University Press, 1986), which represent the most faithful application of the religious side of James's thought, see Henry Samuel Levinson, *The Religious Investigations of William James* (Chapel Hill, NC: University of North Carolina Press, 1981). The writings of John J. McDermott, especially in *The Culture of Experience: Philosophical Essay in the American Grain* (Prospect Heights, IL: Waveland Press, 1987; originally 1976) and *Streams of Experience: Reflections on the History and Philosophy of American Culture* (Amherst, MA: The University of Massachusetts Press, 1986), are brilliantly Jamesian, but as Fontinell shows in *Self, God and Immortality*, Phila., PA: Temple University Press, 1986, p. 179) these writings "tilt" closer to Dewey than to James in that they effectively exclude God and immortality. The brief concluding chapter on religion in Gerald E. Myers, *William James: His Life and Thought* (New Haven, CT: Yale University Press, 1986), is not up to the level of the rest of this acclaimed and surely definitive study of James's thought.

[10]For the perennialists, in addition to the later writings of Huston Smith, see Jacob Needleman, ed., *The Sword of Gnosis: Metaphysics, Cosmology, Tradition, Symbolism* (Balt., MD: Penguin Books, 1974); Seyyed Hossein Nasr, *Knowledge and the Sacred*, The Gifford Lectures, 1981 (NY: Crossroad, 1981).

[11]See Huston Smith, "Beyond the Modern Western Mind-set," in *Beyond the Post-Modern Mind* (NY: Crossroad Publishing Company, 1982; for a full-length treatment of the shrunken Western conception of knowledge, see Douglas Sloan, *Insight-Imagination: The Emancipation of Thought and the Modern World* (Westport, CT: Greenwood Press, 1983).

As a complement to both of these positions, the present paper calls for an increase in meditative-imaginative thinking, or spiritual-scientific philosophizing, by which to make the history of philosophy and contemporary philosophizing more revealing concerning the secrets of the evolution of consciousness.

Drawing on Steiner's theory of cognition and method of Spiritual Science which complements his account of evolution, this essay will recommend a spiritual scientific methodology that seems to me more productive—or at least more promising of creative results in the long run—than Huston Smith's perennialism or Jamesian pragmatism. In effect, I am asking whether Steiner's Spiritual Science might enable us to supplement, and perhaps deepen and transform, these positions. I am claiming that the chaos and despair which characterize our present situation can be overcome by a sympathetic, sustained meditation on the spiritual meanings and forces operative in the evolution of consciousness, including its origin, modus operandi and possible goals. My reference to meditation is meant literally: the strengths of these two positions—and of similar philosophical polarities such as Platonism and Aristotelianism, or, that between James and Royce—can be maintained and the gap between them can be closed by thinking within them, or through them, meditatively. Or—dare we say it: lovingly.

1.

In his lecture on "History of Ideas: Evolution of Consciousness," Owen Barfield reminds us that we tend to divide the history of man-as-knower into two periods, the period before the birth of philosophy and the period after it, and that in relation to such a divide, philosophy, and later science, have always performed a dual role:

> They have operated both as effect and as cause: as effect, inasmuch as they start from and are limited by a mode of perception common at the time of their origin; as cause, inasmuch as, in the further course of time, they themselves help to bring about the formation and fixation of habits of thought divergent from those that prevailed before them. And it is from these divergent habits, from this different perception as their base, that subsequent philosophers will be starting in their turn. [12]

[12]Owen Barfield, *History, Guilt and Habit* (Middletown, CT: Wesleyan University Press, 1979), p. 4.

The term evolution of consciousness refers not merely to the history or evolution of ideas—with respect to ideas, or thoughts, history and evolution can be used synomymously—but rather to the changing mode of perception and thinking by which particular ideas, and not others, appropriately come into being. Great intellectual and cultural movements—referred to, since Thomas Kuhn's *Structure of Scientific Revolutions* as paradigm shifts[13]—are not, though they are generally thought to be, merely a new set of ideas or metaphors. Rather a change in consciousness involves the revision of a pervasive, unconsciously accepted framework, or of a root metaphor, or community of assumptions, which make the old ideas implausible and the new ideas obvious.

The mode of consciousness in and through which an experience or idea is put forth must affect its truth and meaning both at the time and subsequently. When we as a culture finally outgrow the Newtonian and Cartesian, and effectively replace it with a contemporary paradigm—whether Einsteinian, Jamesian or Joycean—we will also feel estranged from modern Western consciousness. This existential estrangement is so real that those of us who have begun to experience it often regard those who have not done so as innocent.[14]

Although it is useful to regard Nietzsche's death in 1900 as a symbolic marker of the transition from modern to post-modern, from meaning to angst, transitions between epochs of consciousness, or between paradigms, tend to more gradual and unevenly accomplished both from one culture to the next and within cultures. Earlier transitions were also gradual and uneven. This includes the uniquely important shift during the sixth to fourth centuries before Christ from archaic or mythic to historical self-reflective consciousness. In its drama and influence that revolution provides one of the best examples of the degree to which a comprehensive paradigm shift alters not only ideas and their meanings, but the mode of thinking which produces certain kinds of ideas and not others.

Even a brief survey of the thinkers and their influence during the sixth to fourth centuries before Christ provides a reminder of the mode of thinking before and after this period: In Greece, the beginning of philosophical speculation by Thales and other Pre-Socratics, culminating in the singular genius and influence of Socrates, Plato and Aristotle; in Israel, the moral and universalist insight of the prophets Isaiah and

---

[13]Second edition, enlarged (Chicago, IL: University of Chicago Press, 1970).

[14]For a brilliant description of this estrangement in terms of Bateson's "double bind," see Richard Tarnas, "From an Archetypal Point of View," *Cross Currents* (Fall 1989), p. 261. And, as the existentialists remind us, the world promises a meaningful reply but then holds us at bay. We wait for Godot.

Jeremiah; in Persia, the prophet Zoroaster, whose experience of Ahura Mazda as well as the spiritual and ontological reality of darkness and light, profoundly influenced Christianity and Islam and served as the basis of Zoroastrianism; in India, Gotama the Buddha and the crystallization of the teaching contained in the Bhagavad Gita; in China, the teaching of Confucius and Lao-tzu who, in their complementarity, established the core of Chinese philosophy and culture for the subsequent two and a half millennia (including the convulsive developments in the present century).

Consciousness prior to this period in these same cultures may be broadly characterized as mythic or pre-reflective. In this mode of consciousness the self does not yet experience itself as thinker, as separate from the divine and natural world—or, rather, from the as yet undivided natural-divine world. Experiences which we take to have been profoundly transformative and revelatory, or too remarkable to be believable, might take on a quite different meaning when understood in the context of the consciousness of that time. Whereas our naturalistic, and perhaps positivist,[15] reading of archaic and early historical experience—e.g., the consciousness recorded in the Upanishads, in Genesis and Exodus, and in Homer—tends to reduce ancient accounts of beings and realities, these experiences might be as characteristic of the second millennium B.C. as they are improbable and unintelligible in the modern (scientific) West.

Perhaps the most helpful way to understand the panorama of paradigmatic experiences—whether termed mystical, revelatory or transformative—is to regard the past two and a half millennia as a steady decline in immediate access to the divine. Owen Barfield refers to this phenomenon as the loss of participation.[16] Our fascination with, and desire to recover, the examples of archaic consciousness exhibited by traditional cultures stems from a longing for the unity lost to the fragmenting function of the intellect. Hence, the popularity of the works of Jung, Mircea Eliade and Joseph Campbell.[17] These thinkers, however, miss the other half of the drama: as the evolution of consciousness reveals a general (though irregular) loss of participation,

[15]Owen Barfield suggests that we are all imbued with "a residue of unresolved positivism." See *The Rediscovery of Meaning* (Middletown, CT: Wesleyan University Press, 1977), pp. 11-13, and *History, Guilt and Habit* (Middletown, CT: Wesleyan University Press, 1979), pp. 70-75.

[16]See especially *Saving the Appearances* (Middletown, CT: Wesleyan University Press, 1988; originally 1957), and *History, Guilt and Habit*.

[17]See especially C. G. Jung, *Man and His Symbols* (NY: Doubleday & Co., 1964); Mircea Eliade, *Patterns in Comparative Religions* (NY: Sheed & Ward, 1958), and Joseph Campbell, *The Mythic Image* (Princeton, NJ: Princeton University Press, 1974).

it also reveals a corresponding (and equally irregular) gain in intelligence.

Loss of immediate participation is complemented by a gain of the mediated, rational and scientific consciousness. Since, in archaic consciousness, the unity of mysticism is given, an initiate could be trained, and could train others, to apprehend the divine and its secrets.[18] In the modern West, the mystical is exceptional and dubitable because the individual has grown through separation from original unity with nature and the divine. Contemporary consciousness has been fashioned by the past two and a half millennia of thinking.

It is doubtful whether consciousness prior to the sixth century B.C.—the century of early Greek philosophers, Buddha, Confucius and their approximate contemporaries—should be understood as thinking. Obviously, the Egyptians, Moses and the teachers of the Upanishads produced important thoughts, but they apprehended, or saw, ideas as living realities. We experience these ideas as cold and crystallized, finished products removed from the mystical experience, or mode of awareness, from which they proceeded. It was just such an ability to see, and then to communicate, such ideas, that Plato attributed to the previous Golden Age and which he wanted to reclaim through his Academy.[19] He believed in the Ideas but could not quite see them. His great achievement was to facilitate, by a combination of intuitive memory and dialectical argument, the transition from seeing to thinking. It was Aristotle who practiced and taught, for the first time, the art of thinking, and thinking about thinking (i.e., logic), without recourse to myth or mystery knowledge.[20]

In the medieval Christian West, seeing ideas was even less possible. Rather, in the face of this loss of participation, the medieval thinkers developed belief as a complement to reason for those realities, and corresponding levels of knowledge, which could not be reached by reason alone. Philosophers who read the history of philosophy so as to disregard the medieval period—or more likely, the two thousand years

---

[18]For initiation, see Rudolf Steiner, *Christianity as Mystical Fact and the Mysteries of Antiquity* (London: Rudolf Steiner Press, 1972; originally 1902).

[19]For the significance of Orphic mystery wisdom for Plato, see Vittorio D. Macchioro, *From Orpheus to Paul: A History of Orphism* (NY: Henry Holt, 1930), pp. 175-185, and Frederick Hiebel, *The Gospel of Hellas* (NY: The Anthroposophic Press, 1949).

[20]According to Rudolf Steiner:

But what identifies the philosopher, and what appeared in Aristotle, is that he worked with a pure-conceptual technique and he necessarily rejected other sources of knowledge, or they were inaccessible to him. And since this is the case for the first time with Aristotle, it is therefore also not without world historical reason that it was precisely he who founded logic, or the science of thought technique (*Philosophy and Anthroposophy*, pp. 8-9).

between Aristotle and Descartes!—miss the drama contained in the evolution of consciousness: the medieval thinkers represent the transition from the Greek memory of seen ideas to the apparently complete loss of participation in the modern West. The nine hundred years between Augustine and Aquinas represent a loss of illumined reason and a corresponding gain in empiricist epistemology which would lay the foundation for a mode of philosophizing, three centuries hence, based on and supportive of empirical science.[21]

If Greek philosophy represents a transition from Greek myths and mysteries to dialectical reason, and medieval philosophy represents a transition from Greek intuition and argument to modern scientific philosophy, modern philosophy itself can be understood not only on its own terms, but equally as a transition. And, in a way which resembles the previous transitions, there may be an overall direction, accompanied and abetted by many less important currents, some complementary to and others in polar relation to, the prevailing paradigm. The Greeks produced Sophists, Stoics and Epicureans as well as Socrates, Plato and Aristotle, as 17th century French philosophy includes Montaigne and Pascal as well as Descartes, and the 19th century includes Emerson, Kierkegaard and Newman as well as Comte, Marx and Mill.

Every field of contemporary thought includes a bewildering array of positions and a polar opposite for each. If we take a long view of philosophy in evolution, we can nevertheless offer a broad characterization of 20th century philosophy which clearly distinguishes it from the thought of earlier periods, and, presumably, of periods to come. To be adequate, any such characterization must await the full unfolding of explorations of schools and movements such as those working out of Wittgenstein, Heidegger, Marxism, Asian and comparative philosophy, as well as the two positions with which we are concerned in this essay, the pragmatic tradition of James and the mystical-perennialist tradition as defended by Huston Smith.

2.

Huston Smith leaves no doubt that a philosophy based on mystical experience, or intuition of a perennial truth, stands at the opposite side of the philosophical spectrum from Jamesian pluralism and pragmatism:

---

[21]See Rudolf Steiner, *The Redemption of Thinking: A Study in the Philosophy of Thomas Aquinas* (NY: Anthroposophic Press, 1983; originally 1920).

Is there any way we can take seriously the possibility that our own cultural-linguistic epoch, say, may have taken a wrong turn; and again, if so, by what criterion? Pragmatic outcomes seem to be the only court of appeal, but though useful for provisional purposes, pragmatic criteria never tell the whole story, for if cockroaches are to inherit the earth, that would not induce us to consider them our superiors. Cultural-linguistic holism stammers answers to relativism; it can counter "vulgar relativism" by appealing to currents of consensus that underlie superficial differences. But this no more saves the day than the structural sturdiness of a house redeems it if it is about to slide off its mountain perch.[22]

In sharp contrast to the cultural-linguistic relativism tolerated by a pragmatic criterion of truth and meaning, Smith espouses a view which he synonymously refers to as traditionalism, perennialism and primordialism:

Ontologically, primordialists claim that we are bound to the ultimate so completely that in the end it is difficult if not impossible to differentiate us from it.... Epistemologically, they claim that we can know our divine identity. Historically, they claim that the first two claims constitute the core of the Revelation that has spawned and powered the world's enduring religions.[23]

Smith argues that the Absolute, or more accurately the esoteric or mystical experience of the Absolute, solves the problem of relativism and at least two of its corrollaries, the problem of evil and the conflict of religions. Smith's grasp of ordinary experience, with its built-in limitations and evils of all kinds, as well as his profound, first-hand experience of the world's religions, would not permit a facile disregard of the temporal and historical, but it does sustain his view that the historical is not an absolute. In addition to the temporal, there is the eternal:

In the strict sense of the word, the Absolute is eternal: it is beyond time. As the rise of process theology suggests, the modern world's absolutizing of time has made God's eternity the greatest stumbling block of traditional theol-

[22]"Philosophy, Theology and the Primordial Claim," pp. 281-82.
[23]*Ibid.*, p. 283.

ogy; Whitehead and Hartshorne concede timelessness to God's abstract outlines, but not to the concreteness those outlines contain.

Translated to the phenomenal plane, the absolutizing of time produces historicism. The traditionalist does not dispute the obvious fact that we are historical beings, or even that we are radically such. The question is whether we are totally such, which is to say historically without remainder.[24]

There is surely something true in this claim that we, and indeed the universe, are not merely historical, but have an eternal dimension. As philosophers, theologians and ordinary believers have sought to know since the dawn of philosophic thinking in the sixth to fourth century B.C., however, the difficulty is to hold to the eternal dimension without sacrificing the meaning and value of the historical. The evolution of consciousness is again relevant in that it provides a picture of those epochs in which, or for which, the eternal was given in experience as real and immediately accessible. In recent centuries, as a result of the shift in consciousness which produced, and has in turn been captured by, the scientific-historicist-relativist paradigm, the experience of the eternal-absolute has been almost entirely out of reach except at the expense of the temporal.[25]

Immediately following the text quoted above, Huston Smith points to a phenomenon which he takes as support of the ability of a thinker such as Anselm to transcend his own time and thereby serve as an exception to "unrelieved historicism":

Anselm once said that St. Paul understood Moses far better than he and his contemporaries could. In so saying he acknowledged time's toll; he admitted that it had disadvantaged his generation in comparison with Paul's on the point in question. What in return does historicism concede to Anselm by way of his capacity to transcend his times enough to recognize that Paul's times allowed things his own did not while the age of Moses allowed even more? Unrelieved historicism is unrelieved relativism in its tem-

---

[24]*Ibid.*, p. 287.

[25]Perhaps the most forceful account of the degree to which an affirmation of the eternal drains one's commitment to the temporal is to be found in John Dewey, *The Reconstruction of Philosophy* (Boston, MA: Beacon Press, 1957; originally 1920) and *The Quest for Certainty* (NY: Capricorn, 1960; originally 1929).

poral mode, and as Hilary Putnam has stated outright, relativism is unlivable.[26]

Without sacrificing the reality of the eternal for which Huston Smith argues so compellingly, and the possiblilty of our experiencing the eternal in the temporal, I nevertheless want to urge that this example has a different lesson: assuming that Moses, Paul, Anselm and a spiritual genius of our own time—e.g., Sri Aurobindo or Rudolf Steiner—possess comparable powers of understanding, then the difference between them is not merely what their respective times allow, but that they exhibit quite different modes, qualities, capacities of consciousness.

Moses transmitted the will and words of YHWH, the God of the Hebrew People.[27] Anselm lived in, and of course, as do all great thinkers, transcended his time, but not so completely as not to experience the contrast in consciousness characteristic of his time and consciousness at the time of Moses. Paul was not only closer in time to Moses than was Anselm, but was a beneficiary of spiritual forces wrought by Jesus Christ into the community for which he was spokesperson. Anselm was a Christian contemplative—i.e., a meditator—as well as a philosopher and theologian, but neither he nor the consciousness of his age gave him access to the consciousness of Moses.

Because the modern Western (scientific) consciousness in which almost all of us participate severely restricts what counts as knowledge, it limits our access with respect not only the consciousness of Moses, but also to Anselm and Paul, and other figures for whom spiritual realities were directly knowable. It is the more remarkable—and for most, the more unbelievable—that a figure such as Rudolf Steiner should break the seemingly unbreakable hold of the age by penetrating the consciousness of all of these figures, as well as the consciousness of other such paradigmatic figures as Buddha, Krishna and Zoroaster. The supersensible powers of clairvoyant figures like Swedenborg and Steiner are so at odds with the limits set by their age that they are perhaps best understood—much like Krishna, Buddha, Confucius and Lao Tzu—as heralds of a new age.

We do not know the extent of transformation which is possible in our time, but Steiner's uniquely revealing three hundred and fifty vol-

---

[26]"Philosophy, Theology and the Primordial Claim," p. 287.

[27]Moses had previously been initiated into Pharaonic mystery wisdom. See Rudolf Steiner, *Turning Points in Spiritual History* (Blauvelt, NY: Garber Communications, 1987), and Emil Boch, *Moses* (NY: Inner Traditions, 1986).

umes[28] might be an indication of a dramatically new capacity. They offer, at least, a vast array of claims—and a method by which to test them—concerning figures like Moses, Paul and Anselm, and their meanings in the context of the evolution of consciousness from their time to the present.

In one of his memorable texts, Huston Smith compares the esotericist intuition to the awareness of light:

> Blue is not red, but both are light. Exoterics can be likened to people who hold that light isn't truly such, or at least is not light in its purest form, unless it is of a given hue. Meanwhile academics have become so fearful that a hue will be overlooked or that some that are known will be victimized—marginalized is the going word—that they deny the existence of light itself....
>
> The primordialist believes that there is such a thing as light in itself—pure white light that summarizes all the wave-lengths—and that it is the Light of the World.[29]

Smith is undoubtedly justified in his portrayal of academics as so motivated more by a desire to know, and particularly not to miss, the particular hue that they remain ignorant of the idea in itself.[30] But the perennialist position not only can easily miss, and undervalue, the various hues in the quest for the Light, but generally fails to show the relationship to various colors both before and after the experience of the Light.

For the Perennialists, as well as mythologists like Mircea Eliade and Joseph Campbell, fundamental shifts in consciousness, or shifts from one to another hue of historical and cultural expression—e.g., from archaic to classical to modern—seem to be of little or no consequence. Eliade offers vivid accounts of archaic consciousness but pays little attention to the place of the archaic in the evolution of consciousness. But the most flagrant lack of historical and evolutionary awareness is to be found in the works of Joseph Campbell, for whom spiritual beings and historical figures of widely disparate times and cultures all figure in his mythological grids without any regard to their personal biographies or historical missions.

---

[28]The authoritative *Gesamtausgabe* (collected works) in German number 354 volumes; more than 200 volumes have been translated into English and are listed in *The Essential Steiner,* pp. 423-38.

[29]"Philosophy, Theology, and the Primordial Claim," p. 288.

[30]William James pointed out that most philosophers of his day were willing to miss the truth in their desperate effort to avoid error.

Huston Smith is more sensitive to cultural and historical differences than Eliade or Campbell, but his case for the mystical experience and perennial philosophy runs a high risk of missing the ways in which the cultural and biographical context actually adds to the meaning, and helps to account for the truth of mystical experience. Smith's perennialism seems to me an inadequate solution for the present situation because it does not disclose the inner meaning of particular contexts— e.g., the mission of Krishna and Buddha relative to the Christ, or the genius as well as the limitation of Greek and Christian philosophy, or the meaning and destiny of the West, and of America. Spiritual Science calls for a meditative, spiritually penetrating focus on these questions which issue from, and attempts to join, the individuality of the thinker and the spiritual realities which stand behind the thinker.

Meditation on the problem of an ineffable Absolute in relation to the relative can call up an image of a divine source expressing itself positively as and through the natural and the human, the spatial and temporal. By meditation, the gap between either-or can be transformed into both-and: the mystic knows by earned experience that the created world, and particularly the individual human being, has its being in and through the divine. Or, in some accounts of mystical experience, the human and natural, when fully and truly grasped, are divine. The more thoroughly the mystic knows the world, the more revealingly and creatively he or she can articulate its divine source and content in a way which serves the human as well as the divine.

3.

In opposition to Smith's case for an experience of the ineffable which is impervious to cultural relativism, I side with pragmatic contextuality for all truths and meanings. Whereas Smith divides religious experience into esoteric and exoteric (or mystical/religious), I want to affirm contextuality and degrees of difference, and put all claims for the absolute and the privileged to the pragmatic test. Spiritual Science is a difficult but promising way of apprehending the kind of realities to which the Jamesian pragmatist seeks access.

Without a transformative spiritual discipline, and an epistemological account of such transformation, a pragmatic faith would seem to be inadequate. Such faith may be necessary for a start but as unable as ordinary religion and ordinary science to penetrate to the inner meanings of natural, personal and historical realities. Pragmatism as a philosophic method may be necessary and productive of positive results but as a vision or metaphysics it needs to be supplemented by a spiritual or meditative discipline which can combine, and transform, the mystical and the practical. The Spiritual Science formulated by Rudolf Steiner might prove itself a radical empiricism capable of this transformative power.

As applied to mysticism and processive pragmatism, a radical empiricism based on Steiner's Spiritual Science would strive to join, or experience the joining, of the spiritual and the perceptual in every act of thinking. In so doing, the radically empirical thinker would become conscious of the fact that we typically regard as thinking what is in fact passive observation, and as a result fail to develop a truly self-conscious method of thinking. Such a practice might take as its ideal the advice offered by Emerson in the opening paragraph of "Self-Reliance":

> A man [person] should learn to detect and watch that gleam of light which flashes across his mind from within, more than the lustre of the firmament of bards and sages. Yet he dismisses without notice his thought, because it is his.[31]

Because we do not think actively, we miss the inner reality, and settle for the appearance, for the idol—the image without its inner meaning. Barfield's definition of idol and idolatry is worth pondering:

> The difference between an image and a thing lies in the fact that an image presents itself as an exterior expressing or implying an interior, whereas a thing does not. When what begins by being an image becomes in course of time a mere thing, we are justified in describing it as an idol. And a collective state of mind, which perceives all things and no images, may thus fairly be characterized as idolatry.[32]

The task of exposing and overcoming the idolatrous habit of mind may well be the most pressing task of philosophy—simultaneous with rather than subsequent to the obvious first priority of nuclear-free peace, for the arms race is itself a manifestation of idolatry. Both the mystical and the practical can be turned into idols. So can Anthroposophy—and in a way which is reminiscent of the sad fate of religions, since it was brought into the world by Rudolf Steiner at the

---

[31]For an insightful explication of this passage, as well as a revealing comparison between Emerson and Steiner, see Gertrude Reif Hughes, "Emerson's Epistemology with Glances at Rudolf Steiner" (*Journal for Anthroposophy*, Spring/Summer 1986, 38-44).

[32]Owen Barfield, *History, Guilt and Habit*, p. 70.

beginning of this century, many of its enthusiasts have reduced it to an image without its inner meaning.

When the processive and the practical are idolized, we get the merely pragmatic, process without *arche* (foundation, original stucture, principle) and without *telos* (aim, purpose, modus operandi). James was extremely effective in exposing excesses (i.e., idolatry) within and about science and religion, and in this respect his thought is nicely supplemented by analyses of science and religion in Steiner, Barfield and Kuhlewind. But Barfield seems to me to go furthest in exposing all manner of idolatry, including the degree to which openness to novelty and a corresponding aversion to *arche* and *telos* can themselves be made into idols. Although James resisted a too easy agnosticism by his exhaustive, and exhausting, study of the varieties of religious and psychic experiences,[33] a too easy pragmatist, he was not entirely successful in devising a method for allowing the concrete, whether objects, events or ideas, to disclose their spiritual contents.

As an antidote to a pragmatism which knows too little, or too hesitantly, the source, the inner meanings and the possible goals of the evolutionary process, I think that, instead of relying primarily on James, it would be more promising to build on Royce's Beloved Community[34] or the vision of a transformed world articulated by Sri Aurobindo,[35] and more promising still is the combination of the evolution of consciousness and the method of Spiritual Science as formulated by Rudolf Steiner and extended by Owen Barfield and Georg Kuhlewind.[36]

The problem with Smith's position is nearly the reverse of James's Although he recognizes the limitations of ordinary thinking for the solving of the ultimate questions, and affirms a something-more

---

[33]For the importance of psychical research in relation to James's philosophical and religious thought, see Robert A. McDermott, "Introduction," William James, *Essays on Psychical Research* (Cambridge, MA: Harvard University Press, 1987), pp. xii-xxxvi.

[34]See Josiah Royce, *The Problem of Christianity* (Chicago, IL: University of Chicago Press, 1968), and Frank M. Oppenheim, *Royce's Mature Philosophy of Religion* (Notre Dame, IN: University of Notre Dame, 1987).

[35]In addition to *The Essential Aurobindo*, see Robert A. McDermott, ed., "Sri Aurobindo: His Life, Thought and Legacy," *Cross Currents*, Special Issue, Winter 1972. For a comparison of Royce and Aurobindo, see Robert A. McDermott, "The Absolute as a Heuristic Device: Josiah Royce and Sri Aurobindo" (*International Philosophical Quarterly*, 1972, 171-99). See also Eugene Fontinell, "A Pragmatic Approach to *The Human Cycle*" and Robert A. McDermott, "The Life Divine: Sri Aurobindo's Philosophy of Evolution and Transformation," in Robert A. McDermott, ed., *Six Pillars: Introductions to the Major Works of Sri Aurobindo* (Chambersburg, PA: Wilson Books, 1974).

[36]See Georg Kuhlewind, *Stages of Consciousness* (1984), *Becoming Aware of the Logos* (1985), and *From Normal to Healthy* (1988), all published by Lindisfarne Press, West Stockbridge, MA.

methodology, his epistemology is inadequate because it fails to give sufficient priority to the distinctive needs and opportunities of contemporary consciousness. In tying historical epochs and cultural forms to an experience of ineffable unity, Smith removes his focus—and that of his reader—from the peculiar tasks of our time. Hence my recommendation of Spiritual Science, a methodology developed for the distinctive crises of consciousness experienced in this century. Exemplified and expounded by Rudolf Steiner, and extended by Owen Barfield, Georg Kuhlewind and others, Spiritual Science, also called Anthroposophy, is a way of spiritual and esoteric cognition, related to, but distinguished from, science and religion. Steiner writes:

> The natural scientist reaches an outer world which cannot be grasped by our inner world; the mystic reaches an inner life that clutches at nothingness as it tries to grasp an outer world for which it longs.[37]

Working from the perspective of Huston Smith's claim for the mystic, we would recommend a meditative appreciation of the ways in which the evolutionary process in its specificity reveals the divine; from the perspective of a Jamesian processive pragmatism, we would meditate on spiritual realities to be revealed even in and through a universe which we rightly experience as pluralistic, or, in James's memorable term, as "buzzing, blooming confusion." Thinking, or at least ordinary intellectual thinking, will not be enough to bridge the gap between the divine espoused by perennialism and pragmatism: active, imaginative receptivity will be needed to transform ordinary thinking into an illumined seeing-thinking by which we might apprehend something of the divine source, or sources, behind everyday consciousness. This mode of thinking is what Steiner refers to as Anthroposophy:

> Anthroposophy is a path of knowledge to guide the spiritual in the human being to the spiritual in the universe. It arises in man as a need of the heart, of the life of feeling; and it can be justified only in so far as it can satisfy this inner need.[38]

If we read the evolution of consciousness along these lines it will follow that neither science nor mysticism is the most effective complement to philosophy in our time. Rather, what seems to be needed, and is here recommended, is a mode of cognition which resembles science and mysticism but aims to be more will-filled, wide-awake and individu-

[37]*Philosophy and Anthroposophy*, pp. 4-5.
[38]*Anthroposophical Leading Thoughts* (London: Rudolf Steiner Press, 1973), p. 13.

ally based. It is by a conscious, sympathetic meditative reflection on the evolution of consciousness, and particularly on the present crisis in philosophy as a symptom of a profound spiritual crisis, that I have come to be convinced of the need for this approach to philosophy—or, more boldly, of this means of transforming philosophy into Spiritual Science.

Whereas mysticism and science function in polar, and no doubt creative, tension with philosophy, this account of the evolution of philosophy, and of philosophy in evolution, calls for a metamorphosis of philosophy into spiritual discipline. In some measure, it represents a return to the origin of philosophy in the Greek mystery teachings which so influenced Plato, but it is also distinctively contemporary in its democratic instinct: whereas in the time of Plato, philosophy was a way of life available only to initiates in mystery centers, in principle anyone can take up the discipline of spiritual-scientific thinking as a way to achieve an intuitive understanding, for example, of the evolution of consciousness, and of the distinctive task of philosophy in the service of contemporary consciousness.[39]

---

[39]Steiner writes:

There slumber in every human being faculties by means of which he [or she] can acquire for himself [or herself] a knowledge of higher worlds. Mystics, Gnostics, Theosophists—all speak of a world of soul and spirit which for them is just as real as the world we see with our physical eyes and touch with our physical hands. At every moment the listener may say to himself: that of which they speak, I too can learn, if I develop within myself certain powers which today still slumber within me.

In ancient times, anterior to our history, the temples of the spirit were also outwardly visible; today, because our life has become so unspiritual, they are not to be found in the world visible to external sight; yet they are are present spiritually everywhere, and all who seek may find them (*Knowledge of the Higher Worlds—And Its Attainment*, NY: Anthroposophic Press, 1947, pp. 1-3).

Can Western Philosophers Understand Asian Philosophies?

Roger Walsh

Interest in Asian cultures and philosophies continues to grow and increasing numbers of Western philosophers are now studying them. Among these Asian philosophies, a number—such as Yoga, Vedanta, Buddhism and Taoism—are clearly mystical in nature. These schools were molded by individuals who were obviously first-rank intellectuals but were also first-rank yogis or contemplatives. That is, in addition to intellectual training they had gone through a rigorous ethical, psychophysical and spiritual discipline designed to prepare them to grasp the special knowledge that is the goal of these traditions.

Almost invariably these philosophers claim that their philosophies are of a different order from mundane ones. As Edward Conze notes "nearly all Indian, as distinct from European scientific thought, treats the experiences of Yoga as the chief raw material for philosophical reflection."[1] They therefore claim that intellectual analysis by itself is insufficient to grasp the deepest profundities of realization and that intuition is essential. Moreover they claim that these traditions are fully

---

[1] E. Conze, *Buddhist Thought in India* (Ann Arbor, Michigan: University of Michigan Press, 1967), p.17.

comprehensible only to those who have undergone a preliminary discipline like their own.

This message was first delivered to the West some 2,300 years ago when Alexander the Great arrived in the Indus Valley. Seeking out some Indian philosophers Alexander's generals found "fifteen stark naked chaps sitting motionless on a sun baked stretch of rock so hot that no one could step on it without shoes." The Greeks were informed in no uncertain manner that they were most unlikely candidates for philosophy and that any candidate—"did he come from God himself—should first be naked and have learned to sit peacefully on broiling rock."[2]

Although sitting naked on broiling rocks is not a common prerequisite, the preliminary disciplines demanded by most of the great Asian mystical philosophies are still sufficiently daunting to grey the hair of most Western philosophers. For example the 15th-century text known as the Vedantasara, "the essence of the doctrines of the Vedanta"[3] responds with an eye-opening list of requirements to its own question, "who is competent, and consequently entitled, to study the Vedanta in order to realize the truth?". Only two of the requirements on this list, textual study and intellectual discrimination, are on the list of most Western academics. However the Vedantasara also specifies the additional prerequisites of faith, renunciation, calm, a turning of attention away from the outer world towards the inner, cessation of sensory perception, endurance, and continuous concentration. Equally imposing disciplines are found in other traditions and the practices appear to be of four main types: a rigorous discipline of ethics, emotional transformation, attentional training and cultivation of wisdom.[4]

Not surprisingly the typical reactions of Western academics to these demands have been disbelief or disregard. Some have laughed, perhaps embarrassedly, while others have pointed out that these demands would require years, perhaps decades, of preliminary work and only a handful of people would probably be successful. They have then gone right on with their purely intellectual analyses.

This reaction is completely understandable. After all, it's a bit insulting to be told that one isn't adequate even to begin training in, let alone understand, another's school of philosophy. In addition, the demands seem elitist and esoteric and quite contrary to Western beliefs that philosophy "is supposed to be open to the approach and accred-

---

[2]J. Campbell, *The Masks of God: Oriental Mythology* (New York: Penguin, 1962), p277.

[3]Nikhilananda, *The Bhagavad Gita* (New York: Penguin, 1962), p. 277.

[4]R. Walsh, "Two Classical Asian Psychologies and their Implications for Western Psychotherapists," *American Journal of Psychotherapy* (1988): 543-560.

ited investigation of every intellectual who can meet the general requirements of a) a basic education, and b) some specialized intellectual training to enable him to keep up with the argument....In modern times, a high school education and four years of college are supposed to open an access to the *sanctum sanctorum* of ultimate Truth."[5] But in addition to their elitism, these disciplines appear overly demanding for additional reasons. After all, the requested prerequisites appear to have little face value and some, such as faith, even seem antithetical to the unbiased pursuit of truth. Likewise while Spinoza, Hume and James may have been fine human beings there is little evidence that highly ethical, loving people have been significantly more successful Western philosophers than less pleasant ones.

Then again, Western philosophy usually assumes that conceptual analysis in and of itself is the royal road to philosophical understanding. This analysis is meant to lead to rational, verbal and publishable products and nonrational, nonverbal intuitions are not the coin of the Western philosophical realm. Tenure and promotion committees are hardly likely to look kindly on such intuitions and especially on those who argue that they can't be expected to publish anything this decade because they are preparing themselves by doing Yoga.

So Western philosophers have almost completely ignored these Asian caveats. The question arises, therefore, has anything been lost? After all much work has been done, much literature been produced and some ancient systems have even been reconstructed in contemporary philosophical terms, e.g. Advaita Vedanta.[6] Likewise some Western philosophers, none of whom would probably claim to be enlightened, have assisted with the rebirth and relegitimization of Chinese philosophies in their home country.

Clearly, much has been gained by Western philosophers pursuing purely intellectual analyses of Asian traditions. But this still leaves the question of whether anything has been lost. Recent research on states of consciousness suggests that, disturbingly, the answer may be yes. Even more disturbing is that what may have been lost may be the most profound aspects of these traditions. Indeed, my central claim is that recent states-of-consciousness research may pose a major challenge to, and demand a radical reappraisal of, our approaches to the study of mystical Asian philosophies. Let us therefore examine the relevant research on states of consciousness.

[5]H. Zimmer, *Philosophies of India*, ed. J. Campbell (Princeton: Princeton University Press, 1969), p.47.

[6]E. Deutsch, *Advaita Vedanta: A Philosophical Reconstruction* (Honolulu: East West Center Press, 1969).

Research on States of Consciousness

After a long gap since William James, consciousness is again becoming a respectable topic for research in Western psychology. One of the major areas of this new interest is in nonordinary (altered or alternate) states of consciousness. The range of alternate states under investigation has expanded from dreams and alcohol intoxication to encompass lucid dreams, hypnosis, psychedelics, meditation, yoga, peak and mystical experiences. This expanding range reflects a growing appreciation of William James's much quoted statement that:

> Our normal waking consciousness, rational conscious-
> ness as we call it, is but one special type of consciousness,
> whilst all about it, parted from it by the filmiest of screens,
> there lie potential forms of consciousness entirely differ-
> ent. We may go through life without suspecting their exis-
> tence; but apply the requisite stimulus, and at a touch they
> are there in all their completeness, definite types of men-
> tality which probably somewhere have their field of appli-
> cation and adaptation. No account of the universe in its
> totality can be final which leaves these other forms of con-
> sciousness quite disregarded. How to regard them is the
> question—for they are so discontinuous with ordinary con-
> sciousness. Yet they determine attitudes though they can-
> not furnish formulas, and open a region though they fail to
> give a map. At any rate, they forbid a premature closing of
> our accounts with reality.[7]

These forms of consciousness, or states of consciousness as we would now call them, are distinct experiential-functional patterns of psychological activity. Charles Tart describes a discrete state of consciousness as "a unique, dynamic pattern or configuration of psychological structures."[8] Different states are associated with different tendencies and patterns of experience and function. Experience and function may vary within states and in some cases it may be appropriate to talk of continua rather than discrete states, e.g., the continuum between drowsiness through normal alertness to hyperarousal.

[7]W. James, *The Varieties of Religious Experience* (New York: New American Library, 1902/1958), p.298.

[8]C. Tart. *States of Consciousness* (El Cerrito, CA: Psychological Process, 1983a, originally published in 1975), p.5 and p. 208.

However in other cases, even though experience and function may vary, discrete states may be clearly identified and differentiated, e.g., alcoholic intoxication and sleeping dream states. A state is called altered or alternate if it varies significantly from some baseline state, most commonly from the ordinary waking state and is "a qualitative alteration in the overall pattern of mental functioning, such that the experiencer feels his consciousness is radically different from the way it functions ordinarily".[9]

One of the characteristics of specific states of consciousness is that they may display what is known as "state-specificity." What this means is that certain capacities such as learning, memory and understanding that occur in one state of consciousness may be specific or tied to that state and show limited transfer to and accessability in other states.

The best studied of these state-specific capacities have been learning and memory. State-specific learning has been observed in both animals and humans under a wide range of conditions. For example, both animals and humans tend to learn and remember more poorly when under the influence of depressant drugs such as barbiturates. However, if something is learned during mild barbiturate intoxication it is subsequently easier to recall when once again under the influence of barbiturates than when sober.[10] This occurs even though learning and memory skills usually function better in the sober state. In other words the memories acquired in the drug state display state-specificity and show only limited transfer to the nondrug state. State-specificity may be the basis for the old folklore that if you lose something when drunk, you're more likely to remember where it is when you are again drunk. Even the relatively mild alterations in states of consciousness induced by different emotions may be sufficient to produce state-specific learning since material learned in a particular emotional state is best recalled when again experiencing that same emotion.[11]

These findings raise the question of just how many other capacities may show state-specificity. For example, may certain types of understanding and insight occur in specific states of consciousness yet be relatively inaccessible or unmeaningful in the ordinary state? This has certainly been demonstrated for decades in hypnotic states and there is also considerable anecdotal evidence for their occurrence in other

---

[9] *Ibid.*

[10] D. A. Overton, "Discriminative Control of Behavior by Drug States," in *Stimulus Properties of Drugs*, eds. T. Thompson and R. Pickens (New York: Appleton-Century-Crofts, 1971).

[11] G. H. Bower and E. R. Hilgard, *Theories of Learning*, 5th ed. (Englewood Cliffs, NJ: Prentice Hall, 1981).

types of altered states.[12] In his classic *The Varieties of Religious Experience,* William James described a number of insights gained under nitrous oxide or ether anesthesia that seemed extremely important at the time to those having them but somehow could not be fully comprehended in the ordinary state. Subjects who have experienced altered states induced by other means, e.g. meditation or marijuana, report similar experiences, though experimental support remains minimal. James himself felt that the insights he gained under nitrous oxide were philosophically valuable. "Looking back on my own experiences," he said, "they all converge towards a kind of insight to which I cannot help ascribing some metaphysical significance. The keynote of it is invariably a reconciliation. It is as if the opposites of the world, whose contradictoriness and conflict make all our difficulties and troubles, were melted into unity." Compare the third Zen Patriarch's advice to "Be serene in the oneness of things" since "dualities come from ignorant inference."[13] In any event, these experiences left a lasting mark on James and appear to have made him more receptive to Hegel.

There are also many anecdotal reports of state-specific communication but as yet this has not been adequately tested experimentally. The concept of state-specific communication implies that insights or understandings gained in a specific state of consciousness, e.g. a meditative state, may not be fully communicable to someone else who is not in that state, especially if the other person has had no prior experience of that state. James provided a possible example of state-specific communication when he attempted to describe his insights gained under nitrous oxide. While he attributed metaphysical significance to these insights he also acknowledged that his attempts to communicate his experience resulted in only "a dark saying, I know, when thus expressed in terms of common logic, but I cannot wholly escape from its authority."[14]

Other examples could be given from drug and meditative experiences. Experienced marijuana smokers, for example, claim that they can understand someone else who is intoxicated even though they themselves are not. This could be interpreted as an example of a partial transfer of state-specific knowledge to the ordinary state of conscious-

---

[12]C. Tart, *States of Consciousness* (El Cerrito, CA: Psychological Process, 1983a, originally published 1975), p.5 and p.208.

[13]Sengstam, *Verses on the Faith Min,* trans. R. Clark (Sharon Springs: Zen Center, 1976).

[14]W. James, *The Varieties of Religious Experience* (New York: New American Library, 1902/1958), p.298.

ness.[15] Meditators often feel that their experiences and insights cannot be fully appreciated or understood by those who have not also entered the corresponding states of consciousness. Indeed the Buddha went so far as to forbid nuns and monks to discuss higher meditative experiences with lay people because he felt that such communications would result in misunderstandings and confusion. Likewise in most traditions meditators and yogis are held to be capable of assessing other peoples' experiences and insights only if the assessors have themselves attained the corresponding meditative states and stages.

In summary, both ancient ideas and recent research suggest that there exists a wide range of states of consciousness and that there may exist state-specific constraints on the extent to which memory, insights, understanding, and communication can be extended to other states. Considerable research will be necessary before we can be clear how just precise and powerful these state-specific limitations are. However, even now they may hold powerful implications for our understanding and study of Asian mystical philosophies, and indeed, for Western mysticism as well.

Mystical States as Altered States of Consciousness

What then is the relevance of these findings of state-specificity to mystical Asian philosophies? Simply this: these Asian philosophers have sought, described, argued and trained for, and have spoken from, altered states of consciousness induced by the techniques they employ.

Indeed, the mystical Asian philosophies describe and eulogize not just one state but whole families of altered states. These include highly concentrated states such as the yogic samadhis or Buddhist jhanas; witness consciousness states in which equanimity is so strong that stimuli have little or no effect on the observer; and states where extremely refined inner stimuli become the objects of attention such as the faint inner sounds of shabd yoga or the subtle pseudonirvanic bliss of Buddhist vipassana meditation.[16,17] Then too there are unitive states such as in some Zen satoris in which the sense of separation between self and world dissolves;[18] there are states in which all objects or phenomena disappear such as in the Buddhist nirvana or Vedantic

[15] C. Tart, *States of Consciousness* (El Cerrito, CA: Psychological Process, 1983a, originally published 1975), p. 5 and p. 208.

[16] J. Goldstein, *The Experience of Insight* (Boston, MA: Shambhala, 1983).

[17] D. Goleman, *The Meditative Mind* (Los Angeles: J. P. Tarcher, 1988).

[18] P. Kapleau, *The Three Pillars of Zen* (Boston: Beacon, 1965).

nirvikalpa samadhi; and states—bhava samadhi, for example—in which all phenomena are perceived as expressions or modifications of consciousness.[19]

The range of states of consciousness that Asian philosophies aim for and describe is broad indeed. A full training program may take a student through a specific sequence of these states, as do the Buddhist vipassana meditation "stages of insight" and the yogic stages of samadhi.

In addition to these ancient claims recent research also supports the idea that Asian practices induce specific states of consciousness. This research includes phenomenological reports by Western researchers of their own experience,[20,21,22,23] quantitative analyses of meditators' subjective reports, studies showing significant electroencephalograph changes,[24] and changes in the nature and speed of perceptual processing.[25,26].

Asian philosophies have long claimed that certain skills may be enhanced in specific states of consciousness. Such skills include evoking increased calm, equanimity, concentration, and psychosomatic control, greater perceptual and introspective sensitivity and acuity, and stronger emotions of love, joy and compassion. Experimental research evidence is available to support the claims for greater calm, psychophysiological control of somatic processes, and perceptual sensitivity, speed and acuity.[27,28,29] Interesting aside, a recent study also supports the vener-

[19]Free John, *The Dawn Horse Testament* (Clearlake, CA: Dawn Horse Press, 1985).

[20]D. Shapiro, *Meditation: Self Regulation Strategy and Altered States of Consciousness* (New York: Aldine, 1980).

[21]C. Tart, "States of Consciousness and State Specific Sciences, *Science 176* (1972): 1203-1210.

[22]R. Walsh, "Initial Meditative Experience: Part I," *Journal of Transpersonal Psychology 9* (1977): 151-192.

[23]R. Walsh, "Initial Meditative Experience: Part II," *Journal of Transpersonal Psychology 109* (1978): 151-192.

[24]D. Brown, "The Transformation of Consciousness in Meditation," a paper presented at *The Greater Self,* a conference sponsored by the Noetics Institue and held in Washington, D.C. in 1987.

[25]D. Brown and J. Engler, "The Stages of Mindfulness Meditation: A Validation Study, Part II. Discussion," in *Transformations of Consciousness: Conventional and Contemplative Perspectives on Development,* eds. K. Wilber, J. Engler and D. Brown (Boston, MA: New Science Library/Shambhala, 1986), pp. 191-218.

[26]D. Shapiro and R. Walsh, eds., *Meditation: Classic and Contemporary Perspectives* (New York: Aldine, 1984).

[27]D. Brown, "The Transformation of Consciousness in Meditation," a paper presented at *The Greater Self,* a conference sponsored by the Noetics Institute and held in Washington, D.C. in 1987.

[28]D. Brown and J. Engler, "The Stages of Mindfulness Meditation: A Validation Study, Part II. Discussion," in *Transformations of Consciousness: Conventional and*

able yogic claim for enhanced longevity. A group of geriatric (average age of 81) nursing home patients taught transcendental meditation were all still alive three years later whereas approximately a third of the controls had died.[30,31]

A particularly important form of skill is the ability to attain state-specific knowledge, understanding and insights. Asian meditators and mystical philosophers have long claimed that they obtain state-specific knowledge that is at least partly unavailable to untrained subjects. They claim that the trained mind which has developed "the keenness, subtlety and quickness of cognitive response required for such delicate mental microscopy"[32] is able to perceive the workings of mind and the nature of reality with penetrating subtlety and acuity far beyond the capacity of most of us. Thus it is said that only the trained mind capable of entering the appropriate states of consciousness can comprehend transcendental wisdom (*jnana* or *prajna*). Specific Buddhist examples of this wisdom include an understanding of the constituents and processes of mind (the Abhidharma), the three marks of existence: change, unsatisfactoriness, and egolessness (*anicca*, *dukkha*, and *anatta*) and the emptiness of all phenomena (*sunyata*).

Two lines of recent research support these Asian claims for enhanced introspective skills and state-specific knowledge. The first is that a number of Western mental health professionals have provided phenomenological reports of their own initial meditative experiences that support the idea of state-specific knowledge.[33] The second line of research is the finding of enhanced perceptual speed, sensitivity and acuity in meditators.[34] Advanced Buddhist practitioners proved capable of perceiving stimuli that were significantly more subtle and brief than

Contemplative Perspectives on Development, eds. K. Wilber, J. Engler and D. Brown (Boston, MA: New Science Library/Shambhala, 1986), pp. 191-218.

[29]D. Brown, M. Forte and M. Dysart, "Differences in Visual Sensitivity among Mindfulness Meditators and Non-meditators," *Perceptual and Motor Skills 58* (1984): 727-733.

[30]C. Alexander, et al, "Transcendental Meditation, Mindfulness, and Longevity," *Journal of Personality and Social Psychology* (in press).

[31]E. Langer, "Minding Matters: The Consequences of Mindlessness/Mindfulness," in *Advances in Experimental Social Psychology*, ed. L. Berkowitz (New York: Academic Press, 1988).

[32]Nyanaponika Thera, *Abhidharma Studies* (Kandy, Sri Lanka: Buddhist Publication Society, 1976), p.7.

[33]R. Walsh, "Initial Meditative Experience: Part I," *Journal of Transpersonl Psychology 9* (1977): 151-192.

[34]D. Brown and J. Engler, "The Stages of Mindfulness Meditation: A Validation Study, Part II. Discussion," in *Transformations of Consciousness: Conventional and Contemplative Perspectives on Development*, eds. K. Wilber, J. Engler and D. Brown (Boston, MA: New Science Library/Shambhala, 1986), pp. 191-218.

those detected by nonpractitioners. Part of this enhancement of perceptual processing speed and subtlety was found only when practitioners were doing an intensive meditation retreat and presumably experiencing the various altered states that occur during such practice. However, part of the enhancement remained when practitioners were not in retreat and not doing intensive practice. In the latter case an altered state had resulted in an enduring altered trait.

These experimental findings support the phenomenological reports of meditators. They claim that during intensive practice they enter altered states in which their perceptual and introspective sensitivity and speed are sufficiently increased to allow them unprecedented insight into, and understanding of, the nature and workings of mind. After they leave the intensive retreat practice these states and capacities tend to diminish though the insights and understanding they afforded may remain. Further evidence for a residual enhancement of perception comes from findings that meditators may display more accurate empathy than nonmeditators.[35]

One particular type of state-specific knowledge and its effects seem particularly important to an understanding of Asian mystical philosophical claims that may seem incomprehensible or even illogical and impossible from our usual perspective. This is the type of state-specific knowledge that causes a re-evaluation of knowledge previously obtained in other states, including the ordinary one. This re-evaluation process is described by the Sanskrit term *Badha* which means contradiction and which Eliot Deutsch[36] translates as subrationing.

Asian philosophers claim that in certain alternate states traditional knowledge, and even logic may be subrationed. That is, our usual knowledge, understanding and logic are recognized as state-specific and limited, and are consequently accorded less scope and validity than the knowledge which subrationed them. However, it is important to recognize that the subrationing knowledge, understanding and logic to which the mystical philosopher accords greater than usual validity may appear quite incomprehensible or illogical to one who has not entered a requisite state of consciousness.

It is also important to note that for Asian philosophies the deepest types of insight and understanding are not primarily intellectual in nature. There is almost universal agreement among the Asian mystical philosophies that the deepest subrationing insights, the deepest understandings that constitute the transcendental wisdom of *jnana* or *prajna*,

[35]D. Shapiro and R. Walsh, eds., *Beyond Health and Normality: Explorations of Exceptional Psychological Wellbeing* (New York: Van Nostrand Reinhold, 1983).

[36]K. Wilber, *Eye to Eye* (Garden City, NY: Anchor/Doubleday, 1983).

are intuitive in nature and usually inaccessible to the discursive intellect. "Not by reasoning is this apprehension attainable" (Katha Upanishad 1, 2, 4) "Words return along with the mind not attaining it" (Taittiriya Upanishad 2, 9, 1). Indeed, according to the third Zen patriarch, "to seek mind with the discriminating mind is the greatest of all mistakes."[37] From this perspective all purely conceptual knowledge is regarded as inherently dualistic and fundamentally illusory whereas the knowledge sought by the Asian disciplines is held to be beyond dualities, categories, words and concepts; hence nondual, transverbal, and transrational.[38]

Indian View of Philosophy

Western philosophy is a primarily conceptual enterprise that seeks the deepest type of understanding through intellectual analysis and logic. The Asian mystical philosophies, however, say that the deepest types of understanding are inaccessible to the intellect. They therefore tend to use the intellect, not as the primary means for revealing these deepest understandings, but to point towards and describe (within the limits imposed by concepts) a previously recognized nonconceptual understanding and the disciplines that can lead others to this same understanding.

This is not to deny that intellectual analysis and logic can be valuable adjuncts in the search for the deepest types of understanding. Indeed, they are probably used to varying extents in all authentic mystical traditions and particularly in jnana-yoga, the yoga of knowledge and discernment. However even jnana-yoga "is not a merely logico-analytic or speculative inquiry"[39] but includes various components of meditative raja-yoga and the final understanding remains beyond words and concepts.

This orientation is clearly embodied in the Indian terms that are often translated as philosophy and philosopher. The term *darsana* refers both to a school of philosophy, especially "a thought system acquired by intuitive experience and sustained by logical argument" and to " a spiritual perception, whole view revealed to the soul sense."[40]

[37]Sengstan, *Verses on the Faith Mind*, trans. R. Clark (Sharon Springs: Zen Center, 1976).

[38]K. Wilber, *Eye to Eye* (Garden City, NY: Anchor/Doubleday, 1983).

[39]R. Puligandla, *Jnana-Yoga—The Way of Knowledge* (Lantham, MD: University Press of America, 1985), p. xii.

[40]Radhakrishnan, *Indian Philosophy, Vol. I* (London: Allen & Unwin, 1929), pp.43-44.

This *darsana* is regarded by Indian philosophy as "a distinguishing mark of a true philosopher." From the Indian perspective, then, philosophy and profound intuitive vision are almost synonymous. This view is reinforced by a term commonly translated as philosopher, namely *Paramartha-vid* meaning he who knows *(vid)* the paramount object or fundamental reality *(Paramartha)*.

Asian Mystical Philosophies as Multistate and State-Specific Systems

Contemporary research, then, suggests that there may be multiple states of consciousness and that capacities in these states may exhibit state-specificity. Asian mystical philosophies and disciplines aim for, describe, and philosophize from, the perspective of multiple states of consciousness and claim that these states provide insights, understandings, intuitions, logics and philosophical views less obtainable and sometimes incomprehensible in our usual state. In short the Asian mystical systems are multistate philosophies and significant parts of their knowledge are state-specific.

The idea of state-specific disciplines is not new and state-specific psychologies, technologies and sciences have been suggested. Daniel Goleman[41] infers that the Buddhist Abhidharma is a state-specific psychology originally conceived in, and only fully comprehensible and testable in, the highly refined states of consciousness engendered by advanced meditation. Likewise Charles Tart[42] has suggested that mystical religions may also be regarded as transpersonal psychologies or state-specific technologies designed to induce transcendent states.

Tart went further and suggests the development of state-specific sciences. These he proposed as disciplines in which participant experimenters or yogi-scientists would learn techniques for inducing altered states, then attempt to observe their experiences in these states as objectively as possible and compare their reports with others. Applying the term *science* to purely introspective observations is using the term broadly but perhaps legitimately: as Hilary Putnam[43] observed "I don't believe there is *really* an agreement in our culture as to what is 'science' and what isn't".

[41]D. Goleman, *The Meditative Mind* (Los Angeles: J. P. Tarcher, 1988).

[42]C. Tart, ed., *Transpersonal Psychologies* (El Cerrito, CA: Psychological Processes, 1983b, originally published in 1976).

[43]H. Putnam, "The Philosophy of Science," in *Men of Ideas*, ed. B. Magee (New York: Viking Press, 1978), p. 233.

The responses to Tart's proposal for the development of state-specific sciences have been dramatic. Both Ernest Hilgard[44] and Gordon Globus[45] responded with strong critiques. Globus immediately sent a critical letter to *Science* which had published Tart's paper. However in what must be one of the most dramatic turn-arounds in scientific history he then happened to reread Tart's paper while in an altered state of consciousness. To quote Globus' own words,

> To my great amazement—his proposal that a science specific to a given ASC may be independent of sciences specific to other ASC's now seems quite correct. *I therefore immediately drafted this letter while in the ASC.*....I am struck, then by the extraordinary paradox that Tart's proposal for state-specific sciences seems absurd to me in an ordinary state but quite correct in terms of my "incorrigible experience" while in an ASC.

Equally remarkable, and just as amusing, is the fact that when he returned to his ordinary state of consciousness Globus again found himself disagreeing with Tart and added to his letter the following :

> Again in an ordinary state, I would argue in favor of one science for all states of consciousness and trust that there is an explanation for my experience that while in an ASC, the ASC seemed clearly incomprehensible to an ordinary state. It seems obvious to me that I can remember what happened in the ASC, but I can't remember it in the way I experienced at the time, i.e., the memory is not veridical. There seems no way to retrieve the experience in the ASC without entering again the ASC which supports Tart's thesis [of the importance of developing state-specific sciences].[46]

So whether or not we in the West can develop state-specific sciences in the future, it seems that Asian philosophers may have accessed state-dependent knowledge and created both state-specific and multi-state philosophies centuries ago.

[44]E. Hilgard, "Consciousness in Contemporary Psychology," *Annual Review of Psychology 31* (1980): pp. 1-26.

[45]G. Globus, "Different Views from Different States," in *Beyond Ego: Transpersonal Dimensions in Psychology*, eds. R. Walsh and F. Vaughan (Los Angeles: J. P. Tarcher, 1980), pp. 213-215.

[46]G. Globus, "Different Views from Different States," in *Beyond Ego: Transpersonal Dimensions in Psychology*, eds. R. Walsh and F. Vaughan (Los Angeles: J. P. Tarcher, 1980), pp. 213-215.

Limitations on our Comprehension of Multi-State Philosophies

If these Asian philosophies are indeed multi-state systems and contain state-specific understandings, it follows that those of us who are not adequately trained will be unable to comprehend them fully. By adequate training I mean the traditional disciplines, or faithful variations thereon, of ethics, emotional transformation, attention and cultivation of wisdom designed to train the mind so that it can voluntarily enter the altered states that are the goals and source of these philosophies. Such is certainly the claim of the people who practice these Asian traditions.

> Without practice, without contemplation, a merely intellectual, theoretical, and philosophical approach to Buddhism is quite inadequate....Mystical insights...cannot be judged by unenlightened people from the worm's eye view of book learning, and a little book knowledge does not really entitle anyone to pass judgement on mystical experiences.[47]

From this perspective without contemplative training we are incapable of entering the necessary altered states and consequently we lack "adaequatio".

> If we do not have the requisite organ or instrument, or fail to use it, we are not *adequate* to this particular part or facet of the world with the result that as far as we are concerned, it simply does not exist. This is the Great Truth of "adaequatio."[48]

If state-specific knowledge, logic and communication do in fact limit our ability to fully comprehend the profundities of Asian philosophies, then what exactly is it that is lost to us and how are we likely to respond to our truncated vision of them? These are particularly important questions since state-specific knowledge may appear incomprehensible or even nonsensical to anyone without experience of that state.

[47]B. Vimilo, "Awakening to the Truth," *Visaka Puja* (Thailand: Ann. Public Buddhist Assoc., 1975), p.70 and p.73.

[48]E. Schumacher, *A Guide for the Perplexed* (New York: Harper and Row, 1977), p.61 and pp. 42-43.

One common response is simply to assume that these Asian philosophies are nonsensical products of primitive thinking and to dismiss them from serious consideration accordingly. Such has traditionally been the most common Western response to Asian philosophies, psychologies and religions. In such cases the entire wisdom of the traditions is lost to us.

But there may be another type of response in which the loss is more insidious. This is the loss that may occur when Western intellectuals, including highly intelligent and well intended philosophers, approach Asian philosophies without the requisite yogic-contemplative training. What may then be lost are the more subtle, profound, state-specific depths of these philosophies. "Their true meaning," said William Stace, "can only be understood if we have in our possession a knowledge of the profoundest depths of the mystical consciousness."[49] Purely intellectual inquirers will not recognize that they are overlooking more profound depths of meaning.

What are being lost are the higher "grades of significance." An illustration based on one given by Tyrrell[50] who coined the term, may unpack its meaning. Let us imagine the different responses and grades of significance that the same object may elicit. To an animal a book may be an oddly shaped black and white object and of course the animal is right, the book is a black and white object. To a person from an illiterate tribe the book may be an oddly shaped soft flexible object with strange markings on it. Again this is correct, although the response is at a higher level of significance than the animal's response. A Western child may immediately recognize the object as a book while a Western adult may recognize it as a particular type of book—one that makes incomprehensible, even ridiculous, claims about the nature of reality. Finally, to a physicist it may be a profound text on quantum physics.

What is important to recognize is this: all the observers were correct in their characterization of the book, but all of them except the physicist were unaware how much more meaningful, more significant the object was than they could recognize. The book was a black and white object, it was a soft, flexible object with squiggly markings, it was a book. And, most important to the nonphysicist Western adult, it was a book whose contents seemed incomprehensible, even ridiculous. What this example so nicely demonstrates is that when we are incapable of comprehending higher grades of significance we can come away from an observation with the mistaken feeling that we have understood the object as fully as possible. As E.F. Schumacher points out:

---

[49]W. Stace, *Mysticism and Philosophy* (Philadelphia: Lippincott, 1960), p. 168.
[50]G. Tyrrell, *Grades of Significance* (New York: Rider, 1947), p.61.

> Facts do not carry labels indicating the appropriate
> level at which they *ought to be* considered. Nor does the
> choice of an inadequate level lead the intelligence into fac-
> tual error or logical contradiction. All levels of significance
> up to the adequate level, i.e., up to the level of meaning in
> the example of the book—are equally factual, equally
> logical, equally objective, but not equally real....When the
> level of the knower is not adequate to the level (or the
> grade of significance) of the object of knowledge, the
> result is not factual error but something much more
> serious: an inadequate and impoverished view of reality.[51]

A central thesis of this paper might be stated as follows. Research
on altered states of consciousness supports the millennia-old Asian
claim that without appropriate prior yogic-contemplative training
philosophers may not be adequate to the higher grades of significance
embodied in Asian mystical philosophies and may be unaware that
these higher grades of significance are being overlooked.

In a way this caveat is similar to one uttered by Western philosophers themselves to the first Western students and translators of Asian
philosophies. Long before Western philosophers took these Asian systems seriously philologists were studying, translating and commenting
on them. When philosophers did begin to investigate them they recognized that the philologists' lack of philosophical sophistication had left
them vulnerable to missing and misunderstanding certain philosophical subtleties. The implication of state-specificity is that just as these
philologists without philosophical training were not fully adequate to
certain philosophical subtleties of the Asian traditions, so also philosophers without yogic-contemplative training may also not be fully adequate to certain subtleties and higher grades of significance of these
traditions.

Other Lines of Support for these Theses

Three other lines of evidence may offer further support for my
theses. These include the reports of Westerners doing Asian practices,
the parallel arguments of Ken Wilber, and the effects of psychedelics.

During the last decade I have met a number of Western philosophers and psychologists who have taken up meditation and/or yoga.

---

[51]E. Schumacher, *A Guide for the Perplexed* (New York: Harper and Row, 1977), p.61
and pp. 42-43.

They consistently report that meditation experiences have deepened their conceptual understanding of the traditions and the few reports that have been published appear to support these claims.[52,53,54] The recently formed meditation and philosophy group of the American Philosophical Association appears to be largely composed of members who have observed a similar impact of meditation on themselves.

Ken Wilber has presented a sophisticated argument for the necessity of contemplative practices in order to understand mystical traditions of either East or West. Wilber's thinking is too rich to summarize adequately here. Suffice it to say that he argues that the intuitive insight sought by mystical traditions represents a distinct epistemological mode that must be cultivated before these traditions can be understood and their validity can be assessed. Wilber's argument appears to parallel and complement the one offered here.[55]

A third, and highly contentious line of support concerns the effects of psychedelic experiences. The question of whether drug-induced mystical experiences are genuine and whether some of them are identical to or even similar to those encountered and described in Asian philosophies has been hotly debated.[56,57,58] For our purposes it is enough to note that some drug-induced experiences bear striking resemblances to mystical experiences[59,60,61] and that after such experiences, subjects may report greater appreciation and understanding of Asian philosophies and may be drawn to undertake yogic meditative practices.[62,63,64] Unfortunately it is difficult to have a rational discus-

[52]R. Walsh, "Initial Meditative Experience: Part I," *Journal of Transpersonal Psychology* *9* (1977): 151-192.

[53]R. Walsh, "Initial Meditative Experience: Part II," *Journal of Transpersonal Psychology* *10* (1978): 1-28.

[54]K. Wilber, "Odyssey," *Journal of Humanistic Psychology* 22:1, (1982): 57-90.

[55]K. Wilber, *Eye to Eye* (Garden City, NY: Anchor/Doubleday, 1983).

[56]H. Smith, "Do Drugs have Religious Import?" *The Journal of Philosophy 61* (1964), pp. 517-530.

[57]W. Stace, *Mysticism and Philosophy* (Philadelphia: Lippincott, 1960), p.168.

[58]R. Zaehner, *Mysticism, Sacred and Profane* (New York: Oxford Press, 1961).

[59]S. Grof, *The Adventure of Self Discovery* (Albany: SUNY Press, 1988).

[60]H. Smith, "Do Drugs have Religious Import?" *The Journal of Philosophy 61* (1964), pp. 517-530.

[61]L. Grinspoon and J. Backalar, *Psychedelic Reflections* (New York: Human Sciences Press, 1986).

[62]S. Grof, *Realms of the Human Consciousness: Observations from LSD Research* (New York: E. P. Dutton, 1976).

[63]F. Vaughan, "Perception and Knowledge: Reflections on Psychological and Spiritual Learning in the Psychedelic Experience," in *Psychedelic Reflections*, eds. L. Grinspoon and J. Bakalar (New York: Human Sciences Press, 1986), pp. 108-114.

sion about psychedelics since the topic is highly charged for most people and the media have distributed gross misinformation.[65] Suffice it to say here that reports from psychedelic research appears to be consistent with the claims of this paper.

Comparisons Between Asian and Western Philosophies

Several important implications arise from comparing Western philosophy and Asian mystical philosophies from a perspective of states of consciousness. The first of these comparisons involves the number of states of consciousness that the respective philosophies describe and from which their practitioners philosophize. The key difference is of course that mainstream Western philosophy is predominantly a unistate enterprise where Asian philosophies are multistate enterprises.

It is important to note that 20th-century mainstream Western philosophy is *predominantly*, though not exclusively, a unistate enterprise because there are of course notable instances of significant understandings gained in alternate states. William James's sympathetic insights, gained under nitrous oxide, into an Hegelian-like synthesis of opposites, have already been noted. These apparently left their mark since James's original antipathy to the Hegelian system apparently mellowed subsequently.

Dramatic historical examples that have reverberated through Western philosophy for a millenium or more include the philosophy of Plotinus and Anselm's ontological argument. Anselm reports that this argument came to him in a dream.[66] I am doubly indebted to James Cutsinger for pointing this out to me when this paper was first presented to the Revisioning Philosophy group. For when he did, Huston Smith exclaimed that he had once dreamed Anselm's proof and that in the dream, and only in the dream, it made perfect sense to him. We might, perhaps, have here a case of state-specific understanding, although against this is the fact that Anselm claimed that the argument also held in the waking state. Of course partial cross-state understanding can certainly occur so Anselm's claim does not rule out the possibility of state-specific understanding. Of course it goes without saying that

[64]R. Walsh, "Psychedelics and Psychological Well-Being," *Journal of Humanistic Psychology 139* (1982): 1525-1526.

[65]T. Reidlinger and J. Reidlinger, "The Seven Deadly Sins of Media Hype Considered in the Light of the MDMA Controversy," *Psychedelic Monographs and Essays 4* (1988).

[66]St. Anselm's 'proslogion,' with 'a reply on behalf of a fool' by Gaunilo and 'the author's reply to Guanilo,' trans. M. J. Charleswort (Oxford, 1965).

the fact that an argument appears to make sense (in any state) does not necessarily establish its validity. In any event it is clear that some alternate states of consciousness, namely dreams, have certainly been a source of inspiration and creativity in both Western and Eastern philosophy (e.g., Anselm, Descartes and Tibetan dream yoga), as well as in diverse fields such as literature (Robert Louis Stevenson and Samuel Taylor Coleridge), painting (William Blake), music (Mozart, Beethoven, and Wagner), psychology (Freud and Jung) and science (Kekule's discovery of the molecular structure of benzene and Loewis's Nobel prize winning experiment on nerve conduction).[67]

A similar multistate-unistate comparison emerges when we consider the number of dimensions of personality or being that Asian or Western philosophies train. Western philosophy takes itself to be primarily unidimensional training of the intellect alone whereas the Asian philosophies employ multidimensional training and regard intellectual cultivation as only one aspect of a fuller essential discipline.

From this perspective Western philosophy might be regarded as predominantly a state-specific philosophy whose observations, concepts, investigations, descriptions and logics may be specific to, and at least partly limited to, the usual waking state. In other words Western philosophy may not be fully adequate to, descriptive of, or veridical for certain other states of consciousness and their possible world views and philosophies.

Because they are multistate and unistate systems respectively, the Asian philosophies may be inherently broader and more encompassing than Western ones. This is by no means to deny the obvious fact that Western philosophy has examined and conceptualized certain areas of our usual state experience in vastly greater detail and depth than have Asian systems. It is simply to say that there appear to exist other important states of consciousness that Western philosophy has not addressed but which certain Asian traditions have accorded great importance and have examined in detail.

A useful simile here may be the comparison between Newtonian and Einsteinian models in physics. The Newtonian model applies to macroscopic objects moving at relatively low velocities compared to the speed of light. When it is applied within these conditions it is highly accurate and valuable yet when applied to high-velocity objects it is no longer valid. The Einsteinian model, on the other hand, encompasses both low and high speeds and from this broader perspective the Newtonian model and its limitations are all perfectly logical and understandable (applying Einsteinian and not Newtonian logic of course).

---

[67]S. La Berge, *Lucid Dreaming* (Los Angeles: J. P. Tarcher, 1985).

However the reverse is definitely untrue, for the Einsteinian is not comprehensible within a Newtonian framework. Furthermore from a Newtonian framework reports of incongruous findings such as the constancy of the speed of light and objects increasing in mass at high speed are incomprehensible, illogical and suspect. In technical terms, the Newtonian model is a limiting case of the Einsteinian model.

In terms of set theory the Newtonian model might be seen as a subset nested within the larger Einsteinian set. The properties of the subset are readily comprehensible from the perspective of the set but the reverse is necessarily untrue. The general principle is that to try to examine the larger model or set from the perspective of the smaller is inappropriate and necessarily productive of false conclusions.

The implications for the comparison and assessment of Asian mystical philosophies are now apparent. From a multiple states of consciousness model traditional Western systems can be seen as relativistically useful models provided that, because of the limitations imposed by state dependency, they are not applied inappropriately to the phenomena of altered states outside their scope. However, from the Western unistate perspective the Asian multistate models may appear illogical, incomprehensible and nonsensical.

Implications For Western Philosophy

Given that Western philosophy is essentially a unistate discipline, what then are some of the further implications for Western philosophy of multiple states of consciousness and state-specificity? First there is the obvious question of whether we have any reason to assume that philosophical knowledge can be best or even adequately sought in only one state of consciousness especially now that we have nonwestern traditions, and some Western philosophers, claiming that other states may even be superior.

Another implication concerns the possible necessity of re-evaluating the philosophy of mysticism. This paper has focused exclusively on Asian mystical philosophies since these have been worked out in greater detail and some of their practitioners appear to have had more ready access to mystical states than most of their Western counterparts.[68] However the general argument that has been advanced towards the Asian systems can obviously also be applied to Western mysticism which may well have been partly misinterpreted, pathologized and

---

[68]W. Stace, *Mysticism and Philosophy* (Philadelphia: Lippincott, 1960), p. 168.

prematurely dismissed by many philosophers. It would clearly seem important to re-evaluate mysticism in the light of state-specificity.

Then there is the very large question of whether any of the many contemporary impasses that bedevil Western philosophy might yield to multistate perspectives and investigations. For example, Western philosophers are increasingly recognizing, and being frustrated by the limitations of the intellect. Since these limitations have been recognized for millennia by Asian mystical philosophers, it might be valuable to see if these traditions can throw any light on this conundrum.

Conclusion

In the light of recent research on states of consciousness and state-specificity, it is clear that claims that contemplative practice may be an essential preliminary for understanding Asian mystical philosophies now have significant experimental and conceptual support. Without such practice we may lose access to the most profound aspects and highest grades of significance of these traditions yet not recognize that we have lost them. Clearly we and Western philosophy are faced with an enormous challenge.

But we are also faced with an enormous opportunity. Asian philosophies, teachers and techniques are now available to us in the West as in no previous time in history. To the extent we use them, say Asian philosophies, to that extent will our understanding of these traditions deepen and our own wisdom grow. And what these traditions claim to offer in their depths is remarkable indeed: awakening, enlightenment, liberation, moksha, sat-chit-ananda, limitless consciousness-being-bliss. Are these claims true? The Asian philosophies' answer remains the same as it has been for millennia: "to see if this be true, look within your own mind. The ultimate testing ground and goal lie within you and are you. The only tool you require is your own trained awareness." As is said in Zen you can do the practice and become rich or you can read about it and become the rich people's bookkeeper. We in the West may have been primarily bookkeepers but the Asian mystical philosophies invite us to become rich.

Acknowledgements: The author would like to thank the many people and institutions that have helped in the formulation of this paper. The National Endowment for the Humanities provided fellowships to a summer seminar with Huston Smith on the Great Chain of Being and to the University of Hawaii's summer institute on Asian Philosophies. Michael Murphy, Jay Ogilvy, Huston Smith and Laurance Rockefeller created the Revisioning Philosophy seminar which partly inspired this paper and whose members provided valuable feedback on earlier drafts. Veronique Foti, Gordon Globus, Philip

Novak, and Donald Rothberg were especially generous with their feedback. The assistance of Dianne Miller Lesty and Robert McDermott, the support of Frances Vaughan, and the secretarial and administrative support of Bonnie L'Allier are all gratefully acknowledged.

Afterword

David Appelbaum

What is meant by "revisioning philosophy?"

After the diverse contributions, the question sounds all the more loudly. First questions make their appearance only at the end. An afterword provides a fitting occasion to confront that which calls the Revisioning Philosophy Program into being.

That ambiguity infects the question of revision is obvious. Ordinarily, revising a manuscript or a set of plans suggests the need for editorial assistance, a mid-course correction, or a new spin. The basic matter is not in question. A mere revision will do. A favorite story of Heinrich Zimmer reveals the other, deeper meaning.

An abandoned tiger cub was adopted and reared by a flock of sheep. It grew up knowing the ways of grazing, following the abundance of grass from season to season. It bleated like a sheep. It was content. One day, the flock was attacked by a pride of tigers. The huge cats over-ran the sheep, killing at will. The adopted tiger, nearly full-grown, tried to escape, fearful, with the rest of the flock. Just then, one of the marauders caught the fleeing tiger. "What are you?" it roared, thrusting the young one's maw deep into sheep's blood. The first taste was instantaneously familiar and pleasant. The second brought the young tiger's first roar as it remembered who it was. It then loped off with the attackers, finishing the job.[1]

The demand for revision in this other sense does not call for a new look from the editor. It brings the question of vision, what it means to look at all. It turns us toward another direction of inquiry, toward what calls us to look upon the matter of philosophy as the content of a vision, a vision that continually stands in need of renewal.

In what does vision consist? The tendency of the tradition to which we belong is to confuse a content with an action, the field of knowledge with the knower of the field, or a state of consciousness with consciousness of a state. "And," as Wittgenstein reminds us, "nothing in the visual field allows you to infer that it is seen by an eye."[2] We respond to the question by citing the object of vision, in the case of sense perception, that red chair, this birch, those sparrows. The extreme passivity of our human part–and the narrow, mentalistic range of response involved– has been criticized by several contributors, including Murphy, Johnson, and Walsh. The result is a philosophy of the object, but a philosophy without vision.

What of the act by which the object is constituted? To seize on Kant's Transcendental thought is to fall prey to revisionism, revising in the shallow sense. Kant takes the visioning act to be exhausted by the automatic workings of the conceptual scheme that governs comparative thinking. We may be deceived by his rhetoric. While Kant speaks of his "Copernican revolution," he accepts wholeheartedly the passive role that Hume assigns to intelligence. From it follows the cage of concepts that everywhere makes the object known and everywhere limits our visioning power. Kant states, "The conditions of the possibility of experience in general are at the same time conditions of the possibility of the objects of experience."[3] From Kant's thought, we feel the lack of possibility of experience. Sight, if anything, contains the power of discerning possibility. Our need is to see with vivacity enough to taste the blood.

To penetrate the names and forms of things to the things themselves demands a new strength of presence. Memory of this strength is preserved in the family of Latin words including videre (to see), vivere (to live), vibrare (to shake), and vigere (to be vigorous), all of which are related to the vi- root clearest in vis (force). When we return to the

---

[1]Adapted from Heinrich Zimmer, *Philosophies of India* (Princeton: Princeton University Press, 1951) pp. 5-8.

[2]*Tractatus Logico-Philosophicus*, tr. D.F.Pears and B.F.McGuinness (London: Routledge, 1961) 5.633, p. 117.

[3]*Critique of Pure Reason*, tr. Norman Kemp Smith (London; Macmillan, 1950) A 158 = B 197.

memory, we are recalled to the question of vision. This question asks, whence arises the force of seeing and how does it relate to the world of objects?

Only when we acknowledge that our insights lack force are we recalled to that which commemorates vision. What is the missing ingredient? That our devitalized, desensitized mode of apprehending things contains a great clue echoes through the thought of Cashman, Griffin, and Wilshire. In our philosophical thinking, the heart has been lost.

What is required, Panikkar urges, is "an enlightened, loving, and thus healing involvement." An open and unprogrammatic response to the world provides such fruit.

When compassion is felt, so are the limitations on what is called vision. How does vision function when cut off from the vitalizing force of memory? Ordinarily our sight (perceptual and otherwise) springs from the act of focus. A circle is drawn within which pours the light of awareness. What lies inside is lighted, what lies outside, not. In the brightness, we learn of the object and how to profit from its use. In the dark, nothing. The primary discovery of our mentalistic epoch is how to operate an attention without sense of origin. This is focus. Descartes did not exaggerate when he proclaimed that each one of us is no other than this focal vision, this bright consciousness. "I focus, therefore I am."

The sediment from which selective or voluntary attention arises lies very deep. The devotion to maintaining focus–and the object world it calls forth–accounts for much of our social makeup. William James, a pioneer in the study of attention, noted that "the faculty of voluntarily bringing back a wandering attention, over and over again, is the very root of judgment, character, and will."[4] The education of our children concerns the development of a knowing subject able to retain focus. Only the fruits of focus themselves—the different intellectual disciplines—are held to be appropriate for training in such a classroom. The faculty of manipulating symbols-mathematical, syntactic, and semantic–is felt to exhaust an intelligence that we experience in fuller moments as thinking with heart and feeling with mind.

With the focal habit firmly entrenched, it becomes quite difficult to recognize the selectivity of focus. That which passes for knowledge occupies the bright area. Dark vision–of the periphery and below–is the vanishing-point of objects, and so does not exist. Only the moment of crisis, of life- or love-threatening momentum, reveals the background conditions of selectivity. From Augustine to Descartes to Husserl to the present, the history of our tradition of thought lives from one crisis to

[4]*The Principles of Psychology,* volume 1 (New York: Dover, 1950) p.424.

the next. Why? The investment in focal awareness and its attainments is immense. The wheel, fire, agriculture, hunting, architecture, writing, this machine that I work on: all the Promethean children of humankind, all technologies, are applications of focus. To let the attachment drop would be unthinkable. It would be to risk the unlit, unknown.

That it drops is an undeniable experience. In the shift from focus to defocus, the conditions of selectivity become perceivable tensions within the field of vision. In the concomitant shift in lighting, the dark backdrop moves to the center. "Field reversal" signifies an opening to vision. The attention, whose selectivity was focussed on representational thinking, broadens, deepens, and grows fluid. Seeing includes not only brightness (that features fixed objects) but opacity (that includes energic movements.) In terms of Wittgenstein's image, the eye itself is in the seeing.

That an appropriate understanding of visioning is new is also undeniable. It is also fragile, perishable, and fleeting—marks of an emergent capability, as Murphy conceives it. The idea of a permanent, unchanging substratum of experience is a product of the comparative mind's categories. Fixity of the object is what gives it the property of being repeatedly identified. Contact with insight and intelligence, by contrast, is intermittent. Nothing is the same for long yet vision constantly awaits our return. How to align ourselves with creative novelty? Gabriel Marcel warns us to be on guard. "We must," he says, break away once and for all from the metaphors which depict consciousness as a luminous circle round which there is nothing, to its own eyes, but darkness. On the contrary, the shadow is at the center.[5]

The opaque is no longer the limit of vision but its possibility. All philosophy of vision, therefore, is a philosophy of mystery.

The milieu of philosophical thinking—the unthought—thereby receives a concrete meaning. That in which thought-experience takes place is the body.

Incarnation—the central "given" of metaphysics. Incarnation is the situation of a being who appears to himself to be, as it were, bound to a body. This "given" is opaque to itself: opposition to the cogito.[6]

So Marcel expresses the fact of embodiment. Our incarnate situation—that the place of human experience is the organism—becomes itself a theme for several contributors. Its objectless, earthbound, and receptive qualities lead Griffin to think of the feminine. The recovery of lived time lies with the life experienced as the body. Citing Dewey's tes-

---

[5] *Being and Having*, tr. Katherine Farrer (New York: Harper & Row, 1965) p. 14.
[6] *Ibid.*, p. 11.

timony, Wilshire goes a step farther, saying that "if consciousness cannot grasp its own conditions in the body, it must wait for the body to generate a new consciousness." A new thought is just a new body–though not the body we think of.

The fact of embodiment gives rise to the force allowing vision to come alive. It enables us to see what we are here for. We taste the blood and while tasting know infallibly our identity.

To free the attention from focus, to cultivate a nonfocal awareness, brings a surprising clarity to philosophical thinking–though one different from Descartes' clarity and distinctness. A primary interest of focus is self-interest: how can the object be used to advance our stake in the world? To be bent on figuring out the usefulness of a thing results in a one-sided approach. Utilitarianism is, in Cashman's terms, an idealism responsible for the self-centered, compassionless rape of the planet. When not preoccupied with knowing how to use a thing, we are available to relation. To allow a thing to be what it is, in lieu of projecting the categories of self-interest onto it, is to recognize its suchness, its unique, unalterable essence.

To speak of the process of emergent reality as emotionally neutral is misleading. We are called to confront our attachment to knowledge, its controlling power and its comforting fruits. In the encounter, anxiety over the loss of order may set the dominant tone. The weight of refusal should not be underestimated or misconstrued. Yet the translucent light of disinterest reveals, not chaos, but a meaningful array of entities–really, a new world order or kosmology, to use Panikkar's suggestion. It is a look into the heart of things. To take the look to heart lies at the center of the work of vision.

From the look arises another question. It too can be heard throughout the contributors' thought since it is very much the question of the day. It asks, "What is the use of philosophy?"

Two kinds of answers abound in our time. The first answers, "No use whatsoever." To the nihilist, no reply is possible because none is solicited. Nihilism, a philosophy of despair, is a disease and a philosophy of vision, no therapeutic. The latter's feel and orientation are that of healthy-mindedness. The nihilist is obstructed from receiving the beneficent effects of visioning until the dis-ease is directly addressed. So-called remedies for nihilism are rife. But since composure and setting the mind at-ease demand an inner willingness, the direction of cure must arise from the person. Herein lies the double-bind of the nihilist. The nihilism that wants to be cured of its own misgivings at the same time holds to its suffering as verification of its truth. There is no exit that is not a change of heart.

The other answer takes philosophy as a means to achieve a limited end. That philosophy is an instrument of conceptual clarification, scientific rigor, or codification of ethics has been proclaimed loudly and self-assuredly by many thinkers of our century. The responsibility for honing the tools of objectivity falls to the inheriters of Kant. Sharpening, ever sharpening, attacks and counterattacks, object philosophy refuses to confront the question of selectivity and focus. In claiming that its is the place of thought, it rejects Griffin's observation that "there is no objective location." The rush to achieve rigor achieves only rigidification. The comparative mind's categories of distinction are never subject to the question of vision since they themselves presuppose the brightness of mental focus. What is their use?

Another sort of answer is given by Chung Tzu, who tells the story of Shih, the master carpenter. Shih passed by a gigantic oak by the village shrine. In its shade, ten thousand oxen could rest, it towered above the hilltops, more than ten of its branches could be made into boats, and under it were crowds of people as in a marketplace. Shih's apprentice was impressed and said, "Never have I seen timber as beautiful as this. Yet you, master, pass by without stopping. Why?"

Shih said, "Stop! Such a tree is useless. If you made a boat from it, it would sink. A tool would split, a coffin would soon rot, a door would ooze sap, and a beam would have termites. The timber is worthless and of no use. That is why it has attained a ripe old age."[7]

We are reminded that the question of use is still hidden from our thinking. When seen through the eyes of self-interest, philosophy is guardian of knowledge. Its usefulness lies in securing the compound of the known. Such is our use, not its. To acknowledge that the door to "scientific philosophy" oozes and the beam that supports our conceptual scheme has termites requires an act of humility. To recognize that the use of philosophy is not yet known is to admit that we do not yet stand in front of the question, what does the vision of philosophy serve? What calls us to re-vision philosophy?

That every "use" to which we put philosophical thinking is empty is the key to master carpenter Shih's perception. The hidden uselessness of the oaktree gives value and makes it fit for ordinary things, like a long life. Our attachment to problem-solving and the development of technologies makes it difficult to listen to and live with the question of use. As Cashman argues, the same attachment commits us to killing off biological species of the planet–the ones that are of no use to us. This

---

[7]Adapted from *Inner Chapters,* tr. Gia-Fu Feng and Jane English (New York: Random House, 1974), chapter 4.

fact highlights the suicidal aspect of our understanding. It underlines the imperative in front of us: heed the question of use, or else.

"Everywhere," Huston Smith writes, "thoughtful people have sensed the presence of another, more fundamental world underlying our familiar, quotidian one." A subtle shift in inner alignment enables us to be more receptive to that which is ordinarily concealed from perception. Degree and duration of receptivity can, moreover, be cultivated once thinking is supported by what McDermott calls a "transformative epistemology." What does a new way of knowing involve? The way requires a sensitivity to impressions that empties the object of knowledge of its fixed categorial form. The way relates the thing to the formless background of all phenomena, the noumenal possibility of all experience. And it must show, as master Shih's oaktree, that to do anything with the object is ultimately useless. Thought then would play its part in transforming us from users (and abusers) to witnesses. Thinking would be a bridge between the two worlds.

A thing's use is related to what it is, its uniqueness and simplicity. The relatedness in ourselves, when thinking with vision, opens us to the hidden heart of things. Only when all things take their place in the heart does the use of any one thing become manifest.

Even with all this said, a crucial aspect of discussion is missing. Vision belongs to any person who feels need to understand his or her humanity in the deepest and fullest sense. In isolation, a single person, however, can do little. Until one is with others, able to exchange without fear and mistrust, the tough crust of individualism, as Ogilvy discovers it, is not likely to break. J.S.Mill's eulogy of the individual has entered our character with our mother's milk. Individualism is in fact linked closely to selective attention and focal perception. What thereby follows—our cultural heritage of going it alone—must be examined and let drop. The shared commitment to a emergent "new realism," as Cashman suggests, is essential to nourishing each one's vision. Community is the mother-liquor of a crystallizing philosophy of vision.

Philosophy from its beginning has enjoyed a necessary connection to political life. For Plato, justice governed an equilibrium of aspects within a single person just as it ruled the aspects of the polis. If the testimony of his Seventh Letter is to be believed, philosophy serves political life in a special way. "The generations of mankind," he writes, would therefore have no cessation from evils until either the class of those who are true and genuine philosophers came to political power or else the men in political power, by some divine dispensation, became true philosophers.[8]

[8]Letter VII, 326a.

That there is little agreement today about the philosopher's aptitude for political leadership may disclose the unclarity surrounding his
skills more than anything else. To ask, "What is philosophy good for?" is
also to raise the question of life with others.

When we recall the act of vision–the heart of philosophy–we witness
a dynamic of exchange. Different thinkers have given different names.
Plato spoke of dialectic, Nicolas de Cusa, of reconciliation, Hegel of
synthesis. In all cases, the confrontation of opposing viewpoints, the
"yes" and the "no," results in a remarkable event. The viewpoints
opposed to one another have one thing in common: they stand on the
same level. The unpredictably new point of view, by contrast, reveals a
movement to another, higher level. It contains the initial oppositions in
the way that an airplane pilot's vision contains two cities, twenty miles
apart, where each can only see the other. Elevation is the crucial factor.

That the direction of creative novelty, of a new vision, emerges
from the meeting of affirmation and denial, is a fact of tremendous
import for the political order. It means that certain communal provisions are required to welcome the manifesting vision. Plato's thought
along similar lines may have led him to urge the need for the demos,
the democratic order of things. When opposition is suppressed, we are
deprived of, in Kant's terms, the "possibility of experience." Your "no"
to my "yes," or my "no" to your "yes," itself provides the opportunity for
a "transformative epistemology" to operate. The novel viewpoint that
arises fulfils Whitehead's principle that the many are increased by one
and become one–the keynote of emergent phenomena. Unpredictable,
shocking, and astonishing visioning has force because it conveys the
force of unity. Thus Zimmer's tiger cub discovered.

Philosophical thinking of this pitch takes place only against a
democratic background. It draws its life-giving power from the clash of
opposites whose energy calls to it a more adequate, inclusive point of
view. In light of its appearance, the direction of inquiry stands revealed.
Dewey is the able spokesperson for such a movement. "Democracy," he
notes, "is a name for a life of free and enriching communion."[9]
Communion, the standing together on common ground, is, however,
not a given but a result of effort. Its work is to abide with the inquiry in
the face of opposition until a unifying thought is revealed. From the
work follow the traditional values of a democratic life, tolerance,
courage, forthrightness, and hopefulness.

We need also to ask to what extent the democratic "experiment" of
our nation provides the ground necessary to inquiry. Do we fully sup-

[9]"The Public and Its Problems," *Later Works of John Dewey*, ed. JoAnn Boydston,
(Carbondale, IL.: Southern Illinois University Press, 1986)

port a pluralistic society? Acknowledgement of fascistic tendencies in us and around us is requisite to facing the question. An impatience for resolution foreshortens the confrontation and struggle through which thought is re-visioned. The urge to annihilate opposing points of view calls for an attentiveness that derives from a source of value that also penetrates our opponent.

Rockefeller's embrace of "the urgent challenge of creating a global community" is a concrete response to the demand for kosmology, a new world order. We need to measure both the nearness and distance of such an aim. The deeply entrenched habits of object-making stand very much in the way of meeting the other as other. To use, manipulate, and control another person are impulses of focal selectivity, our facility for accomplishing priorities. They leave us indifferent to the other as a partner in a vision-laden way of thinking. We lack compassion.

Much nearer and hence more hidden is relation and mutuality. The moment in which objectification is recognized as such frees us to an exchange of substance with the other. This fact, moreover, holds throughout the range of encounter, environmental, personal, and cosmic. To let drop the category and stand face-to-face does not annul the otherness but affirms it. In the space between us passes the force of vision that belongs to neither. For the moment that stands always awaiting us, we are witness to the logos of difference. When we forget and fall back into conflict, separateness, and isolation, the strength of a logos of sameness overwhelms us. Only with the help of the other are we able to break through the concealment and recover that which joins us as one.

That we fluctuate between the two attitudes, control and permission, reveals our duality as humans. We push toward the new through old soil. To be contemporary, to be in this time, is a demand on a fluid awareness. What philosophical thinking discloses of newness is quickly old–and made into a conceptual scheme, a representation, a theory, an ideal. Rigidification of thought is the sole vice of philosophy. I mention this by way of explaining a matter I have skipped over: the re- of "revisioning philosophy." Renewal of vision, realignment of the attention, recovery of contact with the fact of incarnation, relatedness, realization. The re- is found in each concern just as it is in repetition. Once again, vision returns, movement recurs, and we are reminded that content in philosophical thinking is forever secondary to activity.

Notes on Contributors

David Appelbaum

David Appelbaum is a Professor of philosophy at State University of New York at New Paltz. His central concern is the transformation of consciousness. His publications include: *Contact and Attention: The Anatomy of Gabriel Marcel's Metaphysical Method* (University Press of America, 1986); *The Interpenetrating Reality: Bringing the Body to Touch* (Lang, 1988); *Making the Body Heard: The Body's Way of Existence* (Lang, 1988); *Voice* (SUNY Press, 1989); and with co-editor Jacob Needlebaum, *The Real Philosophy* (Penguin, 1990).

Robert N. Bellah

Robert N. Bellah is Elliott Professor Sociology at the University of California at Berkeley. He was educated at Harvard University, receiving a B.A. in 1950 and a Ph.D. in 1955. His publications include: *Tokugawa Religion, Beyond Relief, The Broken Covenant, The New Religious Consciousness* and *Varieties of Civil Religion*. In 1985 he published the Pulitzer Prize winning book, *Habits of the Heart: Individualism and Commitment in American Life* (University of California Press; paperback, Harper and Row), written in collaboration with Richard Madsen, William Sullivan, Ann Swidler and Steven Tipton. His most recent book is *Uncivil Religion: Interreligious Hostility in America* (Crossroad, 1987), edited with Frederick E. Greenspahn.

Tyrone Cashman

Tyrone Cashman holds a Ph.L. in medieval philosophy, and a Ph.D. in philosophy of science from Columbia University. He has practiced "applied" philosophy of science and systems theory in medical research, ecological research and engineering R&D. He served as renewable energy system planner in the California Governor's Office and as president of the American Wind Energy Association. At present he is developing a philosophy of natural systems.

313

Joanne B. Ciulla

Joanne B. Ciulla is a Senior Fellow in the Department of Legal Studies at the Wharton School of the University of Pennsylvania where she teaches business ethics in the MBA program and the Advanced Management Program. A Ph.D. in Philosophy, Ciulla was the Harvard Business School Fellow in Business and Ethics. In 1989 she was Visiting Scholar at Green College, Oxford University. She has just finished a book called *Honest Work*. Her current research is on international business ethics.

Hubert L. Dreyfus

Hubert L. Dreyfus received his Ph.D. in Philosophy from Harvard University, where he was also a Research Associate in Computer Science. He has taught at Harvard and M.I.T. and is now Professor of Philosophy at the University of California at Berkeley. He specializes in contemporary continental philosophy and has been an observer and critic of work in Artificial Intelligence for the past 20 years. In this area he has published many articles and two books: *What Computers Can't Do: A Critique of Artificial Intelligence*, and (with his brother Stuart Dreyfus), *Mind Over Machine: The Power of Human Intuition and Expertise in the Era of the Computer*.

Susan Griffin

Susan Griffin is a writer and social thinker, author of several works of prose and poetry including *Women and Nature: The Roaring Inside Her* and *Pornography and Silence: Culture's Revenge Against Nature*. She is currently completing a book entitled *A Chorus of Stories: The Private Life of War* about women this century and the gender issues related to nuclear weapons.

Don Hanlon Johnson

Don Johnson is Director of the graduate studies program in Somatic Psychology and Education in New College of California, and director of the Esalen Project in Somatic Education and Research. He is the author of two books, *The Protean Body*, and *Body*, and several articles on the body. He is also contributing editor of the journal, *Somatics*, and the French journal, *Somatotherapie*. His principal focus is on how one's experience and definition of "the body" reflect social and cultural forces.

Robert A. McDermott

Robert A. McDermott is President and Professor of philosophy, California Institute of Integral Studies, San Francisco. He was formerly Professor and Chair, Department of Philosophy, Baruch College, New York. Author, *The Essential Aurobindo* (West Stockbridge, MA: Lindisfarne Press, 1988), and *The Essential Steiner* (NY: Harper and Row, 1984). "Introduction," *The Works of William James*, Vol 16: *Essays in Psychical Research* (Cambridge, MA: Harvard University Press, 1987).

Michael Murphy

Michael Murphy is the founder of Esalen Institute, subject of a *New Yorker* profile, coiner of the phrase, "human potential movement," and author of several books about extraordinary human functioning, including *Golf in the Kingdom* and *Jacob Atabet*. He is the author of *The Future of the Body*, forthcoming from Jeremy Tarcher.

James Ogilvy

James Ogilvy is Director of the Revisioning Philosophy Program at Esalen Institute. He taught philosophy for twelve years: seven at Yale, four at Williams College, one at the University of Texas, Austin. From 1979 until 1987 he was at Stanford Research Institute where he served as Director of Research for the Values and Lifestyles Program. He is the author of *Many Dimensional Man: Decentralizing Self, Society and the Sacred* (Oxford, 1977; Harper & Row, 1980), and editor of *Self and World: Readings in Philosophy* (Harcourt Brace Jovanovich 1971 and 1980), and co-author, with Peter Schwartz and Paul Hawken, of *Seven Tomorrows: Toward a Voluntary History* (Bantam, 1982).

Raimundo Panikkar

Raimundo Panikkar himself partakes of pluralistic traditions: Indian and European, Hindu and Christian, Sciences and Humanities. Born in 1918, he has lived and studied in Spain, Germany, Italy, India and the U.S.. He holds doctorates in Philosophy, Science, and Theology.

Ordained a Catholic priest in 1946. Former Professor at the Universities of Madrid, Rome and Harvard. At present he is Professor Emeritus of Religious Studies at the University of California, and lives most of the time in Spain and India. Among his 30 books: *The Silence of God: The Answer of the Buddha*, NY (Orbis 1989); *Blessed Simplicity. The Monk as Universal Archetype*, NY (Seabury Press 1982); *Myth, Faith and Hermeneutics*, NY (The Paulist Press 1979), Second Edition Bangalore (Asian Trading Corporation 1983); *The Vedic Experience. Mantramanjari: An Anthology of the Vedas for Modern Man and Contemporary Celebration*, LA, Berkeley (University of California Press) and London (Darton, Longman & Todd 1977); *The Intrareligious Dialogue*, NY (The Paulist Press 1978), Second Edition, Bangalore (Asian Trading Corporation 1984). He has published approx. 300 major articles from Philosophy of Science to Metaphysics, Comparative Religion and Indology. Among his many honors is his invitation to offer the Gifford Lectures at the University of Edinborough in 1988.

Steven C. Rockefeller

Steven C. Rockefeller is Professor and Chairperson in the Religion Department at Middlebury College in Vermont. He has a special interest in the cross-cultural dialogue between Buddhism, Christianity, and American humanistic naturalism. He is the editor, with Donald S. Lopez, Jr., of *The Christ and the Bodhisattva*, and has just completed an intellectual biography of the American philosopher John Dewey which gives special attention to his moral and religious thought. He has been a student and practitioner of Zen Buddhism since the mid-1970s.

Naomi Scheman

Naomi Scheman teaches philosophy and women's studies at the University of Minnesota. She has written on the connections between politics and epistemology both in philosophical texts and in works of Shakespeare, Henry James, and Freud, as well as in movies and photographs. Her work focuses on the ways in which the social construction of epistemic authority meshes with the social construction of gender, race, class, and sexuality.

Huston Smith

Huston Smith is Thomas J. Watson Professor of Religion and Distinguished Adjunct Professor of Philosophy Emeritus, Syracuse University. Prior to that appointment he was for fifteen years Professor of Philosophy at the Massachusetts Institute of Technology. His other teaching appointments were at Hamline University, Washington University in St. Louis, and the Universities of Denver and Colorado. Author of over 50 articles in professional and popular journals, his *The Religions of Man* has been for 25 years the most widely-used text-book for courses in world religions and has sold over two million copies. His other books are *The Purposes of Higher Education, The Search for America, Condemned to Meaning, Forgotten Truth,* and *Beyond the Post-Modern Mind.*

Robert C. Solomon

Robert C. Solomon has spent much of the past 20 years thinking about (and feeling) the gamut of emotions and reasserting their proper place in philosophy. He is author of *The Passions* (Doubleday 1976); *Love: Emotion, Myth and Metaphor* (Doubleday, 1981); and *About Love* (Simon and Schuster, 1988), as well as numerous books on European philosophy. He is currently Quincy Lee Centennial Professor at the University of Texas at Austin.

Francisco J. Varela

Francisco J. Varela was born in Chile. He was trained as a biologist (Ph.D. Harvard 1970). His interests have centered on the biological basis of knowledge and its epistemological horizons. Over a hundred articles in scientific journals; his most recent book is, *The Tree of Knowledge* (with H. Maturana). Currently Professor of Cognitive Science and Epistemology at Ecole Polytechnique, Paris.

Roger Walsh

Roger Walsh is a Professor of Psychiatry and Philosophy at the University of California at Irvine. His interests and work include spiritual traditions and practices, especially meditation, Asian philosophies and psychologies, and contemporary global threats to human survival.

Bruce Wilshire

Bruce Wilshire is a professor of philosophy at Rutgers University. From 1978 until 1985 he served as Convener of the Committee for Pluralism in Philosophy. He is also Vice Chairman of SOPHIA (the Society of Philosophers in America). His books include *Role Playing and Identity: The Limits of Theater as Metaphor,* Indiana, 1982), and *The Moral Collapse of the University: Professionalism, Purity and Alienation* (State University of New York Press, 1990). He is currently working on a book entitled *Ecstasy Deprivation: The Problem of Addiction and the Need for Wilderness.*